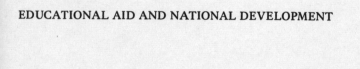

EDUCATIONAL AID AND NATIONAL DEVELOPMENT

EDUCATIONAL AID AND NATIONAL DEVELOPMENT

An International Comparison of the Past and Recommendations for the Future

Nancy Parkinson

First published 1976 by
THE MACMILLAN PRESS LTD
London and Basingstoke
Associated companies in New York
Dublin Melbourne Johannesburg and Madras

SBN 333 14176 8

Typeset by Santype International Ltd.
Coldtype Dept.
Salisbury, Wiltshire

Printed in Great Britain by
Billing & Sons Ltd.
Guildford, London and Worcester

To Etienne Parkinson
and all his fellow nine-year olds
of all races and creeds

Contents

Acknowledgements

In a book covering such a wide variety of countries, organisations and subjects, there are inevitably a large number of organisations, both official and unofficial, and individuals in many parts of the world who have given generously, both of their wisdom and time, to the author and consultants.

The governments, universities and many individuals and organisations in Chile, India, Kenya, Senegal, Tunisia and Turkey afforded the consultants who visited their countries much assistance, without which the chapters on the developing countries could not have been prepared. The high commissions and embassies in London, and also the embassies of Senegal and Tunisia in Paris, gave valuable initial help.

The author paid several visits to France, the Federal Republic of Germany and the Netherlands, and had numerous discussions with government departments, official and unofficial organisations and individuals. The visits were always encouraging, and she is also grateful for the considerable assistance provided by the ambassadors and staff of the London embassies concerned. Apart from a number of meetings at UNESCO headquarters, and OECD in Paris, visits were arranged by the Geneva Office of the United Nations Institute for Training and Research in Geneva, when it was possible, to have discussions with people at the headquarters of the United Nations agencies, or with liaison officers, if the agency was not based on Geneva.

In the United Kingdom amongst government departments notable help was given by the Foreign and Commonwealth Office and the Ministry of Overseas Development; the British Council, both in the United Kingdom and in the countries abroad included in the project, were endlessly helpful; many universities, official organisations, including Commonwealth ones, unofficial organisations, and numerous individuals spent much time and thought in providing helpful information.

It was not possible to visit the United States of America, but both government departments in Washington, various universities, the Ford and

Rockefeller Foundations, and other organisations and individuals were generous with information and comments, both through correspondence and talks in London. Three successive cultural attachés gave much assistance, namely the late Dr Edward D. Myers, Professor Robin Winks, now of Yale University, and the late Dr Wayne Wilcox, tragically killed in the Turkish air crash at Orly in March 1974.

The United Nations and United Nations agencies have also been most patiently helpful, in particular UNESCO in Paris; the United Nations Institute for Training and Research, both in Geneva and New York; the United Nations Information Office in London and the United Nations Development Programme, which not only provided some of the consultants with office space when they visited developing countries, but have supplied a constant flow of valuable information.

To all the people and organisations who are included in the preceding paragraphs, and they run into many hundreds, we would express our grateful thanks.

A survey of this nature has to be financed, and have a base from which the work can be directed. The project would not have seen the light of day without the very generous grant made by the trustees of the Leverhulme Trust Fund. Not only did the trust fund provide a fellowship for the author, but also met the expenses of the three consultants based on the United Kingdom, and of the Indian consultant and his two assistants. For the major part of the duration of the grant the Director of the trust fund was Lord Murray of Newhaven, and we owe much to his constant and understanding encouragement. Bedford College (University of London), which administered the Leverhulme grant, provided a beautiful place from which to work and most generously gave a subvention towards the completion of the task. I am deeply grateful to the Council of the college, to the successive principals, Mrs E. M. Chilver and Dr John Black, to the Department of Sociology, not only for providing a room, but also for their kindness, and to many friends amongst the staff and students.

All concerned owe much gratitude to the Netherlands Universities Foundation for International Cooperation, who appointed the consultants to Kenya and Senegal, and financed their visits to those countries; Dr H. G. Quik, Director General of the Foundation until February 1974, in particular gave us endless help and cooperation.

The author owes especial gratitude to the consultants: for Chile, Dr Harold Blakemore, Secretary of the Institute of Latin American Studies (University of London); for India, Dr L. S. Chandrakant, Director of the Institute of Applied Manpower Research (New Delhi), assisted by Mrs Muriel Wasi and Mr K. Rangachari; for Senegal, Dr Adri Kater of the Netherlands Universities Foundation for International Cooperation; for Tunisia, Dr Robin Ostle of the School of Oriental and African Studies (University of London); for Turkey, Professor Paul Stirling, University of Kent at Canterbury; and for Kenya, Dr Mustafa Tuqan, of the Netherlands

Centre for the Study of Education in Changing Societies. To all of them I am deeply appreciative, both for their contributions and for their friendship which has endured and survived despite the inevitable role of editing which the author has had to play. To Robin Ostle, who has helped so much in discussion and by reading drafts in the latter stages, I owe especial gratitude.

In a task such as this there is a great deal of 'research-office' work, a stupendous amount of 'translating' tape recordings and the author's illegible writing, much reading and checking, and the maintenance of complicated records. Throughout the project all these tasks have been handled by the sole full-time assistant, Miss Winifred Close, and to her I shall always be deeply grateful.

For much of the last year of work the author has led a more restricted life than usual, much of it in King Edward VII Hospital for Officers in London; to the Matron and the exceptional staff for providing such a kindly and cheerful atmosphere, and for the patience of Drs Walter Graham and Lawson McDonald, I have particular gratitude for enabling me to finish the job.

Finally, I would like to express my appreciation of the kind encouragement of Macmillan's, and in particular the cooperation of Mr T. M. Farmiloe.

September 1974 N.P.

PUBLISHERS' NOTE

The publishers regret to say that Dame Nancy Parkinson died in December 1974.

They would like to point out that much of her editorial comment in this book was still in draft form at the time of her death; they nevertheless feel that it is of sufficient clarity to publish without further revision.

They would like to thank Dr Harold Blakemore and Professor Paul Stirling for kindly agreeing to read the proofs.

The publishers wish to thank the following ministries and organisations which have kindly given permission for the use of copyright material: Association of Commonwealth Universities; British Council; Inter-American Development Bank; Ministry of Education, Nairobi; Ministry of Education, New Delhi; Ministry of Overseas Development; Organisation for Economic Cooperation and Development; State Institute of Statistics, Turkey; United Nations Development Programme; World Bank.

The publishers have made every effort to trace the copyright-holders, but if they have inadvertently overlooked any they will be pleased to make the necessary arrangement at the first opportunity.

Part I

1 General Problems of Development Aid

Origins of the project

This book is mainly concerned with people, the way they are used as the chief resource in aid development, and more particularly in the field of education, using the term in a broad sense. That development is really about people seems sometimes to be lost in a miasma of regulations, administrative restrictions, pockets of in-built power, whole volumes of the results of conferences which frequently result in little, if any, positive action for the human beings who are the object of the operation.

The project as originally conceived was to be based on the experiences of the author after nearly thirty years of working with both developed and developing countries, United Nations organisations, and foundations. At first there was no particular limit on the number of countries involved, or on the actual aid processes to be examined. It became speedily clear, however, that there was a need for an examination of the aid processes in the general field of education, and for such an examination to be useful that there must be a limitation on the number of countries and organisations invited to cooperate. It was also obvious that one person could not do everything, so specialists with knowledge of the languages and of the developing countries included in the project were appointed as consultants to the six countries concerned. In the short acknowledgements preceding this introduction, they are referred to in detail.

Methods used

The consultants and author had three separate meetings: one in London in the autumn of 1971, another in The Hague in the spring of 1972, and a third just before Christmas in the same year. The Indian consultant and his associates were not able to attend the discussions but received all the papers relating to them.

Two major results emerged from these discussions. Firstly there was general agreement on the rough format that the chapters on the developing countries, Chapters 3–8, should take. As a result of the consultants' own efforts and some general editing, a reasonably even scheme of publication has been achieved, with the same background and approximately the same problems examined in the six very different countries. Secondly, our original idea had been that the preliminary chapters should be devoted to the background problems of general development, and more particularly as follows.

i. Educational expansion, which is the main problem of this book, can only be seen in true perspective against the background of development aid as a whole. In the following chapters questions such as the dangers of the transfer of educational systems from one country to another, without enough thought of the effect on the developing country, and other equally urgent problems are discussed.

ii. The position arising in the international political scene after the Second World War, which resulted by the mid-sixties in the great majority of dependent countries becoming independent states; these new countries had to face formidable problems, not lessened by the fact that their frontiers had been drawn by the colonial powers, based on the immediate problems of colonial eras, and not on the age-old human geography of the lands, linguistic affiliations, and religious and ethnic differences. An additional difficulty was that the vast majority were peasants living in abject poverty, with a very high rate of illiteracy and minimal knowledge of education and the outside world. The remarkable thing is that these countries have developed at all. This is in great part due to their own efforts, though external development aid has played a vital part. Clearly much went wrong, and was badly done, both internally and by external forces. But historically speaking the period of development has been but a second of time, and in retrospect more has been accomplished than is realised, or could have been envisaged.

iii. The lack of coordination and communication between donors and recipients, and within donor countries and developing countries.

iv. The increase in population and pollution, particularly the former, which obviously affects education; the latter can be said to contain the debatable argument on 'the limits of growth'.

v. The gap which has continued to widen between 'haves' and 'have nots' in developing countries, sometimes made more intense by development aid.

In the final event, however, the result of our discussions has been that most of the problems enumerated above are treated to a greater or lesser extent in Chapter 2, but they receive much fuller treatment in Chapters 3–8, on the developing countries. The numerous arguments and counter discussions that can take place around any of these facets of general development aid are not therefore included in this chapter, but will arise in the final chapter of conclusions and recommendations, based on the facts as the author and consultants have seen them, and not on theory.

Visits by the consultants to the countries concerned had to be fitted in with their existing full-time commitments, and in some cases there has inevitably been a lapse of time before the results of their visits could be recorded; the visits took place mainly between late 1971 and 1972.

The first step was for the author to decide which countries to include in the project. The developed countries were her own choice; the developing ones were chosen in discussions and consultations in France, the Federal Republic of Germany and the Netherlands, and by correspondence and discussions in London with the United States. Agreement to participate in the project then had to be secured from the Governments of the eleven countries involved, and also from the United Nations, United Nations' agencies, the Ford and Rockefeller Foundations. Many discussions were held with a wide range of contacts in France, the Federal Republic of Germany, the Netherlands and the United Kingdom; with OECD and UNESCO in Paris, and with the United Nations agencies in Geneva, or with the liaison officers of agencies not based on that city. It was not practicable to visit the United States of America, but many people from universities and official spheres were generous in discussing the project with the author in London, or by correspondence. In agreement with the United States, their overall official activities have not been included, but only those projects which have appeared to be outstanding in the countries concerned.

In many cases, a contact made continued to provide up-to-date material, so the supplies of material have not only been voluminous, but constantly updated. The material collected was either distributed as relevant to the consultants' case studies, or was used by the author in other parts of the book. Inevitably with so much material collected, not all of it can be used, and in some cases language has had to be reduced to an almost 'telegraphese' form. In squirrel-like fashion, many useful, eloquent, and apt quotations have been hoarded, but lack of space has meant that on the whole they cannot be used. Moreover, a remarkable feature in this field is how quickly factors which may seen of enormous importance one moment become rapidly out of date, and their place is taken by another fashionable developmental problem.

In no case has a questionnaire been used, though without doubt some material which we have had has been based on the questionnaire methods of others. It was found, certainly by the author, that provided people are clearly informed in advance of the purpose of an interview or meeting, an hour's friendly discussion can illuminate and clarify policies or methods, while one thousand questionnaires (a mere hundred of which will be satisfactorily returned) may irritate both sides. This may be 'unscientific', but it remains true.

The main aspects of aid examined

After much thought, several principal problems of aid methodology emerged, which are as follows: the administration of aid; educational systems in developing countries; training at home and abroad, from junior to senior levels; experts, specialist advisers, teachers, counterparts, and volunteers; university links and research work; when relevant, the teaching of the language of the developed country in a developing one, and evaluation. All these subjects can be broken down into innumerable facets, and these will be examined throughout Chapters 2–8. The results are then collated and assessed in the final chapter.

Inevitably the major part of our work has been concerned with the official bilateral and multilateral operations, but we have had the good fortune to have useful cooperation from the Ford and Rockefeller Foundations, and many voluntary societies in a variety of countries.

As this book has progressed the world seems to have plunged deeper into violence, hate, mistrust and misunderstanding between countries, and within countries. If our efforts can, even in a very minute way, help in any way towards a greater understanding and humanity of man to man then we shall all feel that it has been more than worth while. Sir Robert Jackson when submitting his report to the President of the Governing Council of UNDP, in a letter of 30 September 1969, said: 'My only reason for accepting the task was the hope that the study may ultimately help people in developing countries. I believe this work transcends any other human endeavour.' This book has been, I think, undertaken for the same reason, but we would go further: all those who have cooperated in this project in the light of their experiences would subscribe strongly to the view that the so-called developed countries have much to learn from that developing world which represents the majority of the human race. This is at least as important as the more usually publicised reasons for development aid.

Part II

2 The Donors

I SOME REASONS FOR THE PROVISION OF AID

The first question to be asked is 'Why give aid?' The reasons can be as variable as the British climate, depending upon when you happen to be writing about them. Many years ago, and also today, amongst most of the younger generation, aid was and is regarded mainly in idealistic terms, particularly if carried out by voluntary or multilateral governmental agencies. But many believe that the principal reasons are those related to foreign policy and trade.

1. Bilateral official aid

Bilateral aid still remains, and is likely to do so, as the source which presents the greatest quantity of aid. Some basic reasons for such aid are as follows:

i. In cases where there has been a metropolitan country with dependent colonial territories, on the independence of the latter there has normally been an established association which continues, and an assumption by both the metropolitan country and the newly independent one that an obligation exists for continued aid. There is usually one major difference from the pre-independence period, namely that the requests for assistance come from the developing country, and it is only these requests that the developed country considers and meets; but often the assistance available has been somewhat unimaginatively unchanged from year to year.

ii. The provision of aid, or as it is sometimes termed 'external assistance', is in the case of most developed countries an acknowledged part of their foreign policy, and one that has come to stay; as a tool of foreign policy it is believed to bring in its train political advantages to the donor country in the field of international relations.

iii. Bilateral aid has an element, sometimes the predominant one, of hoping to promote admiration and increasing the prestige of the way of life of the developed country concerned, the media of language being a major factor. As with other facets of aid, an inevitable element of competition arises between the different developed nations.

iv. Often there is an overwhelming economic motive for aid leading to trade, and it is perhaps in this field that there can be proven benefits to the donor nation. At the simplest level, if a student of engineering carries out his studies at a post-graduate level in a developed country, when he becomes the manager of an engineering concern in his own country he will tend to be interested in the products of the developed country in which he studied.

v. A further economic aspect of aid is that much aid is now 'tied aid'; although strenuous efforts have been made[1] to loosen the strings of tied aid, there has so far not been any very notable change, and if the practice continues it may not only considerably reduce, but eventually nullify the success of some aspects of aid programmes.

2. United Nations and United Nations' agencies

i. In general the United Nations' agencies were founded for international purposes of goodwill. These purposes have to a certain extent been preserved, more particularly in the cases of smaller agencies concerned with one profession, where there has been success in maintaining high professional standards, frequently backed by purposes of an altruistic nature.

ii. But over the years the original ideals of the founders of some of the organisations have become diluted through the political control exerted by the member states who form the governing authority, and who now number 135. When the United Nations started on 24 October 1945 there were fifty member states. There has also been a growing tendency for blocks of countries to vote in political uniformity, which inevitably diminishes the altruistic and professional purposes of the 'United Nations family'.

iii. The United Nations and the agencies have previously, to a certain extent, 'ventriloquised' receiving governments to ask for certain forms of aid in order to keep their particular organisations occupied and well funded. It remains to be seen if the increased authority of UNDP resulting from the Jackson Report will in any way alter this tendency.

iv. The purpose for which aid is given can within the United Nations be tainted by considerations of institutional loyalties and job security for a large number of people. This produces a built-in reason for pursuing continuous courses of action and resisting innovations.

[1] For instance in the forum of the Development Assistance Committee of OECD.

v. A real danger exists that despite many valuable investigations and reports (including Pearson and Jackson) the United Nations family as a whole is heading towards chaos, unable to control itself or, in the case of the agencies, to keep within the confines of the professional purposes for which the organisation was originally created. Chaotic and often unhappy administrations of the United Nations agencies is one of the most formidable obstacles to the original purpose of an aid project being successfully concluded.

3. The private sector

The term 'the private sector' can comprise charitable foundations, voluntary organisations, commercial undertakings, operations by universities or other institutions; indeed any form of aid which is not financed bilaterally or multilaterally from government sources can come within this term. In the context of this book, universities and other educational institutions inevitably loom very large, in the chapters on both the developed and developing countries, and no reference is made to them here. The industrial and commercial world is mainly concerned with economic aid and somewhat rarely with educational aid, except in the form of scholarships, which are very often tied to one undertaking. There is, however, a growing tendency for both industrial and commercial operations to be financed by either bilateral or multilateral official sources to undertake specific tasks of various types in the field of development aid. The comments which follow are mainly concerned with 'charitable foundations' and 'voluntary organisations'.

The difference between charitable foundations and voluntary organisations can be simply defined by saying that the former usually exist because of the generosity of one individual, whereas voluntary organisations have their roots in the membership of people who support their objectives, and provide finance in the form of fees or donations.

The role of both foundations and voluntary organisations in the field of aid has increased considerably; in the major donor countries finance for development purposes amounting to \$m 620·1 in 1969 rose to \$m 889·6 in 1971.[2]

The number of foundations and voluntary organisations are manifold, and it is difficult to give any accurate picture of their full role, which ranges from the alleviation of distress in times of catastrophe to more recognised forms of aid, particularly educational aid. The OECD and the International Council of Voluntary Agencies (ICVA)'s Directory of 1967, together with the Technical Assistance Information Clearing House Documentation of the United States (with over a thousand entries) provide a basis from which it is possible to gain a fairly comprehensive and

[2] 'Reviews of Development Assistance', DAC, 1971 and 1972.

up-to-date picture of the major bodies in these categories now working in the development field, or in partnership with governments or multilateral organisations. To a growing extent such organisations have been invited by governments, either bilaterally, or on a multilateral basis, to undertake operations for which the official parent organisation has provided finance.

One way in which a number of voluntary organisations now act is as pressure points, to encourage governments to do more in the aid field, and in some cases individual organisations in countries have a recognised role in public relations in this respect.

Charitable foundations, more particularly in the United States, have their origins in large sums of money, donated usually by individual industrialists, for the establishment of a charitable foundation with clearly defined purposes, and governed by a group of independent trustees, who have in many cases substantially increased the original sum by investment. Many of the major foundations include international operations in their work, often concerned with the less developed countries, and frequently assisting with education in one form or another. Two outstanding foundations in the United States of America are notable in this field, and have been included in the project, namely the Ford Foundation and the Rockefeller Foundation.

i. The Ford Foundation exists to advance the public welfare by trying to identify and contribute to the solution of problems of national and international importance. Grants are made to institutes in the United States and abroad in the fields of education, agriculture, population, public administration and economic planning.

ii. The Rockefeller Foundation's main purpose is 'to promote the well-being of mankind throughout the world'. It operates primarily through grants, and has career staff stationed in many parts of the developing world.

Voluntary organisations, as has already been said, are numerous. Their purposes are as varied as they are numerous, often being based on religious activities, or the fulfilling of some desperate and obvious need. Many decades ago the first voluntary organisations to bring some education and health improvements to developing countries were the missionary societies of many different nationalities and creeds, operating in various parts of the world, but their work in these early days was often damaged by a lack of understanding of the cultures and social structures of the developing countries, and the enforcement of such western customs as the wearing of western clothes, often totally at variance with climatic and health conditions. Often, and not only in the field of development aid, it has been a small group of dedicated people from a voluntary organisation whose work has affected a major world issue, or highlighted the problem of one individual country. In the past one of the most striking examples was the anti-slavery movement. Now, perhaps, it is the problem of population, environmental difficulties, or simply poverty.

II THE DEVELOPED COUNTRIES

1. General background and policies

France

France's contribution to the development picture, like that of the United Kingdom, has been greatly affected by being an ex-colonial power with a considerable number of dependent territories, the vast majority of which are now independent states. Inevitably this has meant that by far the largest portion of France's resources available for aid have gone to the countries of the Maghreb, Francophone Africa, Malagasy, and French former colonies in the Far East. In recent years there has been some extension of France's geographical interests, for example the average annual contribution to Latin American countries in the period 1960–6 was $m 98·18, and in 1968–70 it was $m 165·57.[3]

From 1967 to 1970 France led the annual averages of the CNP 'share league', and in 1971 she was second; the annual overseas net official assistance provided bilaterally and multilaterally rose from $m 923 in 1961–3 to $m 1087·01 in 1971.[4]

A certain elegance of language and a concept of *civilisation* can be observed in many facets of French life and these are not absent either from the French presentation of the purposes of their aid, or in many cases from the implementation of their programmes.

Development aid has for a long time been a basic factor of French foreign policy, a policy which has in the main supported the expansion of French culture in its widest sense, the development of the former French colonies, particularly those south of the Sahara, and the advancement of French commercial interests. The policy for giving aid within the overall foreign policy has normally three main criteria:

i. That the aid should help in the widest diffusion of French *civilisation*, including the French language, educational standards and methods.

ii. That it should help the development of the former French colonial territories.

iii. That it can be justified in the belief that France sooner or later will derive some commercial advantage from the aid provided.

[3] OECD Review, 1972.
[4] OECD, DAC Reviews, 1971–2, Table 1.

In 1963 the Jeanneney Commission said,

> The first reason, sufficient in itself for a French policy of cooperation with the Third World, is a feeling which France has of her duties towards humanity .... to fail in this duty would be to deny the *civilisation* which she incarnates, to destroy its inspiration, to endanger its flowering.[5]

This attitude to French aid policies has had the effect that the great majority of previous French colonies have very strong continuing cultural, educational and linguistic ties with metropolitan France; this applies at least to the elites of the developing countries, who have, through formation modelled on French education, come to hold positions of responsibility in their governments and professions. In recent years the position has begun to change, both as regards France's own policies and those of the previously dependent states, partly because in the latter case countries other than France have been increasing their aid to these states.

The changes in France's own policy have been recorded in the annual report of the Relations Culturelles, Scientifiques et Techniques. For example in the report for 1968–9 M. Laurent, the Director-General, said:

> ... the road that leads to human and cultural adulthood is that of training. But we cannot ourselves directly provide this training, and we should not do so lest in effect we hold back the advancement of those countries we have undertaken to assist. Cooperation through substitution is neither effective nor durable. In those countries where substitution is still somewhat too prominent a feature of our programme, as in the North African States for obvious historical reasons, it is our duty to reshape our aims and our means of action by directing our major efforts towards the training of teachers and senior management. The time has come to give practical effect to a policy line that has often been proclaimed but too seldom followed in reality, to put an end to the dispersal of resources and concentrate them on getting countries to train their own management personnel and their own educators.

In 1970 M. Laurent's Introduction suggested that the time had come for greater cooperation by France with multilateral programmes than in the past, particularly where duplication could be avoided. He called for a movement away from general education, which had always been the main concern of French cultural cooperation, towards greater emphasis on science and technology, which apart from meeting local needs in these subjects would lay greater stress on the projection of a truer image of modern France.

[5] 'Le Politique de Coopération avec les Pays en voie de developpement', Jeanneney Commission, 1963.

The years 1960–70 had been years of reflection and re-orientation, permitting the French Government to take greater cognisance of the scientific and technological aspects of culture as against the traditional forms of culture such as literature and language.

In 1971 M. Schuman, the then Foreign Minister, in his Introduction re-emphasised the pre-eminence of scientific and technological projects in the field of aid. The Director-General, M. Laurent, stressed that French as a language was no longer a vehicle for one culture, but for a plurality of cultures, and not just a torch-bearer of French civilisation. He stressed how the French language was needed in its new 'technical role' and the importance of all *formation* and manpower training. Finally, it was recorded that there was a move towards decentralisation from Paris, with more initiative being in the hands of the French missions abroad and their local operations.

The Federal Republic of Germany

In the 1950s the Federal Republic of Germany took the first steps towards providing aid for the developing countries. In these early days West Germany was influenced partially by the fact that they had been a recipient of development aid themselves through the Marshall Plan, partly by their central position in world confrontation between the East and the West, and partly because, even before they had reached a state of sound economic development themselves, they wished to be recognised as a State playing a responsible part in world affairs, and particularly in assisting countries with less opportunities than themselves.

In 1960 the Federal Ministry of Economic Development (BMZ) was created; major responsibilities for aid development are also held by the Ministry of Economics and the Foreign Office. Finance available had risen steadily; the annual average in the period 1961–3 of $m 374 rising to $m 734·2 in 1971. In the period 1961–3 they were sixth in the league ranking of the annual averages of GNP, although despite the financial increases by 1971 they had dropped to tenth.[6]

The Federal Republic's policies as regards aid were little affected by any past history, and at the outset there would seem to have been greater moral and idealistic impulses than was the case with some other countries, coupled with what has already been mentioned – the political wish for full recognition of new nationhood. The Federal Republic's efficiency and willingness to try new methods, her attitude both in practice and in fact of not looking over her shoulder at past history, made her aid welcome in the developing world as both efficient and untainted.

As the years have passed, however, and the aid has become more and more massive, there have inevitably been greater overtones of affinity with

[6] OECD, DAC Reviews, 1971–2, Table 1.

political and commercial policies than existed in the early sixties. But even so the Federal Republic's aid remains less criticised by many developing countries than the aid provided by the United Kingdom, France and the United States of America.

The Federal Republic took a long cool look at their development policies in the early 1970s. In October 1970 a conference of eminent personalities was convened to give new impulses and secure public approval of Germany's development aid policies. At this time the Federal President said:

> A policy directed towards the good of world society can, at least at times, conflict with national interest. This conflict can be endured only if a large proportion of the citizens also understand, accept and support decisions that can be at variance with their own interests. The conjointly responsible task of development aid policy must be held in such high esteem that private considerations present no insuperable obstacles to its implementation.

The Federal Government stresses confidently that it does not wish to press political, social or economic ideas upon developing countries, but that all development work must be done in close cooperation with the developing country concerned, and in cooperation with other partners. Development assistance which is subordinate to foreign policy is felt to be doomed to failure. True, or not, aid development has inevitably some political connotations with foreign policy. Aid, it is hoped, develops good relations with the countries concerned and, as the Federal Republic states, it should help developing countries to be independent and efficient trading partners.

The principal guidelines in the early 1970s for German aid policies were:

i. Assisting and promoting assistance of education, orientated towards employment in the environment of the country concerned.

ii. Improvement of the level of subsistence and hygiene.

iii. Assistance and advice in the sphere of family planning.

iv. Projects related to the development of rural districts, special attention being paid to the means of creating new jobs.

The Federal Republic is realistic in seeing that assistance through the United Nations and United Nations agencies is particularly acceptable to developing countries, who as member states of the United Nations have equal standing in the organisation with the so-called developed states. In 1971 West Germany ear-marked twenty per cent of the money available for development aid purposes to multilateral organisations and has undertaken to continue to provide at least this percentage for multilateral assistance in the foreseeable future. They adhere to the basic principle, that within the developing countries bilateral and multilateral efforts must be coordinated with the country's own national development planning, and preferably under the direction of the developing country. This policy is a view shared by the majority of developed countries, but would not at the moment seem a totally practical operation everywhere.

The Federal Republic recognises that human beings are the wealth of the developing countries, even though far too many are underfed, have no training and no job, and cannot in the immediate future contribute to the development of their country. But, realising that human beings are wealth, the Federal Republic places much weight on the United Nations' strategy for the Second Decade development of emphasising social objectives, food, education, employment and health. The Federal Republic, believing that development assistance can help to mobilise human and natural resources as yet not fully used, recognises that nothing can replace the efforts made by the developing countries themselves.

The Netherlands

Development aid provided by the Netherlands expanded considerably in the early 1960s when not only was the financial allocation considerably increased, but their programme was widened geographically. Before 1963 much of their resources available for aid had been concentrated on West New Guinea, Surinam and the Netherlands Antilles. Their programmes were not so affected by the independence of Indonesia because there was a considerable migration of population to the Netherlands at the time of Independence. In addition, for some years there was a certain coolness between the Netherlands and Indonesia which caused the latter not to accept aid from the former. This meant that their past colonial history has not affected their general policies of aid-giving to the same extent as France and the United Kingdom.

The growth of resources can be seen from the fact that in the period 1961–3 the outflow of their official development assistance both bilaterally and multilaterally was \$m 53 and in 1971 had risen to \$m 216·1. In the league table of how donor countries ranked on GNP shares, on annual averages during the period 1961–3 the Netherlands were seventh, but in 1971 they were top of the league.[7]

The aid policies of the Netherlands have always had their roots in the United Nations Declaration of Human Rights. This has logically caused their policies to follow the belief that the developed and developing countries in the process of aid development should act as equal partners; that it is in the interests of the more fortunate country to avoid conflict

[7] OECD, DAC Reviews, 1971–2.

by the change of an atmosphere of distrust into one of cooperation, based on mutual self-interest. This has caused constant emphasis to be placed on the importance of partnership between the aid-giving country and the recipient. The Netherlands believe that such participation will bring about structural changes not only in the developing countries but in the entire world, as the developed countries must be prepared equally to accept such changes. Their attitude to aid is that attacking the root problems of poverty is the best way to help to remove the seeds of conflict and increase mutual interest between all countries of the world, whatever their level of wealth. The alternative to them is that the world could be disastrously split into rich and poor countries, and this would inevitably bring world-wide disasters.

It is recognised that to try and produce an educational system in a developing country based on the Netherlands' system would be totally impracticable. For the same reason there is no large-scale provision of scholarships for students to study at universities in the Netherlands, the language and the type of course being usually unsuitable. In the 1960s a wide range of special courses for people from developing countries were established, many of them under the auspices of the Netherlands' University Foundation for International Cooperation. These courses have over the years provided a unique form of training; the time may now have come when some of the courses are not necessary, and it seems likely that there will be considerable changes in the future. The subject is at present being studied by the National Advisory Council for Aid to Less Developed Countries: the principle aim is to achieve the kind of course which will be as closely as possible matched to the needs of the developing countries, and for the courses to be held in such countries where feasible. There is an inclination that there should be a project approach, instead of the present standard courses – namely, when courses are being planned the specific aim, the resources and the duration should always be established.

There is also a proposal that the present institutes which have run international courses should be incorporated into the universities. It must however be said that during the life of the Foundation's special institutes and courses they have made a unique contribution to international education; many developing countries have benefited from the imaginative way in which courses have been organised, and in many instances the institutes have won world-wide renown.

The Netherlands' Government has, since the mid-sixties, always looked well ahead at aid programmes, and this tendency is clearly increasing. Both in the past and at present the Netherlands provides a remarkable amount of development assistance; their programmes are efficient and probably have had considerable effect, because they have wisely limited their geographical interests so that they can do a really good job in a few countries rather than provide a little aid for many. They have inevitably, with their international approach, been generous in providing finance for multilateral operations, their contributions to such operations having risen from $m 19·9 in 1963 to $m 50·6 in 1972.[8]

Aid provided by the Netherlands is welcomed in developing countries and is well administered. For the period 1973–5, a 66 per cent increase in finance is envisaged. Such a considerable increase may mean a greater alignment of aid policies to those of foreign affairs and trade than has happened in the past.

The United Kingdom

Inevitably by far the largest part of the United Kingdom development aid still goes to the developing countries of the Commonwealth, and to the few countries which are still dependencies. It should however be stressed that quite apart from British aid much aid has been provided by the other richer members of the Commonwealth, such as Australia, Canada and New Zealand, and to a growing extent there are now flows of aid between the different developing countries of the Commonwealth.[9] In these countries professional people and many elements of the population are English-speaking, and not only those who can be regarded as elitist. This had the important result that, since these countries became independent, the United States of America also has not been inhibited by linguistic barriers from providing a massive amount of aid. The position of the United Kingdom has, therefore, been rather different from that of any other ex-metropolitan power, in that newly independent countries were speedily in the position of having a wide variety of sources of bilateral aid from different countries available to them, quite apart from regional schemes, such as the Colombo Plan and the very considerable multilateral operations of the United Nations and United Nations' agencies.

As was the case with other ex-metropolitan countries, the 'overseas services' of the United Kingdom, principally the Indian Civil Service, the Sudan Political Service and the Colonial Service, were staffed with dedicated people, the great majority of whom genuinely believed in and worked for the independence of the countries in which they served.

On Independence, with the exception of the countries of the Indian sub-continent, there was some continuity of personnel, as the independent states requested that members of the relevant services should stay and serve as members of the government departments of the new nations. This inevitably led to an element of continuity of methods and purposes from the colonial days. Both the personnel and purposes have now rightly changed as independent states have become more able to staff the ministries with their own people, and have become more definite

[8] ODI Review, no. 5, 1972.

[9] See section on Commonwealth organisations, ch. 2, pp. 41 ff.

themselves in deciding what is best for their countries. This has probably led to United Kingdom aid becoming more of a foreign policy operation, with trade not following aid, but often in the reverse order. With the return in 1974 of the Labour Government, however, the doctrine has been forcefully reasserted that the purpose of aid is to bring about human development through assistance to the poorest sections of the Third World.

The Indian sub-continent, now India, Pakistan, Bangladesh and Sri Lanka, was in a different position, the vast majority of the British leaving the countries concerned on Independence. There were far more indigenous trained civil servants than in other parts of the Commonwealth, and many of the universities were established in the mid-1880s, awarding their own degrees. The position in the British colonies south of the Sahara was quite different. Degrees were awarded from the University of London, with whom these countries had a special relationship until the 1960s, when the institutions of higher education all became independent universities.

In parts of the world other than the Commonwealth, for example Latin America, Turkey, the Middle East, South-East Asia and the Far East, development aid has been slower to take shape, and probably the principle purpose of bilateral aid was based on trade and historic strategic considerations. The position of the English language is different from any other language in the world, as although the United Kingdom spends large sums of money on the maintenance and dissemination of the English language, English being the common tongue of North America, New Zealand and Australia, it has become the *lingua franca* of trade and technology. It can therefore be said that English is learnt not so much for reasons of *civilisation*, as is French, but because it is the language of trade. This however is an over-simplification, as the literature of every language through the ages has demonstrated the spirit and belief of its country.

The United Kingdom, like the United States, the Federal Republic of Germany and the Netherlands, gives considerable help overseas through the voluntary societies, using voluntary money (some £18 million from the United Kingdom in 1972). Those concerned with policies and practices of this sector of aid believe that the richer should help the poorer, and do their work without the strings of tied aid, foreign policy, or trade, which inevitably affect official aid.

In the period 1961–3, the annual average of net official development assistance, both bi- and multilateral, was $m 431, and in 1973 $m 603·1. The United Kingdom dropped from fourth in the league ranked on annual averages of GNP shares to tenth in 1973.[10] Although 80 per cent of the total gross bilateral aid went to Commonwealth countries in 1973,[11] aid to

[10] OECD.
[11] Ministry of Overseas Development.

other parts of the world was steadily increased; for example, total United Kingdom bilateral technical assistance to Central and South America was £533,000 in 1966 and by 1973 it was £3,797,000.

United States of America

The United States of America's first major experience of aid was the Marshall Plan, when Europeans knew exactly what they needed to restore their war-devastated economics and had the competence of long experience and trained people to do most of the jobs themselves. Then followed a period when the 'cold war' was a major feature of foreign policy, and was also used as a reason for giving aid. This led step by step to aid being almost a weapon of security. So the two programmes, security and aid, particularly of course economic aid, were presented by successive administrations to Congress together, in the belief that economic aid on its own would get absolutely nowhere. This is probably true, though it is widely believed in the US that despite the enormous amount of money and manpower put into aid programmes, the money is sometimes misdirected and the people in the field and at home are not always round pegs in round holes.

The United States has supplied massive aid, and is by far the largest donor in absolute terms, though on a declining scale. In spite of the vastness of their financial contribution they have never been very high in the league based on average GNP shares, dropping from third in 1961–3 to eleventh in 1971. Both the proportion and amounts of finance going to multilateral organisations have, however, increased and are likely to continue to do so.

The deep and generous humanitarianism of the population of the United States, both individually and collectively, is well recognised. Yet the often imaginative initiatives of successive US administrations are some of the least appreciated by developing countries. Over the years the United States has searched unremittingly for the right methods of administering their official aid, and this has resulted in a variation of policies which has also had some adverse effect on their operations. Now AID and numerous semi-voluntary bodies are the main feature of their administration, supported by a wide variety of totally voluntary organisations. There has also been a constant search for the *rationale* for aid which has not been found, and which has left a continuous gap between the dedication of those who believe in aid, sometimes in an unreasoning way, and Congress which has to decide on financial appropriations.

From the experience of the 1960s it would seem that development aid had no overwhelming appeal to Congress and this was reflected in declining levels of finance. The world-wide theme that the gap between rich and poor would continuously widen tended to receive little response;

the theory of those who support the view that aid can be divorced from political aims and purposes seemed unrealistic.

An argument finding favour with US policy is that economically developed countries are better for US trade and commercial purposes, but a minority tend to say that there would be a boomerang effect – namely a developing country becoming economically viable can become a competitor.

The political argument of winning friendship by aid is a doubtful and rather tender plant, but one political motive which may be singular to the United States and difficult for her to handle is that as the richest country in the world she is expected by developed and developing countries alike to provide aid, including economic aid. Professor Samuel Huntington gives five criteria for purposes of allotting aid to selected countries, which have relevance and are as follows:

1. Economic performance, i.e. demonstrated or probable ability of the country to make effective use of aid for economic development and its willingness to commit its own resources and to adapt its own policies to this goal;
2. Security relevance, i.e. the extent to which a country's external security is of major interest to the United States, and the extent to which that security is or could be threatened by another power;
3. Political democracy, i.e. the extent to which the country has a broad based, democratic political system with meaningful elections and protection of individual civil liberties;
4. Historical association, i.e. the extent to which some special, historical relationship has existed between the country and the United States, giving that country an extra claim on United States' consideration and help;
5. Global importance, i.e. the relative weight which the country does have or potentially may have in world politics.[12]

It would seem possible that the United States sometimes overlooks the massive efforts that poorer countries are themselves making to develop all aspects of their national life. The United States are not alone in this, but it may be one reason why there is opposition to aid amongst some developing countries. The United States of America has an especial interest in the economic development of some countries for non-economic reasons, as a part of US overall policy. In the early seventies they have concentrated on three aspects of aid:

humanitarian action aimed at relieving immediate difficulties and the very poor,

[12] Samuel P. Huntington, 'Foreign Aid for What and for Whom', *Foreign Policy*, vol. 1, no. 1, 1971.

general economic grants chanelled through the World Bank and other multinational agencies, for overall economic development of poorer countries, and

bilateral assistance as a part of the United States overall foreign policy.[13]

2. The administration of aid

Introduction

In the past, developed countries were apt to deal with aid without much knowledge of the country for which the aid was intended, and with little discussion with these countries. There was also a lack of cooperation between the policy makers and the operators. Each factor is equally important and neither can disregard the failure or success of the other; both fundamentally involve money, which can be wasted by an unwise policy, or though being carried out by operators who use extravagant and unrealistic means.

The success of the two wings of administration, the policy makers and the operators, depends on the standard of staff, their dedication to their work, and to the countries in which they serve. This section deals mainly with the 'operations', particularly in the field of education. As far as possible the administrations, as they exist today, are described with a modicum of back history.

As the aid operation has increased, so inevitably has the machinery of government relating to aid. The number of people employed in developed and developing countries has in most cases grown annually; frequently there has been a proliferation of organisations despite some strenuous efforts to streamline the operation as a whole. The 'management of aid' has in many countries been subjected to what has been termed 'convulsive changes', and it is likely that this will continue.

It is difficult for people in developed countries to know who is responsible for what, and the picture is still more perplexing for developing countries, themselves contantly subject to change of systems, shortage of staff, and ministerial moves.

The following comments on the administration of the selected donors are therefore written as simply as possible, bearing in mind the confused picture that these administrations are apt to present to those not actually working in them.

France

France and the United Kingdom have had unusally complicated developments in the field of the administration of aid because of their role as past colonial powers. Aid has always been a matter of deep concern to the

[13] For a fuller discussion of this theme see Huntington, op. cit.

French Government and its administration increased considerably with the Independence of the Maghreb States and later of the Francophone countries south of the Sahara, and Malagasy.

There has been continuous reorganisation within the ministries of the French Government in relation to the administration of aid, and this process of change continues. France does not possess a single agency for aid administration, but the Caisse Centrale de Coopération Economique (CCCE) has as its only object the promotion of development, and works in liaison with the other government departments concerned. The CCCE administers inter-governmental loans, assists the Ministry of Foreign Affairs to carry out cooperation and development programmes, and operates as a development bank in the Francophone countries of Africa, and Malagasy.

Much of the responsibility for aid administration rests with the Ministry of Economics and Finance; all contacts with the World Bank, European Investment Bank, and European Development Fund are the Ministry's concern, as is the preparation of the annual reports to the Development Assistance Committee of OECD. Aid is an important part of the overall external policy of the Ministry of Foreign Affairs; through the Direction de Relations Culturelles, Scientifiques et Techniques the Ministry provides technical assistance to countries other than the Francophone states south of the Sahara, and Malagasy; but direct financial responsibility lies with the Ministry of Economics and Finance. Although this position may seem confusing to the outsider there is close and constant cooperation between the Ministry of Economics and Finance and the Ministry of Foreign Affairs, the former having direct responsibility for operations which are in themselves of immediate economic and industrial interest. One such programme is the very large one of industrial training (approximately 3000 persons per annum come to France) and of 'experts' (of whom about 500 go annually overseas); the major portion of the work being done by the Association pour l'Organisation des Missions de Coopération Technique (ASMIC), the operative wing of which is the Agence pour la Coopération Technique Industrielle et Economique (ACTIE).

The Secretariat d'Etat (S.d'E) which is responsible for aid to the Francophone states south of the Sahara and Malagasy, was for many years an independent ministry, but in 1968–9[14] it became part of the Ministry of Foreign Affairs; it has an independent budget and both formulates policies and administers technical assistance for the countries for which it is responsible.

The two wings of the Ministry of Foreign Affairs, the CST and the S.d'E, meet regularly, the meetings being held alternatively in the two different offices. Although many of the same media of aid are used the approaches are somewhat different. In the case of the Secretariat d'Etat

[14] On 6 June 1974 the Secretariat d'Etat became an independent ministry.

their one concern is aid, and aid on a very large scale indeed. In the case of the CST, developing countries, other than the Francophone African states and Malagasy, receive aid, but they are also treated in exactly the same way as any foreign developed country with the full range of cultural and scientific cooperation.

The export of teachers is on an enormous scale, both the Foreign and Educational Ministries recruiting teachers, and in addition various Catholic and Protestant organisations send considerable numbers of teachers abroad. The Ministry of Education also has a responsibility for assisting higher education establishments in the countries south of the Sahara.

Overseas French embassies are the central point of responsibility for aid operations. In the Francophone African states and Malagasy Missions d'Aid Coopération are attached to the relevant French embassies, with the responsibility both for aid operations and for evolving programmes with the countries concerned, and the French Ministry in Paris.

In the case of all developing countries working with the CST there are mixed commissions to consider the policies and programmes. The CST and S.d'E of the Ministry of Foreign Affairs use the same methods, but do not always use the same organisations to assist them, or put the same stress on different activities; the main methods, not necessarily in order of priority in relation to money involved, or manpower used, are:

(a) Training Industrial training under the Ministry of Economics and Finance has already been mentioned. The French programmes place considerable stress on training '*sur place*' in developing countries, and in the establishment in these countries of educational institutions, particularly at the 'middle level'. One of the few institutions jointly established and staffed by two developed countries is to be found in Chile, where France and the Federal Republic of Germany, and Chile, together formed an engineering institution. Scholarships (*bourses*) are not given for training in France, if the subject can be taken in the home country. If there are more candidates in such a subject equipped to take higher studies than places available, then the tendency is for the French to assist the country concerned to expand the facilities within that country rather than to bring students for training in France. Awards for tenure in France are made bearing in mind the '*multiplication*' effect of each award; some French officials however, see dangers in too much stress being placed on this factor, as the multiplication of French methods might nowadays be irrelevant.

The main organisations concerned with the placement and welfare of people being trained in France are:

(i) Centre International pour les Etudiants et Stages (CIES)

This organisation used to concentrate on Francophone Africa and be known as the Centre International des Stages (CIS), but its geographical spheres have been widened; it now places *boursiers* who come to France for three to nine months elsewhere than in universities, such as in laboratories, government research institutions, or in some cases industry (in as far as ACTIE does not do the placing).

CIES seems to be a highly efficient organisation and has representatives in different parts of the country. Apart from people financed by the French Government, they also place some financed by developing countries, and in a few cases those who are self-financed. They have a welfare organisation and like other organisations find that living accommodation is extremely difficult to secure.

(ii) Office de Coopération et d'Accueil Universitaire (OCAU)

This office deals with students from Francophone and ex-Belgian territories south of the Sahara, who are placed in universities. They too have members of their staff in different parts of the country and have highly organised welfare facilities. *Boursiers* are met at the airport and 1800 rooms are reserved at the Cité Universitaire.

(iii) Centre National des Oeuvres Acceuil (CNOA)

The Centre is concerned with the students who are financed through CST, and works very much on the same lines as the OCAU. It also provides welfare services in all the main university centres. It was stressed that because of accommodation difficulties efforts had been made to place students outside Paris. But now all university towns face a similar problem.

These would seem to be the main organisations, but there are a proliferation of smaller organisations and there does not seem to be very much coordination between them.

Selection of people for training in France is made in the first place by a mixed commission in the country concerned, the final decision being made in Paris, subject to satisfactory placement.

There are not very many special courses for overseas people, apart from courses in 'French as a foreign language'. There is however one particularly distinguished institution for courses in public administration, Institut International d'Administration Publique; from 1959 to 1963 the Institut existed for the training of students from Francophone Africa in administration. After General de Gaulle's visit to Latin America in 1964 it was decided that the Institut should also be available for people from Latin America and elsewhere, and by 1966 this expansion was completed. It has the status of a government ministry and the Director works to the Prime Minister's office.

The Institut's main activities are:

the training of people who have been selected to be civil servants and those who are already members of a Civil Service;

research on comparative administration done principally by French researchers.

There are normally about 750 people under training at any one time, about a third are African, a fifth come from Latin America, and rather fewer from the Near East and Asia, and a variety of other countries. A preparatory course in the French language is given in English-speaking countries, and a six-month course of final language instruction at the Institut.

Candidates are put forward by overseas' governments; the courses last for fourteen months, eight months of which are spent on the speciality of the trainee, i.e. diplomacy, administration, etc. For a period, work is done in geographical groups, i.e. Black Africa, Latin America, the Near East, Mediterranean and South-East Asia, so that training may relate to the problems of the students' own country.

The Institut works in close collaboration with schools of administration in other countries and provides excellent facilities for the general welfare of the course members and their leisure time, such as vacation.

The research section concentrates on a special centre for the study of administration and publications which include a quarterly review of the Institut.

(b) The provision of experts, advisers and teachers to developing countries CTS policy in this field comes under two Sous Directions, one dealing with experts and advisers, and the other with teachers at all levels, except in medical and agricultural subjects.

The Ministry of Education recruits teachers, who are civil servants; both wings of the Ministry of Foreign Affairs employ and place them. The operation is on such a massive scale that there are often gaps left in the teaching service in metropolitan France. In addition many teachers are recruited by religious bodies such as Comité Catholique des Amitiés Français dans le Monde.

Every endeavour is made not to send experts or advisers when there are indigenous people available in the subject concerned. The thesis of *cooperation* leading to *substitution*, inaugurated in 1969–70, was intended to lead to only trainers of teachers being provided by France, but this is a long term *opération*, and cannot be done too quickly without damaging the educational services in some developing countries.

(c) Volunteers The main official scheme is the Volontaires de Service National Actif, a system by which a young man can, when he is due to do national service, volunteer to do aid service instead. If accepted he is then attached to a French Embassy in a developing country for the period of his military service. Another scheme of a voluntary nature is the Volontaires des Progrès, which operates only in Africa south of the Sahara.

The volunteer schemes in France have not been in operation so long, nor are the personnel so numerous as those of some other major developed countries. In 1971 France sent 459 volunteers, as compared to 1524 from the Federal Republic of Germany, over 13,000 from the United States of America, and nearly 2000 from the United Kingdom.[15]

(d) Teaching of French as a foreign language This is clearly one of the major activities of France, and is done with great thoroughness and imagination. It is one which of course covers the whole world, not only the developing world, and only a very brief mention can be made of the main organisations concerned with this major French activity.

Three organisations play a major part. The Bureau pour l'Enseignement de la Langue et de la Civilization (BELC), whose main job is the teaching of French as a foreign language, researches into methods of linguistic methodology, provides a documentation centre, and a centre for the training of teachers of French as a foreign language. Courses in Paris last one year and there are shorter courses *sur place* for indigenous teachers of French.

The Centre de Recherche et d'Etude pour la Diffusion Français (CREDIF) researches into problems of French as a foreign language. CREDIF concentrates on audio-visual aids and believes that the same method can be used in every country, whereas BELC uses contrasting methods for different countries. Both organisations are financed by the Ministry of Education, and both are at the service of both CST and S.d'E of the Foreign Office. There are some special courses – for example one at the University of Paris, which concentrates on the teaching of French as a foreign language, and another interesting venture is a centre in the Republic of Malagasy, for teaching French to English-speaking Africans.

Finally there is the world-wide Alliance Française, which with very little government money does a global operation in the teaching of French, and has all the admirable enthusiasm which is often generated when an organisation has to raise money and earn its position through the excellence of its work.

(e) University links and research

i. University links, or *Jumelage* as they are known in France, are not so active as in other countries. There are some financed by the Ministry of Education, between French and African universities.

ii. Research is done on a considerable scale, two forms of which are covered in this paragraph. First of all the type of scientific research carried out by the Office de la Recherche Scientifique et Technique d'Outre-Mer (ORSTOM). ORSTOM is entirely financed by the French Government, but they have juridical and administrative autonomy and are not an emanation of any individual ministry. The organisation is flexible and works wherever it is requested to do so, and where money is available; a corps of scientific research workers count as civil servants, and in addition there are a number

[15] OECD Review, 1972, Table 17.

of contract staff. Traditionally much of the work has been in Africa south of the Sahara, but ORSTOM works for the United Nations, and in Brazil and Peru. Their independent status makes it possible for them to make agreements direct with governments, for example the Senegalese Government, where there are fifty research people in different institutes and projects. *Boursiers* are brought to France, to form *cadres* of research workers in tropical areas; they are placed by CIES under the direction of ORSTOM.

The other form of research is the growing amount being done into development studies in general, and increasingly into educational problems, sometimes by French teams, but in some cases with researchers from the developing countries, particularly the Maghreb and Africa south of the Sahara. France also assists people from these areas to attend seminars and conferences concerned with development research.

(f) Evaluation The cultural and commercial counsellors in French Embassies abroad are responsible in the developing countries for trying to maintain contact with people who have studied in France, sometimes through societies of returned *boursiers*.

The task of evaluating whether a project has achieved its objectives, has been successful or unsuccessful again falls within the sphere of the relevant Embassy counsellors. Sometimes experts from France, usually university people, visit the developing country to assist in evaluation, and in many cases local indigenous experts join in the assessment. A considerable amount of weight is given to these independent reports, but, as elsewhere, evaluation is a fairly new operation.

(g) Professional migration This does not seem to be a problem that worries France at all, possibly because, at any rate in some cases, a person has to have not only a French qualification, but also to be a French national. The main problem seems to arise with Vietnam, and on a smaller scale with Senegal. The only country said to have more teachers in France than in their own country is Togoland.

(h) Notable features of French aid The maintenance of foreign schools, such as the French Lycées, have not been included in this book, but no comment on French aid would be complete without reference being made to the high standing of French Lycées in both developed and developing countries throughout the world.

The other aspect of French policy, the teaching of French as a foreign language, is also a major activity, but its importance is assumed and not detailed in this section.

The most notable factor of French educational aid lies in the large financial volume provided, for example in 1971 it was \$m 488·9, the only higher figure being the United States of America with a contribution of \$m 609·0. The largest part of the educational aid programme is the provision of educational experts, including teachers, administrators and advisers, who together numbered 27,309 in 1971, and if operational personnel and other advisers and volunteers are added, a total of 41,186 personnel is reached, as compared with 22,417 from the United States and 17,639 from the United Kingdom.[16]

Considerable numbers of students and trainees are financed by France, but in this case larger numbers are dealt with by the Federal Republic of Germany, the United States, and nearly the same number by the United Kingdom. It is surprising that there are such a small number of volunteers and university links.

On the debit side perhaps the picture of French aid is more confusing than in some other countries, partly owing to some lack of coordination and the fact that the two wings of the Ministry of Foreign Affairs use different methods and agencies.

French aid administration will undoubtedly continue to change and develop. An interesting theory has been put forward by Yves Berthelot in an Overseas Development Institute Review on French aid performance and development policies.[17] He expounds the theory that an executive agency with flexibility, and able to take speedy action evolved from a re-grouping of all the departments now concerned with aid administration would be the best way forward and would ensure a more integrated assistance programme. A minister, or deputy minister, should be in charge of the agency, and would keep under review other French national policies liable to affect developing countries: this would mean that the Council of Ministers could always be aware of the needs of developing countries; the centralisation of finance would lead to greater efficiency and the agency should be able to work more speedily than the normal Civil Service. This seems sound sense, but many administrative mountains will have to be successfully scaled before this scheme can get further than words on paper.

The Federal Republic of Germany

The Germans take vigorous action to make their methods and their administration clear to the outside world, and for a full description of the whole range of aid activities the reader is referred to publications of the German Foundation for International Development (DSE).[18] The DSE, which is financed by the Federal Ministry for Economic Cooperation (BMZ) has many other activities; it has four centres for special courses and seminars, a well-known one being the Villa Borsig in Berlin; the Food and Agricultural Centre near Munich is also important, and advanced training programmes in administration are run in cooperation with communities'

[16] OECD Review, 1972.

[17] ODI Review, no. 6, 1973.

[18] The names of organisations are given in English: the initials refer to the German titles, which appear in the Glossary on p. 401.

associations, *Länder* towns and rural districts. The DSE's office in Bonn houses the divisions concerned with education, science and documentation, and is a focal coordinating point for many documentation centres and institutions, projects and research studies connected with German development aid.[19]

Apart from a brief general description of the main Federal agencies this section concentrates upon the organisations concerned with one or other aspect of educational assistance.

At the parliamentary level there is a Committee on Development Aid, organisations do, in fact, receive considerable finance from the BMZ, which works in close consultation with the Committee on Foreign Affairs and Budgetary Questions. The main Federal Ministry concerned is the BMZ, a powerful ministry which covers the full range of technical assistance. The Federal Ministry of Economics is concerned with questions of capital aid policy, and the Federal Ministry of Foreign Affairs harmonises the activities of the other two ministries with foreign policy. The BMZ is a vigorous fairly small ministry and a great deal of the work is devolved upon other organs, nearly all of them receiving finance from the BMZ. This is one of the simplifying aspects of the picture of aid administration in the Federal Republic, as the fact that nearly all the agencies and institutions receive money from the BMZ means that the ministry automatically plays a most important coordinating role.

Many organisations which at first sight might appear voluntary organisations do, in fact, receive considerable finance from the BMZ, which evaluate the results of the projects carried out by these organisations.

A complicating factor is that each of the eleven *Länder* have aid administrations and spend quite considerable funds on development aid. To coordinate activities, the *Länder* Committee on Development Aid was established by the BMZ to ensure cooperation between the Federation, the *Länder* and local communities; with regard to the latter there is within the BMZ a coordinating committee responsible for town partnerships.

The role of the Federal Agency for Technical Assistance (BFE)[20] is of particular importance: an autonomous body, it was established by the BMZ in 1969–70, and is entirely financed by it. The agency is responsible for seeing that projects are implemented in the fields of economic and commercial assistance, health and welfare. It also promotes commercial and technical training, educational aid and agricultural assistance. It provides some of the personnel for multilateral projects and international

[19] Note in particular the series of publications 'Organisation of German Development Aid: Introduction to the spheres of activity of the main German institutions concerned with German Development Aid'.

[20] In August 1974 the BFE was amalgamated with GAWI to form a joint society, The Society for Technical Cooperation (Gesellschaft für Technische Zusammenarbeit – GTZ).

organisations. Here, again, many of the tasks are devolved upon other institutions or agencies.

There are a number of other Federal institutions, but the relevant ones are dealt with below under the particular aspect of aid with which they are concerned.

(a) Training This is the Federal Republic's main educational aid activity and involves more people than other operation; in 1971 there were 21,517 students and trainees who received awards.[21] This was the highest figure for any major donor country.

The Carl Duisberg Gesellschaft (CDG) is one of the major organisations in the training field, financed as for 95 per cent by BMZ, and 5 per cent by industry. They also administer some small *Länder* programmes. The CDG is responsible for the major part of training at the middle educational and technical levels, up to the high level institutions of engineering.

On average about 6000 people are trained in Germany each year, and 3000 with German industries overseas, or at trade schools in developing countries which are established with the assistance of the Federal Republic. Of those who come to the Federal Republic, 80 per cent are grouped on courses, but during their time in Germany they are placed individually for periods for industrial attachments; 20 per cent of the trainees are placed on a purely individual basis and do not attend any special course. Candidates are proposed by the government of the country concerned to the relevant German Embassy, who in turn put the proposals to the BMZ. In 1971 the CDG started 'on the spot selection', for example a team went to Tunisia in March 1971 to select personnel for hotel training. Each potential trainee has to have a certificate from an employer and basic training in their own country, except in cases where no such training is available. All the papers are commented upon by a German expert. The CDG has a large network in the Federal Republic of regional offices, foreigners' clubs, and hostels; as far as possible they find accommodation for the trainees, although this has become increasingly difficult.

In the university field the major institution is the German Academic Exchange Service (DAAD). The DAAD works globally and is, therefore, financed both by the Foreign Ministry and by the BMZ. In addition to its headquarters at Bonn/Bad Godesberg, it has offices in various countries throughout the world and wherever it works it evokes appreciation and affection with those with whom it collaborates. The governing body of the DAAD has a large university representation, and, as its name implies, it concentrates on the placement, in Germany mainly at the post-graduate level, or 'export' of university people overseas.

Selection of people for DAAD awards is done in the countries of origin by bi-national committees. The final decision is made in the Federal Republic by committees mainly of academics relevant to the discipline of

[21] OECD Review, 1972, Table 17.

the candidates. The average number of awards per annum is about 9000.

The CDG and the DAAD would seem to be the two major bodies concerned with training, but there are many foundations, such as the Alexander von Humboldt Foundation, the Friedrich Ebert Foundation, and political foundations such as the Konrad Adenauer Foundation, and the Friedrich Naumann Foundation, all of which give scholarships. There are in addition schemes of the Catholic and Protestant churches.

Other Federal ministries assist in placement, always in close collaboration with the BMZ, of specialised Fellows both on German or United Nations agency awards.

(b) The provision of experts, advisers and teachers to developing countries Major organisations in this field are the German Society for Technical Assistance to Developing Countries (GAWI) which in collaboration with the Federal Labour Office through the Central Placement Office in Frankfurt, sends out specialists to government-sponsored development projects. The BFE, also in collaboration with the Frankfurt Office and the Foreign Office, is responsible for sending experts to international organisations; central agencies of the *Länder* recruit public officials for overseas assignments.

The DAAD concentrates on two categories of academic staff, those who go for one year, and well-known professors who spend from three to five months abroad, mainly to teach, but also to advise on such subjects as departmental libraries. The scheme is quite large and well conceived, both from the point of view of finance and of detailed administration. The academic staff are placed within the developing countries existing systems of education.

Teachers in the general school system and in vocational training institutions are recruited by the various Ministries of Education and Culture of the *Länder* and the Secretariat of the Permanent Conference of the Ministers of Education and Culture of the *Länder*.

The Area Orientation Centre of the German Foundation in Developing Countries (DSE) plays an important role by providing orientation courses and other preparatory facilities for institutions sending specialists to developing countries, but not having their own organisation for orientation work.

Both the Catholic and Protestant churches have a considerable number of organisations for the recruitment of teachers for overseas service.

(c) Volunteers The German Volunteer Organisation (DED) is an efficient body, financed entirely by the BMZ. It is, however, an independent company with a board of directors upon which five government departments are represented. The organisation started in 1963, and by 1971 the volunteers numbered 1524.[22] The average age of volunteers is twenty-four, ranging from twenty-one to a few over

[22] OECD Review, 1972.

thirty-five. The applicants must have at least two years' training after leaving school. Ninety-eight per cent are 'middle-men', few are academics. The normal stay in a developing country is for two years, and many volunteer for a further year. About 25–30 per cent of the volunteers eventually go back to work in the developing countries. The host countries make contributions to transport and housing where feasible.

DED recruit by massive advertisement, in general and specialist papers, and through the radio and television. Those selected for interview have long sessions with DED staff, including psychologists and outside experts. Selected volunteers attend preparation courses of eleven weeks, and when necessary language instruction is given. Except in countries where there are a very small number of volunteers, there is a director/coordinator. There are about twenty-five of these globally; they are well paid and, apart from the general direction of projects and the welfare of volunteers, they examine and report upon the projects and assess new ones proposed by developing countries. In some places they have experts on their staff, for example a medical expert if there are a number of medical projects.

Since 1970 there have been team leaders who have not necessarily been volunteers – if they have been volunteers they rarely go back as team leaders to the same country, but will go to the same language area; after two years as team leaders they can become full-time staff members of DED. Like volunteer organisations in other countries they find requests becoming more and more specialised, and volunteers may soon give way to junior experts. Two years of service as a volunteer means indefinite postponement of military service.

Both the Catholic and Protestant aid institutions and smaller voluntary organisations recruit voluntary helpers, mainly for assignments to their own projects in developing countries.

(d) The German language The main instrument for the teaching of German is the Goethe Institute. This has branches in many countries as well as in many parts of the Federal Republic, the headquarters being in Munich. The Goethe Institute is financed by the German Foreign Office. Its methods are admirable and the numbers who come under instruction both overseas and in the Federal Republic are very large indeed.

(e) Research and university links

i. Research on development problems, as one would expect, is well developed in the Federal Republic. There has been considerable action in the field of manpower studies since 1968, but before results are used these are checked with the manpower authorities (if any) of the country concerned. The BMZ has financed research projects on university links, particularly work under the direction of Professor Meyer-Dohm, at the University of Bochum and Professor Havemann at the University of Aachen; there is a vigorous research department within the BMZ which carries out projects on all aspects of aid. Area institutes, such as the

Institute for Asian Studies, the German Institute for African Studies, the Ibero-American Institute, and many others, do specialised research on the countries with which they are concerned. These institutes, such as the Institute of Development Research and Policy of the University of Bochum, and the Institute of International Technology and Economic Cooperation at the University of Aachen, do research in many branches of development and are linked together through the Interdisciplinary Working Group for research on developing countries.
ii. University links have been a well developed feature of the Federal Republic's educational aid for some time. The major costs are borne by the BMZ though comparatively small amounts are contributed from other sources such as the universities themselves, who carry out the detailed organisation. The DAAD is responsible for the administration of the scheme as agents of the BMZ.

References have already been made above to the intensive research carried out to evaluate links in relation to their original objectives and costs. A bi-product of these links are joint research projects; in 1973 there were a large number of active links between institutes in the Federal Republic and those in developing countries.

(f) Evaluation and 'follow-up' The Federal Republic of Germany has given more attention to evaluation and for a longer period than most other donors. The BMZ feel that the fact that the Federal Republic works almost entirely on a project basis makes evaluation work easier; they modestly do not regard their own evaluation procedures very highly, but clearly much research has been initiated and financed by the Ministry, as instanced in (e) above in the field of university partnerships.

The DAAD takes vigorous steps in this field, and returned scholars are provided with annual subscriptions to a professional periodical relevant to their subject; the DAAD, like institutions in other countries, feels that the continuing link is not usually because the person has studied in an overseas country, but because he has studied the same subject in the same country.

Steps are taken to see that German experts going to developing countries under DAAD auspices meet returned scholars in the relevant profession or subject. Some returned scholars are invited back to the Federal Republic for short periods, after a year or so in their own country; at the headquarters of DAAD a member of staff is concerned full time with evaluation work; overseas visits are made from time to time by officers concerned with different geographical areas to 'follow up' scholars in the developing country concerned.

The German Volunteer Organisation (DED) is also active in evaluation work. Each volunteer sends progress reports every six months to the DED director in the developing country, who forwards them to the Bonn headquarters. In some cases teams of specialists from the Federal Republic visit projects, in other cases joint evaluations are done by the 'developing country and German teams'. In some countries the authorities of the developing country report themselves on the success or otherwise of projects and volunteers.

The staff of the CDG seem also to be in fairly close touch with previous trainees, through meetings and seminars in the developing countries to which trainees are invited, and CDG staff pay visits to the trainees after their return.

(g) Professional migration Professional migration is regarded as a problem, though not a desperately serious one. It happens chiefly in the medical and technical field, and mainly from Iran, Turkey and Greece. The large migrant population, particularly from Turkey, can confuse the picture.

Shortage of medical trained people has caused some sources in the Federal Republic to do a certain amount of advertising for medical staff; it is said that there are a large number of Ghanaian doctors working in Germany, many with German wives, and in 1971 there were approximately 2000 Iranian doctors employed in the Federal Republic.

The BMZ has called meetings of all organisations awarding scholarships to discuss some common problems, and one such problem has been professional migration, or the 'brain-drain', and efforts have been made to see whether organisations could pool their knowledge and coordinate their efforts to lessen this problem. In the case of some awarding organisations the problem is very small; for example the CDG estimates that 95 per cent of their trainees return to their countries of origin.

(h) Notable features of the Federal Republic's educational aid Financially the geographical picture is very different from that of other European countries, such as France and the United Kingdom; for example in the early seventies as much finance was provided for Latin America as for Africa and Asia together. The university links have so far been a major factor in educational aid; whether this will remain so depends on the results of completed evaluation research, or research now in progress.

The Federal Republic provides more training awards than any other donor country; on the one hand fewer experts, teachers, etc. go to developing countries, mainly because the number of teachers is comparatively smaller, but on the other hand almost a quarter of the total personnel sent overseas are volunteers.[23]

There is a tendency for more German-financed students and trainees to be placed *sur place* in their own countries. It is contended that such placements are more successful as compared to the more expensive method of students and trainees coming to West Germany, where they also face the difficulty of learning German. The Federal Republic from the outset of UNDP's role of coordinator has been a supporter of such

[23] OECD Review, 1972, Table 17.

coordination, not only of multilateral programmes, but of bilateral ones too. When the question was asked in the early seventies, in various European countries, as to whether aid programmes should be coordinated amongst the then six members of the Common Market, the only positive 'yes' was given in Bonn.

The Federal Republic has undoubtedly learnt much from the mistakes of those who were earlier in the field; and certainly in the sphere of educational aid the lessons have been well learnt and the results appreciated by the developing countries.

The Netherlands

The Netherlands aid policy is coordinated by a high-level Committee on Aid to Less-Developed Countries, chaired by the Minister without Portfolio of the Ministry of Foreign Affairs. The Minister without Portfolio, a post created in the early sixties, is in charge of development cooperation, the administering organ being the Directorate General for International Cooperation, of which the largest section is the Directorate of Technical Assistance. The Minister has responsibility for all aid policy, including Surinam and the Antilles, but for the two latter territories, the administering agency is within the Deputy Prime Minister's Office, and operates more on a 'colonial' basis. A National Advisory Council for Development Aid, representing many economic, social and cultural groups, makes recommendations to the Minister without Portfolio.

Other ministries involved have the following responsibilities, the Ministries of Economic Affairs and Finance for major aid policy, including finance and the World Bank: the Ministry of Agriculture for the World Food Programme, and the Ministry of Education which plays a significant role through its Department of International Relations. The activities of other national agencies, notably the Netherlands Universities Foundation for International Cooperation (NUFFIC), the National Volunteers' Organisation (NVO), and the Foundation for Assistance to Foreign Students (SBBS) are referred to later.

(a) Training Within the Ministry of Foreign Affairs, the Fellowship Section of the Directorate for Technical Assistance places about 1000 people a year in Netherlands' Institutions, mainly until now on the international courses, administered principally through NUFFIC; in a few cases tailor-made programmes are arranged for individual fellowship holders; only very few students are placed in the universities. Industrial placings also come under the Directorate for Technical Assistance, but as elsewhere, difficulty is experienced in meeting the overseas demand for such training. There seems to be a slight tendency for an increase in the number of students and trainees placed *sur place* in institutions in their countries of origin, or in third countries.

In the Ministry of Education there is a Department of International

Relations which handles all UNESCO fellowships, provides a secretariat for the UNESCO Netherlands Commission, and is also responsible for the UNESCO Centre in Amsterdam; another unit of technology, the Foundation for Development Aid (SOA) is concerned with education at school and vocational levels and advises the Ministry of Foreign Affairs and the Ministry of Education, particularly in the field of vocational training.

Apart from courses organised at Philips' International Institute of Technological Studies – financed by the firm Philips and the Centre for Aerial Survey at Delft, which was founded in 1948 and operates partly in India, and receives a grant from the Ministry – all the international courses and centres receive finance through NUFFIC, which in turn receives grants from the Ministry of Education; in 1972, 720 people took part in the courses.[24] As has already been said this was the position up to 1973, but then the whole system came under review.

NUFFIC is responsible for all the welfare, including accommodation, of their course members. The Directorate of Technical Assistance of the Ministry of Foreign Affairs is responsible for those coming under its aegis, but experiences considerable difficulties in finding accommodation, and for this reason does not encourage fellows or trainees to be accompanied by their wives. The Foundation for Assistance to Foreign Studies (SBBS) in Utrecht has as its principal object the welfare of overseas students, other than those on NUFFIC courses or having individual tailor-made programmes. Their main activities are the provision of four-month introduction courses, at a centre at Berkenhoven, on the Dutch language and way of life; through offices in The Hague and Amsterdam, as well as in Utrecht, help is given with personal problems including accommodation, but the Foundation find great difficulties in this field, as the students are in competition with Dutch families at the lower end of the income scales; opportunities are provided for contact with young Dutch people – here again this is not always easy, but endeavours are made to improve the situation through concentration on similarity of interests; finally the Foundation arranges special courses for expert groups such as nurses from Indonesia and Yugoslavia.

(b) The provision of experts and advisers to developing countries

This is the responsibility, both for bilateral and multilateral official schemes, of the Directorate for Technical Assistance of the Ministry of Foreign Affairs. In 1972, 1415 experts went overseas, 37 per cent being employed by consulting firms who had been assigned some operation of technical cooperation; about half of all Dutch experts were involved in some form of agriculture. Selected experts are briefed by the Technical Assistance Directorate and are given specialised and linguistic training as necessary. In addition general background courses at the Royal Institute of the Tropics are available and are also attended by wives.

[24] For a full list of courses see NUFFIC Annual Report, 1972, The Hague.

A major Netherlands' initiative has been the creation of the scheme for 'young associate experts', mostly provided in cooperation with United Nations agencies, and being, as the term implies, midway between a volunteer and a fully fledged expert. The associate expert's length of service has until now been three years, but this has proved to be too short a period in which to ascertain whether the young associate expert can become a fully-fledged United Nations expert adviser. It is likely that in future after a two-year assignment, and consultation between the Dutch and the United Nations agency concerned, three-year extensions will be offered to those associated experts who seem suitable, and are willing to continue in technical assistance work; there is now more supervision of the associate experts in the field, combined with regular reports. Senior expert advisers, working under Dutch bilateral schemes, do not seem to have all that much support and supervision when overseas.

(c) The Netherlands' Volunteer Organisation (NVO) The NVO is a part of the Ministry of Foreign Affairs, the money and the secretariat both being provided by the Ministry of Foreign Affairs. The age range of the Dutch volunteers is twenty-one to thirty, the average being twenty-five. As in the Federal Republic of Germany, volunteers are only accepted after two years' training, after leaving school at eighteen or nineteen. This means that the great majority are 'technical/vocational' men and women, and all serve for two years. About a third of the volunteers, after this two years, remain in the developing country concerned; about 10 per cent eventually go back to do technical work in these countries, and a further 10 per cent go to some other developing country.

The Dutch expect no contribution from the developing country, paying 100 per cent the cost of fares, maintenance, housing, equipment and small salaries to the volunteers.

In developing countries the volunteers are grouped in teams with a team leader and assistant team leader. A few of the volunteers are appointed as technical assistants and assistant team leaders; in large countries apart from the team leaders there are field directors; in smaller countries a general regional leader covers several countries. Twenty-seven months of active NVO service excuses military service, but this is not stressed in publicity about the scheme. There is massive publicity. Time is bought cheaply on all five TV networks and special films of NVO operations are available. Successful applicants are interviewed by a board, including psychologists, candidates having previously had preliminary interviews with an NVO officer.

When a volunteer is accepted, training consists of one week at a Folk House School, nine weeks in Amsterdam on the language and background of the country to which he is assigned, and when he reaches the country a further week's training is arranged, together with four weeks' handover from the volunteer whom he is succeeding; a volunteer can be rejected at any time during the training period.

A Special Board coordinates some forty private organisations which organise volunteer schemes. The Secretary-General of NVO is Secretary of the Board and there is cooperation between official and unofficial volunteers on some projects; when the volunteers of the private organisations are overseas they come under the same administration as the official volunteers, and have similar training. The Secretariat of NVO are alive to the dangers of volunteers being regarded as cheap labour and they also believe that as the developing countries develop, projects will move out of the field of volunteers into the field of experts. In 1972, 782 Dutch volunteers went to developing countries, an increase of 100 over 1970.

(*d*) *The teaching of the Dutch language as a foreign language* The Dutch language is not promoted to any great extent, although courses in Dutch are available through the Foundation for Assistance to Foreign Students.

(e) University links and research In the early 1970s the Ministry of Foreign Affairs made money available to NUFFIC for the extension of links between institutions of higher education in the Netherlands, and similar institutions in developing countries. Each link had to have a definite object to be achieved, and a time limit set for this achievement. There has not as yet been time to evaluate the results, the time limit of a link being five years.

Research into development programmes is an aspect of technical assistance which it is intended should be expanded in the period to 1975, both at the multilateral official level, and bilaterally; in the latter case much of the work is carried out by NUFFIC.

(f) Evaluating and 'follow-up' Evaluation by NUFFIC has been done on a fairly wide basis direct contact being made with previous course members, through the Netherlands' Embassies abroad, and some institutes, for example the Institute of Hydrology, which provides a regular newsletter once a year. Occasional visits have been paid to interview ex-course members, particularly by the staff of the Institute of Social Studies.

The Netherlands Voluntary Organisation (NVO) does much evaluation in the field, both by evaluation of the project in relation to its ultimate object, and the performance of the individual volunteers as separate entities. The general regional directors and team leaders make regular evaluations which are shown to the authority concerned in the developing country before being sent to The Hague, where NVO have one full-time staff member on evaluation work.

A considerable amount of research has been done on evaluation problems, some commissioned by ministries, others done spontaneously by universities. In October 1970 the Government of the Netherlands acted as host to a three-day seminar organised by OECD Secretariat on the theoretical and practical problems of systematic evaluation work. The results of this seminar, and of one held in 1971 at Oxford which was sponsored by Nuffield College and the Overseas Development Administration of the Foreign and Commonwealth Office, which included OECD representation, were taken into account in preparing the OECD report on 'Evaluation of Development Assistance', which was published in January 1972.

(g) Professional migration This is not really a problem for the Netherlands. In as far as people on offical Netherlands awards show any signs of becoming 'brain-drainers' fairly active steps are taken to discourage them.

(h) Notable features of the Netherlands educational aid programme The most obvious feature of the Netherlands educational aid activity is the extent of their programme, which is remarkable for a country of the size of the Netherlands. The stress put on the use of the words 'development cooperation' instead of 'development aid' have their effect, and universities and social and cultural institutions seem to be more deeply and practically involved than in some other countries.

For the decades 1950–70 international education, through courses at the special institutes and centres, mainly under the auspices of the Netherlands Universities Foundation for International Cooperation, was unique, particularly perhaps in the contribution made to higher technical training.

Another original Netherlands contribution was the initiative in formulating the Associate Experts Scheme. Both the official and voluntary schemes seem well coordinated within their own sphere, and on the whole work amicably together.

On the debit side perhaps there is not enough effective action in relation to the welfare of students and trainees, with the exception of those attending courses at the special institutes and centres, and on official Government awards.

It is to be hoped that the reorganisation of courses until now under NUFFIC administration will provide as good a service to developing countries as there has been in the past.

The United Kingdom

The United Kingdom's imperial past is still reflected in the fact that in 1972 official bilateral flows of £163·2 m of aid went to the Commonwealth, and £35·5 m to non-Commonwealth countries; the proportions in 1968 were £144·6 m to the Commonwealth and £15·2 m to non-Commonwealth countries.[25] The main government organ for aid is the Overseas Development Administration (ODA) of the Foreign and Commonwealth Office.

[25] 1973 White Paper on Aid Administration.

This administration has its roots in the Department of Technical Cooperation created in 1963, and mainly staffed by home-based staff of the previous Colonial Office. Some small operational units in the Foreign and Commonwealth Relations Offices were added to the Department, chiefly those dealing with the Colombo Plan, which had existed since 1951.

When the Labour Party came into office in 1964 the Department became the Ministry of Overseas Development (ODM), with a minister in the Cabinet; later in the same government's term of office, the minister ceased to be of cabinet rank, but the organisation remained an independent ministry. It had during this period taken over the coordination of work of UNESCO in the United Kingdom from the Department of Education and Science, and a similar coordinating role for the World Food Programme from the Ministry of Agriculture. In 1971, when the Conservatives assumed office, it became the Overseas Development Administration (ODA) of the Foreign and Commonwealth Office, but with a minister responsible for it, although he in turn was responsible to the Foreign Secretary.[26]

The ODM administers the British Aid Programme, is the main policy maker for aid, and coordinates views not only with the Foreign and Commonwealth Office, but also with other departments of state and ministries who have an 'aid interest'. In 1964 a number of economists joined the Ministry's staff. Although an injection of trained economists of repute was necessary, perhaps this has meant that the stress on economic development in developing countries, in the past, has been somewhat out of proportion in relation to aid in the fields of social development. Nowadays the social dimensions of development are generally recognised and other criteria than economic growth are considered.

There are five ODM development divisions overseas; in the Middle East, the Caribbean, and since 1972 Southern Africa, East Africa and South-East Asia. These divisions in no way abrogate the responsibility of the Head of the British Diplomatic Missions or the British Council, but mean that in certain areas where they are needed, there are operational and professional advisory staff available (see also British Council on pp. 43–4).

The Ministry provides financial aid and advisory services in almost every and any aspect of financial, economic and social organisation, but from the point of view of this book probably the most important unit of ODM is the Education Division, which together with the Education Advisers is specifically concerned with aid to education. They share the responsibility

[26] On the Labour Government coming into office in March 1974, the administration (ODA) again became an independent ministry (ODM); to save confusion with the OECD term 'Overseas Development Assistance' (ODA) the initials ODM are used in this section.

within the Ministry with the Geographical Departments, the Overseas Manpower Division, and the International Division, which keeps in touch with the work of other donors, multilateral and bilateral. Many operations which are financed by the ODM are handled by four organisations, all of whom collaborate closely with each other, and of which brief details follow:

The British Council

The aims of the British Council as defined in its Royal Charter (1940) are the promotion of a wider knowledge of the United Kingdom and the English language abroad and the development of closer cultural relations between British and other countries. It is an independent organisation in which all its powers are vested in an Executive Committee. Nevertheless because of the size of the Parliamentary Grant in Aid (£22,172,000 in 1974–5) the sponsoring departments (the Foreign and Commonwealth Office and the ODM) take an active part in the planning of its work and the development of its funds. The Executive Committee decides the Council's policy, but there is day-to-day consultation and coordination with the two sponsoring departments on matters of common concern. In general policy matters the Foreign and Commonwealth Office keeps the Council informed of the objectives and priorities of British overseas policy, leaving it to the professional judgement of the Council to decide the precise educational and cultural means by which conditions favourable to the realisation of those policies can be achieved in individual countries. The Council collaborates with the ODM in programmes of British educational aid. In most developing countries the Council's representative acts as educational adviser to the British ambassador, or high commissioner, and has responsibilities in the administration of the educational aid programmes.

The Council's approach to educational and cultural relations is not to use them directly to further commercial and political policies, or to impress a culture on another nation. It is a cardinal principle of the Council's policy that anything it does should not only be of benefit to Britain, but should also be, and should be seen to be, of benefit to the receiving country. The Council only operates overseas at the invitation of the 'host' country. Its approach is based mainly upon responding to requests, but the Council on occasion makes suggestions and in this way it seeks to create an atmosphere of friendly partnership with contemporary attitudes to international relations. The Council works on a global basis and it has within it, to a certain extent, some of the policy and most of the functional operational responsibilities of the two wings of the French Foreign Office, the Secretariat d'Etat and the Relations Culturelles, Scientifiques et Techniques, but clearly a body of independent status such as the Council is not so political an organisation as units of government departments are bound to be.

In 1972–3 some two-thirds of the Council's total budget of £20·5 m was spent on behalf of the fifty-six developing countries in which it works: this includes both work that is strictly educational and the more general projection of Britain in the arts, sciences, and professions. Apart from work financed by the Council, acting in an agency capacity, it spends over £2·2 m on educational aid directly on behalf of ODA, and helps to administer the expenditure of a further £9·7 m under various technical assistance schemes, including United Nations schemes. Where bilateral agreements or conventions provide the framework for Britain's cultural and educational relationship with other countries the British Council is the principal administering authority on behalf of HMG.

The Centre for Educational Development Overseas (CEDO)[27]
CEDO was formed in March 1970, by the amalgamation of three existing bodies: the Overseas Visual Aid Centre, the Centre of Educational Television Overseas, and the Centre for Curriculum Renewal and Educational Development Overseas. It is incorporated as an educational charity pledged 'to promote by all means possible the development overseas of education', assisting when requested developing countries to modernise their educational systems and make them more relevant to their needs. Most of the Centre's activities are covered in later sections, the following are not: the development of specific educational projects, mainly overseas of an innovatory nature, and the provision of much information. CEDO's services cover both formal education, from primary to tertiary, and informal education including many aspects of adult education. The organisation's assistance is sought not only by the governments of developing countries, but also by special agencies of the United Nations. Much of the work is with Commonwealth countries, but assistance is also given to non-Commonwealth countries especially those in the Middle East and South America. CEDO receives a government grant through the Overseas Development Administration, and in addition has received financial assistance from the Nuffield and Ford Foundations, and a variety of industrial concerns.

In November 1973 the Minister for Overseas Development made a statement in the House of Commons to the effects that CEDO would be amalgamated with the British Council on 1 April 1974. This decision had been reached because some overlap existed in the fields of work and resources; it was felt that this amalgamation would make more effective and economical use of British experts and resources in helping developing countries to adapt their educational systems to their needs as they see them.

The Inter-University Council for Higher Education Overseas (IUC)
The IUC was established by British universities in 1946, and its original purposes were:

[27] Amalgamated with the British Council, April 1974.

(a) to strengthen cooperation between the universities of the United Kingdom and universities in colonial territories;
(b) to foster the development of higher colleges in the colonies, and their advance to university status; and
(c) to take such other action as appropriate for the promotion of higher education, learning and research, in the colonies.

In 1970 IUC was incorporated as a company limited by guarantee; a step which enabled it to do its work with increased independence and authority, and also to hold funds from sources other than governmental ones; its main source of income however is a grant from the ODM.

The countries in which there are universities with which it is now associated, apart from Ethiopia, Sudan, Liberia and Hong Kong, are all the British ex-colonial territories or protectorates in the Mediterranean (Malta), East Africa, Central and Southern Africa, West Africa, the Caribbean, South-East Asia and the South Pacific.

The IUC works in close collaboration with other organisations interested in the field of higher education overseas, and particularly with the British Council representatives in the countries where IUC have a special relationship with the universities.

The Council for Technical Education and Training for Overseas Countries (TETOC)

TETOC was established in 1962, and is financed by the ODM. In 1972 it was incorporated as a company limited by guarantee and strengthened with experienced professional staff, mainly from industry. This incorporation makes it possible for the Council to seek money from sources other than government money.

Members of the Council are appointed by the Secretary of State for Foreign Affairs, and are charged with the promotion by all means possible, whether in the United Kingdom or elsewhere, of technical, commercial, industrial and managerial education and training for developing countries.

TETOC is essentially an agency which aims to:

(a) identify needs overseas;
(b) identify United Kingdom sources willing and able to meet those needs;
(c) to match the two and monitor the results.

(a) Training The major organisation concerned with training in the United Kingdom is the British Council. There can be very few organisations in the world which are concerned with so many major schemes. Apart from its own scholarship, bursary and other training schemes, it is concerned with all the technical assistance awards of the ODM; with a wide range of awards made by the United Nations and United Nations specialised agencies; with awards under the Commonwealth Scholarship and Fellowship Commission and Commonwealth Education Fellowships; the Council also handles all Colombo Plan and CENTO awards; when

requested the Council assists other governments with the placement of their students and scholars in the United Kingdom.

To do this work, and the numbers involved are over 10,000 a year, the Council has several departments at the London headquarters – for example, the Technical Assistance Training Department, concerned with awards financed by ODM, the United Nations Fellowships Department, the British Council Scholarships Department, the Courses Department, which is concerned with innumerable courses in a wide range of subjects for people from overseas, and the Commonwealth Education Awards Department.

The award of a fellowship or scholarship, is of course, subject to acceptance at a university, or other institute of higher learning. The universities have been generous in maintaining an overall percentage of approximately ten per cent of students from overseas admitted in competition with United Kingdom students.

Outside London, the British Council have twenty-four offices, and the actual placement with universities, or other institutions of higher education, or the administration of individual programmes of inspection and study by senior people, will be carried out in a region by the relevant regional staff.

A great deal of attention is given to the welfare of overseas people visiting the United Kingdom, be they young students or senior visitors of the standing of a rector of a university, or a minister of education. The Council has always believed that detailed attention to the welfare and accommodation of all categories of people are essential if the visit, or period of study, is to be really a success. As in other countries there has been increasing difficulty in securing suitable accommodation for overseas students and trainees. With this in mind about seven years ago the then Government made a special grant of £5 m entitled the Overseas Students Welfare Expansion Programme, the bulk of the money to be expended with existing organisations or institutions to provide more accommodation for overseas people. An essential factor in the scheme has been that any project receiving a grant should have an adequate number of British students within it, so that those from overseas are not cut off from their opposite numbers in the United Kingdom. By 1974, nearly 6600 additional residential places had been made available, 2075 being for married students with children.

Another scheme which is peculiar to the United Kingdom exists because higher fees are charged to students from overseas than to indigenous students. The scheme, the Overseas Students Fee Awards Scheme, exists for granting awards for full fees to students from developing countries whose subjects are in line with the social and economic progress of the countries. The majority are made to students nominated by the governments of the developing countries, through their embassies or high commissions, and a minority are proposed by the universities and other institutions in the United Kingdom. There are on average about 2000 awards a year, with an average value of £250 per annum. The scheme, financed by ODM , with a secretariat provided by the British Council, is tilted towards post-graduate level, and if a subject can be studied in the student's country of origin, an award is not normally made.

The IUC makes awards for training in Britain to academic administrators, library and technical staff from the universities with which they are associated. Within its field of activity TETOC brings people to the United Kingdom for specialised visits and training, and sometimes awards are provided for training in the developing country concerned.

The final selection for awards under both the Commonwealth scholarships and fellowships and the British Council scholarships is normally made in London, subject to a suitable placement.

The fact that so many schemes are administered by the British Council means that the danger of overlap is to some extent avoided, and a more closely related system of benefits under the different schemes can be attained.

Both the ODM and the British Council have a wide spectrum of advisory committees and individual advisers in many different subjects, who will assist the Council to make the most suitable placement.

(b) The sending of advisers, experts and teachers to developing countries Although the numbers are not so large as in some other countries, 2747 in 1972,[28] the administration seems equally complicated. The major responsibility lies with the ODM, which under its various technical-assistance arrangements made 2205 bilateral appointments to operational and advisory posts in 1972, and 265 to multilateral organisation assignments. In 1972 the responsibility for most operational posts, other than in education, was transferred to the Crown Agents for Overseas Governments' Administration; and similar responsibility in respect of technical education, management development, and industrial education was transferred to TETOC. A major element of the work of the IUC is in recruiting staff for the overseas universities with whom it has special links; both indigenous staff fully financed by these universities and British staff whose salaries are supplemented by ODM. The British Council is also an appointing body, but with considerable concentration on the teaching of English as a foreign language. As was to be hoped the demand for primary and secondary school expatriate teachers has declined, and the number of appointments made dropped from 644 in 1971 to 412 in 1972; there was an increase in the number of agricultural advisory appointments.

(c) The British Volunteer Programme The British Volunteer Programme is operated by four independent voluntary organisations, of which by far the largest is Voluntary Service Overseas (VSO). Other organisations

[28] An Account of the British Aid Programme, Cmd. 5445, HMSO, 1973.

are the Catholic Institute for International Relations (CIIR), International Voluntary Service (IVS), and the United Nations Association International Service (UNAIS). Seventy-five per cent of BVP costs are borne by ODM, the other 25 per cent coming from industry and charitable foundations. In 1963 these four societies recruited 250 graduate and cadet volunteers for service in 48 countries; by 1973 the numbers approached 2000, in about 100 countries, two-thirds of whom were assisting in some form or other of education.

VSO in 1970–1 provided 1519 volunteers (1261 graduates, 258 cadets). The main change of emphasis in the programme of VSO is that at the outset of the programme the volunteers were cadets who went overseas between the ending of their school careers and the beginning of some further training or employment. By the middle sixties the trained, or graduate volunteer, was becoming a major element. The swing to the qualified volunteer reflects the types of assignment put forward by the developing countries. Recently the demand for people with technical and vocational skills has been growing.

In many developing countries the British Council acts as the 'overseas arm' for the British Volunteer Programme, collaborating with the British Embassy or High Commission in recommending and evaluating projects, and negotiating terms for volunteers. The Council is responsible for the volunteers' welfare and for giving 'in-country' training and professional support.

(d) Teaching of English as a foreign language The teaching of English as a foreign language has always been a priority in the British Council's work. In May 1972 the British Council consolidated its already considerable resources of English teaching by creating a separate English Teaching Division comprising an English Language Teaching Institute, an English Teaching Information Centre and an English Teaching Inspectorate. Close contact is maintained with organisations whose work relates closely to the subject, in particular the ODM, the Cambridge Local Examinations Syndicate, the Publishers' Association and the Association of Recognised English Language Schools.

The English Language Teaching Institute provides part-time and intensive course teaching for special categories of overseas students, produces specialist materials, and gives practical teacher-training. In the field of teacher-training, members of the Institute's staff offer courses overseas specifically directed to the use of audio and visual aids in language teaching; in conjunction with the Council's courses department, the Institute organises summer courses on the language laboratory in the teaching of English as a foreign language.

By the end of 1972 the Aid for Commonwealth English (ACE) scheme proposed by Britain at the second Commonwealth Education Conference (Delhi, January 1962) had been in operation for ten years. During that period the impact of the scheme upon the teaching of English within the Commonwealth had been considerable: 94 posts were created in 14 Commonwealth countries. In 1972 a second scheme, for English as a Foreign Language (EFL), was launched to support the teaching of English in non-Commonwealth developing countries by providing expert advisers for key posts.

World-wide there is a growing interest in the teaching of English to those who need it for particular, well-defined purposes. Much of the direct teaching undertaken by the Council meets special occupational requirements (eg. for commerce, engineering and agriculture).[29]

(e) University links and research University links have not in the past been so developed by the United Kingdom as they have elsewhere. Until recently links have depended upon the enthusiasm of a United Kingdom professor, or other staff members who have spent a spell at a university in a developing country. The link may therefore dwindle and become extinct when those concerned retire; however, much excellent and spontaneous work has been done in this fashion, at no cost to the tax-payer. The outstanding exception is the very close link involving the exchange of staff and much equipment between the Imperial College of Science and Technology of the University of London, and the Indian Institute of Technology, Delhi.[30]

The picture is changing however, and more and more funds from official sources are being provided; the IUC are increasingly active in this field and more of their links include joint research projects.

A scheme financed by ODM, 'the home-based scheme', involves financing a supernumerary member, or members, of staff of a particular faculty of a United Kingdom university on the understanding that an equivalent number of staff members from the faculty are always serving overseas.

The United Kingdom has a long history of research in connection with developing countries; as early as 1877 Sir Patrick Manson initiated research on elephantiasis, and seventeen years later Sir David Bruce had discovered a parasite in the tsetse fly which was the conveyor of 'sleeping sickness'. The vast rubber planting concerns started in Malaya in 1893 had their roots in work done at the Royal Botanic Gardens at Kew. Today the ODM finances various research centres in the United Kingdom.[31]

A considerable amount of development research is now carried out at universities and other institutions of higher learning; in some cases being funded by trusts and foundations, and in others by a government agency,

[29] British Council Annual Report, 1972–3.

[30] See Chapter 6, p. 216 ff. for details

[31] For fuller details of research institutions the reader is referred to the booklet 'Britain and the developing Countries', Central Office of Information Pamphlet 103, HMSO, 1972.

usually the ODM or one of the research councils. One institution requires special mention, namely the Institute of Development Studies at Sussex, which, apart from carrying out much development research (many of the researchers being from developing countries), organises special seminars for people from overseas on problems affecting development in individual countries, or in groups of such countries. The Institute publishes a useful research register of development studies in the United Kingdom, which is revised annually.[32] The Institute is widely used in a consultancy capacity – for example fellows of the Institute played a major role in the International Labour Office's missions on employment in Colombia, Sri Lanka and Kenya; seventy-five per cent of its funds come from ODM.

Research into various areas of development studies are carried out by individual senior fellows and scholars at many universities, who come to the United Kingdom under the various schemes administered by the British Council.

Another organisation of much value is the Overseas Development Institute. The Institute acts as a forum where those directly concerned with overseas development may exchange views and information; it publishes many excellent pamphlets on development subjects. It also acts as a pressure point to keep development issues before as wide a public as possible. The Institute finances come mainly from voluntary and industrial resources.

(f) Evaluation and 'follow-up' The United Kingdom has not taken much action in these fields, but is aware of the necessity to do so, lack of funds or other projects of greater priority being the major cause for lack of action. The British Council has for many years had a series of returned British Council scholars associations which have been widened to include other people who have trained or studied under official schemes in the United Kingdom: the vigour and positive value of such associations depends very greatly on the returned scholars and their enduring interest; the bond seems to be that of having studied the same subject in the United Kingdom, and not necessarily the mere fact of studying in the United Kingdom.

Recently the Council has been asked by UNESCO to evaluate the operation of UNESCO fellowship programmes in the United Kingdom. Academic and professional supervisors, as well as UNESCO fellows themselves, cooperated with the Research Department of the British Council in the evaluation which was carried out between April and October 1974.

(g) Professional migration This has been an element which is of

[32] Register of UK-based ongoing research: *Development Studies 1973*, 3rd ed., Institute of Development Studies, University of Sussex.

concern to the United Kingdom, and more particularly to organisations awarding fellowships and scholarships. On the whole the percentage of those who are officially financed and who remain in the United Kingdom without permission is small; but it is a moot point as to how many people return to their own countries for a year or so and then come back to the United Kingdom for reasons of better job conditions, better pay, and education for their children. The professional migrant of this type normally stays a few years, and does not settle permanently in the United Kingdom. The largest element has been in the medical field, chiefly from Indian, Pakistan, Bangladesh and Sri Lanka, but there seems to have been an increasing number in the fields of engineering and education.

(b) Notable features of United Kingdom educational aid The United Kingdom was one of the first countries to be active in development operations. The ODM with its vast experience and roots in the ex-colonial empire obviously have had an expertise in various fields which was second to none. The British Council, which came into being in 1934 and received its Royal Charter in 1940, is notable because apart from its autonomous status it has a large staff overseas, particularly in developing countries, the largest being India. The United Kingdom staff are assisted by local appointees, who are nationals of the country concerned. The United Kingdom staff is transferable and one day may be working in Manchester and the next find themselves in Sierre Leone, then back again to London, and after three or four years outwards to India, and later to Europe. This makes for homogeneity in the operations; the Council officer in country 'X' works in partnership with the people of that country in deciding who goes to Britain, or who comes to that country, and his colleagues in the United Kingdom will have the responsibility for making the visit or period of study a success, or selecting the right expert. Possibly the reception of fellows, students and senior visitors in the United Kingdom is more expertly handled than in some other countries because of the Council's long experience in this type of work.

There has been one very obvious advantage over the years in having much development work done by the British Council, because being a body with independent status under a Royal Charter, it has in some circumstances been able to continue operating when diplomatic relations have been reduced to practically nil between the United Kingdom and a particular government. Conversely it has been the Council which has gone back to a country, at that country's invitation, after a break in diplomatic relations, and before a diplomatic mission returns.

On the debit side of the United Kingdom's work as a whole is its lack of evaluation and 'follow-up', its backwardness in putting its own case forward, its rather out-moded method of selecting experts and advisers, with a tendency to rely too much on those who in the old days had experience in the colonial field; and a rather timorous approach to university links, notwithstanding the many difficulties that surround the successful initiation of such links.

The United States of America

The Agency for International Development (AID) has since 1961 been the successor of a series of different forms of aid machinery, which have followed one upon the other since the days of Marshall Aid in the early 1950s. It has been described as 'the only comprehensive agency in the world, being simultaneously a bank, a foundation, management consultancy service, operations agency, economic developer and planner, political manipulator and technical adviser'.[33] With the added factors of unlimited staff and finance, this description was certainly true in AID's hey-day. For a great variety of reasons the Agency in the latter part of the sixties became unpopular, but it still exists on much the same lines, mainly because of the differing views between the Administration and Congress; in this case this tendency has been abetted by an almost total lack of interest in overseas aid on the part of Congressmen.

Since 1968 a variety of reports have suggested widely differing alternatives to AID, the principle ones being:

(a) In October 1958 a report was published of the President's General Advisory Committee on Foreign Assistance Programmes, named the Perkins' Report after its Chairman, James A. Perkins. This in essence recommended a retention of the AID form of administration, but because of AID's unpopularity a change of name was suggested.[34]

(b) In March 1969 a report was published entitled 'A New Conception of Foreign Aid', a joint statement by the National Planning Association's Joint Sub-Committee on US Foreign Aid, and the BPA Board of Trustees and Standing Committee.[35] This took a very different view from the Perkin's Report, proposing that AID should be reduced to a small policy and financing unit. Neither the NPA nor the Perkins' Reports were acted upon.

(c) In September 1969 President Nixon appointed a Presidential Task Force, under the Chairmanship of Rudolf Petersen. The recommendations of the Petersen Report were nearer to the NPA way of thinking than to the Perkins' Report, stressing that developing

[33] S. P. Huntington's article (see note 12, p. 22).

[34] 'Development Assistance in the New Administration', report of the President's General Advisory Committee on Foreign Assistance Programmes, AID, Oct 1968.

[35] NPA special Report no. 64, March 1969.

countries were by then capable of doing their own planning, that external aid was a minor element in development, and that the United States should put more resources into international agencies – and *en route* it abolished AID.[36]

The President accepted the proposals of the Petersen Report in principle, and draft legislation comprising three bills went to Congress in April 1971. Only one bill, dealing with separate treatment of supporting economic assistance, and its administrative amalgamation with military assistance, was passed by Congress. The other two bills failed to get through Congress and thus AID still remains today.

These happenings cannot have been much of a tonic for the morale of the staff of AID, which still remains by far the major organisation in United States aid administration. At present AID remains, to all intents and purposes, an independent section of the State Department, headed by an administrator appointed by the President. Within AID there are strong geographical units which play a powerful role; a Bureau for Technical Assistance has sections dealing with a wide range of specialisations, including education, human resources, science, technology and development administration. The Bureau is not functional but works mainly on research into new developments which may be of use to developing countries, such as detecting obstacles to aid development and recommending remedies; a major portion of this work is farmed out to universities. Overseas there are strong AID missions in some forty countries, staffed in the main by AID personnel, headed by a mission director, who, just like the chief of AID, the administrator in Washington, has much independence of action, although in theory he works to the United States ambassador in the country concerned.

Other agencies with separate responsibilities are the Treasury, including contributions to the Asian Development Bank; the Department of Agriculture, which determines the necessity for food aid; and until 1971 the Peace Corps, which handled United States volunteers overseas.

An inter-agency survey conducted in 1968 for the Congress of the United States by the Department of Health, Education and Welfare made a comprehensive study of all authorised programmes of the Federal Government concerned with aid activities, aimed at improving international understanding and cooperation. This resulted in the listing of 159 programmes, run by 31 different agencies, all with legislative authority, but not all concerned with overseas development aid. It would appear that some 70 of the programmes are concerned principally with developing

[36] 'US Foreign Assistance in the 1970's: A new approach', a report to the President from the Task Force on International Development, Washington, D.C., Mar 1970.

countries, but this is an approximate assessment; the period of time covered by the data in the inventory was 1966–8.[37]

Apart from contracting work out to other Government agencies many tasks are devolved upon universities and other private institutions, not only in the field of research but in the provision of a wide spectrum of technicians and experts to developing countries. In recent years there has been particular emphasis on education, food production, nutrition and family planning.

There are innumerable voluntary organisations working in the field of aid development, the largest number of programmes being in the educational field, and the majority of the organisations having a religious basis. The financial contribution of the United States to technical cooperation is very large indeed, but not proportionately for the richest country in the world. In 1971 the United States provided $m 699·0 for technical cooperation, only $m 121 more than the French contribution in the same year.

(a) Training Within AID the training of people from developing countries is supervised by the Office of International Training. In 1971 there were estimated to be 17,639 students and trainees with United States awards, as compared to 19,242 in 1967. Quite a considerable number are placed in a third country for training, and a smaller number *sur place* in their own countries.[38]

Many agencies, both Federal and private, including universities, assist both in the placement of the students and trainees, and in their welfare. A notable central organisation is the Institute of International Education, which administers international exchange of persons programmes on a global basis, covering foreign students, teachers and specialists. Apart from their Headquarters in New York, there are a number of offices in the United States and field offices abroad, to advise foreign students about educational opportunities in the United States.[39]

(b) Sending of experts and teachers to developing countries More money is spent on experts and volunteers than on any other activity, $m 243·0, excluding volunteers, was spent on 9364 experts (including 5994 teachers), operational personnel and advisers in 1971. The numbers and costs are not excessive when it is realised that France sent over 32,727 people, and the United Kingdom over 14,381 in the same year.[40] Very

[37] Inventory of Federal Programmes Involving Educational Activities Concerned with Improving International Understanding and Cooperation', US Department of Health, Education and Welfare, Washington, D.C., 1969.

[38] OECD Review, 1972, Tables 14 and 17.

[39] See Alvert E. Gollin, *Education for National Development, Effects of United States Technical Training Programmes*, New York, 1969 for a detailed account and evaluation of training.

[40] OECD Review, 1972, Table 17.

large numbers are recruited through the universities and through a maze of official and unofficial agencies.

(c) Volunteers The Peace Corps Act of 1961 established the Peace Corps to handle United States volunteers abroad.

In 1971 the Peace Corps, a name which had become unpopular, was merged with the domestic programme of volunteers 'ACTION', a Federal Agency of which the Peace Corps became the international division. At the outset of 1961 the programme suffered from having too much money and too little experience. These difficulties were to a great extent overcome, but in the late sixties the Peace Corps became unloved, mainly for reasons of political foreign policy not directly concerned with the Peace Corps. This was sad, as experience had evolved methods of recruitment and training which meant that the volunteers were far better equipped for their allotted tasks, and many were doing excellent work. Even so, in July 1972, after the Corps became the international division of 'ACTION', there were 8500 volunteers serving in fifty-six countries. There seems to have been a swing to more skilled tradesmen, nurses and farmers, and likewise an increase in the numbers of professionally qualified people, particularly in agriculture and education; these tendencies follow the needs of developing countries. Training programmes for volunteers last twelve weeks, and in addition at least 300 hours of language instruction are provided. Today more than half the volunteers receive the major part of their training in the country to which they have been assigned; usually the first assignment is for a period of twenty-four months.

(d) The English language The use of English as a foreign language is a considerable activity of the United States of America. It is mainly the responsibility of the United States Information Service, and the United States cultural centres and institutes are much used for this purpose. Teaching of English is pursued particularly vigorously in Latin America, and in the sixties it became an increasing activity in other parts of the world.

In several countries the teaching of English is a joint activity with the British Council of the United Kingdom, and there is close collaboration between the two countries to avoid overlap and thus enable each to do more towards meeting a global demand which is overwhelming.

(e) University links and research University links are numerous and various, the vast majority being spontaneously created by universities in the States and financed by them: their variety is as great as their value. Money and manpower being more readily available in the United States than in some other major donor countries, there is inevitably much research into development problems. Universities have many faculties of sociology, economics and development studies, at which there are numerous ongoing research projects, financed by the universities themselves, by foundations, or by a Federal agency: and the same is true of individual research and specialised area institutes.

(f) Evaluation As for research, the availability of money and manpower have meant that evaluation, including 'follow-up', has probably been done for longer, and on a greater scale, than is the case in other donor countries. Evaluating processes have always been a feature of many aspects of American life, and it is therefore natural that much thought in the range of evaluation should be given to development studies. The booklet 'Evaluating Development Assistance'[41] gives a selected bibliography, including a formidable list of such research by United States universities, various Federal agencies, and notably by AID.

(g) Professional migration Professional migration to the United States is on a quite considerable scale, but is not regarded with the same concern as in the case of the United Kingdom. There are considerable numbers from Latin America, from India, from the Middle East and the West Indies. It is said that many who migrate do so temporarily, whereas more of this category in other developed countries do so with the hope of permanent residence.[42]

However, people from minority groups such as religious minorities or oriental racial minorities tend to have a preference for the United States or Canada, and are likely to be permanent emigrants.[43] In general when a foreign student thinks of emigrating, working conditions and facilities give him a preference for the United States.

(h) Notable features of educational aid of the United States of America As was said in the introduction to this book, p. 5, the compilers have, with American consent, been selective in the field of US educational aid operations, only including those which it was possible to study in the field; there are therefore many omissions of which all concerned are fully conscious. Time has not permitted full cognisance to be given to the enormous programme of the United States, but references to notable features can be made. The outstanding and generous humanity of individual Americans is well known, and in no field or aspect of American life is this better revealed than when dealing with overseas aid operations. A factor in the last few years, which must have been the cause of great frustration, has been the state of suspended animation of AID, with endless Government enquiries leading, one would guess, to a difficulty in recruiting well equipped staff to an organisation in a state of such uncertainty; a further difficulty is that AID, and to a lesser extent such organisations as the Peace Corps, have become the focus for considerable unpopularity in developing countries. This unpopularity usually has its roots in political factors not really concerned in the first place with the aid operation.

41 OECD, 1972.

42 W. A. Glaser, Bureau of Applied Social Sciences, Columbia University, for UNITAR, Sep 1973.

43 Ibid.

Even so, the United States contribution, both in the finance and people involved, is large, and clearly some excellent work has been done. Reference to some individual US Government operations is made in Chapters 3 to 8 on developing countries. A feature, however, which does deserve special mention is the role of the foundations and charitable organisations, and in particular the Ford and Rockefeller Foundations, some of whose operations are also referred to in the chapters on developing countries. In a recently published book[44] reference is made to the fact that of 315 foundations, with assets worth more than $m 10, 95 are American, and account for one per cent of United States' wealth. It was said that the Ford Foundation alone was worth more than the entire sterling area reserves.

The author of *The Foundations* has criticisms of the boards of trustees of most foundations, but not all, as being unrepresentative and supporting the established 'power' of the elite. He also feels that very often work is done which could be carried out by governments. But against this it can be said that government money is available for other aid purposes; at some junctures foundations and voluntary organisations are more welcome in a developing country than a direct governmental operation, very often doing the job for the government and frequently in cooperation with a university, or universities.

A further criticism is that, especially in the field of education, foundations have changed their emphasis from helping the poor to being organisations from which 'an elite' subsidises an elite'. This it is felt is not totally true in the context of this book, and more particularly of the work which the Ford and Rockefeller Foundations have done in the field of education overseas. It was excellent that these two great foundations took the initiative in organising the first global meetings of operators and experts of educational programmes; they had previously taken similar action in the field of agricultural, demographic, and family-planning research. Results of such meetings pinpoint the way to action, sometimes by an individual government, but more particularly by the United Nations, of an active productive nature on some major problems of developing countries. It is significant that in 1971 grants to the value of $m 588·0 were made by voluntary organisations in the United States to developing countries. The total DAC countries' contribution was $m 889·6; the next largest contributor after the United States was the Federal Republic of Germany with $m 108·3, although if the figures are expressed in terms of GNP shares, Sweden reaches the highest percentage, with Switzerland and the United States sharing second place.

The Rockefeller Foundation supports its own programmes in the field and appoints specialist staff to do the work. The Ford Foundation usually

[44] Ben Whitaker, *The Foundations*, London, 1974.

works through government agencies of a developing country, and with special project teams recruited from US universities or elsewhere. The two Foundations have on occasion cooperated; for example under the general banner of 'The Green Revolution' they founded jointly with the local governments concerned International Rice Research Centres, International Maize and Wheat Improvement Centres, the International Centre for Tropical Agriculture, and the International Institute of Tropical Agriculture.

The Rockefeller Foundation has also been much concerned in developing countries with projects relating to problems of population, centres of excellence at selected universities, rural and community health programmes, veterinary science, and reading centres and language laboratories.

2. The image of aid

In recent years there has been growing interest in the public relations of aid operations within many developed countries, often termed 'the image of aid'. In some countries there have been both official and unofficial surveys undertaken in this field and the results of a few of these, and of conversations with people in the countries concerned, are given in the following brief notes on the developed countries included in the project:

France

In 1962 a survey was carried out on behalf of the then French Ministry of Cooperation, in relation to French aid to Africa, and results showed that 37 per cent were opposed to such aid and 41 per cent were in favour. Two years later, another survey produced very similar results, but a lower rating was given to the spread of French *civilisation* as a motive for aid.

In discussion in Paris in 1971 it was said that 1955–6 were years when aid was very popular, but then there was a lessening of interest. More recently, before M. Pompidou paid his first visit to Francophone Africa as President of the French Republic, there had been a considerable debate on television, and a poll was carried out by one of the major French newspapers, on aid to Francophone Africa. The poll had shown that 54 per cent were in favour of the amount of aid then being given to Francophone Africa, and some people favoured more aid being given. This positive evidence of so many Frenchmen being in favour of aid appears to support the view that the giving of aid is accepted by the majority of French people as a normal part of French external policy.

In an article in 1973 by Yves Berthelot on French aid performance and development policy[45] a theory is put forward that the small amount of

[45] ODI Review, no. 6, 1973.

aid provided through charitable sources by France demonstrates 'a general lack of public interest in the developing countries'. The contrast of the volume of this source of aid as between France and other developed countries is shown by the fact that in 1971 finance from private charitable sources accounted for $m 7·2 in the case of France, out of a total of $m 890 for DAC countries as a whole.[46] This argument, as one demonstrating lack of public interest in aid, does not seem totally convincing; large charitable foundations with finance from private sources, of the type that abound in the United States and elsewhere, are not part of the normal French scene, and lack of funds from this source cannot therefore be attributed to lack of interest or support. Members of the professions tend to support aid; understandably people with lower incomes are not always happy with constant state visits by African presidents and ministers and feel sometimes that their taxes, which may be hard for them to pay, are being used to make life easier for elitist factions in Francophone Africa.

The Federal Republic of Germany

For many years a large number of private organisations have been active in informing the German public on problems of development aid, many being financed by BMZ. The German DSE publishes a calendar of events bi-monthly; many youth, political and adult organisations hold frequent seminars and meetings on development aid topics.

The national mass media, television, radio and newspapers, are quite active in providing news about development, and are supported by a number of specialised magazines.

These various methods of informing the people of the Federal Republic through voluntary organisations and mass media is as highly developed in Germany as in any other donor country, and more so than most. In discussions in the Federal Republic, however, it was felt that although in the very early days of aid operations in the late fifties and through to the middle sixties, development aid had been appreciated by most sections of the population, in the early seventies the population in general was not so interested in or stirred by development subjects, and that improving the image of development programmes was a process that had to be aimed at certain sections.

The image of aid in the universities was probably better than it had been nine years ago, and the student population in particular have taken 'Action for the Third World' as their own theme. They have been energetic in forming action committees, and although they are not always well organised, by and large the tendency seems to be a good one.

[46] OECD, DAC Review, 1972, Table II-10.

The Netherlands

Just as the original policies for development aid provided by the Netherlands had their roots in the United Nations Declaration of Human Rights and in sober appraisals of the state of the world, so the presentation of the image of aid to the population of the Netherlands has been realistic and humane; it has stressed that cooperation between developed and developing countries eventually attains joint benefits, and has underlined what the rich and poor countries have in common, rather than their differences.

The Government wants the support of the population for aid programmes and endeavours to keep them well informed by the provision of information through the Development Cooperative Information Department of the Ministry of Foreign Affairs. This is a service which has recently been expanded and provides analyses of government policies, background information on the situation in developing countries, and respective functions of multilateral and bilateral aid. In addition the National Committee on Development Strategy 1970–1980 is responsible for making people aware of development problems. The Committee in 1972 spent $m 1·08 on projects designed to this end, organised as far as feasible by using existing non-governmental organisations. A considerable number of programmes on aid development are shown on television networks at popular viewing times. These constant efforts to present the purposes and practices of development aid to the Dutch people seem to have met with success; there has been an increase in the interest, and also in the amount of private money donated for aid projects. In April 1973 Armand Brunig of the Development Cooporation Information Department[47] said that a survey carried out in 1972 under the auspices of the National Committee on Development Strategy showed that nine out of each hundred Dutchmen felt that aid money could be better used for domestic purposes: in other words 91 per cent of the public of the Netherlands can be said to be in favour of development cooperation.

The good image of aid in the Netherlands must be a factor in causing so comparatively a small country to play such a distinguished and increasing part in the aid development field, or as the Dutch would say 'development cooperation', and herein may be a part of the secret of the Netherlands' success and the overall public support for the programmes.

The United Kingdom

From the time of the Independence of India and other South-East Asian states in 1947, then of Ghana and the Federation of Malaya ten years later, there was a pause, until from 1960 to 1966 twenty-four colonial countries gained independence.

[47] *Development Forum*, vol. I, no. 3, Apr 1973.

The celebration of Independence, both in the countries themselves and in London, were emotive occasions, and generated goodwill to quite a large extent towards the new nations. Problems of development aid were therefore, even if in a superficial and not deeply informed way, fairly frequently brought to the public attention in the United Kingdom.

After the middle sixties there was an increasing lack of interest, and some disillusionment. Informed mention in the more popular press was scarce and programmes of development interest were rarely, if ever, provided at peak viewing and listening hours on the television and radio.

In the last two to three years the climate of opinion has begun to change a little. In universities there is a growing number of institutes concerned with specific regions of the world which have always been centres of development interest. To these have now been added an increasing number of faculties and institutes of development studies, a subject which in some cases now has degree status. Interest in development studies at universities and other institutions of higher education can therefore be said to be on the increase. It is however through voluntary organisations that the most vigorous steps have been taken to get wider and better informed public opinion on aid, and notably through the Voluntary Committee on Overseas Aid (VCOAD), set up through the collaboration of the main fund-raising voluntary organisations, with approximately a quarter of its budget contributed by the Government.

Interest and concern has grown. The churches have built up considerable support and in 1969 presented petitions with over one million signatures. Politically active groups such as the Third World First Movement, the World Development Movement, and Action for Development have sprung up with demonstrations, pamphlets and political lobbying on a large scale. Even so, interest is still limited, and attendance at conferences and seminars still seems rather restricted to a somewhat small cast. What is helpful however is this growing activity among the younger generation, notably those undertaking some form of further education who may be impatient with the usual conference procedures and devise their own ways of bringing pressure to bear.

In 1971 a useful initiative was taken by the ODM at whose request a study was made by the Office of Population Censuses and Surveys, Social Service Division, on the public attitudes, opinions and knowledge of 'Aid and Overseas Development'.[48] The result is an interesting and thorough publication. The survey included interviewing a general sample of the population of Scotland, England and Wales, between the ages of twenty-one and sixty-nine; 3131 individuals from the electoral register were selected, drawn from all local authorities including both urban and

[48] I. Rauta, *Aid and Overseas Development*, HMSO, for the Office of Population Censuses and Surveys, 1971.

rural. Usable questionnaires were completed by 2297 in summer 1969; there was a recall sample of 473 people selected from the original sample, on the basis of the degree of competence shown in answering questions in the first sample; the recall survey took place in the winter of 1969–70. It was found in the full sample that on a superficial level, when asked the question 'thinking about the things that are going on in the world these days, what are the problems you think need tackling most urgently?', the greatest percentage, 29 per cent gave hunger/famine in foreign countries. The idea that richer countries should help poorer countries was widely accepted; four-fifths were in favour, only one-tenth against.

The more domestic question as to whether Britain should help poorer countries did not get such widespread support, three-fifths saying they were in favour, either strongly or on the whole. It predictably transpired that attitudes towards aid were related to the informants' level of education. Eighty-six per cent who had been educated beyond the age of eighteen were in favour of British aid, as against 57 per cent of those who had left school before they were sixteen.

These were indications that many people thought the British contribution should depend upon 'what we can afford in terms of balance of payments'. As to the criteria for deciding which of the developing countries should receive help, most people tended to think of aid as a matter of moral obligation and humanity, and in general that the interests of the developing countries themselves should be consulted. When asked what was meant by the phrase 'under-developed countries', the majority, 49 per cent, thought deficiencies in education spelt under-development, the 49 per cent being almost double any other mentioned aspect of under-development.

But, faced with the question as to what was most immediately urgent, the need for food, medicine and birth control was rated higher than education. On the whole there was a tendency to look upon aid as a charity; during the recall sample it became clear that it was felt that too much stress on the drama of disasters, caused by flood, famines, etc. increased the belief that aid is a charity, and increased the dangers of disregarding the less dramatic and more long-term continuing aspects of aid. In the recall sample, it was stressed that long-term economic independence of the developing countries was in the interests of the world as a whole and that aid assisted this process. It was widely felt that rich people in the developing countries could do more to help their own people, and that students educated overseas should go home to make use of their education there. Stress was put on the fact that there was not enough publicity given to problems of aid, through mass media, although it was also felt that such publicity was often best done by voluntary organisations.

The survey on the whole shows that public knowledge and understanding of aid tended to be rudimentary.; but the survey does not cover the period from 1971 onwards when there seems to be a slow awakening of interest.

The United States of America

Public attitudes, or the images held by the public, of any national aspect are very difficult to determine in small countries, and in a country with such vast geographic and ethnic variations as the United States of America it would seem almost impossible. The tremendous physical and climatic differences between the east and west coasts, between the north, the prairies and the Gulf of Mexico, must affect people's occupations, their way of living and their attitudes and beliefs. The origins of the population are as richly varied as the physical attributes of the country. A sample survey made in 1969[49] showed that 75 million of the approximately 200 million reported that they were one of seven origin categories; in approximate figures 20 million were of German origin, 19·1 were British, 13·3 Irish, 9·2 Spanish, 7·2 Italian, 3·0 Polish and 2·2 Russian. At the time of the survey there were in addition 11 million people living in the United States who were foreign born, the major nationalities being German, Italian, Mexican and British.

Despite these great variations of national origins and climate, and the physical attributes of an enormous country, perhaps the most remarkable thing of all is how speedily a second generation becomes, at any rate on the surface, 'American'. Maybe it is partly because their forbears had to struggle with the climatic and physical conditions of their new country that a real love and respect of their land is soon engendered in people whose parents were definitely 'foreign'. Another fact is that in the past many, chiefly from Europe, had sought freedom and a new life because of some form of political or religious persecution in their country of origin. There is therefore to a surprising degree an overall public attitude to a great many problems; as regards development aid, apart from the generous outlook of the average American, their past history perhaps tends to give them sympathy towards aid, even if it is of an uninformed nature. Recently, in 1973, the Overseas Development Council and the United States Coalition for Development sponsored a nation-wide survey under the title 'World Poverty and Development: A Survey of American Opinion'. A representative sample of Americans were interviewed for one hour each and the survey provides the first overall look at American attitudes on government and public commitment to global development. It

[49] Whitaker's Almanac, 1974, p. 803.

indicates that a majority of the public in the United States is concerned about the problem.

Responses to careful survey questions showed a third of the American public is basically sympathetic to the needs of poorer countries and would support more aid; a quarter are unsympathetic. It was shown that those Americans who support development would appear to be relatively younger, better educated and in the upper income groups, and politically moderate and liberal. It would seem however that regardless of income or education young Americans between the ages of eighteen and twenty-five, or who are black, are sympathetic to the needs of poorer countries, and to the United States helping to solve those needs. As elsewhere the overwhelming size of the problem of world development and poverty is not realised, and there is an inflated idea of the amount the United States is now contributing and no realisation that in terms of relative wealth they are not spending as much proportionately as some other developed but smaller nations. The survey seems to show that most people in the United States consider television the single most important medium of informing the public more deeply about development problems. In other countries stress is put on the role of voluntary organisations in this field of public information, and it is rather surprising that in the United States where voluntary organisations abound the survey has not given any prominence to the part these organisations play in public relations.

There is one feature which maybe has its origins in the make-up of the population and their past history, and that is the belief that America as a very rich country should share with other countries the good things she has been able to create. However a distinguished American[50] has said that this view is held more in the belief that other countries should imitate the United States not because they are wealthy, but because they are good. And this presumed virtue, rather than affluence, is the reason why 'the American way' should be exported to others. It is said that this attitude does affect some aspects of foreign aid programmes, both in Congressional legislation and in the ways in which AID officials go about their tasks.

III THE UNITED NATIONS AND UNITED NATIONS AGENCIES

Ambassador Edward Martin, when Chairman of the Development Assistance Committee of OECD, gave five reasons why the United Nations was particularly important. A précis of these is as follows:

i. That it has an indispensable role to play in world-wide development, as a neutral forum for dialogue between donors and recipients, and sometimes for agreement on common, mutually supporting and coordinated policy.

[50] Personal communication.

ii. It is preferred by some developing countries for technical assistance and as a research agency in a number of fields, either because of its neutrality or because of the expertise it can command globally.

iii. It sometimes gives global leadership to the international community in mobilising action to deal with critical issues.

iv. Because as neither a major donor nor recipient it is reasonably objective in judging the performance of multilateral and bilateral donors and of recipients.

v. It is the only forum for dialogues and perhaps even some coordination of effort among the leading bilateral donors, the members of COMECOM, and mainland China.

This 'Utopia', Ambassador Martin felt, had several handicaps; a lack of public respect as an effective international institution, caused by frequent failure at the political level to stop or limit armed conflict; its prestige has been reduced by its record of passing resolutions on minor subjects that are regularly disregarded; too often, especially in the development field, its debates and votes reflect the international and domestic politics of the developing and developed countries; the United Nations' complex organisational structure is feudal in its relations, including development matters, resulting in much repetition of discussion; the bureaucracy suffers from the rigidities of public organisations, as well as from a number of special ones, inevitable because of its international character; the specialised agencies in the development field seem to be too compartmentalised along the sectorial lines, now dictated by quite different purposes from those of 1945.[51]

Ambassador Martin's article was written two years after the appearance of the formidable Pearson and Jackson Reports, so perhaps the positon is not now quite so depressing as suggested, as particularly in the case of the Jackson Report the recommendations have now turned to action. It is too early to make definitive statements about the role of UNDP, which was clearly strengthened and increased by the acceptance of the recommendations of the Jackson Report. The ultimate success of UNDP in its new role depends on enough staff with the right qualities.

The habit of referring to the 'United Nations family' seems rather odd, except perhaps that it is a human family, with many squabbles and differences within it, the 'family' being born at widely different times – the International Labour Organisation (ILO), the World Meteorological Office (WMO), the International Telecommunications Organisations Union (ITU) being pre-war, and the rest of the 'family' having arrived on

[51] *International Development 1972*, vol. 4.

the scene at various dates after 1944, the newest member being the United Nations Environment Programme, which like UNCTAD is an organ of the General Assembly without the special degree and autonomy of the specialised agencies.

It is questionable whether it is always desirable for a new United Nations organisation to be created when a new world problem raises its head; some surely are passing phenomena and can be cured without the vast expense which a United Nations organisation inevitably means centrally, and for each individual member country.

Brief notes now follow on those agencies which seem to have relevance to this publication. There is a longer section on UNESCO as the organisation has obviously featured particularly prominently in our enquiries and has been more than generous in providing excellent material. There are also further comments on detailed United Nations and United Nations Agency projects in Chapters 3 to 8 on developing countries.

The World Bank and International Development Association (IDA)

The World Bank was established at the United Nations Monetary and Financial Conference at Bretton Woods in 1944 and began to work in 1946; 122 nations were member states in 1973. An increasing prominence has been given to granting loans for direct educational projects; the following examples for 1971 give some idea of the scope of operations in that year:

The International Telecommunications Union (ITU)

This is the oldest international organisation within the 'United Nations family'. It was 109 years old in 1974. The Union gives priority to all forms of training, such as the establishment of training schools in about thirty countries and individual fellowships, many for tenure on specialised courses in the Netherlands, the ILO Centre at Turin, and in the United Kingdom. Finally they are concerned with seminars/working groups in engineering and management, and regional courses grouped by continents, i.e. Africa, Latin America, India. The ITU send specialists to member states who have ITU projects; they link similar institutions, and basic research which arises has until now mostly been done in developed countries and the results applied to developing ones. They have not as yet decided which are the best methods of follow-up and evaluation. They do not really consider professional migration as a serious problem. ITU have tried to coordinate and cooperate at an early stage in operations and they have worked through the UNDP representative. They were the only United Nations organisation which made reference to the fact that in some developing countries people who had had ITU fellowships did a period of compulsory service in rural areas.

Country	Main purpose	Total cost of project	Amount of loan (US $ million) Bank	IDA
Iran	Primary, secondary general, technical agricultural; teacher training; university (education) (T.A.)	41·7	19	
Indonesia	Secondary technical (T.A.)	7·6		4·6
Greece	Post-secondary technical (T.A.)	24·0	13·8	
Dominican Republic	Secondary general and teacher training (T.A.)	8·1		4·0
Tanzania III	Non-formal rural training and post-secondary agricultural (T.A.)	4·7		3·3
Jamaica II	General secondary; teacher training; vocational training; ITV (T.A.)	28·2	13·2	
Congo (B)	Secondary general and technical teacher training; non-formal rural education (T.A.)	4·1		3·5
Ethiopia II	Secondary general and secondary technical and agricultural	13·4		9·5
Brazil	Secondary technical and agricultural, post-secondary technical (T.A.)	21·0	8·4	
Chad II	Secondary technical and agricultural	3·1		2·2
Somalia	Secondary general, technical; teacher training and non-formal agriculture (T.A.)	3·7		3·3
Turkey	Secondary and post-secondary technical; technical teacher training; non-formal management and adult technical training; science equipment production; mass media (T.A.)	17·9	13·5	
Senegal	Secondary general and secondary technical and agricultural	2·3		1·8
Uganda	Secondary general and technical; post-secondary and non-formal agricultural; health and medical training (T.A.)	10·4		7·3

Source: Education Sector working paper, World Bank, 1971.
T.A. = Technical assistance.

The World Meteorological Office (WMO)

WMO is a competent and well regarded agency which celebrates its centenary in 1975, and has succeeded in maintaining continuous and friendly cooperation between its member states on world information on meteorological subjects. WMO provides fellowships at a junior level for training in developing countries, and it also has regional meteorological training schools and provides a few fellowships for highly trained people for further training in developed countries. It has an ingenious method by which it sends mobile schools to developing countries, with one WMO instructor and an equipped caravan, supported by local assistants; it is not much concerned with the linking of institutions or with joint research problems. WMO finds that professional migration is negligible; a recent survey showed that 80 per cent of the people it had trained were still in the meteorological field of work. As to coordination, WMO feels that in an ideal world this should be done by the developing countries themselves, and that overlap will only cease when multi- and bilateral operations are completely coordinated.

The International Labour Office (ILO)

The International Labour Office is large in size compared with some of the agencies, and the breadth of its mandate inevitably means difficulty in defining its spheres of operation and influence. Together with UNDP it finances the excellent ILO Turin International Centre for Advanced and Vocational Training, where courses are held in English, French, Spanish and Arabic. The Office's fellowship schemes concentrate on technicians up to the top managerial class; it trains teachers to instruct technical teachers and arrange courses for trade unionists, and also for people who are to run small industries in developing countries. ILO sends about a thousand experts overseas annually, five hundred in technical and vocational subjects, and many in rural ones. Since its inception it has tried to coordinate its operations with other multilateral ones, and with bilateral ones. It regards as particularly useful the Scandinavian schemes known as 'multi/bi', where both multilateral and bilateral organisations cooperate in the same project. The ILO has some doubts on overall manpower planning programmes, and tends to consider individual projects on a cost and production basis.

The World Health Organisation (WHO)

This is undoubtedly one of the most expert of the agencies; it has little difficulty in determining the frontiers within which it works. Many of its projects are imaginative, for example the experimental schools and colleges of health science in the Cameroons, where doctors, nurses and paramedical staff and sanitarians are being taught from the graduate level together. WHO is responsible for the coordination and administration of the scheme which is financed by the Cameroons, French, Canadian, United Kingdom and United States Governments, and has a Cameroonian as Rector. The Organisation gives priority to educational training, including the training of teachers; it also advises on training schools for auxiliaries in developing countries, but stresses the dangers of having too few fully trained doctors in proportion to auxiliaries. WHO sends a considerable number of experts to developing countries, and as with other facets of its work it stresses that the success or otherwise of many projects depends on the devoted work of people in the developing countries, experts from developed ones, and the staff at WHO headquarters. The Organisation tries to provide equipment for returned fellows, who are always connected with a project and do not receive fellowships for individual specialised interests. It has done quite a lot of work on follow-up and evaluation, consultants going every five years to see what has happened to a sample of returned fellows. A rough estimate is 65–75 per cent success rate, 13 per cent not fully successful, often because their overseas training is not being used correctly, and a 5 per cent failure rate. WHO feels that manpower planning if expertly done is useful in getting the balance of the grade of people in a profession correctly proportioned; it believes that developing countries favour multilateral aid, but the administrative complexity and slowness of some multilateral operations causes many countries in practice to use bilateral schemes. Some personnel of WHO feel that far greater use could be made of the Red Cross in the field of volunteers, particularly in running management schools for volunteers.

The International Atomic Energy Agency (IAEA)

IAEA has a considerable fellowship programme, and is an expert organisation with well defined boundaries; it includes in its programme the training of teachers. IAEA has a coordinated research programme and its experts are encouraged to see ex-fellows in their countries of origin. The organisation, dealing with such an esoteric subject, normally knows a good deal about the progress of ex-fellows. It finds that professional migration is more of a problem than it would wish; there is an urgent need to supply equipment under research contract programmes, and the position is aggravated by there being far too few technicians and maintenance staff. It sub-contract projects successfully to both industries and universities.

The United Nations Institute for Training and Research (UNITAR)

This has as its main preoccupation research. Examples of its recent projects are:

Professional migration	University of Columbia
Environmental problems: techniques and methods of control and enforcement	Dr O. Schachter UNITAR
New methods and techniques of managerial training	Professor Mallick University of Manchester
Transfer of operative technology from enterprise to enterprise	
Peaceful settlement and conflict resolution	A visiting scholar attached to UNITAR

Food and Agricultural Organisation (FAO)

The United Nations agency which it was not possible to visit, and which is relevant to the project, is the Food and Agricultural Organisation (FAO). It carries a global responsibility for better nutrition and greater efficiency in the preserving of all food and agricultural production. FAO provides a network for the international exchange of information in the fields of agriculture, forestry and fisheries; fellowships and experts are provided within a wide range of subjects and the organisation concentrates on the building up of cadres of technicians and agronomists.

Through the Freedom from Hunger Campaign many voluntary organisations and individuals became involved in FAO's work.

The organisation administers jointly with the United Nations a $m 1000 fund of world food programmes for developing countries.

The Technical Assistance Office in Geneva

This handles all the United Nations fellows who come to Europe to study subjects not covered by any specialised agency, or who are granted UNIDO fellowships. The Office is also responsible for recruiting European specialists and advisers, again concerned with expertise not covered by an existing United Nations agency. Finance comes mainly through the social welfare programme of the United Nations. About 600 fellows a year from developing countries are 'placed' in Europe. Apart from the responsibilities for UNIDO fellows, the Office administers a considerable programme for the training of industrial counterparts, financed by the Swiss Government. It has been found that the selection of fellows is better when a project manager is involved in the selection of possible counterparts for the scheme he is managing; in theory fellowships are only granted to people concerned with a project, although in practice this is not always possible.

The United Nations prefer regional training centres to be fully booked before fellows are sent to more remote developed countries; but regional centres are not always totally successful for political or other reasons. Professional migration of United Nations fellows placed by the Geneva Office is a rarity. For the recruitment of experts the Office sends job descriptions to all the relevant European governments, who then arrange for pre-selection. A representative of the Geneva Office then visits the countries concerned to interview candidates; the final selection is made by the host developing country from a list supplied by the UNDP resident representative, who will have assisted the developing country in preparing the original job assignment when requested to do so.

One difficulty in the past has been that job descriptions were often too vague and the unfortunate expert found the task which he was asked to do in no way fitted the job for which he had been recruited. The recruitment of experts is not getting easier; salaries offered are lower than those provided by the World Bank. In 1972 World Bank salaries for experts were about 12,000–13,000 frs per month, tax free, and with post adjustments and family allowances, terms which are far more attractive than those of the United Nations and United Nations agencies, and even more so than those usually available under bilateral schemes. A further cause for recent difficulties is a world shortage in some fields of expertise. Normally experts are recruited for one to three years, some having extended contracts for five years. The United Nations Geneva Office is not involved to any great extent in follow-up and evaluation, this being mainly done by the UNDP representatives.

The United Nations Volunteers (UNV)

The United Nations Volunteers Programme was established by the General Assembly on 1 January 1971. The first target was to be 500 volunteers in the field by 1974; by the end of 1972 it was expected that there would be about 200 UNVs in fifteen developing countries. The administrator of UNDP is also the administrator of UNV. Candidates must be over twenty-one years of age, and meet the health and personal standards laid down by UNV. The main aim of the programme is to encourage the participation of younger people in development aid. UNV sends job descriptions to experienced voluntary organisations in developed countries, who make preliminary selection, followed by technical endorsement by United Nations agencies, the host country making the final selection. Successful candidates receive training in the language, traditions and culture of the host country, and briefing on United Nations development systems.

The 1973 report of the Administrator of UNDP pinpoints some of the difficulties of the UNV programme as encountered in the early stages. By December 1973 there were 170 UNVs serving in 29 countries, clearly fewer than the original target; 31 per cent were serving in FAO executed projects, 30 per cent in ILO ones, and 9 per cent each in United Nations and UNESCO projects. The remainder were distributed in limited numbers amongst other UNDP and United Nations agency projects. Of the various problems the programme has faced perhaps the most difficult is the time-lag caused by the established recruitment and clearance procedures, which have been so long drawn out that they lead to a high rate of withdrawal of potential candidates.

United Nations Educational, Scientific and Cultural Organisation (UNESCO)

UNESCO arose from the Preparatory Conference held in London in 1945 to establish an educational, scientific and cultural organisation. The Preparatory Conference was the culmination of the work of the Conference of Allied Ministers of Education, which first met in 1942 on the initiative of the United Kingdom's President of the Board of

Education, Mr R. A. Butler (now Lord Butler, Master of Trinity College, Cambridge), in association with the Chairman of the British Council. Lord Butler remained Chairman of the Conference until 1945 when, under a Labour administration, the late Miss Ellen Wilkinson became President of the Board of Education. Throughout the Conference's life the British Council provided most of the secretariat, some being provided by the Ministry of Education.

Apart from the European allies, including the Soviet Union, China, Australia, Canada, New Zealand and South Africa, and at a later date the United States of America, participated in the work of the Conference of Allied Ministers. At the Preparatory Conference forty-four states were represented, and in addition there was a strong delegation from the British colonial territories. The Preparatory Conference decided that the headquarters of the Organisation should be in Paris, a decision which over the years no one can have regarded as anything but admirable. Just as it is difficult to agree on a definition for 'education', let alone the words 'culture and science', so it has been problematical for UNESCO to define the precise frontiers of their work and to be certain what their priorities should be. This has sometimes meant much work in the Organisation, and many impassioned addresses at General Conferences, which have not always had direct relationship to the Organisation's purposes and priorities, and have led to a degree of uncertainty and frustration amongst the staff. These difficulties can be mainly attributed to the rapid growth of the number of member states belonging to UNESCO, and the speedy changes in world circumstances, both leading to one priority rapidly succeeding another.

It is now realised that to set targets of 'no illiteracy' in country X by year A, or to decree that all children in country Y should have primary schooling by year B, was an unrealistic way of working; a more attainable target being that each child should have some 'equipment' for holding its own in a changing world, and in many cases this also applied to parents.

The purpose of UNESCO were described in 1971 by the present Director-General, M. Réne Maheu, as follows:

> UNESCO seeks to organise international relations in the intellectual sphere with a view to promoting human rights and helping to establish a just and lasting peace. This is the purpose in view: the aims obviously reach far into the future, but there are imperatives to be observed immediately. Underlying the purpose is the belief in the power of the mind to shape the course of history.
>
> It is paradoxical that it should have been governments, the agents of sovereign States, and as such dedicated to the defence of particular temporal interests, which conceived this purpose and undertook to help its achievement.[52]

[52] *In the Minds of Men*, UNESCO, Paris, 1971.

An echo maybe of the phrase so fresh and hopeful when in 1945 it was first said 'that since war begins in the minds of men, it is in the minds of men that the defences of peace must be constructed.'

UNESCO's priority for the Second Development Decade is stated to be 'the furtherance by all means throughout the world of a process of radical transformation of traditional educational institutions and processes, and the creating of new ones, to fit changing needs of and prospective resources.[53] In other words educational systems suitable for the needs of individual member states should be created, a task which will take all of a decade and more.

Beneath all the torrents of words on paper at meetings and seminars, some steady and good jobs are done. UNESCO was asked to furnish for this project details of all the field missions and fellowships provided to the six developing countries participating in the project, covering a period of two decades: a unique and most helpful piece of work.

The use of fellowships in particular seems to have shown imagination and a willingness to change with the times in order to meet the new needs of developing countries.

The following sums, in dollars, were provided for the period 1961–70 to the six countries concerned:[54]

Chile	3,004,700
India	21,589,800
Kenya	3,719,600
Senegal	2,292,200
Tunisia	2,612,200
Turkey	4,265,300
	$37,483,800

In 1972 three types of fellowships had evolved: *sur place* training, including seminars in the country of origin; fellowships for study at regional centres; and, for people of particular excellence, fellowships for training abroad.

UNESCO has done comparatively extensive follow-up and evaluation of operations, and is now engaged on a global evaluation of their fellowships scheme.

Total planning within UNESCO seems to have been accepted by the early 1970s; this, and the fact that the World Bank and International Monetary Fund projects are now assessed by UNESCO before decisions are taken, should elcarly strengthen UNESCO and make the Organisation's contribution to the whole field of development a more vital one. Many of UNESCO's projects are described in Chapters 3 to 8 on underdeveloped countries.

[53] SCH/MD/9, Paris, July 1970.

[54] UNESCO, Bureau of the Budget, Aug 1971.

IV OTHER INTERNATIONAL AND REGIONAL ORGANISATIONS

Organisation for Economic Cooperation and Development (OECD)

The Organisation for Economic Cooperation and Development came into being at the end of September 1961, succeeding the Organisation for European Economic Cooperation (OEEC) which was created in 1948 at the time of application of the Marshall Plan.

Besides being an instrument of cooperation between the industrialised countries it also undertakes research in different aspects of development. Its membership consists of the countries of Western Europe together with the United States, Australia, Canada, Japan and New Zealand.

The most relevant section of OECD for present purposes is the Development Assistance Committee (DAC). This Committee receives annual statistical reports, together with other material, from all member states which are members of the Committee, some of it being published regularly. The OECD has been very generous in providing material for the project forming this book; they were originally interested in the project because it was on education in a broad sense, and also because it deals principally in the use of people in the development scene.

Turkey is an OECD member state and is one of the few countries within OECD which receives technical assistance directly from the organisation.

OECD material is impressive. It has the advantage of doing very little operational work. Its national membership being smaller and more adhesive than that of the United Nations agencies, they clearly have briefer and more constructive meetings. Through DAC the work that their member states do in developing countries is under constant review.

The Development Centre of OECD has three groups of activities:

i. Research into the essential problems of the developing countries, in the interests of those countries, and in the interests of member states who desire to offer aid.
ii. Supplementary economic training, mainly for senior officials, or economic leaders in the less developed countries.
iii. The communication of experience and documentation in the sphere of development to competent authorities in those countries.

European Economic Community (EEC)

The major factors in EEC's operations which are of interest to this publication are the various forms of assistance given to the countries in association with the Community, which for most of the period of the lifetime of the Community have been the Francophile countries south of the Sahara and Malagasy. The position will presumably change now that the Six have become nine, and the geographical picture will become broader.

Aid which is given through the European Development Fund (EDF) does of course come within the term economic development, and is on a considerable scale, covering four main types of projects – namely, investments; technical assistance including study grants, training progrmmes and financing of experts; aid to marketing and sales promotion; and emergency aid in cases of famine, flood, or falls in export prices.

The EEC takes into account the advantages of 'integrated projects', the promotion of regional cooperation between associated states; the plans and programmes of such states and the need to give special consideration to countries suffering the greatest disadvantages.

The EEC can enter into co-financing arrangements with member states, non-member states or international financing bodies, as well as with organisations in associated states.[55]

Commonwealth Organisations

As has already been said the Commonwealth is a grouping of states with no constitution, no affirmed or definite purpose, and no obvious reasons for being grouped together, except for the fact that at sometime they were all colonies, or dependencies, of the United Kingdom. To attend a Commonwealth meeting can be inspiring, with so many diverse and independent states of every race and colour, the delegates arguing and debating together to reach a particular goal. The major organisations are described below:

1. The Commonwealth Secretariat is an international body at the service of all member countries of the Commonwealth, providing the central organisation for joint consultation and cooperation in many fields. It was established in 1965 by Commonwealth heads of government, who saw it as 'a visible symbol of the spirit of cooperation which animates the Commonwealth'. It is staffed by 180 officers who represent most of the thirty-three member countries, and is financed by proportionate contributions from the member governments; in 1972–3 the total budget was £762,366. The Commonwealth Secretary-General, the Head of the Secretariat, has access to heads of government. Mr Arnold Smith, of the Canadian Diplomatic Service, is the present Secretary-General.

The Heads of Commonwealth governments decided that the headquarters should be in London, and Her Majesty The Queen made Marlborough House available as a Commonwealth Centre.

[55] For a full description of the 'policy and practice of the EEC aid programme' see David Jones, *Europe's Chosen Few*, ODI, 1973.

The Secretariat is the main agency for multilateral communication between Commonwealth governments. In addition to education, trade and commodities, research and international affairs divisions, there are scientific and medical advisers.

The Secretariat promotes consultation and disseminates information on matters of common concern, organises and services meetings and conferences, coordinates many Commonwealth activities, and provides expert technical assistance for economic and social development through the multilateral Commonwealth Fund for Technical Cooperation. Close cooperation is maintained with the Commonwealth Agricultural Bureau, the Standing Committee on Commonwealth Forestry, the Commonwealth Advisory Aeronautical Research Council, the Commonwealth Air Transport Council, the Commonwealth Telecommunications Organisation and the Commonwealth Foundation. It also maintains regular contact with the United Nations and other regional organisations.

Since 1970 when negotiations started for British entry into the EEC the Secretariat has been in close contact with the issues involved. It also keeps in touch with international economic organisations, such as the World Bank and OECD.

The work of the Education Division of the Secretariat is to encourage and assist cooperation among Commonwealth countries, and to keep educational developments under review; it is advised by the Commonwealth Education Liaison Committee (CELC), which was established in 1959, and on which all member governments are represented. The Commonwealth education conferences, which are ministerial-level meetings, are organised by the Secretariat.

The Education Division acts as a clearing house for collecting, analysing and disseminating information on educational developments in the Commonwealth, and is in close contact with international organisations, such as UNESCO and the ILO; the Secretariat is closely associated with the Commonwealth Scholarship and Fellowship Plan. The plan facilitates educational interchange at university level enabling students of high intellectual promise to study in Commonwealth countries other than their own; over a thousand awards at any one time are provided. For a detailed account of the operation of the plan see the chapter on India.

ii. The Commonwealth Foundation was established in 1966 to promote and strengthen links between the professions, their individual members and their societies through the Commonwealth. The Foundation maintains close liaison with the Commonwealth Secretariat and is housed in London at Marlborough House.

The decision to create the Foundation was made by the Commonwealth heads of government at their meeting in London in 1965, and its terms of reference were:

A Commonwealth Foundation will be established to administer a fund for increasing inter-change between Commonwealth organisations in professional fields throughout the Commonwealth. It will be the purpose of the Foundation to provide assistance where it is needed in order to foster such interchanges. The Foundation will be an autonomous body, although it will develop and maintain a close liaison with the Commonwealth Secretariat.

The work of the Foundation lies primarily with the private sector and is in no way an extension of the technical aid machinery of Commonwealth governments. It endeavours to fill gaps where there is little or no help available from other sources. Originally it provided help to the traditional professions, but has recently turned its attention to other specialised activities, such as management, accountancy, youth leadership, etc.

The Board of Trustees of the Fund are independent persons, each contributing country having the right to nominate one member. Commonwealth governments contribute to the cost of the Foundation and its activities on an agreed scale; the Carnegie Corporation of New York augmented donations raised by public subscription, which enabled the Foundation to launch the Andrew Cohen Memorial Bursaries Scheme which assists young civil servants from developing countries to visit other countries.

To overcome the difficulties of newer Commonwealth members, where both members and funds were scarce, the Foundation has sponsored professional centres, which offer practical facilities and also encourage a joint professional approach to problems of education and training, and the provision of advice to governments on questions of legislation, manpower and development planning. Since most of the professional associations and research institutes are private bodies few are able to offer travel grants for attendance at conferences and meetings; here the Foundation is able to fill the gap and assist professional bodies in the Commonwealth to hold conferences, and make awards for attendance at such conferences, or study and research visits by members of the professions to countries other than their own. The Trustees of the Fund have concluded that support of this nature is one of the most useful services they can render.

The Foundation has published a reference book, *Professional Organisations in the Commonwealth*,[56] containing particulars of professional associations and learned societies in Commonwealth countries. Every effort is made by the Foundation to maintain a free flow of information on professional organisations and matters.

iii. The Association of Commonwealth Universities (ACU) is a voluntary society which became incorporated by Royal Charter in 1963: the members are institutions of university standing in the various countries of

[56] London, for the Commonwealth Foundation, 1970.

the Commonwealth. It originated as the Universities Bureau of the British Empire in 1913, and in 1948 became the Association of Universities of the British Commonwealth; the Association is responsible for organising the quinquennial congresses of Commonwealth universities in different Commonwealth countries.

The income of the Association is largely derived from the annual subscriptions of member universities, colleges, and other institutions of recognised academic status, and the rates are fixed according to their size. The Association receives no government grant, but it provides secretariats for certain statutory bodies, such as the Commonwealth Scholarship Commission in the United Kingdom, the expenditure being reimbursed by ODM.

The affairs of the ACU are controlled by a council elected annually, and works in a variety of practical ways to provide contact and cooperation between universities of the Commonwealth. It acts as an agent for individual member universities, and in some cases assists in staff appointments, or the provision of a secretariat for any special operation requested by its member universities.

From its inception in 1913 the Association has regarded the provision of information on matters relating to universities as one of its major tasks, notably the yearly publication of the Commonwealth Universities Yearbook, which contains 3000 pages and has an international reputation as a book of reference.

Part III

The Developing Countries

3 Kenya

Mustafa Tuqan

I THE LAND, PEOPLE, ECONOMY AND EDUCATION

Kenya is not a small country, having an area of some 225,000 square miles. The Rift Valley cuts the country into two parts, and beyond its western rim the land takes its course down to Lake Victoria and the borders of Uganda. The coastal strip is hot and humid, and from there the land rises through dry bush savannah grasslands and fertile well-watered highlands. Nearly all the northern half of the country is arid and only sparsely populated by nomads, whereas the density of population in the southern half of the country is high, being about 450 per square mile.[1]

Only a small percentage of high arable land is at the moment under cultivation. To raise the standard of living of the majority of the population of Kenya, according to the Agricultural Education Commission, 'land and water resources must be used more intensively, production must become more efficient and unit costs must increase . . . To improve technology the farmers themselves must be improved through general education and specific training. The first need is to invest in people'.[2] A second urgent and pressing need, as this study will show, is to invest in those types of rural development which will generate employment opportunities so as to accommodate those educated or trained.

According to the last census, the population of Kenya at the beginning of 1971 was estimated at 11,900,000, most of whom are Africans. They represent some fifty tribes and four different ethnic groups: Bantu, Nilotic, Nilo-Hamitic, and Hamitic. The Asians, originating chiefly from

[1] John D. Gerhart, 'Rural Development in Kenya', *Rural Africana*, winter 1971.

[2] *Report of the Agricultural Education Commission: Weir Commission Report*, Nairobi, 1973.

India and Pakistan, account for some quarter of a million. In the past and until very recently, this minority group controlled the retail trade, provided Kenya with clerks and artisans, and played a dominant role in industry and commerce. In 1960 the European population, mainly British, numbered 70,000, but the Africanisation policy, especially the settlement schemes aiming at placing African farmers on land formerly owned by Europeans and known as the White Highlands, reduced this group by 40 per cent.

Kenya has few natural resources other than land; moreover almost 90 per cent of the population of rural areas, and at least three-quarters of them have to depend for their livelihood on agriculture. Added to this is the fact that the population is growing at the estimated rate of 3·1 per cent per annum. Apart from the fact that this has created a population containing an unusual proportion of children under the age of fifteen, the evidence suggests that it will also upset the balance between the future work force and the capacity of the labour market to absorb it, especially the graduates of the schools at the lower levels of the educational system. Moreover it is anticipated that such a rapid population growth will hinder the government's ability to enrol all children of school age, and to achieve full literacy as quickly as it had been hoped.

Coffee, tea, and sisal are Kenya's chief cash crops. By 1975, the second Development Plan anticipated earnings from an increase in the production of maize. This 'three crop economy', together with some small industries related to it, accounts for 60 per cent of Kenya's exports, and constitutes 40 per cent of the gross domestic product. The Kenyan economy and its growth is thus closely related to the income derived from agriculture and is affected both by adversities of climate and fluctuations of the prices of primary products on the world market.

When colonial rule ended on 12 December 1963, the annual per capita income was rather more than £30, and more than 70 per cent of the African males were engaged in subsistence farming. Therefore the marginal existence of the majority of the population and the largely agricultural base of the economy demanded that special importance should be attached to agriculture in the educational system. However, the decisions to emphasise the Africanisation of the civil service and expand the non-agricultural modern sector of the economy left little room for manoeuvre in this respect.[3]

Having assumed that there exists a direct relationship between formal education and economic growth, education was to serve the state by producing large numbers of highly educated Africans, because most of the top administrative and management positions in the civil service and in the modern urban sector were filled by Europeans, and to a lesser extent by

[3] See Section II.1 below.

Asians. This meant that the major emphasis was placed on expanding the higher levels of the educational system so as to achieve the necessary substantial increase in trained people from secondary schools and the University.

Since however Kenya could provide neither the funds nor the personnel necessary to implement its programme of educational expansion, foreign aid in the form of capital, experts and teachers was inevitable. These were provided on such a scale that the planned educational expansion would have been impossible had it not been for the capital grants and the massive export of personnel to man the new and expanding educational institutions.

Kenyans were convinced that the monopoly of high positions in the modern urban sector held by Europeans and Asians was due to the type and quality of the education they had received. Hence they had no alternative but to allow their educational institutions, at all levels, to be run by expatriates, a substantial percentage of whom came from the former mother country. This situation, coupled with the necessity to find Africans able to take over from expatriates, forced Kenya to proliferate the structures it inherited. Kenya after Independence faced a situation where future development had to depend on the continuation of a system which existed at the end of the colonial era. Despite some efforts to correct the existing pattern, together with the problems associated with external aid,[4] the colonial legacy was inevitably projected into the future. This meant that the colonial education system could not be decolonised immediately, and led to the unfortunate consequences on the evolution of a country like Kenya which are discussed in Section IV.

II EDUCATION AFTER INDEPENDENCE

1. The objectives

Immediately after Independence in December 1963, the Minister of Education appointed the Ominde Commission to 'survey the existing educational resources of Kenya and to advise the Government of Kenya in the formulation and implementation of national policies for education.[5] The Commission, under the Chairmanship of Professor S. H. Ominde, had fourteen members of whom ten were Africans.

African members of the Commission were convinced that the conditions created by Independence were totally different from those under which their predecessors, the colonial committees on education, had operated. Underlying the reports of the latter was the assumption that the different groups in society would remain separate, if not for all time, at

[4] Discussed in Section V.

[5] *Kenya Education Commission Report*, pt. I, Nairobi, 1964, p. 2.

least for a long time to come. The colonial educational system therefore was designed in such a way as to maintain this difference.

Independence, however, signified the birth of a nation. The task that lay ahead was to unite the different racial and ethnic groups and tribes making up the nation. At the same time there emerged a new idea which marked a break with the colonial past. This was the notion of *harambee*, the nearest translation of which is 'pulling together'. Embracing this idea, the Commission stated that education must subserve the need for national unity. Part I of the Commission's report says that education 'must foster a sense of nationhood and promote national unity'.[6]

Three publications had a considerable impact on the Commission's approach to development. They were the reports of *High-Level Manpower Requirements and Resources in Kenya 1964–1970*, the *Development Plan 1964–1970*, and *African Socialism and its Application to Planning in Kenya*. These publications evolved a new principle, namely the existence of a direct relationship between education and economic growth. If education could produce the high- and middle-level manpower so desperately needed by a developing country, then the pace of economic development could be accelerated. Before Independence, education was not viewed as the seed of economic development, but as a social rather than economic service.

Part II of the Commission's report, free primary education, was endorsed as a valid objective of educational policy. Its contribution to economic progress 'both by providing a reservoir of candidates for secondary and higher education and by fulfilling the minimum basic educational requirement for participation in the modern sector of economic life' was recognised by the Commission. But, although it has an economic value, 'it is not so important in this respect as secondary, commercial, technical and higher education. Consequently, too great an emphasis on primary education must not be allowed to hinder economic growth in these other sectors'.[7]

As a matter of fact, the goals of raising educational output at higher levels of the educational system, and that of providing for free primary education, could not be implemented simultaneously (school fees for primary education were abolished on the tenth Independence anniversary, December 1973), except at the risk of lowering the quality of teaching in schools. Kenya simply did not possess the means, financial and human, to create universal elementary schooling fast enough while maintaining standards at the higher levels of learning. This is the familiar dilemma of quality or quantity which faces every developing country when formulating its educational goals. The Kenya Education Commission was aware

[6] Ibid., p. 25.

[7] *Kenya Education Commission Report*, pt. II, Nairobi, 1965, p. v.

of this danger. Part II of its report states: 'The expansion of primary education must not be allowed to debase quality; on the contrary, the present decline in standards must be arrested and reversed'.[8]

The decisions that were taken to solve this problem, namely the recommendations of the Ominde Commission, and the two Kenya Development Plans *show clearly that the Government chose to place the main emphasis on the expansion of higher levels of education and trying to gear these to the manpower needs of the modern sector of economic life, while providing facilities for a slower but steady increase in primary school enrolment.* Three main reasons determined such a choice. One is to be found in Part II of the Ominde Commission's report:

> Although we recognise a measure of economic importance, for the reasons stated, in primary education, we must concede a prior claim to secondary, technical, commercial and higher education. The key posts in our national life require such preparation. The primary schools themselves depend on an output at the secondary level sufficient to furnish the improved staffing standards to which we refer in paragraph 546.[9]

The other two reasons were grounded in political and economic considerations. Politically, the government was pledged to Africanise the civil service and the economy. Arguments advanced in support of this commitment run as follows. In the past only Europeans, and to a lesser extent Asians, could occupy positions of power and wealth in the modern sector of national life. This virtual monopoly was made possible because of the type and high standard of education Europeans and Asians received and because the educational system during the colonial era was so established as to deny Africans access to such education. These benefits, formerly restricted to two groups constituting three per cent of the population, should now be made available to Africans. If the African was to exercise real power in his society after Independence, he had to acquire an education similar to that of the European. Only then would he be qualified to take over those positions in the government and the modern sector of economic life formerly held exclusively by the Europeans and Asians.[10]

Obviously a sufficient number of highly qualified Kenyans was needed to replace British expatriates and Asians. Some idea of the magnitude of the task of Africanisation may be gained from the following statistics. In 1964 almost 50 per cent of total employment in the high and middle level

[8] Ibid., p. 5.

[9] Ibid., p. 3.

[10] These statements are based on interviews the author conducted with some Kenyans. For a fuller discussion of the points raised here, see Donald Rotchild, 'Kenya's Africanisation Programm: Priorities of Development and Equity', *American Political Science Review*, LXIV, 3, Sep 1970, pp. 737–53.

occupation categories was accounted for by Europeans and Asians.[11] More specifically, the percentage of Africans in the public sector in category A occupations, the qualifications for which consisted of at least university education, was 22·7.[12] The share of Kenyans in category C occupations, comprising jobs requiring a minimum of secondary education, amounted to 45·6 per cent.[13] In the private sector, a much smaller degree of Africanisation, especially in category A positions, was achieved. The percentage of Africans in such positions in ten leading motor firms and four leading banks were found to be 1·7 and 1·9 respectively.[14]

Finally, the context within which the required manpower was to be trained had also, gradually, to become African. African teachers should replace expatriates. The curriculum of the primary and secondary schools should 'appropriately express the aspirations and cultural values of an independent African country'.[15] Because Kenyan society is changing rapidly, education is in a stage of transition. Kenya should decide which elements from Western culture it will accept and which African standards it will retain and strengthen. It must also try to merge the selected components of both cultures into a new and unique pattern. Schools must be involved in this process of developing a new societal pattern, and used as the agents for shaping that society.

2. The quantification of needs

As economic development was seen in terms of supply of manpower, an estimate of the required number and types of manpower category became inevitable. This was one of the accomplishments of the report of *High-Level Manpower Requirements and Resources in Kenya 1964–1970*. For the six-year period it was estimated that 5611 persons trained in category A occupations would be needed. Occupations in this category require university training and include both the top professions and the top posts in administration and management. The estimated requirements of category B occupations were 23,814. This category comprises occupational engagements such as primary school teachers with a minimum of Form 4 education, plus two years' teacher training; laboratory, engineering, and medical technicians working in direct support of and under the supervision of professional people; junior accountants; draughtsmen; nurses; radio communication operators, and so on. To be eligible for such

[11] *High-Level Manpower Requirements and Resources in Kenya 1964–1970*, Report of Kenyan Government, 1970, Table A, pp. 16–23.

[12] Ibid., p. 7.

[13] Ibid., pp. 4, 7.

[14] Ibid., p. iv.

[15] *Kenya Education Commission Report*, pt I, Terms of Reference of the Commission.

positions a two- to three-year education is required after Form 4. Category C occupations require 'a secondary school education (Form 4) for adequate performances of the full array of tasks involved in the occupation'. These are highly skilled manual occupations, and involve 'metal working, precision measurements, electricity and electrical machinery and require a more substantial educational level than many of the traditional craft occupations, such as shoemaker, tailor, stonemason, tile setter, painter, etc.' Estimated requirements for the six-year period in this category were 24,958. For the same period it was estimated that 2732 persons possessing category D occupational skills would be required. These are the skilled office, sales, and clerical personnel. The holders are usually required to have a Standard XII education as a foundation, plus at least six months' supervised training in a specific office skill.[16]

Even with the planned increase of manpower in these categories it was reckoned that, by the end of the period covered by the first Development Plan, 1964–70, the demand would not be met, particularly in the top three categories. Significant difference in the demand/supply situation among the various kinds of category A occupations at the end of 1970 were noted by the *High-Level Manpower* survey. In the science/mathematics-based professions and other occupations requiring specialised training shortfalls of 1335 and 864 were forecast. In category B occupations, the estimated supply was 18,975, resulting in a shortfall of 4839 at the end of the six-year period. Amongst principal individual occupations which exhibited significant differences between supply and demand were: primary school teachers 626; engineering and laboratory technicians 649; junior accountants 310. For occupations of categories C and D the shortfalls were estimated at 20,934 and 2348 respectively.[17]

To a considerable extent, the shortfall forecast at the end of the period of the first Development Plan came true. It was also anticipated that significant shortages in many high-level occupations would persist for many years after 1970. At the end of 1969 and 1970 there was a deficit in the supply of teachers at the maintained and assisted secondary schools and at the primary teacher training colleges of 1449 and 1305 respectively. At university, teachers' training colleges, and other institutions of higher technical learning, at least 60 per cent of the established posts are still in the hands of expatriates.

It is clear by now that the course of action chosen after Independence necessitated a major emphasis on the extension of educational facilities at the higher levels of the system. It is also clear that the secondary school output became the key to providing Kenya with the type and level of manpower which it sought relentlessly after Independence.

[16] Ibid., pp. 4, 14, 15, 26.
[17] Ibid., pp. 14, 15, 26.

3. Action to fulfil the needs

As mentioned earlier, it was the formal educational system which had to produce the required manpower described in Section 2 above. Therefore an account of the educational development which took place after Independence will reflect the extent to which the required skills were provided.

(a) Primary schools

From 1964 the government assumed control of the educational system. In 1966 a transition from an eight- to a unified seven-year sequence and a common curriculum for all primary schools in the country was completed.

To improve the quality of instruction, the so-called New Primary Approach was adopted. Under this system English became the medium of instruction from the first day of Standard I (the first elementary class). By dividing the class into small groups, and by letting a warm and informal class atmosphere prevail, children would be encouraged to express themselves, ask questions, and develop habits of self-reliance and cooperation. To assist in the implementation of the new approach, a Curriculum Development and Research Centre was established to prepare suitable teaching materials and to train teachers. However the new approach had serious growing pains.[18]

In the years immediately after Independence, many new employment opportunities were created, particularly in government service. As primary education expanded many teachers left the profession to fill the new posts that became available. It is estimated that in 1964, 75 per cent of the National Assembly's members were former teachers. For the secondary school leaver possessing a first or second division School Certificate, teaching in a village school was not attractive. In 1965, only 8 per cent of the total number of primary teachers had finished their secondary schooling, and 34 per cent were completely untrained. In spite of the new scales introduced in 1964, salaries remained low, and although teachers were provided with houses, the conditions of these were described by the Ominde Commission as being in 'a shocking state of disrepair'.

To make the teaching profession 'as attractive as any other public career in the public service', the recommendations of the Salary Review Commission in 1967, with regard to increasing teachers' salaries, were accepted by the government. To improve the competence of primary school teachers a variety of measures was undertaken. Schemes to upgrade untrained teachers were devised. A Primary Education Supervisory Service was established. In-service courses for headmasters and correspondence courses for teachers were organised. Admission to teachers' training

[18] See Section IV. 4 below.

colleges now needs higher qualifications. In spite of these efforts and for the reasons given later[19] no substantial results were achieved.

At the time of Independence, nearly 50 per cent of children of school age were receiving primary education. At the same time the pressures mounted from almost all groups in society to increase this proportion, and in fact to move as quickly as possible towards universal primary education. In the 1963 election, promises for free universal education were made by the Kenya African National Union, the country's ruling political party. The Union's manifesto stated unequivocally: 'KANU intends that every child in Kenya shall have a minimum of seven years' free education'. Furthermore many Africans with relatively low educational qualifications were taken into government and private employment prior to Independence. This experience strengthened people's belief in the power of schooling to open up for its recipients undreamed of possibilities for personal advancement by way of income, security and prestige.

But, according to the government's goals as sketched in Section II.1, and for the reasons given there, such a rapid diffusion of elementary schooling to meet popular demand could not be effected. Although enrolments did rise, the rate of increase over the period 1964–9 was only 20 per cent: from 1,010,889 in 1964 to 1,209,670 in 1969.[20] The Development Plan 1970–4 aimed to increase enrolments to 1,833,000, thus trying to cover 75 per cent of the primary-school age population in 1974.[21]

(b) Secondary schools

To eliminate former differences between European, Asian, and African secondary schools, curriculum programmes common to all were created. Efforts to desegregate these schools were also made. The Government's policy from 1967 stipulated that at least 50 per cent of the students attending Form 1 classes (the first secondary class) should be Africans. By 1964 94 per cent of the students in all Form 1 classes were Africans.[22] This, in turn, augmented the number of Africans at the higher grades of secondary schooling.

A start has been made to modify the syllabuses in certain subjects. The Nuffield Scheme in physics is an example. The aim here is twofold. First, materials that would help teachers to present science in 'a more lively, exciting and intelligible way' were to be developed. Second, the Curriculum Development and Research Centre would bring together the specialists, the teachers, and the tutors of the training colleges to work on curriculum change.

19 See Section IV.4.
20 *Statistical Abstract 1971*, Kenyan Government, Nairobi, Table 16.3, p. 148.
21 Ibid., Table 17.3, p. 454.
22 Republic of Kenya, *Economic Survey*, Nairobi, 1969, p. 159.

Immediately before Independence, the primary school system underwent a tremendous growth. In 1962 there existed in Kenya 6198 primary schools as opposed to 142 secondary schools with enrolments of 935,766 and 26,586 respectively.[23] Out of this expansion grew a social demand for secondary school places. Another factor that intensified the demand for secondary schooling was the youthfulness of the elementary school leaver. The average primary-school leaving age was now thirteen years, an age which is unsuitable for placement in the labour force. The demand for further schooling became all the greater as everyone began to realise that the KPE (Kenya Primary Education) Plan was no longer the key to personal advancement, but that a graduate in 1963 with a Division I or a good Division II school certificate had a wide range of attractive choices. By entering Form 6 he could possibly pursue his study at a neighbouring university, or get a scholarship to a university overseas. He could also join one of the training courses organised by the several government departments or private establishments. If he completed a diploma course he might earn between £500 and £700 a year. The starting salary of the university graduate in the civil service or business firms would be between £800 and £1000 a year. Compared to the average annual income of the peasant farmer (£20) or the wage of the labourer (£80) in the years immediately after Independence, this income represents a multiple of fifty and ten respectively.

During its inquiry, the Ominde Commission met with a 'popular clamour' for secondary education. This also corresponded in many respects with the previously stated policy of the government to increase the numbers of highly educated Africans. Of course a major extension of the educational facilities since 1964 at secondary and university levels has been effected. Over the period 1964–8 Form 1 intake nearly doubled: from 8956 in 1964 to 15,169 in 1968. The intention was to raise the intake to 21,530 by 1974.[24] This represents an increase of 240 per cent since 1964. The importance that is attached to secondary expansion is also reflected in the distribution of development expenditure on education during the first Development Plan period. The largest share of development expenditure went to secondary schools. From 1956 to 1970, out of a total of K£8,841,000 earmarked for education, K£5,127,000 or nearly 58 per cent was spent on secondary schooling.[25] During the Second Development Plan period the percentage of expenditure on secondary education will be 43 as compared with 0·003 for primary schooling.[26]

[23] *Statistical Abstract, 1971*, Tables 16.2, 16.3, p. 148.

[24] *Development Plan 1970–74*, Kenyan Government, Nairobi, Table 17.7, p. 458.

[25] *Revised Development Plan*, 1966–70, Table 3, p. 313.

[26] *Development Plan 1970–74*, Table 17.36, p. 487.

There has also been a major commitment to the expansion of the pre-university Forms 5 and 6. By 1974 an increase to 9180, an increase of nearly 68 per cent since 1964, was planned,[27] the growth of enrolment in Forms 1–6 having caused this rapid expansion.

(c) The vocational and technical schools

The vocational and technical secondary schools developed partly in response to the Manpower Survey mentioned earlier, and partly as a result of the adoption of the recommendations of the Ominde Commission in 1964. By the end of 1970 Kenya possessed ten vocational secondary schools offering programmes intended to provide students with skills basic to specific occupations. In the strict sense of the word, these programmes are largely pre-vocational rather than vocational. Students are offered an education of a type that enables them to work in industry where they can receive further training as craftsmen or technicians. Enrolment at these schools rose from 1043 in 1964 to 2426 in 1970.[28] The enrolment target called for by the Development Plan of 1970–74 was 3,935. Although enrolment was nearly four times as great in 1974 as in 1970, these schools serve relatively small numbers of pupils when compared with the general secondary schools described in the earlier paragraphs: they had a total enrolment of 2426 in 1970 as against 126,855 at general secondary schools in the same year.[29] The over-emphasis on the expansion of general secondary education is clearly reflected in the projected development expenditure on education during the second plan period: K£788,000 for secondary vocational education in 1974 as compared with K£7,907,000 for general secondary education.[30]

With regard to secondary technical education there are four schools at the moment. These offer a Cambridge School Certificate (now East African Certificate of Education) curriculum, providing four-year courses of general education in which geometric drawing, building construction, and metal work engineering replaced biology and history. Enrolment at these schools was intended to be nearly doubled between 1968 and 1974, rising from an actual enrolment of 1596 in 1968 to a target enrolment of more than 2800 in 1974. The projected expenditure of this type of education for the year 1974 was K£192,000.[31]

The Kenya Polytechnic is substantially a post-secondary institution. It offers courses in engineering, building, printing, catering, science, commerce, etc. In 1969, the enrolment stood at some 2100. The Development

[27] *Development Plan 1970–74*, Table 17.36, p. 487.
[28] *Statistical Abstract, 1971*, Table 16.3, p. 148.
[29] Ibid.
[30] *Development Plan 1970–74*, Table 17.35, p. 487.
[31] Ibid.

Plan of 1970–4 expected an increase of enrolment to 3000 by 1974. Some of this increase will be met by the opening of departments for teacher training, hotel management, and business studies.

(d) Teacher training colleges

In 1968 there existed in Kenya twenty-four primary teacher-training colleges. In the years 1969 and 1970 the colleges' outputs of teachers were, respectively, 2400 and 2500.[32] In order to achieve the required number of teachers, the 1970–4 Development Plan proposed the following first-year enrolments at the colleges for the years 1971 and 1974: 3475 and 4050. According to the plan, these first-year enrolments would produce the following outputs of teachers: 2900 and 3700.[33]

Three major institutions are engaged in the preparation of secondary school teachers in academic and non-academic subjects: the Faculty of Education at the University of Nairobi, Kenyatta College and the Kenyan Science Teachers College. Until 1969 the output of teachers for secondary schools was 380, resulting in a shortfall of 1449 teachers. The 1970–4 Development Plan hoped, through a programmed expansion of teacher-training institutions, to increase the output of teachers for the years 1970 and 1974 to 417 and 670. In spite of this, deficits of 1305 and 272 in the respective years were expected, but the year 1974 was expected to provide a surplus of 169 qualified secondary school teachers.[34]

The Kenya Science Teachers College offers a programme for science and vocational teachers. The college has expanded by 50 per cent since its establishment in 1968. In 1971 it produced 115 teachers who could teach four subjects up to Form 2 level at at least two science subjects up to Form 4 level. In 1972 its expected output was 140. The programme designed to prepare technical teachers is located at the Kenya Polytechnic. The average intake for the years 1968 and 1970 was successively 12 and 61. Over the period 1973–8, presuming no wastage during training, it is hoped to put 459 technical teachers in the field.

(e) The university

In line with the policy of concentrating on the production of high-level manpower, a major investment in the University of Nairobi was made. (Before 1970 this was a university college of the former University of East Africa.) The total undergraduate enrolment from 1964 to 1968 nearly trebled: from 602 to 1743. By 1974, the Development Plan anticipated an enrolment of 3433.[35] Development expenditure for the University is

[32] Ibid., Table 17.19, p. 467.
[33] Ibid.
[34] Ibid., Table 17.22, p. 468.
[35] Ibid., Table 17.29, p. 474.

second only to that for secondary education: K£3,700,000 out of K£16,576,000.[36]

The University now has the following faculties: agriculture, architecture, law, commerce, education, veterinary medicine, science, arts, engineering and medicine. Other parts of the University are: the Institutes of Education, of African Studies, of Adult Studies, for Development Studies, and the School for Journalism.

III FOREIGN AID AND THE FULFILMENT OF NEEDS

As can be seen from Section II, Kenya, at the time of Independence, suffered from a severe shortage of trained African manpower necessary to achieve the educational goals that had been set, and the funds needed to extend training facilities were lacking. Yet Kenya embarked on an ambitious educational programme. Where then, did Kenya get the money, the teachers, the tutors, the vocational and technical instructors, the lecturers, the experts, the African university graduates that were obviously needed to implement such a programme?

A substantial part of the required finance and expertise has been, and still is, provided by foreign aid. The two major sources for the training of Kenyans at universities and other higher educational institutions overseas were the United Kingdom and the United States of America. Large numbers of Kenyan students were engaged in full-time study at British universities and colleges for further education in the period 1964/5–1969/70.[37]

Table 3.5 in the Appendix shows details of the 951 awards made through the United Nations and British sources to Kenyans for study in the United Kingdom during the period 1964/5–1969/70. In addition the Kenyan Government awards scholarships for tenure in the United Kingdom (37 in 1967 and 58 in 1973). Kenyan students at their own or their parents' expense go to study in the United Kingdom in considerable numbers.

The total number of Kenyan students in the United States in the period 1965–9 was 1351. During the same period there were 479 trainees at the various American firms and establishments.[38]

In the year 1966 there were 45, 32, 9, 21 and 20 Kenyans respectively studying at Canadian, French, West German, Dutch and Swedish universities and other post-secondary institutions.

Allowing for a time-lag of three to four years, and an output equal to 80 per cent of entrants to universities and other colleges of higher education, one might expect that by the end of the academic year 1971–2 not less than 2500 Kenyans would have graduated from British institutions

[36] Ibid., Table 17.35, p. 487.
[37] See Appendix, Tables 3.1–3.4.
[38] OECD Development Assistance Committee, DD–235, 4 June 1971.

of higher learning. Applying the same assumptions in the year 1969–70 some 1080 Kenyans were supposed to have completed their studies at similar institutions in the United States, and in the same year about 100 in the other countries mentioned above. Assuming a time-lag of one to two years and a success rate of 80 per cent for trainees, some 500 would have finished their practical training in Britain and 385 in the United States in the year 1968–9. The total manpower thus educated and trained means that nearly 15 per cent of the requirements in categories A and B (taken together) envisaged by the High-Level Manpower Survey of 1965, and at least 30 per cent of category A alone, were met by one component of foreign aid.

Foreign personnel

The main exporters of educational personnel to Kenya was the United Kingdom, as can be seen from a comparison of Tables 3.6 and 3.7 in the Appendix.

Most of the expatriate personnel referred to in Table 3.6, and some of those indicated in Table 3.7, teach at the maintained and aided secondary schools. *That the Kenyan educational programme would have been severely restricted had it not been for this profision of personnel can be appreciated from the following figures. In 1966 and 1969 respectively only 27 per cent and 37 per cent of the total staff in maintained and assisted secondary schools was indigenous.*[39] Early in 1965, the Ominde Commission recognised that it would be 'disastrous' to run down the supply of overseas teachers until 1970. Part II of the Commission's report states: 'Owing to the rapid increase in the number and size of secondary schools in the coming six years, any premature attempt to run down the overseas element might be disastrous'.[40]

With the exception of the secondary trade and trade schools, a comparable situation is found during the period 1968–70 with regard to the staffing of teacher-training colleges, the Mombasa Technical Institute, and the Kenya Polytechnic.[41]

Similarly, the creation and extension of educational facilities at the university level was not possible without foreign aid in the form of both capital and personnel. A sizeable part of the costs of buildings, equipment, instruments and laboratories was covered by grants and technical assistance. The following are examples of some forms of technical assistance to the University – there are of course others. Medical training started with the arrival of various medical experts in 1965 from the University of Glasgow. In 1968 Canadian teams joined the faculty. Since

[39] Filemona F. Indire and John W. Hanson, *Secondary Level Teachers: Supply and Demand in Kenya*, 1971, Table 24, p. 56.

[40] Ibid., p. 46.

[41] See Appendix, Table 3.8.

1962 teams from the Universities of Giessen and Glasgow assisted in the establishment of a Veterinary Faculty, and assistance from UNESCO, starting in 1967, has been directed towards the Faculty of Engineering and the Institute of Education.[42]

The bulk of personnel resources of the University of Nairobi continues to be provided from overseas. In 1967 the percentage of Kenyan citizens employed as science and arts teachers at the University were, respectively, 28·4 and 32·5.[43] In the year 1969–70 the actual number of established posts at the University stood at 304.[44] At the same time, the number of expatriates occupying teaching positions was not less than 215.[45] This means that in the year 1969–70 at least 70 per cent of the staff at Nairobi University were expatriate.

The contribution of the aiding countries mentioned in Tables 3.6 and 3.7 of the Appendix and that of Kenya to the costs of training Kenyans abroad, provision of teachers, educational advisers and experts, is shown in Table 3.9, while Table 3.10 provides a general view of the duration and share in costs of the country projects under the UNDP technical assistance programme.

IV THE CONSEQUENCES OF THE POST-INDEPENDENCE EDUCATIONAL POLICY DESCRIBED IN SECTION II

1. The reinforcement of the colonial conception of the reasons for education

Initially, the Africans in Kenya tended to reject European education. It took some time before distinct changes occurred in the attitude of the African towards Western education. One factor contributing to this change was that 'Europeans were an elite group in African societies, and their characteristics and attainments came gradually to have the prestige and value which commonly are accorded to an elite'. In addition the yearning to discover the secret of the wealth and power of the Europeans caused the Africans to send their children to European schools.[46]

The change was most marked in the later stages of the colonial era when opportunities for young literate Africans began to open up in governmental departments, in the lower echelons of the civil service, in the railways, in the post office, in commercial houses, and in teaching. Entry to these white-collar jobs was determined by the results of competitive

[42] Source of data in this paragraph is 'Technical Assistance to Kenya as at 30 June 1971', UNDP, Nairobi, 1971.

[43] Report of an evaluation survey of university-level manpower supply and demand in selected African countries; UN document no. E/CN.14/WP.6/32, Table A.6, Annex I, p. 5.

[44] Report of the University of Nairobi Grants Committee, p. 6.

[45] Source as note 42.

[46] F. Sutton in *Education and Political Development*, ed. J. Coleman, 1965, pp. 64–5

examinations based on a literary curriculum. In a social order where the majority of the people, especially in the rural areas, were leading a hard and marginal existence, the Africans saw in these newly opened doors their chance to live in a comfortable fashion like the Europeans and the government officials. 'Even a clerkship at, say £50 a year', writes Stabler, 'was infinitely better both in income and prestige than the back-breaking work of subsistence farming'.[47] Hence, the African before Independence had a narrow conception of the usefulness of education. In his eyes, education was a means which would enable him to escape the countryside in order to secure a job in the modern urban sector. Now that the current educational strategy is intent on the provision of sufficient highly skilled manpower to staff and expand this sector, and that a major part of the available funds is allocated to urban development (see Section 3 below) it follows that it is in this very area of the economy that most of the jobs and better rewards of education are to be found. When compared with rural areas, the chances for employment are much bigger, the pay much higher, the prestige at its greatest, and the security at its best. Thus, the highest goal of the individual before Independence, namely to compete with the colonisers in their administrative positions, became after Independence competition with the members of the Kenyan elitist group who, through the education they had received, were also filling that same type of post.

Now that Africanisation of the civil service is virtually completed, and because of the limit imposed on the absorptive capacity of the modern urban sector, opportunities for employment have been steadily decreasing since 1965. In fact, since 1967 it has become increasingly difficult for those with only secondary school education and university graduates of the arts, humanities, and social science faculties to find jobs in the modern urban sector. While the educational system cannot be held entirely responsible for producing a serious number of unemployable school leavers (see Section 3), it must be pointed out that the course of action chosen after Independence both intensified and perpetuated the 'pre-Independence' African evaluation of education, making it more difficult for the products of the system to find employment that would enable them to contribute to the national reconstruction of society.

2. The exclusion of the majority of the young from the full educational system and resultant unemployment

Laying the major stress on the expansion of the secondary and tertiary levels of the educational system, and on the development of the modern non-agricultural sector of the economy, meant that education, especially at the university level, came to be seen as preparation for entry into the

[47] E. Stabler, *Education since Uhuru: the Schools of Kenya*, 1969, p. 11.

'high-status' white-collar jobs. But, as the number of graduates at every educational level substantially increased, and the absorptive capacity of the labour market in the city being limited (again see Section 3), so the chances of employment for those with lower formal credentials were drastically curtailed. An unmistakable sign of this situation was the pressure for higher and higher levels of formal schooling, and the more the market approached a point of saturation, so the desire to reach the highest level of learning was intensified.

Yet the pool of graduates at every educational level is far in excess of the number of places at the succeeding stage. This means vigorous selection and, indeed, an onerous and highly competitive system of examinations at different educational stages has come to constitute the sole criteria of one's eligibility to climb the educational ladder. Since practically all school activities are directed at preparing the pupils for examinations, the main function of the primary school is to select entrants for the secondary school, and the latter has an identical function with regard to admission to university. In this way a large segment of the school population is progressively excluded from the school system. To give some factual data, some 10–15 per cent of the primary school leavers find places in Form 1 at the aided and maintained secondary schools. If we include the unaided *harambee* and other private schools, the percentage of pupils who completed the primary cycle and who are admitted to Form 1 in the years 1967 and 1970 would become 21·5 and 25 respectively. (These percentages were calculated on a basis of the reports of the Ministry of Education.) Of all candidates (at maintained, unaided, and private schools), the percentages of passes at the Kenya Junior Secondary Examination held at the end of Form 2 in the years 1966 and 1968 were 28·3 and 20. From all Form 4 candidates who sat for the General Certificate of Education examination during these years, only 20·8 and 32·4 per cent passed. For the same years 46 and 57·2 per cent for Form 6 candidates who sat for the Cambridge Higher School Certificate examination succeeded.[48]

Not only were the fall-outs unable to pursue further education, but a substantial percentage of them, particularly at the lower levels of the educational system, were left with no alternative as to what to do. They could neither receive alternative forms of training nor find employment in the labour market. In an assessment for 1964, the Kenya Education Commission calculated that of the 103,400 school leavers, 11·5 per cent went to secondary schools, 3·5 per cent found some form of training course, and 19·5 per cent entered wage employment, leaving 65·5 per cent with 'no prospect of wage-earning employment or further education'.[49]

[48] *Kenya Statistical Abstracts, 1967, 1970.*

[49] *Kenya Education Commission Report*, pt. I, p. 135.

The calculations for the year 1965 showed similar results.[50] In 1966, 75,000 out of 147,000 primary school leavers, or 51 per cent, did not find permanent wage employment or formal education.[51] Since 1968 the problem of catering for no fewer than 118,000 primary school leavers has been crying out for a solution.

In 1969, when 14,413 out of 16,973 passed the School Certificate examination, no training or jobs were available for 7529 (or 52 per cent). In 1970, 22,161 candidates sat for the same examination, of whom only 10,814 passed. Skilled job openings were available for 6884 and no training projects were available for the 3920 who also passed, let alone for whose who failed.[52]

In 1970, the total number of school drop-outs in Kenya was a staggering 176,161. Of this number, 15,456 were enrolled in the first years of training at key educational institutions including the University, teacher training colleges, secretarial colleges, and polytechnics. Thus, Kenya was left with 160,705 youngsters who could be on the *Shambas*, self-employed, or looking for jobs. Some repeated the examinations at their drop-out level, but the bulk of drop-outs consisted of those who left the lower stages of formal education when neither work nor facilities for further training or job orientation were available.

While the second Development Plan talks about extending practical education at the secondary schools, virtually no government programme for elementary school leavers exists, and while it appreciates the so-called 'village polytechnics', a rural job-training scheme of the Christian Council, no funds have been allotted to this scheme, so the situation remains unchanged. Each educational level continues to prepare the young for the next; hence, those pupils who leave school are not prepared for the life they will have to lead later. Indeed, they were educated, not for jobs in the country's main occupation, agriculture, but only to go further in the educational pipeline to try and get a white-collar job in the city.

3. The deepening of the urban–rural divide

As post-Independence objectives were heavily orientated towards the urban areas, so the bulk of development resources in the sixties was directed there. Out of K£62 million in private loans and advances from commercial banks outstanding on 31 December 1967, only K£6 million were allocated to agriculture. In 1968 out of a total of K£64 million, the share of agriculture was eight million. In comparison, K£3·1 million and

[50] *Teacher Education*, vol. 8, no. 3, Feb 1968, p. 206.

[51] J. E. Anderson, 'Education for Self-reliance: The Impact of Self-help', Institute of Development Studies, Nairobi, 1968.

[52] B. M. Raju, in a speech at the education exhibition at the Faculty of Education, University of Nairobi, 1972.

K£3·4 million worth of private buildings were reported to have been completed in 1967 and 1968 in Nairobi alone.[53]

The second Development Plan stated that the main emphasis during the period 1970–4 would be placed on rural development. However, the total central government budget over the years 1969/70–1973/4 still shows an inappropriate distribution of resources. (K£39 million for agricultural development and K£2·5 million for rural development as against K£40 million for local government development, of which Nairobi's share is K£25 million.)[54]

Naturally this differential investment resulted in a high rate of migration from rural to urban areas. On the other hand Harbison says that

> . . . at the very most, the modern sector in the typical newly developing country may expand its employment at the rate of 5 percent per annum. If only 10 percent of the labour force is employed in the modern sector, this means that new employment opportunities in the modern sector will absorb only one half of one percent of a country's labour force.[55]

Yet Kenya's population is growing at a rate in excess of 3 per cent a year. One implication of this is that its labour force grows annually at rates in excess of 2·5 per cent. Data on the available labour force and the proportion engaged in wage employment in the year 1969 shows that out of a population of 10,880,000 the potential labour force was 3,808,000, of which 2,491,000 were adult males. There were 528,000 males employed in the modern sector and 300,000 in the traditional sector, thus leaving 1,653,000 adult males with no wage employment, who form the ranks of the unemployed and under-employed.[56] By 1974, there will be an increase of 672,000 in the total labour force of whom 440,000 will be male adults, an increase which is nearly double that of the number of jobs envisaged by the plan. Another implication of this growth concerns the projected enrolment of school age population at primary schools. About 55 per cent of primary-school age children enrolled in 1965. If the present fertility rate remains unchanged, only 62 per cent of the primary school population will be at school in 1990, and the number of uneducated children will double by the same year. If, on the other hand, the fertility rate were to be reduced by 50 per cent, all children of school age would be enrolled shortly after 1985.[57] The products of the schools then will

[53] *Report of Select Committee on Unemployment*, Nairobi, 1970, p. 9.

[54] Ibid., p. 1, 149–51. See also *Economic Prospects in Kenya*, IBRD, Oct 1969.

[55] Harbison, 1969. paper submitted to the Eighth Conference of the Afro-Anglo-American Programme held in Nairobi in 1969, in *Teacher Education in New Countries* vol. 10, no. 2, Nov 1969, p. 101.

[56] *Report of Select Committee on Unemployment*, p. 4.

[57] E. Stabler, *Education since Uhuru*, pp. 160–1.

encounter placement difficulties. Even students possessing university arts degrees who do not acquire marketable skills or specialised knowledge are expected, by the end of the plan period, to experience difficulties in finding suitable employment. And unless the educated youth prefer to swell the ranks of the unemployed, or under-employed, they either must remain on the land or augment the forces in the intermediate sector of the economy.[58]

But here we face one of Kenya's most persistent dilemmas. To begin with, any attempt to change the prevailing conception of the purpose of education (see Section IV.1) is likely to meet with resistance. The evidence suggests that the eradication of attitudes thoroughly absorbed over a long period of time is a painstaking and very slow process. Since the development of these attitudes was born of experience, and given the continued emphasis on training for high-level manpower and the associated provision of opportunities and income, education is still likely to be seen as the route to individual material advancement. Values will remain unchanged.

Furthermore the new emphasis laid on rural development by the second plan raises a fundamental question, namely, the connection between education and rural development. Nowhere in the plan has the role of education in developing and rural areas been made clear. While the basic strategy adopted is 'rural development', there is no mention of these two words in the chapter on education. It is true that in several places the plan made a number of ambiguous statements concerning changes in teaching methods that would enable the school leaver to lead a more useful life in society, but how these changes are to be effected was not clarified.

The second plan suggested certain schemes to be implemented during the period 1970–7, inter alia the inauguration of an experimental rural development programme in some representative districts, a redistribution of benefits in society through the use of increased taxation in the cities, and the generation of more employment opportunities. As to the latter scheme, the Select Committee on Unemployment declared: 'But even if the Development Plan is fully implemented, the problem of unemployment is still with us'.[59] The magnitude of the problem is largely determined by the rate of population growth, the relegation to the background of the development of rural and agricultural life where more jobs have to be sought and generated; and the failure to gear education to the needs of this sector of the economic system.

For all the reasons mentioned in this sub-section, we doubt whether the schemes contained in the second plan will lead to an alteration of the

[58] Harbison, op. cit., p. 105.

[59] *Report of Select Committee on Unemployment*, p. 4.

situation to any appreciable degree. Only major transformations in the socio-economic educational structures will induce students and other members of society to re-assess their prospects, stem the tide in urban–rural migration, and narrow the gap between these two areas in national life by persuading more people to stay on the land.

4. The inability to 'decolonise' the inherited educational system effectively

In the development of an educational policy for tropical Africa, the metropolitan powers and the colonial governments were influenced by two studies on African education produced in the mid-twenties by a group of American and British educators, known as the Phelps Stokes Reports. These reports argued that education 'must be of a character to draw out the powers of the Native African and fit him to meet the specific problems and needs of his individual community life'.[60] This meant the expansion of practical, vocational, and rural-orientated type of education.

In a White Paper of 1925 the emphasis on the need to develop vocational and practical training was reiterated. With the publication of this paper, British educational objectives in Kenya were made known:

> Education should be adapted to the mentality, aptitudes, occupations and traditions of the various peoples, conserving as far as possible all sound and healthy elements in the fabric of their social life; adapting them when necessary to changed circumstances and progressive ideas, as an agent of natural growth and evolution. Its aim should be to render the individual more efficient in his or her condition of life, whatever it may be and to promote advancement of the community as a whole through the improvement of agriculture, the development of native industries, the management of their own affairs, and the inculcation of the ideas of citizenship and service.[61]

But as this educational policy began to take shape, the native Africans became increasingly critical. They observed that Europeans stressed subjects for Africans which were different from those they themselves were taught. They also began to connect the academic educations Europeans were receiving and their positions of power and wealth in society. Moreover, it soon became apparent to the African that the rate of progress in rural areas was very slow because of insufficient capital and lack of technical skills.

This led to increased pressures for school expansion and higher academic standards. The African, focusing mainly on the mobility

[60] *Education in East Africa*, Phelps Stokes Fund, New York, 1924, p. xvii.

[61] Advisory Committee on Native Education in the British Tropical African Dependencies, *Education Policy in British Tropical Africa*, HMSO, 1925, p. 3.

function of the school, hoped that through formal academic schooling he would share in the ever-visible distinctions of the white-collar world, entry to which was determined by the results of competitive examination based on a literary type of curriculum.

All these factors meant that the rural and practical orientations of education of earlier days had to give way to the British literary/humanities tradition in education. In 1949, when the Beecher Committee conducted its inquiry on the scope, content, and method of African education, it found that technical and practical training at the primary schools had almost disappeared.[62]

The British educational pattern was confidently copied in Kenya. With some exceptions, the British curriculum was duplicated, and, in this context, it lacked relevance and imagination. The imported examination system was applied almost intact. Examination standards set up in the mother country came to dominate teaching, curricula and practically all activities at schools which were operating in a radically different environment. Teaching methods were repetitive and laborious. An authoritarian and impersonal attitude characterised the social contacts between teacher and pupil. Subsequently, a high degree of formalism came to be embedded in the educational system – a formalism reflected in the attitude towards learning which stressed the examinable content rather than grasping the essence of what was taught. In many of the schools, the medium of instruction was English. Since language and culture are closely linked, the curriculum, even in the non-language subjects, had a high degree of concentration on content derived from the milieu and culture of the foreign language. One outcome of this was that the educational system became more isolated from the human environment surrounding it. Hence its formalistic nature was accentuated more than ever.[63]

The Africans concentrated on schooling largely as a means through which wires in the city could be pulled, and failed to see how rigid and constricting the habits of actual instruction and examinations were, and that the school was not meeting the requirements of the social and economic evolution of Kenya. When in the latter stages of colonial rule, Europeans began to realise what actually constituted society's needs in Kenya, and they began to redefine their educational conceptions to meet these needs, Africans resisted the new interpretation and pressed for those features of European education most clearly linked with European status and power.

When colonial rule ended, the new government was confronted with public demands for a rapid increase in educational provision, and also

[62] *African Education in Kenya*, The Beecher Report, Nairobi, 1949.
[63] John Anderson, *The Struggle for the Schools*, London, 1970, and E. Stabler, *Education since Uhuru*.

there existed certain immediate needs in the civil service and the modern urban sector of the economy. On the other hand, the large agricultural base of the economy (see Section IV.3), the small size of the urban sector and of the segment of society whose interests are served by its development (see pp. 98–101), the marginal existence of the overwhelming majority of the population, especially in the rural areas, and the conjunction of academic education with elite status and higher living standards, all this demanded that the utmost importance be attached to imparting a new character to the educational system, especially at the lower levels, in a way that would have been useful to a primarily agricultural economy. Had this been done, the educational system would have been realigned to respond to the needs of the majority of the population, and not only to the narrow interests of a minority group, whose members go to university and swell the ranks of the white-collar jobs in the modern urban sector. Furthermore, the educational system would have been enabled to serve the needs of the bulk of students, for whom primary education would have been terminal and, at the same time, it would have provided higher education for the remaining few to meet the real social and economic development needs of the country, as distinguished from theoretical needs based on standards uncritically borrowed from the developed countries (see Section VI).

But the decision to concentrate on the manpower gap at the higher professional levels, and the expansion of the economy in sectors other than the agricultural one, left little room for manoeuvre. This led to a high proportion of the school population entering life with no marketable skills and with little chance of employment. These factors together with the large percentage of capital invested in urban areas caused severe urban–rural imbalance and the exodus to the cities (see IV.3).

When Kenya embarked on expanding the higher levels of the educational system on the scale described in Section II, and at a time when it could not afford such an expansion, it had to seek outside help, including the personnel necessary to man the newly opened schools and other educational institutions. The fact that foreign teachers are seriously limited in their ability to change the existing *status quo* in education, or even to identify necessary changes, is illustrated by the following passage from F. C. A. Cammaerts, formerly Dean of the Faculty of Education at the University of Nairobi.

> There are many excellent young men and women from overseas countries who are fully aware of the needs for change, but both by judgement and by length of service their contribution can be of only limited significance. Their judgement of what is needed is necessarily impaired by their own experience at home in a totally different situation; they can say 'this is all wrong', but they cannot stay long

enough to be able to say 'this is what is right'. The expatriate innovator is liable to introduce innovations which are totally foreign to the country, he is certain to create disturbances by his innovation, and he is very unlikely to be followed by anyone who wishes or who knows how to continue the train of his innovations.[64]

At the primary level, the problem of staffing was complicated by the tremendous growth in enrolments in the period immediately preceding independence. This growth created an enormous demand for primary school teachers. Obviously, the large number of qualified teachers needed could not be found as speedily as the expansion taking place. Consequently, thousands of teachers classified as either unqualified or untrained were hired to operate the newly opened schools. Often these teachers taught 'at and beyond the limit of their knowledge'. In 1968, the Ministry of Education reported that some 27·5 per cent of primary school teachers were unqualified. By the following year this percentage declined to 21·6. In 1965 it was found that not less than 70 per cent of the average primary school staff consisted of teachers who completed primary school education and followed a two-year training course, teachers with two years' training but who did not finish primary school, and teachers with elementary education but no training.[65]

On the other hand, it is difficult to train teachers in such a way as to enable them to take proper advantage of the adopted New Primary Approach (NPA) mentioned on p. 88. The rapid increase in NPA classes resulted in shortages of texts and materials, insufficient teacher preparation, and an inadequate supply of supervisors.[66] Added to all this were the very intricate problems of English as the medium of instruction, and the avoidance of the teaching profession because of the low salary and prestige accorded to it at this level. It is improbable that teachers, under such circumstances, and with such limited education and motivation, could master an approach which, as a method, stresses discovery and exploration, that breaks with bookishness and brings rural life into the classroom; and uses an active and enquiring approach to teaching and learning which can provide a means of developing qualities for curiosity and initiative, readiness to cooperate, and tolerance for change, that are precisely the qualities that young citizens of a developing country need.[67] This is an art, and a very difficult one. In some interviews it was learnt that many teachers resist this approach simply because they are unable to

[64] F. C. A. Cammaerts, 'Kenya', in *Priorities for the Preparation of Secondary School Teachers in Middle Africa*, ed. Frank H. Klassen, International Council of Education for Teaching, Washington D.C., 1969, pp. 118–46.

[65] E. Stabler, *Education since Uhuru.*

[66] Ibid.

[67] Ibid.

understand it. Even if teacher training could be raised to a level whereby the teachers are capable of grasping the essence of the NPA, this would entail raising qualifications and consequently the salaries of teachers, which are already a heavy burden on the budget of primary education. In the final analysis, the NPA has remained more of an ideal than a reality.

With scarcity of qualified staff, the emphasis on high-level manpower and the rush to expand secondary education, not only did the newly established secondary schools have to be heavily staffed by expatriates who had the consequent disadvantage of being unable to innovate, but also little room was left for initiative to experiment with new materials and methods. All this meant that both the new government-aided and self-help secondary schools had to follow the academically orientated models of the colonial era. The curriculum had to remain geared to the Cambridge Overseas School Certificate. Some of the unfortunate features of the Cambridge system are that it does not lend itself to teaching techniques that fit into the Kenyan situation, it permits an imbalance in the selection of subjects and, above all, it involves a great deal of repetition and learning by heart of narrow and irrelevant subject matter.[68] The situation was made more grave when parents, concerned about the future of their children after completion of the primary cycle, began to develop self-help projects. Calling on the notion of *harambee* they established their own secondary schools. By 1968, out of a total of 783 secondary schools in Kenya, 483 were founded on this basis.[69]

One result of the situation that has been described is that most secondary schools cannot, in their present state, effectively follow the lead of the Nuffield Physics Scheme referred to on p. 89, and we must emphasise that it is precisely the grasping of the principles behind the Nuffield Science Scheme that every developing country so badly needs. One effective step then would be the translation of these principles into curriculum according to the Kenyan national educational needs, but within its budget and teaching resources, rather than directly copying ideals which appear to fit into the present pattern.

Many factors combined to hold back innovative thought and action at the University. One is that the expansion of higher education was not motivated by the quest for knowledge; rather, it was the result of the government's policy to produce specialists to meet certain manpower requirements. One outcome of this was that the University's main function in Kenya was to transmit rather than to produce knowledge. Secondly, the highest individual goal is to achieve the highest educational level so as to ensure a high status white-collar job in the modern world of the city (see

[68] For a fuller discussion of these points see Anderson, *The Struggle for the Schools.*

[69] Ministry of Education annual reports.

IV.1 and p. 83). As the degree is the passport for entry into this world. virtually all activities at the schools and the University are directed towards preparing the student to obtain this, and since the salary scales are based on educational degrees rather than on any ability to fill a certain job, the end in view for the student became the degree status, and not the knowledge or competence to which this should testify. Thirdly, when on 1 July 1963 the University College of Nairobi became a constitutent College of the University of East Africa, the traditional British pattern of university education was established. Although in this pattern special emphasis was given to such professional faculties as engineering and veterinary science, the British academic model with entry at A level only was quickly adopted.

Several of the professional faculties suffer from staffing problems. The need to follow British practices imposed overloaded lecture programmes, mechanical teaching, and a strong tendency towards isolation from much of the life of the country. In its turn, isolation tended to create a distinct sub-cultural milieu, obscuring many of Kenya's more relevant needs.

The academic faculties suffered most from the transplantation of the British pattern of university education. Both within the University and in society there is a high regard for British 'standards'. Interchange between faculties seldom takes place. During the second and third years, the general degree pattern requires the study of only two subjects. The effects of the lack of knowledge of relevant supporting subjects have not yet been assessed. On the contrary many departments have now turned to specialisation in one subject only during the second and third years, thus stressing the relation between specialisation, ability and prestige in the minds of many students. Attempts to integrate new subjects into the present curriculum, when made, never materialised. Efforts to integrate physics with managerial studies were in vain. The education option programme, intended to enhance the production of graduate teachers, encountered many difficulties from the arts and science departments. Finally, anxiety not to threaten *standards* led to rigidity in instruction.[70]

Under these circumstances it is not surprising to observe general agreement that many of the students leave university with a limited breadth or perception in their own and supporting subjects, and with an educational experience that has provided them with few analytical tools and little understanding of the dynamics of change. Neither the contents nor the intellectual method have been designed for the tasks they have to face in practical life, nor for those which society actually needs.[71]

[70] The points made in this and the preceding two paragraphs are based on John Anderson's book and the author's conversations with various lecturers at different faculties at the University of Nairobi.

[71] This conclusion was confirmed by the interviews conducted with Kenyans and foreign experts and lecturers.

V PROBLEMS OF AID

1. Aid and the response to the Kenyan request

The main developed countries responded to the needs of Kenya as these were formulated and vigorously pursued by the Kenyans and the Kenyan Government alike. As can be seen in Section III, training abroad was at the senior level. Moreover, the planned expansion programme in secondary and higher education could never have materialised had it not been for the expatriate personnel and other forms of technical assistance. Similarly, with funds from bilateral and other sources, the Government's decision to concentrate on augmenting the modern non-agricultural sector of the economy became feasible. One wonders whether the dependence on external aid to fulfil the Government's educational and economic policy after Independence was a happy situation, given the serious consequences of such a policy (see IV 1, 2, 3 and 4) and the effects these had on the social and economic progress of Kenya.

The developed countries could, of course, have responded differently to the Kenyan request. One possible reaction would have been to withhold aid that tended to magnify and perpetuate the educational system started in colonial days. At first glance, this line of action might seem sensible and sincere, but the question is not really so simple. The aiding country is concerned with the diffusion of its own culture, anxious to secure economic gains by means of aid, and to prevent Kenya from adopting the political and economic order of an opposing group. It feels further handicapped by the mistrust in Kenya that would be caused by any solution departing from the customary pattern, such as the development of rural life and rural education; the adaptation of education to the needs of a fundamentally agrarian economy is perceived as a means to keep the African down by offering him a type of education 'inferior' to the Western one, and the charge of 'neo-colonialism' could well be made.

Yet, in spite of these considerations, it seems an objectionable feature of aid to take the easy way out and give assistance to an educational system that clearly does not enhance the social and economic evolution of a country such as Kenya to any appreciable extent.

2. Multinational participation in educational aid

At the moment, there is in Kenya a steadily increasing trend towards accepting multinational educational aid. Several developed countries are now providing educational aid to Kenya. Generally speaking this trend, under favourable circumstances, has two major advantages. Kenya will come to appreciate that many different educational systems exist in the world, and this may open up possibilities to reconstruct its own educational concepts and methods. Furthermore, if aiding countries begin to see that their own educational systems may not be the only models suitable for

Kenya, and if subsequently, with the active involvement and participation of Kenya, these countries decide to cooperate in a joint search for new and more suitable structural designs, a certain degree of synchronisation more in tune with local conditions and requirements may evolve.

Unfortunately, the evidence collected during the research for this chapter did not show conditions likely to lead to the realisation of this objective. At present, the greater part of aid to Kenya is still provided bilaterally, and this applies to development generally as well as to educational aid in particular. The principal aiding country is this respect is the United Kingdom. On the other hand many of the other donor representatives in the field claim that the British have established an educational tradition in Kenya which is 'strangling' the country's progress. Moreover, they assert that the British personnel operating in Kenya persist in maintaining their influence and resist pressures to change their views. The fact is that other donors, partly because of a dissident attitude towards British educational principles and practices, coupled with the conviction that the British were most unlikely to change them, went their own ways since each believed in the exclusive validity of his own model of education. The Kenyans, therefore, were not presented with one jointly constructed educational scheme, but with British, Canadian, Swedish and German schemes, each of them more or less excluding the others. And in fact, Kenya could only be affected marginally by the ensuing rich crop of educational models, since it was the prisoner of its own actions and reactions to the British type of education during the colonial era (see pp. 95–6), and it was critically dependent on British aid, a major part of the total aid given to the country. Consequently, additional force was given to the existing tendency, whereby the educational system in the recipient country was merely an unadapted copy of the educational system of the principal donor country.

3. Aid and collaboration between representatives of bilateral agencies

Collaboration between representatives of the different bilateral agencies on the spot leaves much to be desired. Although the factors adversely affecting cooperation are still not fully perceptible, the following points may offer some clues: they are derived from the author's experiences in Kenya, in his home country, and in certain of the advanced countries. Sometimes, lack of cooperation may be traced to the ignorance of an aiding agency of what others are doing. But often there are very subtle forces at work; not only does official bilateral aid often mirror historical traditions but, more important, it also has its anchor in deep-seated cultural and political thoughts. These thoughts create certain feelings which, though undoubtedly not justified, are real. Thus, the feeling that, for instance, this developing country belongs to one's 'zone of influence', or that one's own culture is superior in quality or importance to other cultures, has not infrequently caused many different official bilateral aid agencies to coexist rather than cooperate, each pursuing its own policy independently of the others.

In these circumstances, it is obvious that one can hardly speak of coordination of plans and activities. On the other hand, Kenya, and probably every other developing country, seems not really to want coordinated aid. In one of our interviews, the coordination of aid was categorically rejected: 'Let ten institutions render aid in the same field. The fittest will survive and, after all, it is not our money'. Moreover, with untidy aid and a multitude of agencies competing to offer aid, a situation is created that is ideally suited to play off one donor against the other. In many cases, this leads to duplication or overlappoing of activities; furthermore some donors give in to demands to which they are unsympathetic, and provide aid which responds far more to the urge for spectacular accomplishments and international prestige (such as an international sports stadium costing £15 m) rather than to the more urgent and unspectacular needs of the receiving country.

4. Aid and planning in Kenya

After December 1964, the task of planning in Kenya was entrusted to the Ministry of Economic Planning and Development (MEPD). The MEPD has three divisions, one of which deals with technical assistance. This division has two main duties: the coordination of international economic matters and cooperation with other ministries.

The organisation of planning in Kenya has been affected by several factors. (a) All planning functions are centralised within MEPD. The realisation that centralisation is insufficient if policies and programmes are to be adequately developed led to the establishment of 'planning units' at several ministries. The planning unit at the Ministry of Education, established with UNESCO assistance in 1970, only recently was able to make progress. The reasons given for this were the long delay in the recruitment of supporting staff, including the attachment of Kenyans to the unit, and the lack of definition of the relationship and lines of communication between the unit and the ministry's Development Section. (b) Native qualified staff is not yet available in sufficient numbers. One reason for this is that the planning organisation could not be developed fast enough to catch up with the expansion in governmental programmes. This necessitated a heavy reliance on expatriates, with the result that the building up of an indigenous organisational capability and experience, the necessary continuity and long-term viability of planning, became questionable matters. (c) There is little inter-ministerial coordination of policies and programmes. (d) At many Ministries, not all staff are capable of evaluating and planning. In general, the plans that are made lack content. They amount to no more than a mere enumeration of quantified targets to be reached, or a single statistical presentation: e.g., percentage of literacy to be aimed at, number of children to be enrolled, number of classes or schools to be opened, number of teachers needed, given a certain teacher–pupil ratio, amount of expenditure, and so on. In this way the quality of developmental efforts gets little attention. Planning in Kenya at the moment is rudimentary. If the view is accepted that an overall plan producing decisive effects is a prerequisite for effective development, we are then led to an unavoidable conclusion that neither the aiding developed countries and multilateral organisations – see (a), (b) and (c) above – nor Kenya, though for totally different reasons, are as yet advancing in this direction.

5. Aid and the training of counterparts

To a far greater extent, the feelings of superiority mentioned in (3) above were reported to be held by some of the aiding agencies towards the Kenyans.

The Kenya Science Teachers College, one example of Swedish aid, was labelled 'a model of aid'. On enquiring about the reasons for this high evaluation, we heard, 'We have no doubts about the intentions of the Swedes. They really want us to progress and to go ahead and you feel this intention. We don't feel that the Swedes think that we are ignorant. They have faith in the ability of the Kenyan and we have faith in their ability. The personnel provided by them are so hard working and of such a quality that the Kenyan counterparts became enthusiastic and involved'. Some foreign experts and many Kenyans stated that the British method of work is based on the assumptions that 'the British method is the best', that 'Kenyans are not capable', and that, therefore, 'they should be told what to do'. One of these foreign experts added: 'If you don't believe in the capacity of the counterpart, you should leave'. The donor–recipient personal relationship seems to be so important to the Kenyan that one senior man said 'I really would sacrifice a lot of technical expertise in favour of having expatriates with the right personality structure', meaning expatriates with 'personal qualities such as sympathy, understanding, willingness to cooperate, etc.'

It is significant that, in the few cases where 'a partnership on equal footing' is (rightly or wrongly) felt to prevail, cooperation between the two parties taking part in the project, together with government support and fulfilment of 'original plans', were seen to be at their best.

But the evaluation of an effective system of counterpart training is disturbed by other factors. One general complaint by experts and some Kenyans is that 'it is not easy to find counterparts suitable for training'. According to these experts, the difficulties encountered in recruiting suitable trainees are largely to be attributed to the quality of their previous educational experience. Because of 'the long-established British teaching and examination structure', the training could not form a 'foundation on which later effective training can take place'. They did not provide graduates with the ability, or of a calibre that would enable them to follow the training with profit. Even in science and technology, the 'formula' for the graduate 'is the recipe'. He is inflexible in application but finds it difficult to manipulate his skills because he was 'not trained to grasp what stands behind it'. In some cases there are no counterparts at all; the reason for this, it was said, is that projects are often not properly thought out beforehand.

Often the ground is not prepared in advance when the project and its plan of operation are negotiated and concluded at the top level. The trainees are not associated with the project from its inception and often exhibit a sad lack of knowledge of the true nature of the project, its aims, means and ways of achieving these, allocation of resources, etc. Misconceptions with regard to the role of the expert are also bound to occur. Whereas the expert's role is essentially an advisory one, helping counterparts to help themselves, it is often mistakenly thought of as mainly of lecturing. The expert–counterpart situation is worsened by the fact that many Kenyans, especially at the graduate level, do not like to be treated as counterparts. In their eyes being a university graduate is equivalent to being knowledgeable. Training, therefore, is not needed.

Often counterpart training, as a step towards preparing the Kenyans to take over the project, entails scholarships abroad, and the possibility of obtaining a higher degree. On return, however, a great many of the trainees are not posted to the project but to the more remunerative, more status conferring, and secure jobs of the civil service, banks, or other private enterprises. Some of them join the international scientific community. Others stay in the host training country. In many instances this has meant that the handing over of projects could not take place in the scheduled time. The faculties of medicine and veterinary science clearly show the necessity to make one extension after another. At this point it must be stressed that continuous long-term assistance, or the availability of the expert for an indefinite period, may be counter-productive; the conflicting views of many competing experts is another source of difficulty.

Often an expert finds himself in a perplexing situation; before his arrival in the host country he was imbued with the idea that, in his efforts to modernise, he should take into account the existing structures and try to adapt these to the modern demands. But if these structures are archaic, the accomplishment of his task becomes extremely difficult, even impossible. This often leads to a conflict between his duty not to tamper extensively with the traditional structure and what he, as an expert, ought to do. At the same time, the host country accepted an expatriate expert and expects positive, tangible results from him. If his mission is not successful this in all likelihood will be interpreted as a personal failure. On the other hand, the expert is often alone and the time at his disposal is limited. Thus he has to make a choice and, above all, in making his choice he has no alternative but to base himself on his own evaluation of the situation. Since in many instances he lacks adequate training and insight as an expert in a developing country, and can expect little guidance from outside sources, partly because of the lack of suitable development techniques; and since he is often highly qualified in his own expertise, he is limited in its application in the developing country, thus he opts for efficiency at the expense of everything else. Hence the use of more or less totalitarian methods, the reduction of all problems to technology, and therefore because of these reasons the work is done for the developing country and not with it.

6. Aid and the utilisation of training

It is apparent that there is a lack of coordination in the present training structure in Kenya.[72] One outcome of this is that many individual scholarships are granted without regard to the real needs of the country and many individual scholars chose subjects with a similar disregard for Kenya's priority needs.

The better job prospects available to trainees with qualifications from overseas educational institutions cause some Kenyans to follow courses abroad rather than those provided by foreign experts employed locally. The following quotation from Professor W. F. M. Fulton of the Glasgow University team at the Medical Faculty in Nairobi is illustrative of this practice: 'It is surely anomalous that experienced teachers should come here at no small expense to Kenya and to the countries of their origin while the post graduate trainees who might benefit from them are sent to other teachers in the same countries overseas to undergo a primary post graduate training less relevant to the practice of medicine in Kenya than provided here'. Not infrequently, studying overseas produces a psychological and social uprooting effect, which induces some students to stay in the host country, or go to some other advanced country. To my mind, the true causes for what is now termed 'professional migration' are the much more satisfying conditions of life abroad, professionally, socially, and materially. For some Kenyans, conditions at home at present may make a man's training overseas too disjunctive, and by implication too unintelligible to be exploited in a productive way. Kenyans with this type of training are apt to become an enclave in an alien environment.

7. The problem of tied aid

Most of those whom we met in Kenya stated that bilateral aid, with very few exceptions, is not without 'strings'. Most of it is tied to the services, goods and personnel of the aiding developed country. Therefore, it was

[72] See the Ndegwa and the Training Review Committee Reports

argued, one's freedom of action is forfeited in exchange for assured rewards.

The disadvantages of tied aid in the field of investment and trade are increasingly recognised. In so far as bilateral educational aid is concerned, there is, generally, little preparedness to consider other forms than tied aid. Because it nearly always involves an element of national cultural policy, most aiding developed countries are not inclined to award scholarships to be held in a third country. Similarly, and for the same reason, there are very few cases where the developed country is willing to finance the supply of teachers to a developing country from a third country. 'Untied' educational aid falls within the scope of multilateral agencies. It has been suggested that these agencies should be enlarged. However, since their resources are very limited, this postpones a solution to the distant future. Moreover, because of the high dependence of Kenya on foreign aid, and because there is no real basis for presuming that this dependence will diminish in the foreseeable future, bilateral educational aid will continue for some time and it will continue to be tied aid of one sort or another.

VI SOME CONCLUDING REMARKS

One obvious conclusion to this report is that the manpower utilisation model of development, as it was conceived and put into effect in Kenya, proved to be facile. A sizeable part of the estimated trained manpower could not be said to have represented the priority needs of the country. This is borne out by the fact that a substantial amount of the trained manpower produced could not be accommodated in the labour market.

The failure of manpower planning in Kenya, as in many other developing countries, derives from three major interrelated factors. The manpower-utilisation model of development is one based on the conditions of life and needs of a developed society, which itself reflects the views of the classical and new theorists of the welfare of nations, where development is seen merely as a problem of provision of capital and specialised manpower skills to exploit natural resources. The authorities in both developed and developing countries therefore came to believe that the sheer supply of funds and expertise would mean that the developing people would reclaim or develop their natural resources, for the prosperity of all, or at least to the elimination of their poverty, without regard to the causes of this poverty.

The uncritical transplantation of the manpower model of development resulted in seeing development in a developing country as a disembodied problem and, as such:

1. It failed to see that changes made in one or some parts of the system must invariably be linked with similar changes in other parts of the system if they are to produce the intended results.

2. It could not examine and assess the consequences that would be caused by the grafting on to traditional structures, models of development that are not adapted, (and are probably not adaptable) to the radically different circumstances and needs of a developing country.

3. It caused a situation where the consumptive and creative output of schooling were separated into isolated categories.[73]

4. It obscured the path towards comprehensive and long-term decisive answers to the problem of underdevelopment.

Some elaboration of these points is now required.

1. Two basic assumptions underlie the manpower approach to development. First, development is taken to mean economic development. Second, economic development is simply a matter of making available the various manpower skills thought to be needed. From these two assumptions and the fact that the formal education system was considered to constitute the only potent tool for filling the manpower gaps, the conclusion was drawn that the development of society would automatically follow from formal schooling.

But the days of undisputed belief in formal education as a direct and unobstructed road to development are coming to an end. The inadequate functioning of many aspects of the new schools, coupled with the serious tensions produced by the educational output and the capacity of the labour market, makes it clear that the contribution of formal education to development is no longer a question that can be simply posed and easily answered. Strictly speaking, there can be no such thing as education in isolation. Any worthwhile education has to take into consideration not only the specific goals it is seeking to achieve, but also the social consequences generated by its wider relationship with the societal matrix surrounding it. As C. A. Anderson concludes in his article 'The Modernisation of Education': 'The best assurance for a stimulating and constructive educational system is to surround it with a society that has vigorous impulses toward change and initiative. Schools alone are weak instruments of modernisation; but when well supported, they are powerful'.[74]

The manpower model of development emphasised the need to impart certain academic and professional skills to the trainees. In education, this emphasis, among other things, meant the development of science instruction in schools. Consequently, some new ideas in this respect were adopted. But, in the main, these ideas were introduced into the old systems. Thus, side by side with the introduction of the New Mathematics

[73] The word 'productive' in this section, unless otherwise indicated, is used in its widest sense, and not in the narrow sense of economic production.

[74] M. Weiner (ed.), *Modernisation*, 1966, p. 80.

and Nuffield Science approaches to education at the primary and secondary schools respectively, a whole range of traditional educational and social structures, usages and concepts were left intact. For example, the examination systems remained an exact replica of those used in the past, and at present, by the ex-mother country. There are few rational arguments that can be advanced in defence of these systems as they stand today. Although the Certificate of Primary Education (CPE) allows only the best passes to enter secondary education, its validity in measuring the child's educational potential, or even his capacity to absorb important bits of information, is a highly questionable matter. The examination is so designed that only those who can cram so many facts into their heads for the length of time needed to pass the exam are considered eligible to go through to higher levels of learning. At the secondary schools, the story is the same. Here, the psychological pressures exerted by examinations on parents, students, teachers and schools alike, are such as to defeat the true aim of education. They make a virtue of rote learning. This bookish mentality tends to incline students at the secondary schools to view examination results as the only valid criterion of education. More crucial, this mentality is inevitably carried over to university. It speaks for itself then that examinations at all educational levels, reinforcing each other and being as they are, completely nullify the current efforts, to consolidate the revolutionary ideas contained in the New Mathematics and Nuffield Science approaches to education. They also make it difficult for a young nation like Kenya to utilise its trained manpower to the full, since the capacity of its graduates to apply the knowledge acquired in a creative, constructive and responsible way is undermined by rote learning.

The situation is made worse by the fact that, especially at university level, faculties teaching traditional disciplines, with entire bodies of specialised and self-contained knowledge, with traditional standards of excellence and methods of instruction, are still in full operation. Thus, the massive and necessary task of building up a body of knowledge to gain a better conception of tomorrow's society and its needs, is jeopardised. The development of an analytical framework of the future by marshalling and transcending the knowledge contained in the traditional disciplines, is probably a too optimistic and naive hope, because of the high regard for foreign standards of excellence and the rigidity of instruction, which emanates from the desire to maintain these standards. Few analytical tools, and little understanding of the dynamics of change are also manifest. This situation can certainly be attributed to the inflexibility of teaching methods, and the wish not to tamper with standards, together with a high degree of compartmentalisation. A group of graduates, trained in certain subjects that are so strictly defined, cannot be expected to have the impetus to act as agents of fundamental change. Where their local and international professional status, their intellectual competence, and their security are at stake, their inclination to maintain the *status quo* is at its greatest.[75]

The next example concerns teachers. With the coming of manpower projections, the capacity and qualifications of the teacher to transfer the required manpower skills to his students became the most significant attribute of his image. But here, as elsewhere, old structures, practices and concepts remained alive.

(a) There is a very large and vitally important group of teachers who were hired to man the elementary schools, and who remained after Independence. The members of this group can be seen as constituting a huge area of a porous and sedimentary rock, since neither in their total outlook on life or motivational patterns, nor in their academic qualifications or pedagogic competence, are they enabled effectively to put into practice the new ideas now being disseminated. Although many of the members of this group have been undergoing some training courses, yet, for the reasons mentioned earlier, and others to be discussed later, it cannot be said that they could profitably follow the training. This then partly explains their resistance to the New Primary Approach introduced at the primary schools.

(b) A great deal of 'modern' teacher training in Kenya still exhibits many of the features of training of earlier times. Fundamentally, the major emphasis in teacher training is placed on bringing up the trainee to a level of competence in certain classical methods and basic academic or narrowly specialised subjects. There is little regard to pedagogical training grounded in a learning psychology that derives its content and method from the social and cultural realities of the child. This is largely to be attributed to the presence of an immoderately high percentage of expatriates in charge of the training and who are at a disadvantage to innovate, for the reasons given on p. 94 ff.

(c) As we shall try later to show, manpower needs were based on traditional manpower jobs, that called for traditional preparation. In so far as decision makers, educational administrators and inspectors are concerned, herein lay the dilemma of innovation. Innovation means discarding certain attributes thought to be undesirable and adopting new methods believed to be better. In order to reach the target the blessing of the authorities concerned is vital. But to obtain this is difficult or impossible because the *status quo* was a built-in part of the authority structure of the past training.

(d) Two aspects of the quality of the pupil are singled out. The pupil grew up in, and is still surrounded by, a social and cultural environment that is basically non-scientific and non-technological in character. There-

[75] This view has been confirmed by many of the interviews conducted with Africans and expatriates.

fore, it is to be expected that such an environment will not be complementary to – it is even antithetical from – what will be taught at school. Moreover, for parents and children alike, the purpose of schooling is to obtain a passport to open the doors to a career in the administrative services, rather than to acquire knowledge and competence in a specific field of interest, to which a certificate should only testify. Manpower is perceived in terms of the possibilities it may offer in the way of personal advancement, rather than in terms of productivity. In many ways this could be regarded as an effect of the Government's policies to concentrate on producing the manpower to man the modern sector. Lewis remarked that

> the aspirations of people for social and economic betterment are not so much the result of education, which is seen as a means to betterment, but rather the result of the contrast so patently visible between the material and cultural limitations of rural life and the apparent richness of urban life. The power, authority and tremendous material advantages enjoyed by the expatriates, whether government official, trader, plantation manager or missionary working in the colonial dependencies was a greater source of inspiration to the people they lived among than was any of the lessons taught at school.[76]

Since all these environmental factors underlie the behaviour of the student, it is no wonder that he cannot be motivated, or enabled in an effective and constructive manner, to pursue the proper objectives embedded in the new curricular programme.

(e) And exactly as it was in the past, the standard of teaching is considered to be proportionate to the teacher's ability to put a class through the requirements of examinations, and to the number of students sent to university.

All the foregoing centrifugal forces tearing at the educational system illustrate with dramatic clarity the virtually irreconcilable conflict between values, attitudes and arrangements inherent in the new structures and those immanent to the old educational and social institutions. A change in one aspect of the system, if it is to produce the intended results, entails corresponding changes in other sections of the total system. Thus, the conclusion is inevitable that the grafted changes remained peripheral in a situation where the new had to fight a losing battle against the old. Under these circumstances, the new becomes hollow in its presentation and weak in itself; one cannot put new wine into old skins.

The most urgent and most pressing need of every developing country after the winning of Independence is the bringing about of a new and solidly founded identity reflected in a wide range of competencies

[76] Arthur Lewis, CESO, 1969a, pp. 23–4.

sufficiently integrated to toll the bell for the collapse of an order steered by tribal standards, and characterised by a high degree of feelings of inferiority and dependence on the ex-mother country. Prominent among these competencies are: a critical and creative bent of mind, and an independent will to establish their own values of justice, merit, responsibility, flexibility, empiricism, efficiency and their position in a small work group and the community at large.

2. Although practically all the establishments included in the survey were visited to secure the information needed to standardise definitions, the employers' job specifications, in most cases, and especially in government, were accepted and placed into standardised categories. But, by and large, the evidence strongly suggests that these specifications mirrored traditional antecedents, that is, colonial standards regarding the tasks and duties making up the job, the experience, the aptitudes, and the preparations necessary to hold the job, as well as the rewards that should be accorded to the various jobs. This meant that it was accepted that what was needed at the time of Independence was an inflation of the past, or to have 'more of the same'; in this way, the future was made to conform to the conditions which existed when colonial rule ended.

One consequence of this is of particular importance. At the time of *Uhuru*, the most salient feature of the wage structure was the deep chasm separating the highest and the lowest incomes. The importance of this disparity cannot be suffiently stressed, for it is exactly this aspect of the colonial legacy that laid the foundation for later political and economic developments. Politically, it led directly to the formation of classes with conflict interests, namely, a very small elite class of the 'haves' and the rest of the population of 'have nots'. The vested interests of the former nascent class impaired their willingness and capacity to consider seriously the need for social justice by drawing together the two extremes in society and eventually unfolding their potentialities and canalising their energy into the service of social restructuring. From an economic point of view, the huge income differentials provided the basis for neo-classical economics where the valid demand, or the one capable of producing decisive effects, is that which can be upheld by money. Since the elite group had the wealth, resources had to be channelled to meet their demands. This immediately legitimised the existing income structure and, consequently, helped to build an economic structure that could only serve the narrow interests of a small group in society. The same can be said to be valid of foreign enterprises, since these also had capital. Because the patterns of demand of both foreign agencies and the indigenous elite group have a highly consumptive character, and because the nascent elite is not entrepreneurial, or in a position to compete with foreign manufacturers, the demand for foreign consumer goods and the attendant dependence on foreign capital, expertise and technology was inescapable. A necessary, but not sufficient, condition for a way out of the impasse is a substantial redistribution of income.

The importance of the unemployment problem, especially among school leavers at the lower educational level, must be put in its proper perspective. Manpower and educational planning in Kenya could not run counter to what existed in the country when Independence was won, since it was assumed that a developing country could not develop without the necessary capital and skills, and these were thought to be lacking. But the one resource which is plentiful in developing countries – people – existed, though their mobilisation, the harnessing of their energies and potentialities, was thought of only in terms of models of manpower planning which were not appropriate to the actual situation.

3. In the Kenya Manpower Survey, 1964–70, a total of 248 private enterprises and mixed enterprises with 100 or more workers were included, as well as certain industrial groups where there were fewer than 100 workers but where an adequate sample could be obtained. While an attempt was made to collect data on some of the larger agricultural employers, agriculture as a whole was not included because of the sporadic distribution of employees in this sector, the very low percentage of high- and middle-level employment in it, and the fact that various Government land-schemes were under discussion when the survey was made.[77]

Clearly, the bias towards enumerating employers with 100 employees or more engaged in non-agricultural employment could not be said to have been accidental or due to some restraining factors, as the previous paragraph may suggest. It was dictated by the Government's policy in which the manpower skills to be produced were to be at a high level, the assumption that smaller establishments did not employ personnel who could be classified as possessing high- or middle-level manpower skills, and the clear intention to utilise the required level of manpower precisely in these larger organisations. Naturally, this resulted in the major part of the available resources, and a very high percentage of Kenya's high-level manpower skills, being heavily concentrated in the highly paid and status-conferring positions in Government and, to a much lesser extent, in the larger firms in the cities. Thus, the reinforcement of the relationship between high-level formal academic and professional education and high personal gains and elite positions in the urban centres added to the motivation prompting Kenyans to seek this education, and the Kenyan Government to provide it. This education, remaining fundamentally modelled on European principles and practices, resulted in alienation from their background, in memorised packages, and in stifling the imagination

[77] *Kenya Manpower Survey 1964–70*, pp. 2–3.

and disciplined curiosity of the student, rather than acquiring the tools that would have enabled him to participate in the reconstruction of national life, and the commitment to the wider collectivity and its goals. In other words, the consumptive capacity of schooling was not proportionate to an increase in productive capability. Without this the contribution of schooling cannot be a source of measured development.

4. This suggests that all that has been achieved so far in the way of manpower production could at best merely nibble at the problems of underdevelopment. By serving primarily the personal and never explicitly stated interests of a small nascent elite group, by having a very narrow vision of development, by being grafted on to powerful traditional structures, concepts and usages, by covering a very limited span of time, the manpower planning in reality sacrifices any professed political doctrines and prospects for development in return for short-term and micro-level benefits.

All that has so far been said suggests, then, that if manpower planning is to be decisive in its effects, it should recognise that development is much more than mere material production, that development is a comprehensive act directed at all the participants in society and all sectors of national life, and that, therefore, development calls for much more than adjusting a system at the margins. In its turn, adopting new premises implies a change of methods, posing different questions, and getting answers to these. Only in this way is one able to face up to the monumental task of laying the foundation of a new structure in which a clear conception of tomorrow's society, its institutions, and its requirements are rationally integrated. This entails not only the identification of certain political and social objectives and consensus on these; it is also necessary to delineate the kinds of educational, social, political, and economic institutions one hopes to consolidate in the long run.

Such structures can only justify themselves if they can mobilise everyone to live in and do his best to serve his own society. And they can only do that if development is defined in its widest and only meaningful sense. If the concept of development we have in mind is to be viable, it has to curb the drive toward material pursuit and consumptive patterns that are constantly tearing at society and thus frustrating the hopes of millions of others, and depriving many of their legitimate rights to a share, however small the cake may be. This means comprehensive long-term planning of which the basic tenets are: an economy based on man, a clearly defined and defensible concept of social justice, men possessing the abilities and the qualitities needed by a society striving to transform itself, an engagement in the various national activities that represents a positive force in the lives of people, the inclusion of all members of society in the educative process, and an all-inclusive coherently interdependent developmental effort.

Policies in Kenya seriously seeking to consider the type of planning we have been describing depend, to a great extent, on the degree of flexibility the Kenyan Government has in this regard, and the willingness of the developed countries to rationalise their aid process, and the principles or assumptions giving direction and content to these. We are also fully aware of the fact that policies along the lines we are suggesting, if eventually adopted, will have to struggle against great odds. Some of these are: the colonial legacy of the educational and administrative structures; the high dependence on external aid, especially teachers, experts, and capital; and the pervading influence of the rudimentary state of planning. Nevertheless, given the seriousness of the consequences of no change in the social and economic evolution of Kenya, we feel that any analysis in terms other than those sketched in this section will only scratch the surface of the problems with which a developing country is confronted, and with which it has to deal.

It is this analysis which has served as a guideline in this assessment of the educational achievements of Kenya, and of development aid, and it is the context for the concrete recommendations contained in the next and final section of this chapter.

VII SOME CONCRETE RECOMMENDATIONS BASED ON SECTION VI

1. Since neither the amount of money nor the number of teachers, experts, and scholarships put at the disposal of Kenya proved to be decisive in the developmental effort, it is proposed that aid should give priority to projects initiated by nationals, or national institutions, and judged by a panel of experts to have the potential of making an important innovation in the educational system. Criteria for judgement may be whether the project comprises suggestions with regard to new teaching techniques and materials; to replacing the present examinations system by more rational measures as to what could be inculcated in the learner; to ways and means of relating education to the needs of the country, especially those of the rural areas and the urban slums; and, above all, whether the project intends to experiment with the proposals contained in it, and to evaluate them after being put into effect.

2. A major part of the present bilateral educational aid should be rechannelled to the development of the intermediate and agricultural sectors of the economy. The reasons for this are compelling. The intermediate sector produces and sells to the bulk of the population; it constitutes a leverage point *par excellence*, since it permits a line of progress in the sense of making a large impact on the economy without excessive investment; and, if this sector is augmented, it may offset the overdevelopment of the modern sector.

The priority to be given to agricultural development is based on the following facts: (a) The traditional agricultural sector in the countryside will continue to dominate the social and economic panorama in Kenya for a long time to come. It may be argued that the traditional sector is losing ground all the time, because of the continuous process of urbanisation. The truth, however, is much more complicated; the country cannot be urbanised as rapidly as some may believe. And when urbanisation is identified with the development of the modern sector, it is also counteracted by the emergence of the shanty towns, simply because the town will continue to be filled with unemployed youth who cannot be absorbed into its limited capacity. (b) The majority of the Kenyan population will have to depend for its livelihood on agriculture, because of the weakness of the private sector, the extremely slow and deliberate nature of the process of industrialisation, and because of the virtual absence of a scientific and technological culture, of the resources and of the modern skills necessary to trigger off such a process in the foreseeable future. (c) For these reasons, many of the jobs needed to tackle the problem of unemployment have to be generated in the agricultural sector. (d) For the school leaver, the evidence that engaging in agricultural activities will enable him to make money, and enjoy a good standard of living, may be more persuasive to him than the attempts to induce him to stay on and love the land through changes in the curriculum of the primary school. The point has been made very clear by the Uganda Education Commission:

> Our first observation, then, is this: until there has been a substantial breakthrough from relatively unproductive subsistance land use, to much more intensive and profitable forms of farming in which young people can see a return for their efforts, school leavers will continue to seek other means of employment. Hence, paradoxically, the problems of agricultural education are not primarily educational; they are intimately bound up with the solution of economic, technical, and social problems.[78]

(e) As W. A. Lewis observes, 'if agriculture is stagnant, it offers only a stagnant market, and inhibits the growth of the rest of the economy. The core of the doctrine of "balanced growth" is that neglect to develop agriculture makes it difficult to develop anything else'.[79]

3. In order to make a technological character really penetrate into agricultural practices and techniques, the surrounding social and cultural environment should be stimulating, and give support to the new changes to be effected. This suggests that external aid should channel support to

[78] 'Education in Uganda', *The Report of the Uganda Education Commission* (The Castle Report), Entebbe, 1963, paras 106–7.

[79] W. A. Lewis, 'Reflection on the Economic Problem', a paper prepared for the Oxford Conference on Tension in Development, New College, Oxford, 1961.

schemes having as their aim the development of, and experimentation with, a system of educative services capable of releasing the traditional, conservative, non-rationalist structure of rural life from its rigidity. A part of the funds consumed by the present bilateral educational aid could be diverted to finance country programmes of this sort, to be executed by multilateral agencies in collaboration with the Kenyans working at the existing corresponding institutions in Kenya; namely, the institutes for development studies, of rural development, and of adult studies.

4. The previous recommendations mean a shift in the aim, type and level of the educational, technical, and vocational aid that is currently rendered:

i. Instead of the same mass of export of teachers engaging in direct teaching, especially at the general secondary school level, it is high time that educational aid confined itself to supporting schemes aimed at the training of teachers of teachers, particularly in those sectors where internal resources are either inadequate or totally lacking, provided that such schemes are potentially capable of improving the quality of the present teaching–learning pattern in Kenya. The supply of science and technology teacher–trainers merits special attention. But then science teaching can result in little fruition if it lacks a central ingredient. This is creating in the trainee what E. Shils of King's College, Cambridge and the University of Chicago termed 'the disposition of disciplined curiosity and sensitivity'. In technological instruction, judgement and wisdom should be sought as the quality of the educated, no less than technological competence. And, at the core of all training should lie the actual amount of the pedagogical training to be undertaken, rather than the attainment of a level of competence in certain basic subjects, and one anchored in psychology grounded in the realities of the Kenyan social and cultural context.

ii. Instead of exporting experts on a large scale, it is believed that the time has come to concentrate on training Kenyans in key skills, the proper acquisition and practising of which may unlock the door towards real progress and self-sustaining development. One of these skills to which external aid is most suited is development and educational planning. This is a priority in the true sense of the word, since it constitutes the main key to improving returns on every form of aid. The aim here should not only be training in the mere enumeration of targets in purely quantitative terms, or the simple numerical presentation of the number of personnel, or the amount of money needed. If training in educational planning is to have a genuine meaning and value, it should also relate to the whole purpose and aim of the relevant education and, above all, the educational plan must contain within it the seeds of its implementation.

Another key skill that every developing country badly needs is training a sufficient number of citizens in research methods and techniques in general. The aim here is not to train in investigating a particular theme or hypothesis; rather, every effort should be made to assist the trainee to grasp the essence of scientific thought and method and the adoption of this as a way of life. The importance of this for the task of producing knowledge, especially with respect to the true nature of society's problems and how to tackle these, can hardly be exaggerated.

iii. To be able to meet the training needs of the intermediate and agricultural sectors of the economy, and of the informal system of education recommended above, a good deal of the money consumed by the massive training of Kenyans abroad at high levels can be diverted to provide for training that is quite different, both in kind and in level. The kind and level of training we have in mind stems from the nature of the occupational skills needed in these two areas and in (3) above. Very roughly, these skills can be classified into lower and higher middle-level occupations. The former category has to do with functions, the performance of which is necessary for the proper functioning of any modernising society. It includes such jobs as carpenters, plumbers, tailors, electricians, garage hands and many others. For training in such skills neither experts of the kind currently exported, nor a high level of formal schooling is required. Actually simply equipped workshops established and run locally by instructors in skilled labour from an aiding country, and an elementary education on the part of the trainee should suffice. The second category comprises functions necessitated by the need to launch agricultural extension, health and nutrition education, family planning, promotion of citizenship, and community development programmes. The category includes amongst many, such jobs as health educators, community organisers, family planning advisers, agricultural extension workers, small-scale industry manufacturers, etc. If training in these occupational skills is to be carried out successfully, certain basic requirements have to be fulfilled. Adequate rewards in the way of prestige and remuneration should be accorded to these professions. Sympathy with, and the willingness to serve, less fortunate fellow men, devotion to and faith in one's mission, merit and aptitude are among the criteria suggested for selection of candidates for training. Training should take place locally, and preferably in centres established within the rural areas. Also these centres should not escalate to the granting of university degrees. Foreign aid can assist in the training, but:

(a) it should recruit personnel who have experience in the community problems of separation, disunity, and inequality characterising most social groups in the developing countries; such recruits should be capable of designing training programmes and experimental schemes based on a sensitivity to and understanding of these problems. Probably such qualities are likely to be found more among certain volunteer groups than among the highly specialised experts;

(b) it should make it possible for the trainee to visit other developing countries that have had longer experience of experimenting with community development schemes, e.g. India and Pakistan, with the purpose of exchanging views, experiences and probably acquiring new insights.

iv. With regard to the University of Nairobi, both donor and recipient should see that:

(a) No expatriate teacher is appointed at the University unless he is contracted to select his most promising Kenyan students, and concentrate on training them as his successors, and this within a prescribed period of time. This can be done by assigning to the selected trainees certain organisational and supervisory tasks, the volume and importance of which are increased gradually, so that at the end of the study period the trainee is ready to assume full responsibility.

(b) The Kenyan nationals, thus selected and trained, should on completion of the study, be obliged to take over the positions of the expatriates at the University for an agreed number of years.

(c) The Kenyan Government should ensure to these teachers security of tenure, income, promotion possibilities, and other fringe benefits and privileges that are in no way less than those enjoyed by the graduate civil servant.

(d) In his training efforts, the expatriate should bear in mind that the traditional intellectual excellence associated with some universities in developed countries are not necessarily standards needed in developing countries. In such countries the intellectual excellence to be sought should be dynamic, empirical, flexible and oriented towards finding the most suited intellectual tools for analysing and tackling the problems of a society that needs to be transformed and modernised. Among others this means involvement of the University in tackling the problems of society.

(e) The same principles mentioned are valid for the training of counterparts in projects outside the University, and for the Kenyans to be trained in the occupations needed in occupational skills.

(f) In Kenya we were told that some experts were appointed by correspondence. The assignments of others took place on a basis of second-hand interviews. Moreover, there was a complaint concerning the relative utility and effectiveness of the expert. For these reasons and those mentioned throughout this study we recommend that better selection and preparation methods be devised to ensure that the expert possesses certain professional and human qualities, some of which are: adequate knowledge of the country to which he is assigned, especially with regard to its culture and the psychology of its people, the spirit of an educator, humility in approaching problems, and the capacity to act both as a counsellor and student.

(g) Competition between donors and duplication of activities may be minimised by applying the consortium method to educational aid. In principle, such a consortium is merely a free association of the donors active in Kenya. In it, bilateral, multilateral and private organisations can be represented. For its smooth functioning however, no single member should dominate. The fact that a certain member–donor country or organisation has a bigger, or the biggest, share in aid should not be construed to mean that this organisation is entitled to play a predominant role, and others become mere figureheads. And if such a consortium is to prove itself a powerful tool for effective development:

it should aim at contributing to an actual improvement in the quality of education rather than occupying itself with the quantitative (how much money and how many people) and the procedural aspects of aid;

its policy should be determined by a genuine concern for a real social and economic evolution of Kenya rather than by some narrow interests of its members and those of a minority group in Kenya, as well as by the actual, as distinguished from the hypothetical, needs of the country;

it should renovate its means and ways for meeting these needs by searching for, applying, and experimenting with, new methods and techniques more fitting to the circumstances prevailing in Kenya;

it should work in the closest collaboration with the relevant Kenyan official institutions (including the University) and other non-governmental organisations, especially private enterprises;

it should serve as a means through which official, private, national, and international contributions and efforts are pooled, and coordinated action taken by each element in the field in which it is most qualified.

APPENDIX

TABLE 3.1

Number of Kenyan students enrolled at British educational institutions by year and type of educational institution attended

Year	*Type of educational institution attended*						*Total*
	Universities	Technical colleges	Inns of court	Colleges of education	Nursing	Others	
1964–65	392	664	45	31	391	025	548
1965–66	430	682	35	25	372	114	1658
1966–67	456	852	17	18	399	076	1818
1967–68	386	789	4	13	389	132	1713
1968–69	401	812	12	24	323	111	1683
1969–70	447	813	19	15	292	117	1703

Source: British Council, *Student Statistics*, 1959–70.

(The breakdown at British universities appearing on Table 3.1, into type and field of study, is shown in Tables 3.2 and 3.3.)

TABLE 3.2

Kenyan students enrolled for full-time study or full-time research in UK universities by year, type and field of study (1964–5 and 1965–6)

Year	*Type*		*Field of study*								*Total*
	under-graduate	post-graduate	agriculture and forestry	arts	dentistry	medicine	pure science	technology	veterinary science	social studies	
1964–5	330	62	20(4)	83(23)	1	68(8)	67(12)	106(8)	5	42(7)	392
1965–6	347	83	26(7)	71(20)	3	59(8)	65(14)	144(20)	5(1)	57(13)	430

Source: Commonwealth Universities Yearbook, 1966–7.

TABLE 3.3

Kenyan students enrolled for full-time study or full-time research in UK universities by year, type and field of study (1966/7–1969/70)

Year	*Type*		*Field of study*										*Total*
	undergraduate	postgraduate	arts other than language	languages, literature, and area studies	social, administrative, and business studies	education	pure science	engineering, technology, and applied science	architecture, town and country planning, home/hotel management, etc.	agriculture, forestry, veterinary science	medicine, dentistry and health	biological and physical sciences	
1966–7	383	73	17(6)	13(1)	58(5)	38(13)	66(12)	158(17)	4(3)	34(10)	68(6)		456
1967–8	305	81	9(5)	10(3)	49(11)	31(9)		149(25)	11(1)	20(9)	60(5)	47(13)	386
1968–9	312	89	9(5)	9(6)	41(15)	35(20)		171(15)	2(2)	16(8)	60(3)	58(15)	401
1969–70	354	93	8(3)	5(3)	45(9)	30(19)		174(20)	4(4)	19(8)	88(4)	74(23)	447

Source: Commonwealth Universities Yearbook, 1968–71.
Figures in parenthesis represent postgraduate studies.
(The number of Kenyans enrolled in practical training at British governmental and industrial establishments during the period 1965/6–1969/70 is shown in Table 3.4.)

TABLE 3.4
Number of Kenyans enrolled in practical training at British industrial and governmental organisations by year and type

Year	*Type*				*Total*
	business professional	industrial	government	others	
1965–6	77	44		44	165
1966–7	338	47		128	513
1967–8	42	30		20	92
1968–9	52	17		25	94
1969–70	56	24	19		99

Source: as Table 3.1.

TABLE 3.5
Distribution of scholarships to Kenya by year and source

Year	*Source*						*Total*
	British Council scholarships	British Council bursars	UN Fellows	Technical assistance SCAAP	Commonwealth teacher bursars	Commonwealth scholarships	
1964–5	5	7	18	132	20	5	187
1965–6	4	6	15	106	18	4	153
1966–7	3	12	16	103	21	3	158
1967–8	1	8	5	85	19	3	121
1968–9	3	8	15	123	21	3	173
1969–70	3	6	18	116	11	5	159
Total	19	47	87	665	110	23	951

Source: British Council's Central Statistical Unit.

TABLE 3.6

Numbers of UK publicly-financed personnel in education in Kenya specified by year and field of assignment

Year	*Field of assignment*							
	1	2	3	4	5	6	7	8
	Total teachers	Primary and secondary education	University and higher technical education	Teacher training	Technical and vocational training	Educational administration	Educational advisers	Total exports in education
1966	647(29)	547	20	30	50	12	4	663
1967	976(66)	797	92	25	62	9	1	986
1968	1017(86)	933	7	24	53	7	4	1028
1969	980(105)	955	5	–	20	36	4	1020
1970	945(54)	826	32	31	56	33	5	983

Source: ODA London and OECD Development Assistance Directorate, Document DD-235, 4 June 1971.

Figures in parenthesis represent volunteers.

Column 1 = sub-total of columns 2–5 }
Column 8 = grant total of columns 2–7 } excluding volunteers

TABLE 3.7
Number of personnel in education in Kenya by year and exporting country

Exporting country	*Year*	*Number of persons*				
		Educational experts			Volunteers	
		Total	*(of which teachers)*	*Advisors*	*Total*	*(of which teachers)*
	1965	21	21	10	–	–
	1966	38	37	18	35	24
CANADA	1967	39	36	22	58	36
	1968	50	47	36	69	45
	1969	47	44	29	64	44
	1965	9	7	–	25	25
	1966	10	10	6	30	14
DENMARK	1967	14	9	16	46	11
	1968	15	9	16	53	6
	1969	17	13	20	64	7
	1965	10	7	5	–	–
	1966	12	10	11	–	–
FRANCO	1967	17	16	5	–	–
	1968	15	13	7	–	–
	1969	15	13	7	–	–
	1965	9	9	33	16	1
	1966	11	11	46	50	5
GERMANY	1967	34	28	44	65	34
	1968	32	17	24	88	22
	1969	22	16	20	71	13
	1965	–	–	3	–	–
	1966	–	–	4	36	–
NETHERLANDS	1967	–	–	15	70	1
	1968	–	–	32	76	7
	1969	–	–	70	61	6
	1965	8	8	2	–	–
	1966	12	12	10	–	–
NORWAY	1967	15	15	17	–	–
	1968	19	19	22	24	15
	1969	22	22	29	60	25
	1965	7	5	–	–	–
	1966	10	10	15	–	–
SWEDEN	1967	14	12	12	–	–
	1968	34	30	9	–	–
	1969	39	37	11	15	11
	1965	29	–	47	129	39
	1966	27	–	43	234	98
USA	1967	26	–	51	341	175
	1968	36	–	42	334	173
	1969	14	–	68	455	282

Source: OECD Development Assistance Directorate, DD-235, 4 June 1971.

TABLE 3.8
Percentage of Kenyan citizen staff by year and type of institution

Type of institution	*Year*	*Citizen staff (%)*
1. Teachers colleges	1968	36
	1969	42·5
	1970	50
2. Mombasa Technical Institute	1968	10
	1969	10
	1970	20
3. Secondary trade and trade schools	1968	51
	1969	56·5
	1970	66
4. Kenya Polytechnic	1968	11
	1969	20
	1970	25·6

Source: Annual reports of the Ministry of Education, 1968–70

TABLE 3.9

Percentage of development expenditure on education by year, recipient and aiding country (US $)

Country	*1965*		*1966*		*1967*		*1968*		*1969*	
Kenya	1,269,783	(6·2)	2,293,695	(13·9)	1,962,520	(9·68)	5,280,752	(20·64)	7,509,471	(28·32)
UK	13,600,000	(66·43)	7,300,000	(44·25)	10,600,000	(52·31)	9,800,000	(38·31)	6,600,000	(24·89)
USA	4,100,000	(20·02)	4,000,000	(24·25)	4,000,000	(19·74)	4,000,000	(15·63)	5,000,000	(18·86)
Canada	400,000	(1·95)	900,000	(5·45)	900,000	(4·44)	1,200,000	(4·69)	1,500,000	(5·65)
France	n.a.		n.a.		n.a.		n.a.		n.a.	
Germany	800,000	(3·9)	1,200,000	(7·27)	1,400,000	(6·9)	2,000,000	(7·81)	2,000,000	(7·54)
Netherlands	n.a.		n.a.		n.a.		n.a.		n.a.	
Norway	100,000	(00·48)	300,000	(1·81)	500,000	(2·46)	800,000	(3·12)	1,300,000	(4·9)
Sweden	200,000	(00·96)	500,000	(3·03)	900,000	(4·44)	2,500,000	(9·77)	2,600,000	(9·8)
Total	20,469,783	(99·94)	16,493,695	(99·96)	20,262,520	(99·97)	25,580,752	(99·97)	26,509,000	(99·96)

Source: This table is compiled on the basis of Table 5(1), OECD Development Assistance Directorate, DD-235, 4 June 1971, and Table 37(b), Annual Report of the Ministry of Education, Kenya, 1970, p. 91.

(The figures given by the Ministry's quoted report are in K£. These were converted into US dollars at the rate of K£ = 2·80 $.)

TABLE 3.10
Kenya country projects

Project	Agency	Approved by Governing Council	Project duration (years)	Project costs (US dollar equivalent): Total	Governing Council earmarking	Government counterpart contribution
1. Faculty of Engineering, University College, Nairobi	UNESCO	May 1972	8½	5,236,100	1,626,100[1]	3,610,000[1]
2. Kenya Polytechnic, Nairobi	UNESCO	May 1962	9½	5,140,500	2,347,500[2]	2,793,000[2]
3. Survey of the irrigation potential of the lower Tana river basin	FAO	May 1962*– Feb 1966	3	1,273,065	950,065	323,000
4. Mineral resources survey in Western Kenya	UN	Jan 1964*– Oct 1969	3½	992,300	605,300[3]	387,000[3]
5. Surveys and pilot demonstration schemes leading to the reclamation of the Yala swamp	FAO	June 1964*– June 1970	4½	965,000	649,000	316,000
6. Animal Health and Industry Training Institute, Kabete	FAO	June 1964*– June 1968	3	931,700	458,700	473,000
7. Management Training and Advisory Centre, Nairobi	ILO	June 1965	6	1,345,000	932,000[4]	413,000[4]
8. Range Management Division of the Ministry of Agriculture and Animal Husbandry	FAO	Jan 1966	7	4,749,200	2,916,200[5]	1,833,000[5]
9. Operational research on human and animal trypanosomiasis eradication in the Nyanza and Western provinces	WHO	Jan 1967	3	3,156,600	1,211,600	1,945,000
10. Irrigation Research Station, Ahero	FAO	Jan 1967	4	3,271,600	778,600	2,493,000

11. National Industrial Vocational Training Scheme	ILO	June 1967	4	1,294,600	924,600	370,000
12. Training of secondary school teachers, Department of Education, University College, Nairobi	UNESCO	June 1967	5	3,710,500	1,492,500	2,218,000
13. Beef Industry Development, Nakura	FAO	June 1968*– Oct 1969	1	845,800	260,800	585,000
14. Animal Health and Industry Training Institute, Kabete, Phase II	FAO	June 1968	5	2,186,700	1,210,700	976,000
15. Beef Industry Development, Nakuru, Phase II	FAO	June 1969	3	1,387,100	832,100	555,000
16. Industrial Survey and Promotion Centre, Nairobi	UNIDO	Jan 1970	2	649,200	517,200	132,000
17. Research on tick-borne cattle diseases and tick control	FAO	Jan 1970	3	749,200	463,200	286,000
18. Sewerage and ground water survey, Nairobi	WHO	Jan 1971	2½	1,012,900	666,900	346,000

Source: UN Resident Representative, Nairobi.

* Date of completion of field work.

[1] Includes supplementary earmarkings of $739,500 and additional Government counterpart contribution of $2,686,000 approved by the Governing Council at its January 1969 session.

[2] Includes supplementary earmarkings of $919,400 and additional Government counterpart contribution of $1,913,000 approved by the Governing Council at its June 1969 session.

[3] Includes supplementary earmarkings of $65,400 and additional Government counterpart contribution of $22,000 approved by the Governing Council at its January 1968 session.

[4] Includes supplementary earmarkings of $175,500 and additional Government counterpart contribution of $59,000 approved by the Governing Council at its June 1970 session.

[5] Includes supplementary earmarkings of $859,400 and additional Government counterpart contribution of $129,000 approved by the Governing Council at its June 1971 session.

4 Senegal

Adri Kater

I HISTORICAL BACKGROUND

Like most African states, Senegal owes its present shape to the occupation of Africa by the European colonial powers. Before the arrival of the Europeans several kingdoms already existed and were from time to time invaded and subdued by others. In the fifteenth and the beginning of the sixteenth centuries, the Portuguese settled in Cape Vert, Gambia and Casamance, and were later followed by other European powers. Trading was the sole objective of these Europeans, the slave trade being the most attractive and a far from peaceful activity. After the abolition of slavery, it was gradually replaced by trading in groundnuts and gums.

The real conquest of Senegal began in 1854 when the Frenchman Faidherbe was appointed Governor, and in 1891 it was completed. Four communes had been created; Saint Louis, Gorée, Dakar and Ruffisque. The inhabitants of these communes had the same status as French citizens; the people outside the communes were French subjects. The French conquests were not confined to Senegal, and large parts of West Africa came under French rule. In 1902 Dakar became the residence of the Governor-General of French West Africa, while Saint Louis became the residence of the Governor of Senegal. The four communes elected their Municipal Council, a General Council and a deputy in the French National Assembly. This situation remained until the Second World War.

In 1942 the Governor-General, Bousson, who previously had supported the Vichy Government, placed French West Africa on the side of General de Gaulle. In 1944 the Brazzaville Conference took place in which General de Gaulle promised that the colonies would be represented in the French Constitutive Assembly. Two Senegalese deputies were elected members of the Constitutive Assembly: Léopold Sedar Senghor and Lamine Gueye. In

May 1946 French citizenship was granted to all inhabitants of the French colonies in Africa, and thus the colonies became overseas territories in which territorial assemblies were created with important administrative and budgetary powers. The Senegalese elected the members of these territorial assemblies, as well as the deputies of the National Assembly of the French Union and Council of the French Republic.

In 1958 General de Gaulle came to power in France and drew up a new constitution by which the French Community was created, in which it was proposed that the different territories would become independent states. In September 1958 a referendum was held to enable the former colonies to vote for or against this constitution. It was made clear that to refuse the constitution would mean immediate independence for the country concerned, but on the same day France would completely withdraw all its officials and support. Senegal voted by a large majority for this constitution, and on 25 November 1958 became the Senegalese Republic and a member of the French Community. Senghor became Senegal's first President; Mamadou Dia became Prime Minister.

Efforts to create a Federation of West African States within the Community failed. Most former colonies were not in favour of it, so eventually only Mali and Senegal created the Mali Federation, with a Federal Assembly, presided over by Senghor and having Modibo Keita as President and Mamadou Dia as Vice-President. This Federation lasted only until August 1960, when the Senegalese National Assembly proclaimed Senegal's independence; Senghor again became President of the Senegalese Republic and Mamadou Dia Prime Minister. In 1962 a conflict arose between Dia and Senghor; the Assembly supported Senghor, and Dia was imprisoned. In 1963 the constitution was changed; the post of prime minister was abolished and the President of the Republic became also the President of the Council of Ministers.

II SENEGAL TODAY

Policy in today's Senegal to a very large extent means President Senghor's policy. President Senghor is a brilliant exponent of the elite that originated under French rule in Africa. Together with Césaire he is the founder of the Négritude Movement, which stresses the importance of African culture. This is essentially a cultural phenomenon and has hardly any racial meaning. As such it is very different from similar movements in the United States, where stress on colour and search for African origins go hand in hand. The partisans of this *movement* originally fought the idea that African culture is savage, barbaric, primitive and bound to disappear under the tidal wave of Western culture. They pointed to the importance of negro art in the past and its influence on general world culture. One of the most impressive manifestations of Négritude was the World Festival of Negro Art, held in Dakar in April 1966. This Festival was to mark, according to President Senghor, the beginning of a new phase in Négritude. The old one was the phase of defence; the new one that of cultural independence.

Although Césaire is a native of Martinique, most adherents of this Négritude Movement came from Francophone African countries, and it can be asked whether this *movement* is not so much a consequence of the French education of its supporters, as of Negro culture itself. The lack of interest in political, economic, and to a certain extent, in social phenomena, is moreover typical of the *movement*. This lack of interest was one of the main points the critics raised against the 1966 Dakar Festival. For this reason Cuba and Guinea refused to participate, as did the artists Harry Belafonte and Myriam Makeba.

It is not difficult to discover in Senegalese policy this same preoccupation with purely cultural affairs. It is quite clear that the value orientation of Senegalese elite is impregnated with Senghor's ideas. The theatre building, *Daniel Sorano*, in Dakar and the fame of the Senegalese national ballet are only two examples of the priority the Senegalese President gives to cultural manifestations. These manifestations should certainly not be considered as prestige objects. In Senghor's view culture is as essential for the well-being of a people as food and health, and independence should in the first place be cultural independence. Without this cultural independence, political, economic, and social independence cannot be realised.

Senghor considers himself to be a socialist, not in the Marxist sense of the word, but in the African sense. He rejects the Marxist approach as a theory that can only be applied to the nineteenth-century European situation. The Twentieth-century African situation is entirely different.[1] Its clearest characteristics are the colonial situation and the cultural, financial, and economic dependence on the rich countries of Europe. Senghor denies that there is a class struggle in Africa, because classes are non-existent. He does not deny that there are groups in Africa with opposing interests, but these groups are not social classes based on the ownership of means of production.

Senghor's ideas on the African way of socialism are related to those of the group Economie et Humanisme in France, founded by Professor Lebret. This school rejects the study of economics as an isolated subject and propagates an integrated approach to development in which human well-being has a central place and is not confused with economic growth.

These same ideas, amongst others, can be found in Senghor's African socialism as, at the invitation of Senghor, Lebret advised the Senegalese authorities on the drafting of Senegal's first Four-Year Plan. During the

[1] See L. S. Senghor, *Liberté II: 'Nation et voie africaine du socialisme; novel essai de definition*, Paris, 1971.

first years of Senegal's independence, there was a sincere effort to realise this kind of socialism, but soon it became clear that its adversaries were more powerful. After the arrest of Mamadou Dia in 1962, the situation changed and although African socialism is in theory still considered a target of Senegalese policy, its influence on politics is more and more restricted to a very limited number of powerful men, and disappears behind the somewhat opaque walls of party politics.

This in no sense means that Senegal has become a dictatorial state. Senghor is far from a dictator who enjoys power for its own sake. He is a sincere humanist trying to guide his country in the direction he thinks best, taking into account realistically the existing power structure in Senegalese society. He is a typical intellectual, poet, and philosopher, a man who thinks more along broad lines of principle but without forgetting the hard facts of everyday political life. What he wants primarily is that Africans should play their part in the shaping of tomorrow's universal civilisation, and that his country should have a leading role in this effort. It is along these lines that the Senegalese cultural and educational policy should be understood.

'African socialism' is an expression used in different senses. Senghor's is different from Nyerere's, but both have in common the idea that there is such a phenomenon and that it is based on the African tradition. Seghor's emphasis is however on culture, while Nyerere's is on security. Both tend to over-simplify things and tend to neglect the differences which exist inside Africa. Nevertheless a simplified idea about the essence of African society and culture can be very useful for the reconstruction of that society.

III DEVELOPMENT

Senegal's capital, Dakar, is a modern city built to be the capital of the whole of French West Africa. Today it is the capital of a country of three and a half million inhabitants, which has no access of any importance to other countries in the hinterland. More than ever, however, it gives the impression of being a prosperous city; trade and cultural life flourish and the city is clean and busy. To a certain extent this is due to the fact that Dakar is still a regional centre for West Africa. Several regional and international organisations have chosen Dakar for their headquarters, and many countries have chosen Dakar as a place of residence for their representatives, even when they are accredited to other countries, no doubt because of the many climatic and infrastructural advantages Dakar has over the other West African capitals. Being situated at the most western point of Africa, international airlines and shipping make use of Dakar's airport and port facilities. Immediately outside Dakar, however, one is confronted with a poor, relatively dry country, which does not have much to offer.

The Senegalese economy depends on groundnut culture, which is notoriously sensitive to prices on the world market. Most Senegalese farmers live by subsistence agriculture and grow groundnuts for their necessary cash income; an income needed primarily to pay taxes and for social purposes. Senegal's population grows yearly by 2–3 per cent and living conditions in the countryside are far from improving. Thousands of Senegalese leave their villages and settle in or near Dakar where they hope to find a better life. In this respect there is little contrast to other developing countries. Dakar lives from its harbour, its trade, and the international and national bureaucracy.

As has already been mentioned, President Senghor and other leading Senegalese personalities claim that a class struggle does not exist in Senegal, because there are no social classes. It may be more correct to say that there is, as yet, no class consciousness. There are great discrepancies of income in Senegal. The main gap is between farmers who live from the produce of their fields, and those who receive a regular salary. In 1968, during a student strike at the University of Dakar, President Senghor reproached the students, saying that a government grant for a Senegalese student, though moderate, was still five times the annual income of a Senegalese farmer. (The students' answer was that they did not in the first place ask for higher grants, but for lower salaries for ministers and higher officials.)

The salaried classes are mainly concentrated in Dakar. In many respects their interests are opposed to those of the farmers, and living in Dakar they have more influence on the Government than the farmers who are scattered over the country and are not in a position to exert much influence. Moreover the farmers have no suitable organisation to do so. Apart from the salaried classes there are two other groups which influence Senegalese politics to a great extent; these are the traders (foreign as well as Senegalese), and the *marabouts*.

The *marabouts* are a very influential group in Senegal; they are the leaders of the local Muslim congregations and have great power over their followers. In monopolising knowledge about religious matters and acting as intermediaries between their followers and God, they are more than religious chiefs alone. In exchange for the spiritual services they render, the farmers work part-time on the *marabouts*' fields; their leadership is charismatic and they are well aware that education and democratisation are threats to their power. They are certainly not big landowners; though rich, their power does not stem from their economic position but is rooted in the belief and value system of their followers.

It is generally accepted that the *marabouts* were behind the fall of Prime Minister Mamadou Dia, who was arrested in 1962 for alleged conspiracy against the security of the state. Dia, like Senghor, believed in an African way of socialism, but unlike Senghor, was more inclined to put his ideas into practice. The *animation movement*, inspired by adherents of Lebret's school of Economie et Humanisme and aiming at stimulating the participation of the populations in the responsibility for their development, was for Dia the way to African socialism. Although this *movement* does not use a conflict model, the *marabouts* considered it, and with good reason, as a threat to their power, and acted accordingly. The fall of Dia meant the end of efforts to reshape political and administrative structures.

The other influential group in Senegalese politics are the traders. Commercial trade is dominated by foreign trade companies and although Senegalese tradesmen do exist, and are sometimes very successful, trade generally depends on these foreign companies. The Senegalese tradesmen do, however, exert an important influence on Senegalese politics. During the first years after Independence, the Senegalese Government made an effort to reorganise the commercialisation of groundnuts in such a way that the farmers would become less dependent on businessmen, and that the trade in groundnuts would be restricted to Senegalese traders and farmers' cooperatives, through the Office de la Commercialisation Agricole. This Office is, as well as the cooperatives, part of a highly centralised system which is part of the state bureaucracy. They system is intended to give the farmers their share from the benefits of groundnut production, their only cash income.

To a certain extent this system has been successful; the farmers are now less dependent on traders, who used to buy the groundnut harvest before it was ripe, at a far lower price than the one to be expected at harvest time. However, state-organised commercialisation is expensive; the farmers do not really feel responsible for their cooperative and they are cheated by officials and employees. After the fall of Dia, *marabouts* assured themselves of key-posts in the cooperative system.

Moreover this dependence on groundnut growing is risky and income depends on weather conditions and world prices. A few years ago the harvest was extremely bad; the farmers were not able to pay their debts to the cooperative organisation and the state was threatened with bankrupcy. The situation was saved by French action, which made available the necessary funds to pay the farmers' debts, thereby saving President Senghor and the Government. Critics of Senghor's policy maintain that by doing so, the French continued an undesirable situation in which only a few Senegalese benefit, while the masses of the population suffer. However, it can be questioned whether in the present world situation Senegal has any chance of following a policy from which the masses will profit more than they do now. It should not be forgotten that 50 per cent of the national budget is paid by foreign aid. Senegal's neighbours Mali and Guinea have tried to follow more independent courses, in which Mali has failed, and Guinea, despite its important sources of income from mining, does not succeed in giving farmers a better standard of living than in Senegal.

IV THE SENEGALESE EDUCATIONAL SYSTEM

The responsibility for education in its restricted sense of formal education is divided between two ministries: the Ministry of National Education, which is responsible for general education from the primary level up to and including the university level, and the Ministry of Technical and Vocational Training. Besides these two ministries, others are involved in several fields of adult education. The educational system follows in general the French model. In a report by one of the commissions charged with the establishment of the third Four-Year Plan, a critical assessment is made of achievements in the field of education. The main points of criticism are the following:

> The existing system resulting in the threat of a growing proletariat of unemployed at the primary school level.
>
> The growing number of those who failed to enter the sixth form, for whatever reason, and who have not received any adequate training to earn a living.
>
> The failure to make the rural youth literate so that they can take part in the technical, cooperative, and hygienic developments of the rural regions.
>
> The training of many young people, often at high costs, for jobs for which they have no motivation whatsoever.
>
> The continuing devaluation of manual labour.
>
> The diminishing quality of school education hand in hand with too numerous classes and frequent repetition of classes.
>
> The preference of students for literary subjects as against technical and scientific subjects.
>
> The fact that the primary school has become an instrument of social differentiation instead of an institution for democratisation.
>
> The lack of coordination which exists between training and production.

These tendencies and the impossibility of raising, for budgetary reasons, the percentage of children for whom school education is available, caused the Senegalese authorities to rethink the educational system. A result of this rethinking is that an educational reform has been proposed and accepted. This reform, however, does not go as far as could be expected from the announcements which preceded it. In the near future, Senegal does not envisage making school attendance compulsory.

At the start of the third Four-Year Plan the percentage of children of school age, actually going to school, was 40; in the course of the 1969–73 Plan it is expected that it will rise to 50 per cent. For those who will not be able to go to a primary school, an out-of-school training programme was to be established, intended to give a training adapted to the rural environment. It was announced as follows:

> L'adaptation au milieu signifie en premier lieu la formation d'une jeunesse ouverte au progrès technologique, et préparée à occuper une fonction dans la société, en second lieu la création chez l'enfant d'attitudes favorables au developpement. Pour cela, au-delà d'un enseignement primaire rénové qui gardera sa double fonction de communication des connaissances utiles et de formation intellectuelle sera prevue la mise en place d'une éducation non-scolaire, conçue comme un appui pédagogique aux structures d'accueil qui existent et qui ont pour nom village, coopératives, société d'aménagement, entreprise artisanale destinée à préserver l'acquis de l'enseignement primaire et à completer par une formation pratique fascilitant l'insertion du jeune dans un circuit de production. A ce titre une évaluation systematique des diverses expériences faites d'une manière disharmonique au cours de second plan s'avère indispensable avant d'entreprendre une généralisation.

This was written in 1968 and, as could be expected in 1972, one year before the end of the third Plan, the situation was still the same. Many disparate and uncoordinated activities, sponsored by different bodies and with the aid of different countries and their organisations, are still active. One of the most well though-out of these is part of the Animation Movement. As has been pointed out before, on page 141, this *movement* was originally designed to cover the whole country in an integrated approach to development. Through the locally designed *animateurs* all kinds of training would be brought to the villages as part of an effort to involve the villagers in the planning and execution of their own development. As a consequence of the events of 1962 (see p. 141) this *movement* was more and more restricted in its activities.

Half of Senegalese youth will be provided with the chance to follow at least primary education. Today the primary school has five classes. After these five years 20 per cent of the pupils will have the opportunity to attend a *lycée*, while about 30 per cent will go to the *colleges d'enseignement general* (*CEG*), or *colleges d'enseignement secundaire* (*CES*). Those who finish their studies at a *lycée* will have the right to enter the University of Dakar. The others either drop-out or follow technical training. In the third Four-Year Plan the main aims are to maintain the level of school attendance at 50 per cent, the regionalisation of the colleges and the deconcentration of the *lycées*. This regionalisation means that every year thirty *CES* should be constructed, a number that certainly will not be attained.

The educational methods used in primary and secondary schools are the traditional ones inherited from the French period. The Senegalese Government does not intend to change the programmes of these schools. The idea behind it is that, apart from providing the manpower it needs for its development, Senegal should be able to provide a sufficient number of university-trained people of the highest level, so that the country can make its contribution to intellectual life on a world level. It is clear that the present Senegalese Government considers this as the first aim of education. The reason for the decentralisation of the secondary schools is to prevent the growth of masses of educated unemployed in the cities, where they can be a source of unrest. It is doubtful if this result will be achieved. The poor conditions of life in the rural areas cause people to migrate to the cities whether they are educated or not.

Technical education and professional training belong to the Ministry of Technical and Vocational Training. The kind of schools operating under this ministry are secondary technical schools, regional technical training centres for women, regional technical training centres for men, agricultural training centres, centres for training in agricultural handicraft, regional centres for professional orientation, and the national school for merchant shipping as well as schools for training in fishery, water and forest management, cattle breeding, graphic arts, handicrafts, rural staff, public works and secretarial work.

If we look at the different types of schools under this ministry, we see that some of them are orientated towards trade and industry, and supply workers for the urban industrialised part of Senegal, while others are directed towards the rural areas. Some of these schools, like the schools for water and forest management, for public works and training of rural staff, train future government officials. Most of the pupils study on government grants and have a contract which forces them to enter government service after finishing training. The effect of this contract is, however, more in the interest of the pupils than of the Government, because it obliges the Government to supply them with jobs, or if no vacancies are available, to pay them their salaries. The last situation is by no means exceptional.

As can be seen from Table 4.3 (see Appendix) the total investment in general education is more than half of the total budget for education, training and cultural information. Though this cannot be deducted exactly from the amounts given in these Tables, it can be estimated that only 10–20 per cent of this total investment is destined for those who will not be able to enter primary education. This group embraces, according to the targets of the third Four-Year Plan, half the total number of children of school age. The question arises as to how realistic these plans are and in answering this the results of the second Four-Year Plan may give some guidance. For technical and vocational training the percentage achieved was in general 25, ranging from 0 per cent for the fisheries school to 100 per cent for the school for training of assistants in water and forest management. Comparable numbers for general education were not available, but are probably better. It may therefore be assumed that the results of the third Four-Year Plan will not alter the situation, sketched by the Commission charged with its preparation.

V THE UNIVERSITY

The University of Dakar has an important place in the Senegalese educational system. Like Dakar itself, it has been created by the French, as a French university for the whole of French West Africa. Its students came from all French territories in Africa and, after independence, from all French-speaking countries in Africa. Besides these Africans, a considerable number of French students studied at the University of Dakar. Until October 1971 the University was financed by the budget of the French Ministry of Education, and its diplomas had the same value in France as those of other French universities. In 1968 more than half the students came from other African countries. In that year, however, the situation started to change, no doubt influenced by the situation in Paris in May of that year, when students occupied the University in protest against a cut in their grants. They announced that they were prepared to accept the cut if ministers were also prepared to lower their salaries. Riots broke out, the police intervened and hundreds of students were arrested. As a result, 442 foreign African students were sent back to their own countries; the University was temporarily closed and a reform was announced. The reform was published in August 1968 and stated that the University should in future have a regional African character and concentrate its teaching and research on the special problems of Senegal, Guinea, Mali, Mauretania, Upper Volta and the Niger.

The other African countries, however, became aware of the fact that their students were too dependent on the goodwill of the Senegalese Government, and a demand which already existed for national universities was strengthened. This led to the creation of faculties, which became universities in other African countries. As a consequence of this, France was no longer prepared to maintain a French university in Dakar. The Senegalese government on the other hand was prepared to take over full responsibility for the University. Senegalisation meant, however, that the diplomas of the University had no longer validity in France nor in the other African countries. At present the Government is trying to achieve recognition of full validity of the University of Dakar's diplomas, at least in the other French-speaking African countries.

In October 1971 the University had four faculties: the faculty of law and economics, the faculty of medicine and pharmacology, the faculty of science, and the faculty of literature and the humanities. A veterinary institute has been created and will become a veterinary faculty, and a technological institute will also grow into a faculty. Besides these institutes, a school for librarians and archivists has been set up within the University. In close relationship with the University, without being part of it, a Higher Teachers Training College has been established, primarily to train teachers for the colleges for secondary education. Although the University is now Senegalese, 80 per cent of the teaching staff is still French. The system is equally French and there is little indication that the curriculum is now more adapted to the actual needs of the country than it used to be. The Sociology Department, for instance, is more interested in macrosociological theories and philosophy than in research into practical problems of the rural populations. In this respect President Senghor's interest is apparent. In March 1972 he intervened in a debate that had been going on for some time in the Dakar newspaper *Le Soleil*. The issue was the presumed influence of African culture on ancient Greek culture. In his intervention Senghor stressed the necessity for more research in this field. For this reason, he stated, the study of African pre-history should have high priority among the subjects studied at a Senegalese university.

VI FOREIGN AID TO EDUCATION

The aid given to Senegalese education cannot be separated from aid given to Senegal in general. The lion's share for foreign aid given to Senegal comes from France. As Senegal is part of the monetary zone of the French franc there is no national currency, but a West African currency and banknotes, freely interchangeable against French francs. For the moment it seems that there are more direct advantages than disadvantages in this situation, the main drawback being the French control over Senegalese finance. In addition to this dependence, Senegal's budget is supported by France. French intervention in the difficult situation that existed when the farmers were not able to pay off their debts has already been mentioned. The motives for France's readiness to give such a large amount of aid to Senegal are not always very clear and moreover they are complicated. Without pretending to rank them in order of importance, or to be a complete list, the following motives should be mentioned:

French defence interests: Being situated at the most western point of Africa, and having a well-equipped harbour, Dakar is of strategic importance in the defence of French interests, not only in Senegal but in the whole of Africa.

French commercial interests: France is the main supplier to Senegal and the main buyer of Senegalese groundnuts and other products. French capital is invested in Senegalese harbours and industry and many Frenchmen earn a living in Senegal.

French cultural policy: The French are, it can be said, very self-conscious of their cultural achievements. All over the world the French make an effort to spread the French language and culture. French official representatives in foreign countries put more accent on their language and culture than any other nation in the world. It is characteristic that French aid to countries which were not members of the former French Union, falls under the same Department of the French Foreign Office as do the French cultural services and missions in developed countries. The missionary zeal with which the French make their cultural achievements available to the whole world was strongly stimulated by President de Gaulle. For him too, the *grandeur* of the French Republic was based, not on its military or economic power, but on its civilisation. This cultural argument may very well be the most important motivation for French aid. From this point of view it is clear why the French make such a tremendous effort in giving educational aid to developing countries.

French foreign policy: Another motive for French foreign aid is the political one. Bilateral aid policy is part of foreign policy and subject to it. Aid can be used to gain a country's support in international politics. Quite often one country gives aid to another in order to prevent a third country from doing so. Ten to fifteen years ago the aid policy of even a small country like the Netherlands was in the first place motivated by the fear of Communism. During the sixties there was a silent but permanent struggle going on in Africa between France and the US, both trying to enlarge their zones of influence. In this struggle aid was one of the weapons. It is clear that many developing countries, or more exactly, many governments of developing countries, have profited from this situation.

All these motives apply to French aid to Senegal, including the cultural motive, explaining why France gives such an important amount of aid to education. Table 4.4 (see Appendix) gives a review of the number of French personnel engaged in assistance to education by means of French bilateral aid. It can also be seen from this Table that the number of French teachers in primary education and in the colleges for secondary education has been drastically reduced; their places have been taken by Senegalese. On the other hand it should also be noted that other foreign nationals teach in Senegalese schools, through other aid programmes or on individual contracts.

The question as to how far foreign aid influences national educational policies is difficult to answer. One can hardly say that the Senegalese system of education has been influenced by the French; it was created by the French, it is supported by the French and, in short, it is French, and it is still so by choice of the Senegalese, because on the whole the Senegalese who are responsible for educational policy have themselves been educated in this system, a system that has more influence in shaping the intellectual life of those who went through it than any other system in the world. Many Senegalese intellectuals feel as much at home in France as in their own country.

It cannot be denied that by its policy of aid to education, France influences Senegalese education; it manifests itself on different levels and goes through different channels, as follows.

The Senegalese system was created by France; Senegalese teachers have received their school education from Frenchmen or in France; all educated Senegalese have been immersed in the French educational system. For most of them education is French education.

The French language is a strong binding force among Francophone Africans. Results of research in the field of education are easily available to them. By undertaking this kind of research, by organising seminars, etc., France makes available the channels through which knowledge is spread. If more and more attention to questions about the ruralisation of education is given, this is a result of thinking on an international level about these subjects. International conferences and seminars deal with educational policies, and in this way influence the policies of individual countries far more than the individual countries do themselves.

France influences Senegalese educational policy both by its participation in the activities mentioned above and by the organisation of conferences and seminars on educational subjects. France finances research in the field of education, makes available teachers, receives students from Senegal, and constructs teacher training colleges.

By doing this France enables the Senegalese government to maintain the educational *status quo*, and does not exert any influence on Senegal to change its educational policy. The Senegalese have the prime responsibility for their own educational policy. The reason why France provides aid for this policy is only to a certain extent influenced by the ideas developed by French educational research on what the purposes of education in developing countries should be.

VII EDUCATION IN THE SECOND AND THIRD FOUR–YEAR PLANS

Tables 4.1 and 4.2 (see Appendix) give a recapitulation of the budgets of the Ministry of Education and the Ministry of Technical Education and Professional Training for the years 1969/70–1972/3.

France is by far the most important donor in the field of educational aid. The number of French teachers is shown in Table 4.4. The costs to the Senegalese for this kind of assistance are not negligible. For every technical assistant, including teachers, houses are given free of charge and a sum of 55,000 CFA a month is paid to the French Government. The large role that France plays in Senegalese education is in part the result of the assimilation policy during colonial times and the years of the French Union. The ideal was that all these African colonies would finally assimilate French civilisation, and in that way become French citizens and bearers of French culture. The fact that colonial practice did not seem to be in a hurry to achieve this goal does not mean that the principle itself did not work. The educated Senegalese were educated as Frenchmen.

Senghor never rejected this assimilation policy completely; he once said he interpreted it in this way: 'We want to assimilate, not to be assimilated', which means that he wants to accept the many good things France has to offer without rejecting the positive values of Africa. The French influence on Senegalese educational policy is channelled more through technical assistance in the ministries and their pedagogical offices, than through the teachers themselves. Even where the educational system begins to deviate from the French model, there is still a French influence behind it. The idea of creating *CEG* and *CES* (see p. 143) which give general secondary education for a shorter period than the *lycées* is not limited to Senegal, but has been elaborated by Frenchmen and Africans in close cooperation. The same applies to the efforts for the ruralisation of education, which is not as yet very far developed.

Some authors, mostly Anglo-Saxon, are inclined to criticise this situation and to see the Francophone African countries as victims of French cultural imperialism. For the most part this is a consequence of the language situation. *La Francophonie* is an important phenomenon. French-speaking ministers of education meet annually, as do French-speaking economists. The French-speaking African States have created the OCAM – the Common African and Malagasy Organisation – of which former Belgian colonies are also members. *Francophonie* has an appeal to French-speaking Canadians, Belgians and Swiss as well. Though de Gaulle's original idea of creating a French Union has never been realised, *Francophonie* can certainly be considered as a kind of cultural union.

If we forget for a moment the less idealistic motives for giving aid, such as foreign policy targets, commercial interests, etc., we must conclude that all countries give aid because they are convinced that they have something to offer that is better than that which exists in the poorer countries, although lip service is paid to the idea that countries should decide for themselves which values they want to accept or reject from the developed countries. At the same time democratic countries are favoured more than dictators and donors want to help these countries to create equal opportunities for everybody and to promote the idea of fundamental equality for all.

The transition of French colonial policy to foreign aid policy has been very gradual. The presence of the French in Senegal and other former colonies is more evident than that of the British in their ex-colonial territories, and the influence on daily life too is more obvious in Francophone countries. The degree of dependence is impossible to measure, certainly if one does not wish to limit the measurement to legalistic and economic facts. It is therefore impossible to pretend that Senegal is more dependent than, for instance, Kenya, and it is quite open to question whether we should make 'independence' the crucial factor of human well-being.

This preponderance of French aid is as impressive as it is intriguing. To many other Europeans, it is highly irritating as well. Senegal is the most French-influenced country in Africa and, although the number of Frenchmen in Senegal did not increase after Independence as it did in most other former French colonies, many Frenchmen still feel very much at home in Dakar and St Louis. Many other Europeans who live in Dakar resent this French presence, and the fact that the French still feel at home, and do not consider themselves as real expatriates. Rita Cruise O'Brien[2] seems to be one of these other Europeans. She suggests that behind every important Senegalese official is a French adviser who does the real work and takes the decisions, and that in this way the key posts in the Senegalese government are under direct French control. She considers education as one of these key spheres and the efforts made by France to aid Senegalese education as a method to maintain French colonial grip on Africa. Many other Europeans and Americans, certainly those who come from Anglophone countries, share this opinion. Coming themselves from countries with a different system of education and having a different language, they get the impression that the French form closed, separate cliques into which other nationals are not admitted.

One cannot deny that the French still play an important role in Senegal. Is this a sign of re-colonisation, as Rita Cruise O'Brien suggests? She certainly exaggerates as far as the Ministry of Education is concerned. The number of Frenchment in the central, policy-making services of this department is very limited. If we define colonisation as the exploitation of

[2] Rita Cruise O'Brien, *White Society in Black Africa*, London, 1971.

one country by another, there is no indication that Senegal is any more exploited than Kenya or Nigeria. Of course, French firms play an important role in the exploitation of Senegal, but other national and international firms do so to an even greater extent. This however has little to do with cultural influence, nor with aid to education. France could be blamed for the fact that the educational system it helps to maintain and to expand in Senegal does not take into account the real needs of that country. Many Frenchmen in Senegal would agree with this criticism. The Senegalese Government considers this system to be the right one for the moment, placing the needs of the country on another scale of priorities than donor countries. Thus the dilemma of French aid to education as far as it concerns Senegal is the same as that for all donors giving aid to the Third World: do we give help according to our priorities, or to theirs?

VIII BRITISH AID

British aid to Senegal consists of making available teachers, and the creation of the British Institute. The Institute is not an integral part of the Senegalese educational system and it organises language courses independent of any other educational institutions. President Senghor has shown remarkable interest in the Institute, and has on certain occasions stated that Senegal should be a bilingual country. No doubt he had political reasons for saying so: on the one hand to warn the French not to diminish their efforts, on the other hand he might have thought of future ties with Gambia. The British, on their side, are apt to forget that the Senegalese constitution states that French is Senegal's official language.

IX CANADA

Canadian aid to Senegalese education is very important. In financing the construction of colleges of general education, Canada contributed in an important way to the realisation of Senegal's Four-Year Plan. Besides this, about sixty Canadian teachers teach at secondary schools and at the higher teachers training colleges. The reason for this Canadian interest in Senegal is in the first place to be found in Canada's internal politics. By giving attention to Francophone countries, it gives French-speaking Canadians their share in the formulation of Canada's foreign policy. Besides, being bilingual, the Canadian teachers are in a favoured position as teachers of English. Canada does not, however, limit itself to language teaching; its contribution to natural science teaching is also important. Though important in size, one cannot say that Canada is exerting an influence on Senegalese educational policy. It enables Senegal to pursue its policy; it does not however try to change it and had no part in shaping it. The same can be said of other kinds of bilateral aid. The United States give aids as grants and loans, while the Peace Corps volunteers taught English.

This policy cannot be said to motivate the aid given by international organisations. They have established a development policy of their own and give aid only in those cases where Senegalese needs fit into this policy. This is true of the World Bank in its financing of educational projects, and of the European Development Fund. For both organisations the educational projects in Senegal are only a minor part of their total aid programme for Senegal.

X UNITED NATIONS DEVELOPMENT PROGRAMME (UNDP)

The main UNDP project in the field of education is the project Sen-11, a Special Fund project which started in 1963. The technical assistance is given by ILO and FAO, and the Ministry of Technical and Vocational Training is responsible for the project. The project is threefold; one sub-project is concerned with agricultural techniques, the second with handicrafts and the third with education of women in rural areas.

The first of these aims is to improve agricultural methods. At a centre at Guerina, agricultural assistants receive a training for two years, after which they are posted to centres of agricultural improvement. In these centres they train 'pilot' farmers. These farmers receive not only training but also simple, but improved equipment.

The second sub-project aims at creating the local craftsmen who will build and maintain this equipment. For this purpose technical assistants receive two years' training at a centre at Kaffrine, and are later attached to handicraft improvement centres in which they teach local farmers to make and repair their own equipment and build workshops and houses. It is not the intention that these farmers establish themselves immediately as full craftsmen. They will continue to do their farming, but will at the same time improve their own and their co-villagers' equipment. In this way they will not be obliged to give up their farms for a future as craftsmen before it is proved that such a future is viable.

The third sub-project aims to train women in the social, as well as in the agricultural field. For this purpose female trainees receive a two years' training at Thiès. After this training they are employed at the Centres d'Expansion Rural.

This Sen-11 project trys to be an integrated project in two senses: its different parts should form an integrated whole and it should be integrated into other activities in the rural areas, notably community development. Though every project is successful in itself, the integration into a total integrated development policy is lacking, not least because such a policy does not exist. Care should be taken that urban producers and importers of more sophisticated and expensive machines which are difficult to repair, do not sabotage the project.

Another completely different ILO activity is the creation of a school for the training of managers' secretaries. This school is intended to provide properly trained secretaries for the management of industrial and commercial enterprises. A *raison d'être* for the school is the fact that practically all directors' secretaries are expatriates, and this training is necessary for the Senegalisation of these functions. However, until now foreign enterprises do not seem to be very interested in Senegalisation. The school is well equipped, and well attended, but the future of the pupils is not certain.

XI PROFESSIONAL MIGRATION

Senegalese authorities were not inclined to stress the importance of the emigration of trained Senegalese to Europe or elsewhere. In this respect they even stated that Senegal was giving technical assistance to other countries. On the other hand, measures are taken, by the French Aid Mission also, to ensure that grants for study in France are given only for work in those disciplines that cannot be studied locally or regionally. Study by Senegalese in the West African region is, however, very rare.

XII CONCLUSIONS

It is clear that a research worker, however short and limited his research has been, is indebted to the country and people who received him, helped him, and at the same time were the subject of his research. The only thing he can do to repay part of that debt is to try to create understanding for them among others and eventually to give recommendations for possible improvements. I will therefore try to conclude by giving my ideas about Senegalese development and education, but only after I have made clear my own point of departure.

I do agree with many others that certain social structures are blocking the road to development. I do not believe, however, that breaking down these structures will in itself create development; the demolition of existing structures is by no means a guarantee for development. Development is not created by structures but by the men who make up these structures, and these men should possess the knowhow, the mentality, the power and the opportunities for development. Development aid should be directed towards the creation of these opportunities and knowledge; aid can eventually help to transform attitudes; but should it not refrain from interfering in power structures? Before answering this question in the negative, we should be well aware that aid has its influence on the power structures, whether designed to do so or not. We should also be aware that all aid means interference. Whatever lip service we pay to the responsibility of the recipient in the choice of the kind of aid he wants to receive, the donors only give aid when they, according to their own judgement, using their own values, agree that it is a good thing to so. This means that in judging the aid to Senegalese education, we should ask whether this aid contributes to a development that we consider as a good thing for the Senegalese. In doing so we should not forget the realities of the situation.

Hence the problems of education and aid to education in Senegal cannot be considered out of their context, the total social and economic situation of the country. It cannot be denied that in the present world economy, this country cannot continue to exist on the level it does now, let alone develop, without external aid. This aid is given for a number of reasons, only one of them being the aim to develop the country in order to improve the well-being of its inhabitants.

Senegal inherited its educational system from the French model which deeply influenced the thinking of the Senegalese elite educated in this system. It is this elite that is in power at the moment though it has to share its power with the Muslim religious leaders. The educational system reflects the values of both: education of a high degree that can play its role in cultural and scientific developments on a world level, and limitation of the educational facilities of those who are under the influence of the *marabouts.* This approach can certainly be called an elitist one, and as long as the word 'elitist' is not value-loaded, it can be discussed whether this elitist approach will promote the well-being of the masses or not. Dumont claimed[3] that the *marabouts* could very well play a role in Senegal's development. In the same way it should not be assumed that the educated elite will not be conscious of the needs of the masses. The Animation Movement which made such a promising start in Senegal was created by members of this elite. It is a pity that more powerful forces have been able to shunt this *movement* on to a dead-end track, and have made it to a large extent subordinate to political purposes.

France, the main donor of aid to Senegal, has stimulated quite a lot of thinking and research about the role of education in developing countries. This has been done by government-sponsored institutes, universities and private initiatives. However, the application of the result of all these efforts, as far as Senegal is concerned, does not go very far. Though the Four-Year Plan does pay attention to education adapted to rural conditions, the achievements do not reflect a first priority on the part of the Government. It is clear that achievement in the established educational system is far ahead of that which aims at the adaptation of education to the needs of the rural population. Senegalese primary education is almost exclusively given by Senegalese teachers which certainly is an important achievement. We may expect that the Senegalisation of secondary education is only a matter of time and continued assistance.

However we may regret this, we should not forget that rural schools do not initiate rural development, however well adapted they may be. If we

[3] Cited by J. Serreau, *Le développement à la basc au Dahomey et au Senegal*, Paris, 1966, p. 121.

aim at a development from which the masses of the population will benefit, we should see development as a total process in which know-how improves, opportunities are created, and outlook is changed. Participation techniques should aim at stimulating the masses to participate in this total process of development, and not limit themselves to incidental activities. The Animation Plan as it was originally elaborated for Senegal[4] is based on this conception of development. No plan, however realistic it may seem from a financial and technological point of view, will be realised if the will and power to implement it are lacking. It is perfectly clear that this approach met resistance from those who were likely to lose power in this process and those who had conflicting economic interests. Only when the elites which guide development are sufficiently powerful and motivated to make the plan succeed, can we hope to move in the direction of development along these lines.

How realistic are we in expecting this to happen and how far is aid to Senegalese education aid in this direction? Critics of Senegalese policy state that the Senegalese authorities are trying to maintain the *status quo* in their own and foreign interest: I am not sure they all do so. As long as Senegal depends to such a great extent on foreign aid, and as long as no alternative is offered, they have little choice, and the possible alternatives that can be reached on the national level are limited. Education in the sense of the Senegalese system of general education can play an important role, however unadapted to the Senegalese situation and out-dated in the eyes of modern western educationalists it may be. Critics may, with reason, point out that the educational system favours the existing elite and is far removed from the needs of the masses. They should not forget, however, that they are able to make this criticism because they went through that same system. Education has always had this quality of the sorcerer's apprentice. We can expect that, also in Senegal, it will eventually reinforce an elite that has the know-how and the will to guide the masses and to shift the internal balance of power. It is the task of the specialists in the aid-giving countries to influence the motivations for giving aid, so that they will be less dictated by business interests and the aims of foreign policy.

[4] On Animation see: Cisse ben Mady, 'L'animation rurale, base essentielle de tout développement', *Afrique Documents* no. 68, 1963. Cisse ben Mady, 'L'animation des masses, condition d'un socialisme authentique', *Développement et Civilisation*, 12, 1962. R. Colin, 'De la tradition à l'évolution consciente ver le développement authentique ai milieu rural'. *Développement et Civilisation*, 28, 1967. R. Colin, 'Animation rurale en Afrique Noire', *Archives Internationales de la Sociologie de la Cooperation*, no. 20, 1966, 133–99. H. De Decker, *Nation et développement commun utaire en Guinee et au Sénégal*, Paris-La Haye, 1967. J. Serreau, op. cit.

TABLE 4.1
General education (in million francs CFA)

Operations	*Year of realisation* 1969/70	1970/1	1971/2	1972/3	*Total*	*Source of finance*
1. PRIMARY EDUCATION						
Construction and equipment of 1200 classrooms	300	300	300	300	1200	FED
Extension of canteens and gardens	4·1	4	4	3·5	15·6	NB
Centres of rural training	28·5	26	26	19·5	100	
Extension of primary inspectorate	36·9	36·9	24·6	24·6	123	NB
Regional inspection	7	14	14	7	42	NB
Medical inspection in schools	24·8	33·6	13·4	18·2	90	NB
2. TEACHER TRAINING						
Construction and equipment of 2 teacher training schools	200	100			300	FAC
Improvement of the teacher training school at Kaolac	25				25	NB
Permanent centre for refresher courses for teachers		12·5			12·5	NB
3. SECONDARY EDUCATION						
Construction of 30 colleges for secondary education	250	250	250	240	990	Canada and World Bank
Improvement of *lycées*	35	35	35	35	140	NB
Construction of boarding house at Lycée Blaise Diagne	150				150	Canada
4. HIGHER EDUCATION						
University Institute of Technology	50	53			103	World Bank
Veterinary Faculty	35	120	120	225	500	FED
Improvement of Higher Teacher Training College (Ecole Normale Supérieure)	40	40			80	Foreign
Cité Universitaire (first part)	220				220	FAC
Cité Universitaire (second part)	215				215	?
Calculating Centre Faculty of Science	6	6	11		23	?
Faculty of Literature	12			15	27	NB
Faculty of Medicine	50	50	48		148	FED
Total	1689·3	1081	846	887·8	4504·1	

Source: 'Enseignement et Formation, Culture et Sports, Animation Urbaine Information Emploi', *Rapport de la Commission no.* 7, 3éme Plan de Développement Economique et Social (1969–73), Apr 1969.

FED = European Development Fund   NB = National budget   FAC = French aid

TABLE 4.2
Technical and vocational training (in million francs CFA)

Operations	*Year of realisation* 1969/70	*1970/1*	*1971/2*	*1972/3*	*Total*	*Source of finance*
Technical teacher training school men	200				200	FAC
Technical teacher training school women	90				90	Foreign
Regional centre for educational orientation	9	3			12	NB
Centres for agricultural and rural improvement	84	56			140	Special fund
Family houses for rural training	34	35	40	47	156	NB
Merchant Navy and Fishing School	157				157	World Bank
Regional fishery training centre	20				20	?
Four regional centres for female technical training	260				260	USAID
Regional centre for male technical training		65			65	?
Centres for home economics	16	16	16	4	52	NB
Handicraft training centre	105		10		115	NB
Technical training centre	133				133	USAID
Complementary improvements and equipment	138	71	17	3	229	?
Totals	1246	246	83	54	1629	

Source: as Table 4.1.

TABLE 4.3
Financial review of the operations in the field of education, training and cultural information in the third Four-Year Plan (in million francs CFA)

	Total	*National budget*	*Foreign aid Grants*	*Loans*
General education	4496	960	2018	1518
Technical and vocational training	1727	661	619	447
Cultural, youth and sports information	814	638	132	44
Total public operations	7037	2259	2769	2009
Private operations	361	–	305	56
Total	7398	2259	3074	2065

Source: as Table 4.1.

TABLE 4.4

Numbers of French teachers and experts in Senegal, made available by French aid

Educational and training institutions	*1966/7*	*1967/8*	*1968/9*	*1969/70*	*1970/1*	*1971/2*
1. MINISTRY OF NATIONAL EDUCATION						
a) Central services	5	5	6	5	5	5
b) Primary education	62	51	35	28	22	19
c) Short secondary education (CEG + CES)	129	176	88	46	17	16
Long secondary education:						
Lycée Van Vollenhoven, Dakar	77	80	77	78	82	78
Lycée Blaise Diagne, Dakar	67	64	64	58	54	56
Lycée John F. Kennedy (JF), Dakar	29	33	33	40	43	46
Lycée Mixte de Rufisque	32	28	30	31	39	40
Lycée Malick Sy, Thiès	33	36	37	35	38	33
Lycée Gaston Berger, Kaolack	31	34	40	40	51	51
Lycée Djignabo, Ziguinchor	23	24	27	27	34	37
Lycée Faidherbe, St Louis	19	20	17	23	27	27
Lycée Ameth Fall (JF), St Louis	18	14	15	17	17	19
Lycée Charles de Gaulle, St Louis	32	38	39	45	45	45
Total lycées	361	371	379	394	430	432
d) Teacher training						
Pedagogical bureau	8	19	25	28	32	32
Teacher training colleges	24	17	18	14	16	13
Pedagogical training centres	13	4	–	–	–	–
Total teacher training	45	40	43	42	48	45
e) Higher education						
Higher teacher training college	7	10	12	12	14	11
University	10	15	7	10	16	23
Total higher education	17	25	19	22	30	44
Total national education	619	668	570	537	552	561

TABLE 4.4 (*cont.*)

	1966/7	1967/8	1968/9	1969/70	1970/1	1971/2
2. MINISTRY OF TECHNICAL AND VOCATIONAL TRAINING						
a) Central services	19	12	10	13	13	14
b) First technical classes						
Female technical training centre, Dakar	16	17	12	7	7	3
Female technical training centre, Diourbel	5	6	4	4	2	2
Centre for technical qualification, Dakar	9	6	4	5	5	5
Centre for handicraft training, Dakar	8	9	5	3	4	4
Regional technical education centre, Ziguinchor	3	4	3	1	—	—
Regional technical education centre, Kaolack	1	—	—	—	—	
School for agricultural assistants, Louga	6	5	7	4	4	4
School for agricultural assistants, Ziguinchor	4	5	3	4	4	6
School for water and forest management assistants, Ziguinchor	6	3	4	3	4	4
School for fishery and oceanography assistants, Thiaroye	5	6	2	3	2	3
Centre for horticultural professional training, Cambérène	3	3	2	2	2	2
Centre for professional training in the hotel trade, Dakar	3	3	4	3	2	2
Total first classes	69	67	50	39	36	40
c) Secondary technical classes						
National school for maritime training, Dakar	9	8	8	11	10	9
National school for rural officers, Bambey	13	16	13	10	13	11
National school for public works, Dakar	19	22	17	18	14	13
Training school for the improvement of secretarial personnel, Dakar	2	6	3	3	5	6
Total second classes	43	52	41	42	42	39

d) Technical teacher training colleges							
Male technical teacher training college, Dakar		–	1	1	3	6	4
Female technical training college, Dakar		9	7	6	8	5	5
	Total technical teacher training colleges	9	8	7	11	11	9
e) Vocational training							
Centre for fishing handicrafts training, M'Bane		1	1	1	1	1	1
Interprofessional training centre for staff, Dakar		1	3	3	3	3	3
	Total vocational training	2	4	4	4	4	4
f) Technical colleges							
Lycée Maurice Delafosse		117	117	100	95	91	93
Lycée André Peytavin		36	32	31	32	33	31
	Total technical colleges	153	149	131	127	124	124
g) University Institute of Technology, Dakar		6	6	6	6	6	6
	Total technical and vocational training	301	298	249	242	239	244

TABLE 4.4 (*cont.*)

	1966/7	1967/8	1968/9	1969/70	1970/1	1971/2
3. MINISTRY OF CULTURE, YOUTH AND SPORTS						
Arts school	6	4	4	3	3	3
Tapestry school	–	1	1	1	1	–
Total culture	6	5	5	4	4	3
Sports education	19	20	9	16	14	20
Physical education in lycées	37	27	23	17	11	11
Youth	6	11	3	2	–	–
Literacy	3	–	2	–	–	–
Total youth and sports	65	58	37	35	25	31
Total culture, youth and sports	71	63	42	39	29	34

4. DIFFERENT MINISTRIES						
National school for public administration	–	1	1	1	1	1
Centre for administrative training and improvement	12	4	3	3	4	4
Preparatory military school, St Louis	19	23	21	24	24	25
Institute for economic development and planning	1	1	1	1	1	1
National school for applied economics	4	8	7	9	7	7
Urban community development	3	3	2	2	–	–
National police school	6	9	11	4	5	6
Customs school	1	1	1	1	1	1
Public works training centre	1	1	1	1	1	1
National PTT school	7	7	6	5	3	3
National social assistants school	1	1	1	–	4	2
School for nurses	1	1	1	1	–	–
Sanitary assistants school, Khombole	1	–	–	–	–	–
Hygiene assistants school, St Louis	1	–	–	–	–	–
School for veterinary assistants	4	5	4	3	3	3
UNESCO pilot project (Ministry of Information)	9	7	7	4	2	–
Total different ministries	61	72	67	59	56	54
5. RECAPITULATION						
National education	619	668	570	537	552	561
Technical education	301	298	249	242	239	244
Culture, youth and sports	71	63	42	39	29	34
Different ministries	61	72	67	59	56	54
Total	1052	1101	928	877	876	893

Source: The French 'Mission d'Aide et de Cooperation' at Dakar.

TABLE 4.5
Aid in the field of education to Senegal from different developed countries and international organisations given in 1969

Country/organisation	*Type of aid*
CANADA	Building and equipment of colleges of secondary education
	Boarding-school: Lycée Blaise Diagne
	Teachers and professors
EUROPEAN DEVELOPMENT FUND	Higher Pedagogical Institute
	School for rural officers
	School buildings
	Centres for vocational training
	Centres for rural training
FRANCE	Primary school buildings
	Teachers and professors
	Construction and equipment for teacher training schools
	Running costs of University and affiliated institutes
	Technical and vocational training centres
GERMANY	Educational material
	Teachers
	University professors of philosophy
NETHERLANDS	Home economics training centres
UNITED KINGDOM	Teachers: British Institute
UNITED NATIONS	Urban and rural vocational training
	Higher teacher training colleges
	Experts in different educational fields
USSR	Teachers in Russian language
USA	Primary school inspectorate
	Building and equipment of lycées
	Peace Corps volunteers (teachers)
	School for social workers
	Centres for vocational training
	University student housing
TUNISIA	Teachers of Arabic

Source: as Table 4.4.

(The list is not detailed and does not give the costs involved, because the sources from which they are taken had been established for other purposes and had different classifications.)

5 Tunisia

Robin Ostle

I INTRODUCTION[1]

Modern Tunisia occupies some 125,000 sq. km between the two large neighbouring countries of Algeria and Libya. Despite its small area, there is much variety in the land and the activities which it supports. Agriculture in various forms has long been the principal source of livelihood for the majority of the inhabitants; olives and cereals are two of the staple products. The northern areas are mountainous and well wooded and have the heaviest rainfall in the country. The coastal plain of this northern section is fertile and reasonably well watered, and produces citrus fruits and market-garden crops. The principal olive-growing region is the eastern coastal strip known as the *Sāhel*, traditionally one of the most vigorous and active areas of Tunisia. The gently sloping coastal shelf supports an important fishing industry based on such ports as Sousse and Sfax. In the south and the interior outside the oases, animal husbandry provides a subsistence livelihood for an often semi-nomadic population.

Apart from the produce of the land and sea, Tunisia is not well endowed with other natural resources, in sharp contrast to Algeria and Libya. There are some lead mines in the region of Béja in the north-west, iron ore is found along the Algerian frontier, but only phosphates are mined in considerable quantities. The textile industry has been developed and expanded since Independence, and the value of tourism as a source of foreign currency increases annually. With the growth of tourism, traditional arts and crafts have been organised and encouraged on a national

[1] Much of the material in this brief introduction is taken from Wilfrid Knapp's excellent general book, *Tunisia*, London, 1970.

scale, and administered through the National Artisanate Office. Basing calculations on the last national census in 1966, it has been estimated that on 1 January 1970, the population was something over 5,080,000.[2]

This small country known to the Arabs as *Tūnis Al-Khadrā* (Tunis the Verdant), inherits a long and proud tradition extending back to the beginnings of Mediterranean civilisation. The Island of Jerba was the legendary home of the Lotus Eaters; the site of the Phoenician city of Carthage lies some few kilometres up the coast from the modern capital of Tunis. After a long and distinguished period as a province of the Roman Empire (from 146 B.C.), in A.D. 670 the armies of the Arab Omayyad Caliphate in Damascus established a garrison town at Qayrawān, and Tunisia became an important base for the extension of the Arab conquests along the North African coast, and beyond into Spain. The new invaders brought the Arabic language and the religion of Islam, and created a cultural tradition which in many respects has remained unbroken until the present day.

The city of Tunis was the capital adopted by the Hafsid dynasty which ruled the area for some 300 years from A.D. 1207. As a port it developed in importance with the growth of European trade, whilst the land-locked city of Qayrawān became correspondingly less significant. At the end of the fithteenth century, Tunisia, along with Algeria and Tripoli, became a Regency of the Turkish Ottoman empire and continued as such until the nineteenth century, when France, anxious to preserve her position as a great European power, occupied the country and established the French Protectorate in 1881. Thus began the period during which Tunisia, in common with other Arab countries, experienced a direct if often unsought contact with the power and the culture of Western Europe.

After the initial shock of colonisation in its various forms by the European powers, the Arab countries were not slow to react with ideas and aspirations often drawn directly from the political and cultural traditions of those European nations, in particular France and Britain, who seemed in their eyes to possess such inherent power and superiority.[3] Under such pressures, the traditional religio-political concept of the Islamic Caliphate gradually declined to be replaced throughout the Arab world by nation states after the European model, increasingly aware of their identities, and ever more demanding for self-determination; above all, they were deeply conscious of the great disparity between their own situations and the power and technology of the European countries. In

[2] Werner Plum, *Facharbeiterbedarf in Tunesien*, publication of the Forschungsinstitut der Friedrich-Ebert-Stiftung, Mar 1971, p. 4.

[3] For a comprehensive and scholarly survey of this topic, see A. H. Hourani, *Arabic Thought in the Liberal Age*, Royal Institute of International Affairs, Oxford University Press, 1962.

such an atmosphere, the modern state of Tunisia began to emerge. Not unnaturally, education was seen as one of the fundamental causes of the apparent gulf between French civilisation and their own; before the Protectorate was established in 1881, the Tunisian modernist Khayr al-Dīn Pāshā al-Tūnisī reorganised the teaching of the Zaytouna Mosque, and in 1875 he founded the Sādiqiyya College, intended to train civil servants and produce graduates for the liberal professions. The new college retained an important part of the syllabus for traditional Islamic studies, but now alongside the old Islamic disciplines, French and Italian were taught, and also modern mathematics and science.

Throughout the period of the Protectorate, the Sādiqiyya College was to create and foster Tunisian nationalism. The very acquaintance with French culture which it provided, gave its graduates the stimulus and the experience to develop their own ideology of the Tunisian nation and community. They also had the advantage of the cohesion which came from graduating from one institution, frequently spending further years of study together in France without losing contact. From this small closely-knit elite of politically aware people grew the varying movements which played a role in the ultimate achievement of Tunisian Independence, even though they were not all by nature nationalist in themselves. The so-called Khaldūniyya and the young Tunisians were active around the turn of the century, but the first really decisive movement for Tunisian nationalism came after the First World War, with the creation of a new party, the Destour (Constitution) Party. Although it did much to create and articulate the cry for nationalism and emancipation from the French in Tunisia, this party left much to be desired in organisational terms, and many of the younger, more radical-minded members were far from contented. Concrete expression was given to this dissatisfaction in 1934 with the foundation of the Neo-Destour Party led by Habīb Bourguiba. Operating from a much wider and more proletarian base, with greatly improved organisation, the party and Bourguiba advanced gradually towards Independence and the reform of Tunisian society.

In 1955 the Mendès-France Government first agreed to grant Tunisia complete internal sovereignty, and when France was obliged to grant independence to Morocco after her failure to subdue the nationalist movement there, Bourguiba demanded complete independence in his turn, and this was granted on 20 March 1956. Subsequently, President Bourguiba and the Neo-Destour Party have remained firmly in control of the country. The Neo-Destour is the only party of government (a small Communist party was suppressed in 1963), and only its candidates are presented in elections. The political atmosphere is pleasanter and less oppressive than in most one-party states, although significant opposition must expect to encounter a firm reaction from the Government.

II TUNISIAN EDUCATION IN THE DEVELOPMENT DECADE

1. The Protectorate

As Wilfrid Knapp has observed, the most effective system of education in Tunisia under the Protectorate existed primarily for the benefit of the French settlers, and was extended to take in only a very limited section of the Tunisian population.[4] This system was quite separate from the traditional Muslim education of the *kuttāb* or Qur'ān school, the basis of which was the learning by heart of the Qur'ān, the principles of Arabic grammar, and reading and writing in classical Arabic. The only form of subsequent higher education was available at the Zaytouna mosque in Tunis, or in its annexes which existed in certain other Tunisian towns. While such an education was not without its virtues, its beneficiaries could not look forward to any significant degree of advancement in Tunisian society under the Protectorate. Pressure for a French-style education led to a very diverse system. There were four categories at the primary level: (a) Those schools for French nationals only, of which some were co-educational. French was the only medium of instruction, and the teachers and curricula were also French. (b) The so-called Franco-Arab schools existing mainly for boys, with only a very few girl pupils. Here again, French was the main medium of instruction, but some Arabic was taught. The curricula and the text-books remained French, and Muslim pupils in this category would need some knowledge of French to be admitted. (c) The *kuttāb* schools as described above. (d) Modernised *kuttāb* schools which in effect were based on the Franco-Arab schools of category (b), but which concentrated much more on classical Arabic.[5]

At the secondary level, the French model of the *lycée* leading to the *baccalauréat* was the predominant category. Here French was the only medium of instruction. Then there were the Zaytouna annexes providing the traditional Muslim form of higher education, with Arabic as the medium of instruction.[6] Between these two extremes in the later years of the Protectorate, it became possible at some secondary schools to prepare for the diploma course in the Sādiqiyya College, a course which was progressive and up to date, and retained at the same time a significant proportion of Arabic studies. The Sādiqiyya diploma was usually the first step towards higher studies in France, and this path became the main aspiration of the select group who were to guide their country towards Independence. Even today the majority of the elder statesmen and those

[4] Knapp, *Tunisia*, pp. 119 ff.

[5] Ibid.; see also Pablo Foster, *Introduction to Tunisian Education*; a survey produced for the use of foreign teachers in Tunisia, unpublished at the time of writing.

[6] This traditional Muslim education would concentrate on the study of the Qur'ān, Islamic tradition or *hadīth*, and jurisprudence or *fiqh*.

close to the centre of power, including President Bourguiba himself, are former Sādiqiyya graduates. Apart from the Zaytouna University mentioned above, the only other form of higher education possible was to go directly to a French institution in France itself, or to pass via the Institut des Hautes Études in Tunis, a first-year annexe of the University of Paris.

It must be emphasised that during the Protectorate, the relatively few Muslim Tunisians who received any education at all did so in the primary sector. In 1953, of the estimated 775,000 Tunisian children eligible for primary education (age-range 6–14 years), 95,000 or 12 per cent attended school. In the same year, 1953, there were only 6682 Tunisian pupils receiving secondary education.[7] By the date of Independence, the total number of Tunisian pupils benefiting from some form of education had risen to about 260,000; of these 226,919 were in the primary sector, and only 32,924 in the secondary.[8] Only a small proportion of both categories would be girls. In other words, in 1956 about 26 per cent of the school-age population were receiving some form of education.

2. The United Nations Development Decade, 1960–70

Not surprisingly, the low proportion of educated children was seen as one of the great weaknesses of the newly independent Tunisia: 'Education is one of the state's most urgent duties. It is the fundamental basis on which her foundations rest securely. Indeed, education is the factor which guarantees conditions of progress and general well-being, which ensures a decent standard of living for all'.[9]

Well before Independence, the future leaders of the country had been preoccupied with this subject: 'During that period I was already convinced that if we gained control of the state, we would attack the problem of education as a priority'.[10] In the face of this unequivocal political commitment, Tunisia made an early choice in favour of what was then seen as an essentially long-term investment in a human infrastructure, as opposed to more short-term projects which would yield quicker results in economic terms, but provide training and employment for only a limited section of the population.

[7] Foster, *Tunisian Education*, p. 3.

[8] Chedly Ayari, *Aperçu Quantitatif de la Scolarisation en Tunisie*, publication of the Tunisian Ministère de l'Education Nationale, Apr 1971, p. 4 Table I. See also A Bsais and C. Morrisson, 'Les Coûts de l'Education en Tunisia', *Cahiers du CERES*., Série Economique 3, June 1970, pp. 73 ff.

[9] Extract of a speech by President Bourguiba delivered in 1957, quoted by Bsais and Morrisson, 'Les Coûts de l'Education', p. 34.

[10] Extract of a speech by President Bourguiba delivered in 1958, quoted by A. Chouikha, 'Conception et Résultats de la Réforme Tunisienne de l'Enseignement de 1958', *Revue Tunisienne des Sciences Sociales*, Dec 1969, p. 39.

This urgent desire for rapid action was given material form in 1958 with the Ten-Year Plan for the Reform of Education, introduced by the Minister at the time, Mahmūd Messadi.[11] His initial objective was to reduce the state of imbalance between the archaic Muslim Arabic system as it then existed, and the totally French pattern at the other extreme; he wished to create a new intermediary process theoretically capable of embracing all Tunisians, and responding to their newly fostered aspirations. The state assumed responsibility for ensuring that all eligible Tunisians should have free education; it was originally envisaged that the system should be gradually re-nationalised in terms of personnel and the language of instruction. Curricula were revised, particularly in literature and the arts, history, and geography, so that they provided more of an authentic grounding in Muslim Arabic culture than that of Metropolitan France. It was hoped that compulsory primary education would be available to all Tunisian children by 1968. The plan also made projections of the buildings, the personnel and the considerable numbers of foreign teachers who would still be necessary for its implementation.

The system which emerged from the Messadi Plan remained in force until 1967, and at the primary and secondary levels as follows:

i. Primary The duration of these studies was theoretically six years, from the age of six to eleven; these being the minimum age requirements for admission to each year of primary school. For the first two years the programme consisted of 15 hours per week, and 25 hours per week during the final four years. French was introduced as a medium of instruction after the first two years. The basic model for the arrangement was still the French primary schools of the Protectorate system, but inadequate resources made it necessary to reduce the duration from seven to six years, and also the number of hours taught per week.

ii. Secondary This consisted basically of six years in a French-type *lycée* or three years in a *collège moyen*. The *moyen* version of secondary education was designed to replace the former system of centres of technical training vhich both in recruitment and in their general standards had been judged unsatisfactory. Recruitment for the *moyen* category took place through the same entrance examination as for the *lycée*.[12] Many of the pupils in this former category were those who finished the primary stage at a very retarded age, often between fifteen and seventeen years old.[13] Pupils would find themselves in this unhappy situation as a result of irregular attendance, constant repetition of the various years of primary education, or merely late entry to the primary school. Within the *lycée* system itself, a fairly rigid system of selective vocational training was

[11] See Chouika, 'Conception et Résultats', pp. 39–54 for a summary of this plan.
[12] Bsais and Morrisson, 'Les Coûts de l'Education', p. 50.
[13] Chouikha, 'Conception et Résultats', p. 48.

envisaged: some were to be trained as primary school teachers, some were destined for the University, while others would be deployed within very vaguely defined 'technical spheres of life'.[14] These vocational choices were supposed to take place after the first year of secondary education. Agricultural training was available in institutes which have been the responsibility both of the Ministry of Agriculture and the Ministry of Education (see below, pp. 188ff).

Since 1967, education in Tunisia has been a consistent source of crises for a variety of reasons which will be discussed in more detail below (p. 184ff). This period of uncertainty has been marked by no fewer than five ministerial changes between 1967 and 1971. By 1967 the danger signs were already becoming apparent: costs had continued to rise astronomically, wastage rates were consistently high, and the vocational streaming system of the Messadi Plan proved increasingly unpopular. The Arabicisation of the system was not succeeding both because of the complex linguistic situation in Tunisia (see pp. 190–1), and the lack of properly trained teaching personnel to use Arabic as an effective medium of instruction suitable for the educational process of a modern state. In 1968 Ahmad b. Ṣalāḥ,[15] the powerful Minister for National Planning and Economics, became in addition Minister of Education, and attempted certain reforms of the Messadi system. The vocational streaming was delayed until the fourth year of secondary education, after an initial period of three years which were common to all.[16] French was introduced into the first year of primary school, and bi-lingualism was accepted as one of the objectives of education. In September 1969, Ben Ṣalāḥ was removed from all positions of power following the widespread discontent caused by the system of cooperatives which he favoured (see p. 184), and further changes took place in the Ministry of Education towards the end of 1969. This constant change and confusion caused much doubt and uncertainty throughout the educational world in Tunisia: the now endemic problems of the desperate need to stabilise expenditure, to reduce the appalling wastage rates, to make language instruction effective either in French or in Arabic, were not really approached in a radical, long-term manner.

Following the ministerial change of June 1970 when Chedli 'Ayārī replaced Muhammad Mzālī, modifications were introduced which have produced the system which exists at present (1970–71). Primary education still lasts for six years (age-group 6–11), with French now being introduced during the second year. At the end of the primary stage, all those who gain 50 per cent in the final examination may pass on to some form of secondary education.

[14] Foster, *Tunisian Education*, p. 5.
[15] For a brief biography of Ben Ṣalāḥ, see Knapp, *Tunisia*, pp. 215–16.
[16] Foster, *Tunisian Education*, pp. 9–12.

The secondary level is notorious for the diversity of its institutions, but the following broad divisions exist: first there is the traditional *lycée* course which is comparable with its French model. Those destined for the *baccalauréat*, which leads in turn to University entrance, spend three initial years known as the *premier cycle*. They then spend a further four years preparing the *baccalauréat* with options in the arts, economic sciences, applied sciences, pure science and mathematics. These represent the elite of the system, and are usually referred to as the *section générale*. Then there is a technical section of the *lycée* system which lasts for six years; after the initial three years which represent the common *premier cycle* both for the *section générale* and the *section technique*, those in the technical section spend a further three years preparing either a *brevet de technicien* or a *diplôme de fin d'études secondaires*. The pupils of these two sections of the *lycée* system are those who are no older than fourteen years by the end of the primary stage. Those who have passed this limit or who are judged unsuitable for this type of *lycée* training may be directed towards the *écoles professionnelles*, where they exist; these are Technical Schools giving a four-year course in industrial training for boys and secretarial training for girls: such a course leads to the *brevet professionnel*. Or they may attend the institutions of the *moyen* or intermediary grade of the secondary system where they would gain rather rudimentary formations in the fields of general education, or commercial and industrial training. In this category, the *collèges d'enseignement général* provide only three years of instruction while *lycées d'enseignement général et professionnel* provide three- or four-year courses. Finally, those who wish to train as teachers for the primary schools go to the *écoles normales d'instituteurs*, which are also included in the secondary level of the educational system.[17]

At this stage one should point out that the *écoles professionnelles* of the Ministry of Education (see above) represent only one section of technical training in Tunisia. The responsibility for this is divided amongst many ministries and institutions, according to whether a more general or specific type of training is given. The principal bodies offering broad technical training are: (a) L'Office de la Formation Professionnelle et de l'Emploi, created in 1967. Originally this was intended to be responsible for all technical training activities, but this has not proved to be the case. (b) The Ministry of Education itself. (c) The Ministry of Agriculture. Other ministries such as Post and Telecommunications and Public Health provide training for their specific needs. As one might guess, it seems that cooperation between the separate responsible bodies has often left much to be desired.

Higher Education since 1960 The University of Tunis was founded only in 1960, and incorporated the former Institut des Hautes Etudes (see

[17] Bsais and Morrisson, 'Les Coûts de l'Education', pp. 87–9.

p. 169), the Bourguiba Institute of Modern Languages, and the Zaytouna University itself. The Zaytouna remains the centre of traditional Islamic studies, with a strong emphasis on theology and Islamic jurisprudence. The main function of the Bourguiba School is to provide language courses for adults and students; it was founded in 1957 with the help of the United States Government, although the main source of external assistance since 1964 has been the Ford Foundation. The main body of the University is divided into the following faculties: arts and social sciences, sciences, law, agronomy, medicine, theology (the Zaytouna), and the Ecole Normale Supérieure, which produces graduates to teach in secondary schools. Until recently, the latter was a largely residential institution, the students of which followed the normal university courses with no special provision for teacher training. Steps have now been taken to rectify this. The so-called Ecole Normale des Professeurs Adjoints (re-named in 1971 the Ecole Normale des Professeurs de Collège) differs from all the other institutions of higher education in that it does not require the *baccalauréat* as an entrance qualification; its graduates are teachers destined for the *premier cycle* of secondary education only, i.e. those not involved in the long type of *lycée* formation.

Apart from the faculties, there are other more specialised institutes of higher education which are attached to the University and conceived very much in the manner of the *Grandes Ecoles* of the French system. These include the Ecole Nationale des Ingénieurs de Tunis (engineering), the Institut Supérieur des Gestions des Entreprises (a business school, for post-graduates only) and the Institut des Hautes Etudes Commerciales. In addition, particular ministries control specialised institutions to supply their specific needs: for example, the Ecole Nationale de l'Administration is attached to the Prime Ministerial Office. Other similar institutes include the Ecole de Santé Publique, the Centre de Formation Bancaire, the Institut National de l'Education Physique et Sportive, the Ecole des Beaux Arts (mainly for architecture), the Institut Bach Hamba (journalism and documentation), the Ecole Nationale du Service Social, and the Ecole de l'Aviation Civile et de la Météorologie. There are various research institutes all of which are situated in Tunis.

Education in Private Institutions These occupy a fairly insignificant position in the national scene overall: usually directed by religious organisations, there are fewer than fifty such establishments in the country, providing a variety of general and technical education. About 80 per cent of these schools are to be found in the region of Tunis itself. They account for about 16,000 pupils, or two per cent of the national total.

The Education Explosion in Tunisia The initial political idea (see pp. 169–70) which saw education as a basic means of propagating more democracy and equality in post-Independence Tunisia, led to a rapid, massive expansion of the system in quantitative terms. The progress made since Independence in purely statistical terms is quite remarkable, and the majority of the studies and reports undertaken hitherto have been largely statistical and quantitative by nature. Thorough critical examinations of the effectiveness of the system have still in the main not been undertaken. From 1956 until 1971, the total numbers of pupils and students in Tunisia increased from some 261,193 to 1,122,979; this is an overall increase of 861,786, or an average annual increase of about 27 per cent.[18] The numbers of pupils in primary schools grew from 226,919 in 1956–7 to 922,861 in 1970–1. At the secondary level, the numbers increased from 32,924 in 1956–7 to 181,909 in 1970–1. In higher education, between the years 1961–2 and 1970–1, the numbers of students increased from 1911 to 8859.[19] Of the three sectors, the most dramatic explosion occurred at the secondary level where the increase took place in the amazing proportions of 1 to 6, as opposed to 1 to 4 at the primary level, and 1 to 4·5 in higher education. While in 1959–60 some 41·5 per cent of the educable population of primary school age were receiving instruction, since 1970 this figure has gone beyond 80 per cent. For secondary schools, the equivalent percentage increase has passed from 8 to 30 per cent. Very few developing countries can match such a record in statistical terms, and be at least within sight of total scholarisation at primary level after a period of some twenty years since Independence.

The costs of education are borne by the Tunisian Government, and this places a crippling burden on state expenditure. Naturally, the educational process is continuous and unending, and rapidly becomes the *tonneau sans fond* for financial resources. With the increasing popular demand for more participation in the destiny of the country to be achieved through education, even when costs escalate out of all proportion, it becomes an impossibility in political terms to halt the process. Ever since 1960, the state expenditure on education has seen a staggering average annual increase of 14 per cent![20] In 1960, the total expenditure on education can be represented by 2·8 per cent of GNP. By 1970 this had risen enormously to 7·37 per cent GNP. In that same year, 31·68 per cent of the national budget was devoted to education alone; according to present trends, it can be estimated that in 1975, the Ministry of Education alone would spend 39 per cent of the national budget, or 14·7 per cent of GNP.[21]

It does not seem possible that this spiralling trend be allowed to continue indefinitely, particularly in a country so poor in natural resources and apparently lacking in industrial potential according to present evidence. Such figures also emphasise the extreme urgency of undertaking studies on the effectiveness of the system, and the wastage rates which remain extremely high. Here one may point out that countries such as the

[18] Ayari, *Aperçu Quantitatif*, p. 3.
[19] Ibid., p. 4, Table I.
[20] Bsais and Morrisson, 'Les Coûts de l'Education', p. 34.
[21] Information made available through UNESCO.

United States, the Soviet Union, Japan, the Netherlands and Sweden, which lead the world in their efforts devoted to education, use from 5 to 7 per cent of their GNP's in the process.

As previously stated (pp. 169–70), this massive educational expansion was seen as a future investment in a human infrastructure, and the remarkable growth took place as it were intuitively, and quite autonomously of the country's economic development as a whole. Economic development since 1956 has given rise only to gloomy prognostications for the future, with no significant change in the depressed conditions of the labour market.[22] Agricultural production during the 1960s has more or less stagnated, food imports have risen while exports have fallen.[23] The same is true in general of mining production, with isolated exceptions such as zinc and superphosphates.[24] The important fruit and fish canning industries have shown a decline since their high point in the mid 1960s. On the positive side, the production of building materials has shown an increase since 1968. Tourism became by far the most important and rapidly expanding section of the economy during the 1960s, and a particularly vital source of foreign currency.[25] The huge expansion of education since Independence, particularly at the primary and secondary levels, has meant an ever-burgeoning pressure to get jobs for the 15–19 year-old age group. Indeed the population of Tunisia as a whole is extremely young: it has been calculated according to the census in 1966 that some 50 per cent of the population was less than 16·8 years old. At the same time it was calculated that some 15·3 per cent of the available labour force was unemployed, and it was suspected that unemployment in the 15–19 age group was three to four times as great as in the 35–55 year-old group. With so much social prejudice in favour of the traditional 'general' education of the *lycée*, with the high drop-out rates, and technical education very much the poor relation of the system, unemployment amongst those leaving or dropping out of secondary education has become one of the crisis points in Tunisian society.

III THE DONOR COUNTRIES AND INTERNATIONAL AID[26]

Since Independence, Bourguiba's Tunisia has exploited astutely a special position within the Arab world and the Third World as a whole. For a country of such small size, relative poverty, and strategic insignificance, the input of foreign aid during the 1960s from such a variety of donors has

22 Plum, 'Facharbeiterbedarf', pp. 11–16.
23 Ibid., pp. 19–20.
24 Ibid., p. 23.
25 UNDP sources, Tunisia.
26 Much of the material in this section is based on information kindly made available by the UNDP mission in Tunis, and on conversations with staff of embassies and aid missions.

been nothing short of remarkable.[27] Technical assistance has always formed an important proportion of such aid: in 1970, Tunisia received about 12·8 million dinars under technical assistance programmes (1 Tunisian dinar is the approximate equivalent of $2 or 10 francs, or £1.05). This represented about half the total quantity of grant aid (24 million dinars), and 14 per cent of the total capital assistance (90·5 million dinars). The principal donor countries and other organisations in 1970 were France (4 million dinars), UNDP (2 million dinars), West Germany (1·2 million dinars), United States (1·2 million dinars), Canada and Belgium (1 million dinars).

France is the donor country most heavily involved in the provision of technical assistance within the broad field of education and technical training. Although other donors have made considerable contributions here, by comparison with both the size and the continuity of the French effort, they can be described as marginal, often centred on specific, limited, pilot schemes, quite unlike the extensive involvement in education which has been the French role throughout the 1960s. Broadly speaking, one can suggest as reasons for this a reluctance on the part of other donors to enter a domain which by tradition has belonged to France, and also because the financing of any part of the educational process can become a long-term investment where quick returns are rarely apparent. Once a donor becomes committed, subsequent withdrawal is difficult, particularly where the aid is in the form of experts and teachers on whom the system might begin to depend.

France

Unlike French financial aid, technical and cultural cooperation between France and Tunisia was uninterrupted during the 1960s. In 1964 financial aid from France was suspended completely following the nationalisation of French-owned land by the Tunisian government, and was not resumed again until 1967. One may take 1968 as a typical year to illustrate how the total programme of French technical assistance was organised: total expenditure was 3,907,800 frs covering the services of experts, teachers, fellowships and equipment. The following are examples of the individual programmes, although *only proportions of the sums of money mentioned are programmed for one year*, as most of the grants are spread over longer periods.

i. A sum of 500,000 frs was granted to the National Cancer Institute to supply X-ray equipment. This was opened in 1969 and modelled on the Institut Gustave Roussy in Paris. Tunisian doctors and researchers are sent to France for certain periods, and scholarships granted to nursing and technical personnel for necessary training abroad. Books and documents are also supplied to the library.

27 [illegible], *The Aid Relationship*, O.D.I., London, 1968, p. 114.

ii. One million frs were granted to the Institut National Technique. This is an institute to train engineers at university level, constructed originally with Soviet aid. France agreed to supply laboratory and workshop equipment, French would be the language of instruction and French teaching staff would be supplied. Scholarships and practical training would be available for some 300 students expected to enrol from October 1969.

iii. In 1968, two million francs were approved to construct and equip the Ecole Normale Supérieure pour l'Enseignement Agricole. This school is designed to train agricultural education teachers, and is one of the three agricultural institutions existing at the tertiary level (the other two being the Ecole Supérieure d'Agronomie, and the Institut National de la Recherche Agronomique). France helped to prepare the teaching and training programmes, and short- and long-term scholarships were granted for training in France.

iv. A total credit of 1,700,000 frs was approved to construct and equip an annex to the Ecole Nationale de l'Administration (200,000 frs was programmed for 1968). France has supplied teaching staff, civil servants on short missions, books and fellowships. The school gives training basically in French methods to Tunisian civil servants at all levels.

v. 200,000 frs was granted to the Centre d'Instruction et de Perfectionnement Electrotechnique; this was established in 1959 with the cooperation of the Gas and Electricity Company of France to give technical training to employees of the Tunisian Electricity and Gas Company (STEG). This centre is modelled on the Centre de Cury-le-Châtel in France, and has had a regular supply of experts and equipment since 1963.

vi. 500,000 frs to the Mission de Vulgarisation Agricole, the Agricultural Extension section of the Ministry of Agriculture. This section has employed four French experts since 1967.

vii. 500,000 frs to the French Productivity Mission which is assisting the National Productivity Institute in studies on tourism, and the textile and leather industries.

viii. 300,000 frs for equipment and materials for a chemistry and physics laboratory in the University Science Faculty. Other amounts have been granted for the training of public works inspectors, for equipment for the National Institute of Oceanography, and for hydraulic studies.

By far the most obvious symbol of the technical and cultural cooperation between France and Tunisia is the large numbers of French personnel working as experts, or in the majority of cases, as teachers. These *co-opérants* are either civilians, or military volunteers who opt and are selected to do this work rather than the normal form of military service. The *co-opérant* is employed under very favourable terms, receiving almost the double of his salary in France. There are two types of contract,

A and B. Under the former, two-thirds of the salary is paid by the Tunisian government and one-third by the French. Under the 'B' contract, the Tunisian government pays the total remuneration. Naturally the military personnel are much cheaper than the civilians. Those on contract 'A' are paid 78 dinars plus 358 frs a month, while those 'B' are paid 118 dinars a month. These teachers now work exclusively at the levels of secondary and higher education, as the primary sector now employs only Tunisians, with the exception of a few French school inspectors. Because of the high costs involved, the number of civilian *co-opérants* is being gradually reduced, while that of the military personnel is being correspondingly increased. In 1967, there were 2515 civilian teachers in Tunisia, and 387 military, while in 1968, there were 2261 civilians and 797 military. While this makes sense in economic terms, it gives reason for concern in other respects: the military volunteers are not usually as well qualified or as experienced as the civilian teachers, and most have an essentially short-term view of the period which they will spend as military servicemen and the tasks they will perform. Although the numbers of the civilian proportion are decreasing, overall there is no sign of any decrease: in 1971 there were 2984 French *co-opérants* working in secondary education alone, and 269 in higher education.

The United States of America

The United States has been an important source of aid to Tunisia since 1957, when a bilateral agreement for economic and technical assistance was signed; at this stage, technical assistance as such was not considered a particularly important part of the American programme, it being more of an extension to the large aid-financed capital projects such as the Tunis–Carthage Airport, the Kasserine Pulp Mill, or the Oued Nebaana Dam. From 1967–8, American financial and technical assistance now administered by AID began to concentrate on four general areas: agricultural production, industrial and mining production, development of human resources, and assistance with planning and economic policy formulation.

In the educational sector, American technical assistance has concentrated on agricultural training and higher education. The Chott Maria Agricultural School was constructed and equipped with the aid of an American loan to finance the necessary foreign exchange costs (see pp. 188–9 for agricultural training). Similar loans have been granted to the Faculty of Law and Economics, and the Business School (ISGE). The Chott Maria School was completed in 1968, and AID financed a contract with a team from Texas A. & M. University in order to train Tunisians to staff the school and to develop curricula. Further technical assistance activities in the agricultural sector include personnel training in soil conservation methods, flood prevention, and help with the development of the Medjerda Valley project.[28] A bureau of economic studies of the Ministry of Agriculture has also been created to do research and analysis of agricultural produce and marketing, and to train agricultural economists. This project is being carried out by a team from the University of Minnesota, acting on behalf of USAID.

In the University Faculty of Law and Economics, the University of Minnesota also supplied a number of visiting professors who conducted short courses and seminars, generally helped strengthen the teaching staff for economics, and assisted in introducing new and improved teaching methods. At the ISGE, a project was started in 1966 to train new entrants to the management field, to provide entrants to the management field, and advanced training for executives in both public and private enterprises. First a technical assistance contract with Harvard University, and subsequently one with the University of Illinois, were intended to provide a Master's degree in business administration training for Tunisians. These inter-institutional links are interesting and relatively recent experiments. On an individual level they seem popular on both sides, but at the official level of administration they have proved complex and difficult to organise.

In 1967, a so-called 'general training' project was begun to meet on a selective basis some of the Tunisian Government's training requirements for senior and middle-level personnel. By 1969, 36 fellows and participants had benefited from the project: for example, 20 people were in the United States studying hotel administration, 5 students were studying engineering, and others were engaged in individual disciplines to Ph.D. level. This 'general training' programme has to some extent forced the issue of the recognition of US academic qualifications in Tunisia, a problem which is now virtually solved in theoretical terms, even if there still remains much practical prejudice against qualifications which are non-French in origin. Through this programme it was also hoped to convince the Tunisian Government of the necessity to install an evaluation and follow-up system for all trainees, whether US-sponsored or not.

The Ford Foundation

In a manner similar to the USAID programmes in Tunisia, the Ford Foundation has been particularly active during the 1960s in agriculture and higher education. In cooperation with USAID, the Foundation has sponsored a highly successful project to increase wheat production by the introduction of high-yielding varieties of Mexican wheat. Alongside this, there exists a training programme for agricultural technicians, designed to give specialised training to key technicians whose training hitherto had been of a rather general nature. It had been anticipated that most of these

[28] See Knapp, *Tunisia*, pp. 195ff., for a brief description of this project.

trainees would become officials of cooperative agricultural units, and that some of the trainees would later be assigned to the wheat project.

The Ford Foundation has been closely involved with the Ecole Nationale de l'Administration during its recent period of reform and reorganisation (see p. 177). A three-year grant of $300,000 was made in 1965, and another of $275,000 in 1968. These funds were used mainly to pay the salaries of foreign teaching staff, and to develop the library and research centre of the school. In 1967, the Foundation began a project to assist with vocational and technical training, in conjunction with the OFPE (see p. 172). This involved the provision of two experts, and a grant of $148,000 in 1968 for an overseas training programme, purchase of equipment, and specialised consultant services.

Since 1963, the Foundation has been connected with the Centre for the Promotion of Investments (CPI), which was developed to encourage foreign private investment in Tunisia. A terminal grant of $35,000 was approved in 1968. The Foundation also provides advisory services for the ISGE.

One of the most significant contributions of the Ford Foundation to higher education has been its help in the creation of the Centre for Economic and Social Research (CERES), and its subsequent support for its development throughout the 1960s. With a flourishing programme of teaching and research, and the regular production of a respected periodical, this institute has become one of the most stimulating parts of the University of Tunis.

Since 1964, the Foundation has cooperated with the Bourguiba Institute of Modern Languages, originally founded with the help of the US Government in 1957. Since 1964, Foundation funds have helped to purchase audio-visual equipment, and to provide scholarships for long- or short-term training abroad. Tunisian teachers of English have also been sent on tours and study courses both in the United States and the United Kingdom.

In 1969, the Foundation together with the British Council began a project to prepare new text books for the teaching of English in secondary schools. This seems a valuable scheme from several points of view: it recognises the great desirability of modern, up-to-date teaching manuals prepared by professional linguists who bear in mind the specific complexities of the linguistic and social situations in Tunisia. In other words, it lays stress on the improved effectiveness of teaching by relating the teaching materials to the Tunisian environment as closely as possible. It is also an impressive example of close cooperation between two donors eminently suited to combine their resources for this particular project, a type of cooperation which will probably set the pattern for bilateral aid in the future either officially or *de facto*, particularly amongst the smaller donors.

The United Kingdom

The fact that North-West Africa has never been a traditional area of British influence is reflected in the minor role played by the British Government in technical assistance to Tunisia. There are two British *lecteurs* attached to the University of Tunis, and gifts of books have been made to the University and the ISGE in particular. The most significant current project is the British Council participation in the preparation of new text books for English teaching at secondary school level (see above). Along with the Ford Foundation, the British Council supplements the work done by the linguists with the organisation of summer courses for Tunisian teachers of English: in 1971, a party of such Tunisian teachers attended a summer course in Colchester, although subsequent evaluation indicated that *sur place* training would in future be much more effective. The increasing demand for more English tuition from the secondary level upwards is likely to lead to demands for greater involvement of British cooperation and assistance in the future.

The Netherlands

The Netherlands programme of capital aid and technical assistance to Tunisia dates back to 1964. The agricultural sector has been of prime importance with two centres of instruction: one for cattle-raising at Sidi Thabet, and a market-gardening and fodder production centre at Saida. Individual experts are also provided by the Netherlands in certain specific cases: for example during 1968–9 an hydraulic engineer, a statistician, an agricultural teacher and two veterinaries were made available.

The Netherlands Government also provides fellowships for studies in the Netherlands: for example in 1968 five scholarships for the Higher Hotel School at Maastricht were awarded, and one for an agricultural course of six months.

The German Federal Republic

Tunisia has ranked remarkably high on the list of the many states receiving development aid from West Germany. In 1969, it held seventh position overall and received more aid than any other country in Africa. In general it seems to have been considered by the Federal Government as a pilot country for that continent. Capital aid was begun in 1962, and in 1965 the aid programme saw a significant expansion, consisting of some 40 million DM annually in the form of repayable credits, and 10 million DM of technical assistance in non-reimbursable grants.

Once again, the agricultural sector has played a major part in German technical assistance, with an impressive number of projects. A pilot farm to improve dairy farming was set up between 1960 and 1965 at Béjaoui (Medjerda Valley). A similar centre was also created at Sedjenane (West of Bizerta), including sheep-raising and the cultivation of food crops. West Germany has also participated in the Netherlands' pilot farm project at Sidi Thabet. Two agricultural cooperatives have been created at Dar Chichou and Bordj Toum, and there is a forestry training project at Ain Draham. Assistance has also been given to the Agricultural Research Institute in Tunis.

Technical training (sometimes referred to as 'professional' or 'vocational' training) has received a particular emphasis in the German technical assistance programme. The so-called Vocational Training Centre at Menzel Bourguiba was created in 1963: its object is to produce skilled workers to use machine tools, general mechanics, automobile mechanics, diesel mechanics, and people able to repair and maintain agricultural machinery. Equipment and German teaching staff have been provided. The *Land* of Baden-Wurttemberg has cooperated in this project which has now been handed over to the Tunisian Government. Teachers and equipment have also been supplied to the Hotel School at Bizerta designed to train hotel staff.

A German volunteer service has existed in Tunisia since 1966; in 1969, there were some 120 such volunteers working in Tunisia, mostly attached to the Ministry of Public Health and in the Agricultural Division of the Ministry of Planning.

Trainees in 'vocational' and managerial training have been sent to Germany: during 1969 for example, the quota was fixed at sixty Tunisians.

Some interesting contacts have been made by individual German institutes: in 1964, the Friedrich Naumann Institute established the Ali Bach Hamba Institute for adult education, with the collaboration of the Tunisian Government. The Friedrich Ebert Stiftung also cooperates with the Parti Socialiste Destourien in organising seminars.

United Nations Development Programme

In common with most of the other donors, the UN agencies and UNDP have not been heavily involved in the traditional educational sector, but they have concentrated to a large extent on agricultural and technical training. It should be stressed that as far as Tunisia is concerned, multilateral assistance is coordinated by UNDP, and the Tunisian Government has given no sign that it wishes to see any separate agency representation established in Tunisia. The Resident Representative acts on behalf of the specialised agencies, and as their representative.

Between 1965 and 1970, the Tunisian Government and UNESCO were involved in the creation of the Ecole Normale des Professeurs Adjoints (now the Ecole Normale des Professeurs de Collège, see p. 173); this school produces teachers for the *collèges d'enseignement moyen* and the *collèges du premier cycle*. A further project in which UNESCO is involved is the further development and organisation of archaeological remains, particularly in the Tunis–Carthage region.

As might be expected, FAO and ILO have been the most active specialist agencies in Tunisia, with a long list of projects. For example FAO has had a joint project since 1965 with the Reforestation Institute in Tunis to increase and diversify the country's resources of wood; experiments and demonstrations have been organised with the production of fruit, market-garden products and animal food-stuffs. Studies have also been made to improve irrigation and drainage techniques. In 1969, an agreement between the Tunisian Government and FAO was concluded to help reinforce the extension service of the Institut de Génie Rural et de Machinisme Agricole. FAO is also involved in the proposed future development of the fishing industry, and has helped with a scheme to train farm managers.

The ILO's interest in technical training in Tunisia is demonstrated by schemes to assist the activities of the Institut National de Formation et de Perfectionnement Professionel, the Institut National de Productivité, and the OFPE itself (see p. 172). Since 1969, the ILO has helped in the creation of the hotel and tourism training institute at Monastir, and along with appropriate training and educational programmes it has been involved in the development of cooperative enterprises.

The efforts made by the bilateral and multilateral donors referred to above may be summarised in the following general terms: France occupies a unique position in her involvement at every level of the educational process, from the few remaining *conseillers pédagagiques* in the primary schools to the *co-opérants* and experts working in various branches of higher education. This situation obviously owes much to political history and dates back to a period when many of the problems existing today were either not apparent or not considered by both donor and recipient alike. The United States and the Ford Foundation have paid particular, though by no means exclusive, attention to some of the important, prestige-laden institutions of higher education (Faculty of Law and Economics, ISGE, CERES, etc.) where the intellectual elite of the country would be expected to congregate. The other donors such as the UN agencies, West Germany and the Netherlands have concentrated heavily on agricultural and technical training at the lower and middle levels, very often in the form of restricted individual pilot schemes. Significant technical assistance from West Germany and the Netherlands dates mainly from the mid-1960s, when many official outside observers were beginning to think more realistically about the relation of a country's overall development to its system of education. Hence the concentration on agriculture and the various forms of technical training, activities which most foreign observers consider vital to Tunisia's needs: unfortunately this view is not always echoed wholeheartedly by many Tunisians, nor is it necessarily borne out by the performance and apparent potential of the Tunisian economy.

IV THE SITUATION AFTER THE DECADE OF DEVELOPMENT

The fact that even today the educational system in Tunisia has maintained such a high degree of continuity with the French model of its Protectorate predecessor is easily explained: in 1956 it seemed that the obvious way to redress the uneven balance in the relationship was to imitate as closely as possible the system of the strong developed country. In addition, twenty years ago the ideas of the developed countries themselves on the content and nature of all education were much more universally accepted than is the case today. For a country such as Tunisia, when so much had to be created from nothing, the educational system is inevitably a reflection of the ideals and aspirations of those political leaders who have tried to mould society according to their own visions of the sort of country Tunisia should be. Hence it becomes pointless to consider the educational system apart from a wider political context; many of the problems which on the surface belong to the realm of the classroom, in fact are of a much wider relevance, affecting the future pattern of the country's life. Unfortunately, once one generation of politicians has created a system of education, subsequent change becomes a difficult, sometimes practically impossible process, and initial mistakes may take generations to rectify. The confused, conflicting atmosphere in Tunisian education over the last five years is symptomatic of the country's problems in general.

In 1968, the powerful Ahmed b. Ṣalāḥ, Minister of Planning and Economy, also took personal charge of the Ministry of Education, attempting to relate education more closely to the needs of social and economic development as he saw them. University authorities began to try to guide students more towards studies linked with the development drive; in 1968–9, a quota system was introduced for each faculty, heavily slanted in favour of careers in agriculture and teaching. The Co-operative Movement was Ben Ṣalāḥ's most important venture: large areas of land were taken over by the Government to be organised into state cooperative, a measure which caused widespread discontent and bitterness amongst many small land owners whose property was usually the first to be nationalised.

Between September and November 1969, Ben Ṣalāḥ was removed from all positions of power, tried and subsequently imprisoned. He had been the most dominating figure in Tunisian politics since 1961, with the exception of Bourguiba himself. These events along with the natural disaster of the worst recorded floods in Tunisian history, made the autumn of 1969 extremely dramatic for the country. The subsequent changes amounted to nothing less than a complete national reorientation. Prior to the overthrow of Ben Ṣalāḥ, there had been an ever-growing commitment to the cooperative system throughout the economy. This trend was now completely reversed, and much of the land previously taken over was returned to its former owners. Widespread changes were effected throughout ministries and state-owned enterprises, right down to middle-level officials. Subsequently, the Government has shown a greater tendency to withdraw from directing the economy too closely and rigorously; the signs are that more private investment is being encouraged, with the possibility of attracting foreign capital through the so-called *sous-traitance* system.[29] When the situation is so generally uncertain, constructive long-term technical assistance of any form and from any type of donor is extremely difficult to plan.

The problems in Tunisian education remain enormous; they are most apparent and acute in the primary and secondary schools. An enduring Tunisian contact with France and French culture is ensured by the fact that the educational system is bilingual. At present (January 1972) the study of French begins during the second year of primary school (10 hours per week, 15 hours in Arabic), and during the final three years of primary education these proportions are reversed. As secondary education progresses, French gradually takes over as the principal medium of instruction, particularly in the prestige-laden *section générale* of the *lycée* leading to the *baccalauréat.* At university level, French is almost exclusively the medium of instruction, Arabic being restricted to such subjects as Islamic theology, Arabic literature, history, and civilisation. Since Independence, the Government has clung tenaciously to this idea of bilingualism which would supposedly bring the enrichment of a 'double culture', enabling Tunisia both to maintain its traditional identity and to keep in step with the modern world, through this contact with a highly industrialised occidental state.

It is not for outside observers to decide whether the theory of this bilingual education is the correct one for Tunisia, but there would seem to be a number of serious deficiences in the system which have not been properly studied. The massive expansion of primary education forced certain manpower economies on the authorities: one of the methods of making maximum use of the available teaching personnel was to cut down the number of teaching hours per week over a range of subjects, including French. Those who complete the primary stage receive something between 1600–1800 hours on instruction in French, while educationalists have suggested that 4000 hours exposure would be a minimum to guarantee 'mastery' of the language.[30] Whatever the accuracy of such figures, they

[29] *Sous-traitance*: a form of sub-contracting by manufacturers to the Tunisian government, whereby only a part of a given industrial process would take place in Tunisia, taking advantage of the abundance of cheap labour.

[30] Foster, *Tunisian Education*, p. 17.

indicate a serious deficiency which is borne out by facts: even the more gifted pupils who go on to the *lycées* frequently do not achieve this 'mastery' until well into the secondary stage of education, and much time and energy is wasted in grappling more with language problems than those posed by curriculum content.[31]

Another grave problem has been the quality of the primary school teachers themselves. The Tunisification of the primary school system was achieved in the mid-1960s: this was a desirable step from the point of view of national principles, and because of the heavy costs to Tunisia of employing the French *co-opérants* (see p. 178). But this did not take place without sacrifices to quality. Many of the teachers did not undergo proper courses of instruction, and were not properly qualified: these are the *moniteurs* as opposed to the qualified *instituteurs*. In fact between 1960 and 1969 the percentage of qualified primary teachers has actually diminished (from 78 to 62 per cent) while the percentage of monitors has increased from 22 to 38 per cent. Such figures are explained by the extremely low wages and the poor working conditions, in particular the very overcrowded classes (anything from 40–50 pupils per class). Many of the monitors have completed only 2–3 years of secondary education, and their own grasp of French is often rudimentary. Methods and manuals of teaching are usually somewhat archaic.

Large numbers of the primary school children come from illiterate, often semi-nomadic family backgrounds. While people may sincerely believe that education is the means to achieve more democracy throughout the nation, for such children this scarcely applies. In principle, everyone has the same opportunity, but the conditions described above and the peculiar difficulties of the bilingual system tend to operate to the disadvantage of those most in need of real equality of opportunity. The pupils who become most proficient in French, the key to success in secondary education and beyond, are those who may have a French parent or who come from a family where French has always been a medium of communication. For the average child of the average peasant or unskilled worker, there is often little hope. The few critical statistics which have been prepared bear out these impressions.[32] It has been estimated that of the pupils who enrol in primary schools, some 46 per cent do not complete the primary stage. These may be pupils who drop out before taking the entrance examination for secondary school for reasons of family economics; but very large numbers are those who either fail the secondary school examination, or who by reasons of their

[31] A situation frequently described in numerous conversations with French *co-opérants.*

[32] Chouikha, 'Conception et Résultats'. See also by the same author, 'Rendement Scolaire et Cadres Enseignants en Tunisie', *Revue Tunisiene des Sciences Sociales*, Mar 1969, pp. 65–79.

advanced ages become too old to proceed. The advanced age of many primary school pupils is a chronic problem more particularly in rural areas where school attendance may have been anything but regular.[33] There are very few institutions to receive or guide these young people who leave school, and the great majority find themselves amongst the unemployed *dans la rue.* Encouraging such young people to try to live off the land and adapt more to their rural milieu is made difficult by the very contact, however brief, with a type of education which is anything but rural-orientated. The aspiration of the majority would be 'a job in the town'. Between 1961 and 1967, about 18 per cent of the pupils dropped out annually on failing the secondary school examination, and more than 40 per cent repeated this sixth or final year. The method of repeating years known as *redoublement*) is in itself one of the least attractive features of the system: the pupil simply repeats the course which he failed the previous year, with little or no attempt made to meet his or her special educational problems. On average, 30 per cent of the pupils repeat at least one of the years of primary education. It is difficult to avoid the conclusion that to operate this bilingual education effectively and justly from the primary stagc onwards, would require the use of highly trained personnel and advanced materials and techniques on a very large scale; in fact resources which a country already crippled by the costs of education does not seem to possess.

The basic educational model which has seen such an explosion during the 1960s, absorbing so many internal and external resources, has remained predominantly geared to the traditional type of general education, leading to the *baccalauréat* and university, however much the Government has attempted to modify it. This is a system originally evolved in a highly developed and varied economy, in a sophisticated society with a labour market of great extent, variety and fluctuation. Obviously there is no such situation in Tunisia, nor is there likely to be in the near future. The ultimate aspirations in this cycle are centred on the liberal professions or executive roles in the process of industrial development. The technical sectors of the educational system suffer from the same social stigmata all too familiar in other countries, both developed and developing: this *enseignement professionnel* (technical teaching and training) is seen as the last resort for those who have failed in the general education which retains most of the social cachet and prestige. During the 1960s at the secondary level, the pupils in the technical teaching sectors have actually decreased in number, while those in general education now represent between 70 and 80 per cent of the total numbers.[34]

[33] Chouikha, 'Conception et Résultats', pp. 53–4.

[34] Ayari, 'Aperçu Quantitatif', pp. 36 ff; Bsais and Morrisson, 'Les Coûts de l'Education', pp. 86–91.

The *écoles professionnelles* or schools providing technical training usually have the least gifted pupils, and instructors not always of high quality. Such institutions also require the installation of expensive machinery and workshops to function effectively. The whole secondary system seems much too heterogeneous to remove the vicious circles of social prejudice against anything which is not quite the same as the traditional *lycée*. Many young people drop out of the *lycées* before completing their course, frequently because of the pressures of family economics. They are the doubtful products of a general education which has been anything but technical, and present a chronic employment problem. Some may obtain an indifferent *baccalauréat* and go on to university courses for which they are ill-equipped. At university level there are still sufficient vacancies for graduates willing to teach in secondary schools (as at January 1972). For those with no desire to teach, for science graduates, and engineers in particular, the situation is becoming increasingly serious, the only concrete hope in many cases lying in emigration. As yet, the problem of unemployment for the graduates has not been so chronic as for those who come on to the labour market lower down the educational ladder.

The same stigmata as those described above operate equally strongly against a career in agriculture. Here again, the wider political context has had an inhibiting effect on this area of education, in particular the reversal of the cooperative policy after the fall of Ben Ṣalāḥ. The Government has subsequently been ambiguous about the whole future of the cooperative idea. At present the Ministry of Agriculture is responsible for agricultural training at all levels, although during the academic year 1968–9 the *lycées agricoles* were experimentally placed under the control of the Ministry of Education.

There are altogether ten agricultural secondary schools in Tunisia, one being for girls. In 1971, these were occupied to 60 per cent of their capacity, and in the view of one experienced UN expert, the teaching has been far too theoretical and not enough practical work is done. The period which these *lycées* spent under the Ministry of Education left a rather traditional academic trace on the curricula. There are sufficient numbers of teaching staff, but they too suffer from a lack of practical agricultural experience. The heads of these establishments talk openly about the lack of motivation in many of the students. An agricultural career is not seen as a noble activity; many students entering these *lycées* see them more as an avenue to a job as a civil servant or to further higher studies, rather than to a practical career on the land. Prior to 1969, the cooperative policy offered many of the students from these schools guarantees of jobs in the civil service: this is now much less sure and recruitment has become correspondingly more difficult. Agricultural production generally continues to stagnate, the present cereal production is quite insufficient for the country's needs, and vital opportunities to increase production in all sectors do exist. Even so, agriculture alone would still not solve the basic unemployment problem.

During the past two years, the multilateral agencies in particular have insisted on the need for more effective manpower planning in Tunisia, and a more realistic integration of the educational machine and what are rather vaguely described as the country's developmental needs. This view is also implicit behind many of the bilateral donor's technical assistance projects in agriculture and other areas of industrial and technical training, rather than in general education. There is certainly room for improvement in manpower planning, but one feels bound to point out that if the proportions of pupils from general education and those from technical education could be reversed (see p. 187), it is difficult to see where such people would find employment other than through emigration, at the country's present stage of economic development. Tunisian workers emigrate in increasing numbers every year: 9000 left the country in 1969, and 13,000 did so in 1970. These figures *do not* take into account the unrestricted emigration to France. This emigration is a carefully organised process, and is controlled by the OFPE (see p. 172) in cooperation with the foreign agencies concerned. Bilateral agreements exist with West Germany, the Netherlands, Austria and Belgium. Increasingly the demand is for skilled workers, and there are centres in Tunisia to provide appropriate training for future migrant workers.

One cannot emphasise too strongly that many of the problems which may appear specific to education, lie in reality in wider fields of political and cultural controversy. As explained, the principle behind bilingualism is that the conjunction of two cultures should be doubly enriching, but for most people the opposite is usually the case. In Tunisia the cultural problems can be quite as acute as any economic crisis, and many of the country's intellectuals are troubled by the following complex: Islamic civilisation and the Arabic language are identified with all that was weak, old-fashioned and ill-attuned to the modern world. It was an Islamic society which was colonised and reduced to subservience by the apparent power and superiority of Western Europe. The period of the Protectorate dislocated the type of rational balance advocated by K̲hayr al-Dīn-al-Tūnisī (d.1889), one of the leading Islamic modernists in the nineteenth century, and similar in outlook to Muhammad 'Abduh and Jamāl al-Dīn al-Afgh̲ānī. They believed in Islam's capacity for regeneration from within, albeit with a certain amount of adaptation from Western ideas and institutions. Up to the present time, French has been one of the keys to success in Tunisian education and society. Most of the intellectual elite of the country have doctorates from French universities. The power and the glory that was France are still too close and too evident to be discounted by most Tunisians. Yet this is also the country of Ibn Rashīq (d. A.D.

1066), Ibn Khaldūn (d. A.D. 1405), the holy city of Qayrawān, and the great mosque and University of the Zaytouna. The dilemma for many modern Tunisians is how to achieve a balance between the two poles of European culture and their own Arab-Islamic environment.

At the moment the defects of the bilingual system penalise those most in need of the benefits of education; the most logical step to introduce more realistic democratisation into education would seem to lie in making Arabic the principle vehicle of instruction. Yet the process of Arabicisation is by no means as simple or automatic as it may at first seem. The enormous social cachet which attaches to the knowledge of French and its widespread use in education has greatly inhibited the development of Arabic itself as a modern living language acceptable throughout society. Arabic within Tunisia is a remarkable conglomerate of linguistic varieties: altogether five principal registers have been identified in Tunisia by the linguists:[35]

i. Archaic classical Arabic as used in the mosques, the Zaytouna, religious sermons and the language of religious instruction.

ii. Modern literary Arabic – the medium of newspapers, magazines, radio and television, creative writing and the language of education where taught.

iii. The Arabic known as *Arabiyya Muhadhdhaba*, a form of polite, *spoken* Arabic which is a modified form of the first two categories much influenced by Tunisian vernacular.

iv. The Tunisian vernacular itself, being the language spoken by 95 per cent of the population, and having no established written form.

v. *Frarabe* which is a disorganised mixture of Arabic and French in varying proportions.

To decide which category or rather combination of categories of the above should be the medium of Tunisian instruction and culture is not something to be chosen artificially and arbitrarily. Once the decision to Arabicise has been taken in principle, the language will doubtless develop under its own dynamism, probably as a combination of the vernacular, modern literary and the *Arabiyya Muhadhdhaba*. Yet questions concerning the use and nature of the Arabic language are never devoid of deeply-felt religious and cultural considerations which cannot be ignored by the Government. This is an area where language is still frequently an accurate indication of an individual's view of and place in society, and the values which he is likely to hold. One must add that if the teaching of French in

[35] Muhammad Ma'amouri, 'The Linguistic Situation in Independent Tunisia', *American Journal of Arabic Studies*, vol. I, 1973, pp. 51–65.

Tunisian schools is somewhat archaic, then this is certainly true also of Arabic.

Further to the problems of cultural identity and language described above, the educational system suffers like the remainder of the country from extreme centralisation, the focal point being the city of Tunis itself. The University is there,[36] and all the country's research institutes; the best of the schools are there, at least by reputation. A man out of work may go to Tunis not necessarily in the hope of finding work but in the expectation that there his children would find decent schools and a higher standard of teaching. Not only does Tunis exercise a magnetic attraction for inhabitants of the countryside but also for those who live in the provincial towns even of some importance. The towns in the interior of the country very often serve as no more than staging-posts in the great drift towards Tunis. The rural exodus leads to an inter-urban exodus, both of which culminate at Tunis.[37] The *bidonvilles* are a well-established feature on the peripheries of the city. Already in a country of five million people, one million have congregated in the Tunis region, and the capital's population is still growing. The paradox of this enormous drift to the city becomes clear not even twenty miles outside the city boundaries, as one sees how much could be achieved through the reform and social rehabilitation of agriculture as a way of life. Meanwhile the average age of those workers employed on the land increases annually.

This trend towards extreme centralisation is accentuated by two factors: the first is probably a legacy from the centralised pattern of metropolitan France duly passed on to Tunisia and now operating very much to the country's disadvantage. Second, the physical nature of the country has always emphasised the latent tensions between the urban and rural semi-nomadic environments. The long but narrow coastal strips have long-enshrined centres of sophisticated urban civilisation such as Sousse, Sfax, Mahdiyya and Tunis itself. The harsh hinterlands form a brusque contrast and were a frequent source of attack and pillage by nomadic or semi-nomadic raiders. This constant tension was analysed perceptively by Ibn Khaldūn in the fourteenth century. Whatever the combination of reasons, the result in educational terms is often too clear: a primary school teacher from the *Sāḥel* region will be sent to a post in some remote area of the south or the interior. He considers his appointment as some form of exile, and has great difficulty in identifying with his working evironment. Consequently he finds little to stimulate his interest in the peculiar educational problems of the children of illiterate, semi-nomadic families who will form the majority of his class.

[36] At the time of writing (January 1972), proposals for moving parts of the University of Tunis to Sfax were under consideration.

[37] P. Sebag, A. Bouhdiba and C. Camelleri, 'Les Préconditions Sociales de l'Industrialisation dans la Région de Tunis', *Cahiers du CERES*, Série Sociologique I, Aug 1968, p. 88.

V CONCLUSIONS

In many developing countries the system of education is subject to the will and ideas of the government in power in a very direct manner. That government is ultimately the sole channel through which all development aid will pass. Projects often succeed or fail according to the extent to which they have the political backing of the government for a long-term, sustained period. When the educational system has such a short history in its overall development as is the case in Tunisia, then the effects of outside interference, however benevolent, are all the more accentuated.

While the bilateral and multilateral donors may have great reserves of technical expertise, this expertise usually does not and should not extend to deciding what is best to suit the patterns of education in individual cultural situations. Most bilateral donors are realistic enough to admit that their development aid is not an entirely altruistic process, and that bad decisions may be taken in some development project because of pressures from another unrelated area of political activity. The United Nations agencies are in the best position to be more genuinely altruistic, but they too have to deal with politicians whose interests are at best uneasy compromises between short-term pressures and long-term objectives in the 'national interest'. All these are very serious limitations within which aid and technical assistance must function under the present methods of their administration.

If development projects are to have any chance of overcoming these limitations which are basically political, then studies undertaken at all stages of the development process should obviously be as de-politicised as possible. Governments should encourage even more the use of the people well-equipped to perform such tasks, namely those independent of the official institutions connected with development aid either as donors or recipients. They should obviously have the greatest possible specialist knowledge of the peculiar local conditions which exist in each country. Most importantly, their studies must have the benefit of both 'official' and 'unofficial' material. Without criticising the hard work and dedication of government officials, no country, developed or developing, is ever free of the danger of poor communication between the central government and the problems existing in specific, local situations in the country at large.

It is tempting to attach much of the blame for Tunisia's current problems in education to the massive French involvement throughout the system. This would be both facile and unhelpful; the French involvement dates back to a time when both donor and recipient were happy to accept that the rapid expansion of this form of education would eventually fulfil the country's needs. In addition, the transition from Protectorate to Independence took place without the same degrees of violent conflict as those experienced in Indo-China and Algeria. At the present time, although the number of *co-opérants* in Tunisian schools remains extremely high, it is recognised, if somewhat cynically, that this situation will not long continue. This is not because of high costs, but because teaching is virtually the only large-scale employment possibility for Tunisian graduates.

The safest and most useful solutions for the donors at present seem to lie in restricted, individual pilot-projects such as those developed by West Germany, the Netherlands and the multilateral agencies (see pp. 181–4). Because of their restricted nature, their effects on the cultural patterns of the country are marginal, yet they could be vital models for development provided that the country as a whole decided to move in the directions indicated by these projects. These particular donors have also been able to benefit from the wisdom of hindsight as their involvement began at a later stage, when the relationship between the former Protectorate and metropolitan France was already established. They have all concentrated heavily on agriculture where there is great potential for development, but the possibilities of the projects will not be fully realised until they are sustained by firm and consistent government directives.

These donors have also been much concerned with the fact that technical education and training at middle and lower levels have been neglected. There are undoubtedly some adjustments to be made in the manpower requirements and the training at present available, but until the country's longer-term directions of development become clearer it is difficult to make reasonable recommendations on the extent to which such training should be developed.

As for the present predominance of a general, French-type education, it goes without saying that curricula must be evolved which will foster aspirations more capable of realisation within the Tunisian context, rather than vice versa. The solution to this does not lie with any donor of development aid. The bewildering proliferation of different types of *lycée* and *collège* in secondary education exacerbates social prejudice and misunderstanding in an area which is highly emotive in any country. A more 'comprehensive' type of secondary system would have great advantages, and possibly lend itself more easily to flexibility and adaptation following the fluctuations in the country's future development. If a basic curriculum could be devised containing more technical and practical components, then so much the better.

Sooner or later the Arabicisation of the educational system must become more than a principle to which lip-service is paid. For Arabic to become a successful medium of instruction from primary school onwards will demand nothing short of a revolution in teaching methods and materials, probably making as much use as possible of audio-visual aids on a large scale. There is certainly sufficient expertise within Tunisia to produce appropriate materials and to organise such a programme, but a lot of financial aid would be required to provide the technical infrastructure in terms of equipment and trained personnel. In the secondary system, this should lead logically to a greater variety in the foreign languages taught, a desirable step as Tunisia's economic future will almost certainly be linked closely to the European Economic Community. Here again the relevant donors could do worse than bear in mind the example of the joint Ford Foundation/British Council English language teaching project. The Bourguiba Institute (see p. 173) could well play a leading role in developing a greater variety in foreign language teaching in secondary schools, as it already has annexes in some of the main provincial towns outside Tunis. One must stress that there is no reason why French should not always be the first foreign language in Tunisia; this would be only logical. At present (January 1972) French has more than the status of a foreign language; it remains the principal means of communication for the country's social and intellectual elite.

The most ironical aspect of education in Tunisia is that the basic French model has been an object of severe criticism within its own society, particularly since 1968. In those technologically advanced countries which permit open debate and relatively free expression of opinion, there has been a great deal of self-examination and criticism around the nature and objectives of education; those countries to which many former colonies or protectorates looked for the secrets of progress and power have lost the air of omniscience which in some way accompanied their apparent omnipotence. Such a situation would seem to demand a more restricted type of development aid for education. In Tunisia there will long remain urgent needs for donor countries to provide appropriate finance and equipment for educational purposes, but beyond that the country has sufficient intellectual potential to create its own cultural destiny.

6 India

L. S. Chandrakant, assisted by M. Wasi and K. Rangachari

I HISTORICAL INTRODUCTION

India is among a dozen of nearly seventy developing countries which are at the bottom of the scale of economic growth because of an annual per capita income of less than Rs. 100 and a low rate of increase in the GNP. Yet, like China, she stands apart from most of the others by reason of her size, history and cultural heritage. The people of India were exposed to modern Western ideas in the nineteenth and twentieth centuries, like all other inhabitants of former colonial territories who have now gained independence; but there was a difference in the impact of the ideas on the minds of Indians. There was both acceptance of, and resistance to Western influence for reasons largely rooted in the social and cultural patterns which were the legacy of the country's long and troubled history. The partial acceptance accounts for the endurance of democratic institutions grafted on the political system which, in other areas, have either disappeared or come under serious strain. It also explains the growth of a modern sector which in parts compares well with that of some developed countries, and also India's pioneering efforts in economic planning through democratic institutions. The partial rejection or non-acceptance of modern ideas in some areas is seen in the slow progress towards the elimination of social inequalities and traditional practices which impede national integration and slow down the adoption of improved techniques of production in agriculture and rural occupations.

India's unity through history lay in its culture, not in its nationalism; this culture has its roots in antiquity and many of the oldest traditions have been preserved without a break to this day. The consciousness of the antiquity of their heritage among the Hindus and the exaggerated importance attached to it may have been responsible for the resistance to social change owing to the fear that change would involve a loss of social or cultural identity. The Indus Valley civilisation, usually known as the Harappa culture, belonged to the early part of the third millennium B.C.; it owed little to the cultures of the Middle East but showed a highly-developed capacity for town planning, with bathrooms and sewers for each house, thus anticipating by several centuries the drainage systems of the Romans. The Harappan culture used implements of copper and bronze and handled a pictographic script. 'Pre-Aryan India', says Basham, 'made certain advances in husbandry for which the whole world owes her a debt.' But the Indus Valley culture left no living tradition for later generations. India's history begins with the Aryans, who entered the country in the second millennium B.C. and later composed the Vedic hymns handed down by word of mouth with few changes until the present day. Collectively, the Vedas show the Aryans as a pastoral and agricultural people, without a city culture; the religious ideas of the Vedas have survived to the present day and contribute a living tradition, influencing the religious and philosophical ideas of present-day Hindus, including those who have had access to Western scientific education.

Sanskrit had even then developed as a fine and sophisticated language to express the hymns of the *Rig Veda*, and its vocabulary was furhter enriched in the early years of the first millennium B.C.; phonetics and grammar was evolved until the great grammarian, Panini, stabilised and standardised the structure of the language in the fourth century B.C. Basham observes: 'Panini's grammar is one of the greatest intellectual achievements of any ancient civilisation and the most detailed and scientific grammer composed before the 19th century in any part of the world.' Sanskrit gradually became the mother of all Indian languages and though it was never the language of the masses, it served as the *lingua franca* for the intellectuals interested in the philosophical and religious commentaries and controversies and as the langauge of the great epics, authoritative texts on astronomy, mathematics, medicine, logic, architecture and sculpture and the medium of India's finest literary works by great masters like Kalidasa, Dandin and Bhavabhuti which have received universal acclaim. In southern India, Tamil had similarly developed its own style and grammar and the Tamil literary academics mentioned by tradition, though not conclusively established by historical evidence, existed several centuries before the Christian era.

Great dynasties rose and fell in the Indian sub-continent between the time of Alexander's invasion (326 B.C.) which coincided with the founding of the great Mauryan empire (the most illustrious descendant of which was the Emperor Asoka) and the end of Hindu hegemony after the Muslim invasions at the end of the ninth century A.D. The most highly sophisticated treatise on a model administrative and governmental organisation under an absolute monarchy was produced by Kautilya (or

Chanakya) in the fourth century B.C. and his Arthasastra can well compare with Machiavelli's *Prince*. The early years of the Christian era were marked by a literary efflorescence of which Kalidasa's poetry and drama are the finest examples. Greek astronomy probably influenced the Indian signs of the zodiac and the seven-day week, but Indian astronomers made much headway on their own because of their superior mathematical attainments. Indian notions of cosmology were such as to invite Macaulay's ridicule in the nineteenth century but the astronomer Aryabhata, who lived in the fifth century, suggested that the earth revolved round the sun and rotated on its own axis. India had developed mathematics to a stage far more advanced than any other nation. Largely because of the clearer conception of abstract numbers by Indian mathematicians, the rudimentary algebra based on a simple decimal notation facilitated more complicated calculations than the Greeks could manage with their mensuration and geometry. Later, the Arabs carried back to the West these mathematical attainments – including the decimal system, zero and infinity and the value of π developed by the three great Indian mathematicians, Brahmagupta, Mahavira and Bhaskara who lived between the seventh and twelfth centuries A.D.

The indigenous systems of Indian medicine as they are practised even today, owe their basic ideas to the textbooks of Charaka (first century A.D.) and Susruta (fourth century A.D.). Interest in this field was stimulated by the Indians' curiosity about physiology arising out of the practice of yoga and the missionary activity of the Buddhist monks in healing. An empirical type of surgery was also evolved for bone-setting and plastic surgery to remove deformities. Because of the intense interest in metaphysical problems the Hindus had also developed a distinctive system of logic contained in Gautama's Nyaya Sutras written in the early centuries of the Christian era. That the Aryans knew the heptatonic scale in music is evident from the Sama Veda, which laid down rules for liturgical chanting; a complete system of 'classical' music and dancing was developed later in Bharata Natyasastra which is followed even to this day. Finally, only bare mention can be made here of the progress of architecture, beginning from the utilitarian brick houses of the Harappa culture to the Buddhist *stupas* of the period before the Christian era at Sanchi and Bharhut and the cave temples and, finally, of Pallava architecture in the south and the excellence of mediaeval temple construction based on earlier models and principles. Similarly, sculpture and painting, though largely inspired by religious themes, show great vitality and adherence to certain traditional forms and rules laid down for their practitioners.

Throughout these centuries Indians always had some contact with the Hellenic world, particularly with the Romans with whom they traded, and with the peoples of South-East Asia who still retain traces of cultural and religious influences from India. An understanding of India's cultural heritage is relevant to the appreciation of the Indian response to the challenges posed first, by the Muslim and later, by the British conquest of the country and the search by intellectuals for new equations with Western science and political ideas after the achievement of independence. These achievements did not perhaps benefit the masses of the people who continued to till the soil or provide hard manual labour for construction, living in their stagnant village communities, impervious to changes around them. The caste system, which has remained rigid throughout history, prevented any fair sharing of the common heritage. There was hardly any advance over the brilliant work of the astronomers and mathematicians during the succeeding centuries. Partly perhaps as the result of Muslim rule during this period, intellectual achievement was confined to the theologians. Cultural stagnation and internal decay had set in with the Muslim conquest, perhaps as an inevitable consequence of the loss of political freedom and of royal patronage which generally encouraged arts and letters. Jawaharlal Nehru in his *Discovery of India* says:

> The Indian social structure had given amazing stability to Indian civilisation. It had given strength and cohesion to the group, but this came in the way of expansion and a larger cohesion . . . So long as that structure afforded avenues for growth and expansion, it was progressive; when it reached the limits of expansion open to it, it became stationary, unprogressive, and later, inevitably repressive.

However, it is possible to compare and contrast this Indian stagnation under Muslim rule with the response (even while being denied political freedom) to the opportunities opened up by English education and the contact with Western science and modern ideas. Barbara Ward, who regards the British conquest of India as the catalyst required for change, mentions the 'wise, liberal and moderate response on the Indian side to the intellectual and spiritual challenge offered by British rule and ideas.' A momentous step was taken by the British in 1834 when Lord William Bentinck and Macaulay decided to impart Western education and a knowledge of science to Indians in English. English replaced Persian as the court language and the medium of higher courts of law; the codification of public laws completed by 1861 opened up, according to Percival Spear, an area in which Indians attained a high position and 'their subtle minds had the fullest play'. In a sense these constituted the real beginnings of Western educational aid to India and set it on the road to modernisation. The flow of English teachers and books to India and the opposite movement of students and publicists to the West to make or renew contacts with Western institutions, created a fruitful partnership.

Thc limitations of the caste system still continued to restrict educational and other opportunities to the socially privileged groups; but

India was able within a century of the introduction of English education to produce its own professional classes – lawyers, scientists, engineers, doctors, civil servants, military personnel, accountants, businessmen and, not least, politicians – and to achieve self-reliance in the supply of trained personnel in all but a few complex branches of modern science and technology. This was undoubtedly due to the eagerness and enthusiasm of the Indian middle class to benefit by the new opportunities, even though its first result was to underpin colonial rule by producing trusted subordinates for the British Raj. This highly receptive middle class was the product of the same caste system which was believed to have caused the stagnation of the Middle Ages. After the encounter with the West, it helped to fill a vacuum in Indian public life by providing timely leadership in many fields which needed it on the withdrawal of the foreign power.

The moral of this brief excursion into Indian history is that the absorptive capacity of international educational aid to India has always been very high, and for that reason the scope for providing it in the last two decades, unlike the trend in other developing countries, became limited and has gradually shrunk.

II BACKGROUND TO ECONOMIC PLANNING

During the quarter of a century since India's independence, political, social and economic conditions have undergone considerable changes, though the basic problems of poverty, illiteracy and low rate of economic growth remain to be solved. Over 186 million people, constituting over 50 per cent of the population in 1947, have been added during these twenty-five years; in spite of frequent periods of drought and food shortages, these additional people have been fed, most of them perhaps at bare subsistence levels. This was no mean achievement, considering the constraints on resources and economic growth. A parliamentary system has been in operation and five nation-wide elections have been held on the basis of adult suffrage (many more in some states). The working of the basic democratic processes, promoting increasing consciousness of the citizen's rights and providing opportunities for the periodical expression of his rising expectations and dissatisfactions, offers a striking contrast to their failure in many other developing societies. So does the working of a complex federal polity after the successful integration of politically, socially and economically disparate units consisting of the British-administered areas and nearly six hundred Princely states. They have all held together in spite of the diversity of interests and aspirations, promoted freedom of movement and removed barriers to trade, commerce and communications which might otherwise have impeded unity and growth.

One political party – the Indian National Congress – has provided the leadership for what has been achieved and it still remains the only viable party to provide stability in the administration of the nation's affairs, in spite of some brief setbacks since 1967. The parliamentary system is to that extent incomplete, but continuity has been a major gain of this dominance by one party. Similarly the administrative services organised under the British Raj have survived, though their quality has suffered by expansion, and have reinforced stability provided by the Congress party. In spite of declining efficiency, both the party and the services have shown an inclination to review their shortcomings from time to time and have tried to take lessons from other systems. In this respect, however, both have been slower learners than the Armed Forces, which have been repeatedly challenged to prove their worth; except for the major reverses in 1962 against China, they have risen to the occasion and also shown a capacity to learn the use of modern weapon systems and be self-reliant in defending the country. The Indianised army has also maintained the best democratic traditions by its subordination to political authority and its willingness and readiness to help it out in difficult situations, but only when called upon to do so. These three centres of stability – political, administrative and military – have drawn extensively on Western practice and experience to find solutions to their problems, largely because historically they were trained to do so. This is also true of the Indian press and the judiciary which by and large have fulfilled their roles, finding their models in Western democratic systems. At the institutional levels, therefore, the obstacles to modernisation have been fewer in India than in many other traditional societies marching on the same road. At the social or personal levels, however, the experience has been different and varies widely because of the strong influence of caste and custom.

An important area in which India's leadership has been responsible for innovation is in launching a centrally-planned economic development long before it became respectable in Western democratic systems. The Indian Planning Commission was set up in 1950 as an extra-constitutional body immediately after the Republican Constitution came into force. To this day it continues to influence decisions on investment, both public and private, and to determine economic policy despite the uneven results of the four Five-Year Plans so far implemented. The task of dovetailing private sector programmes in industry, agriculture, transport and other services into the Government's own plans is a complex one; equally so is coordination of the programmes of the State Government which are autonomous in their field of constitutional powers. Coordination has however been successfully accomplished because of the Union's own wide-ranging authority over foreign trade and aid, its role in mobilisation of resources through taxation and borrowing and their allocation, and, not least, by the continued sway of a single political party over the centre and in several, if not all, of the states. The Government's wide powers for licensing industry, control of investment and prices of essential articles, and for regulation of joint stock companies have been adequate to make the private sector fall in line with the Government's policies. In all these respects, the Indian authorities have gone further than the Western democracies from which they very often derived their inspiration or ideas. This institutional basis was firmly laid long before foreign aid flowed in to supplement domestic saving on a substantial scale after 1956; only technical assistance under President Truman's Point Four and the Colombo Plan were generally under discussion before 1956.

Economic and social development during the period since 1950–1, covered by four Five-Year Plans and three annual plans, may be broadly divided into three phases. The first was a period of stabilisation of the economy which lasted until the beginning of the second Five-Year Plan in 1956, which enabled it to recover from the effects of inflation during the Second World War and the distortions created by partition of the subcontinent. This phase is also marked by the foundations laid for institutional changes relating to the operations of the private and public sectors. Economic growth to the extent achieved belongs to the next phase covered by the Second and Third Plans (1956–66), although there were many critical periods marked by a foreign exchange crisis, inflationary prices and the distractions of a war with China in 1962. These difficulties, aggravated by failure of rains and another war with Pakistan in 1965, compelled a planning holiday for the next three years (1966–9) which meant mere annual outlays to continue work on on-going schemes. The Fourth Plan period (1969–74) has more or less continued the stagnation which began in 1966, with two major exceptions; the first was the spurt in agricultural production after 1967–8 until it was interrupted by the severe drought of 1972–3; the other was the success in export promotion in 1968–9, almost for the first time since Independence, which has been maintained since.

The results of this chequered course of Indian planning may be briefly described in quantitative terms. The increase in population during these two decades at a rate of 2·3 per cent per year largely neutralised the gains of growth, which has never risen above an average annual rate of 3·5 per cent. The rate of saving in the economy has nearly doubled, from less than 6 per cent at the beginning of planning. The state's share of the national income secured through taxation has risen from less than 7 per cent in 1950–1 to nearly 17 per cent now. Food production has increased sufficiently to take care of the additional population in good years, though the fluctuations in bad years are too large to admit of self-reliance. The period of agricultural prosperity for five years from 1967 to 1972 witnessed a revolution in wheat production but only modest improvements in all other crops brought about by more irrigation, supply of modern inputs, offer of price incentives and use of improved varieties.

The industrial structure has been diversified by the creation of substantial capacity for steel making, engineering products including railway wagons and coaches, aircraft manufacture, machine-building units, production of many modern chemicals and drugs, installation of oil refineries and petro-chemical complexes besides further expansion of established industries like cement, sugar and textiles. Substantial investment in railway transport has more than doubled the capacity for carrying goods traffic on one of the world's largest railway networks covering 60,000 kilometres of track. Power generation has increased tenfold but is still far below the increasing demand from industry and agriculture. All this has involved considerable inflationary financing particularly after defence-needs secured equal priority with development. As a result prices have risen steeply, particularly during the sixties. While no reliable estimates are available for the employment generated by the Plans in the rural and unorganised sectors, it appears that in the organised sector covering both public and private employment, the annual rate of increase of about 6 per cent until the middle of the sixties has now declined to about 2 per cent a year. In the rural areas, however, five years of relative agricultural prosperity may have softened the effect of this sharp decline in new job opportunities.

The strengthening of the social infrastructure for development is one of the major objectives of planning and here again the results are much below expectations. The percentage of literates in the population has risen from 17 to 30 in these two decades; not all children of school-going age are yet in school and female literacy is still below 17 per cent. While much work has been done for the eradication of communicable diseases, the effects of which are seen in the higher average life expectation (over 50 years), health and medical services have not been sufficiently extended to rural areas. However, there are more roads and post offices; many more villages have been electrified. The direction of these many-sided efforts in planning has been unquestionably right but progress has been less than adequate and the failures have not been entirely the result of unforeseen developments though these have contributed much to them.

III EDUCATION AND SOCIETY IN INDIA

'The destiny of India is now being shaped in her classrooms', began the Education Commission Report published in 1966. 'This, we believe', it went on,

> is no mere rhetoric. In a world based on science and technology, it is education that determines the level of prosperity, welfare and security of the people. On the quality and number of persons coming out of our schools and colleges will depend our success in the great enterprise of national reconstruction, whose principal objective is to raise the standard of living of our people.

In 1974 there is nothing particularly revolutionary about such a statement, and even in 1966 it reflected advanced thinking in India, but to pre-1947 India it would have come as a shock. For one thing, the concept of national education is comparatively new. Pre-1947 India thought, for the most part, in terms of an elite that had been provided for throughout the nineteenth century, and that, it was assumed, would govern India at that unspecified date at which she became a self-governing dominion. Besides, the crucial importance of education in national development is comparatively new. Gone are the old Socratic ideas of truth as the objective of education. By 1966, and even earlier, it had become clear that people are, or should be, educated in relation to the needs of a given society. Into this society they must fit as if moulded for it, to add to its wealth and well-being. The close connection between education and the economic well-being of a people (and not merely a few million individuals) was now articulated with the confidence that this was the only acceptable way to educate for the twentieth century.

The Education Commission left little to the imagination. It spelt out its meaning by indicating the nature of the democratic educational revolution that had taken, and was taking, place in India.

> This direct link between education, national development and prosperity . . . exists only when the national system of education is properly organised, from both qualitative and quantitative points of view. The naive belief that ALL education is necessarily good for the individual or for society, and that it will necessarily lead to progress, can be as harmful as it is misplaced. Quantitatively, education can be organised to promote social justice or to retard it . . . a social and cultural revolution has been brought about in a system where equality of educational opportunity is provided and education is deliberatley used to develop more and more potential talent and to harness it to the solution of national problems . . . It is only the right type of education provided on an adequate scale that can lead to national development; when these conditions are not satisfied, the opposite effect may result.

Of the sort of education that had prevailed before 1947, the Commission had this to say in brief:

i. It did not reflect the supreme importance of agriculture which was neglected at all stages and did not attract an adequate share of the top talent of the country.

ii. The system was too academic to be of material help in increasing national wealth.

iii. Schools and colleges were largely unconcerned with the great national effort at reconstruction and their teachers and students were generally uncommitted to it. They were often unaware of its principles and rarely had opportunities to participate in its programmes.

iv. Several features in the educational system promoted divisive tendencies instead of social and national integration. Caste loyalties were encouraged; rich and poor were segregated in schools.

v. Education did not emphasise character formation and made little effort to cultivate moral and social values and particularly interests and attitudes that were needed for a democratic and socialistic society.

In purely quantitative terms, what was the relative position at focal points in education between 1950, which, for all practical purposes provides the figures at Independence, and 1972?

The total number of children in primary schools in classes 1–8 covering age group 6–14 years in 1950 was 16–17 million. In 1972 it was 75·5 million. Enrolment in secondary schools covering age group 14–17 years rose from 1·8 million in 1950 to about 7 million in 1972. Undergraduate enrolment rose from 18,000 in 1950 to 165,000 in 1972. Professional course enrolment rose from 263,000 in 1950 to approximately 365,000 in 1972. The total expenditure on education in 1950 was Rs. 1444 million. in 1972 it was Rs. 10,938·6 million approximately.

Nor was the change merely one of dimension. The quantitative expansion in fact reflected a radically changed attitude towards education that was not confined to India but that characterised postwar educational development all over the world. The end of the Second World War saw the beginning of a period of liberation, of deliberate national planning for masses of under-privileged peoples and of faith in education as the most potent single instrument of change. To this, more than to anything else, millions of people looked with hope and faith. In many traditional societies such as India's, awareness of the need to move towards modernity and that proverbial place in the sun was bound up with the belief that this was possible only through education. The clamour for education in the big cities and towns was insistent, and even the rural areas of the country were not untouched by the prospect of a better life through learning. A new ferment in education set in, that has grown with the twenty-six years of Indian Independence.

In its preamble, the Indian Constitution, promulgated in 1950, crystallised the new aspirations of the Indian people:

We, the People of India, having solemnly resolved to constitute India into a Sovereign Democratic Republic, and to secure to all its citizens:

JUSTICE, social, economic and political,

LIBERTY of thought, expression, belief, faith and worship;

EQUALITY of status and opportunity; and to promote among them all

FRATERNITY assuring the dignity of the individual and the unity of the nation in our Constituent Assembly, this twenty-sixth day of

November 1949 do hereby adopt, enact and give to ourselves this Constitution.

The egalitarian spirit of the Constitution was reflected in its directive principles of state policy. Thus, Article 38 read: 'The State shall strive to promote the welfare of the people by securing and protecting as effectively as it may a social order in which justice, social, economic and political shall inform all the institutions of the national life.' Article 43 read: 'The State shall endeavour to secure by suitable legislation or economic organisation or in any other way to all workers, agricultural and industrial or otherwise, work, a living wage, conditions of work ensuring a decent standard of life and full enjoyment of leisure and social and cultural opportunities.' Article 45 read: 'The State shall endeavour to provide within a period of ten years from the commencement of this Constitution for free and compulsory education for all children until they complete the age of fourteen years.' Article 46 read: 'The State shall promote with special care the educational and economic interests of the weaker sections of the people and in particular of the Scheduled Castes and Scheduled Tribes and shall protect them from social injustice and all forms of exploitation.'

The four Five-Year Plans that have characterised the twenty-six years of Indian Independence tend to give the impression that the concept of planning and of educational planning began with Independence. This is not entirely so. There is evidence in the Report of Post-War Educational Development in India (more generally known as the Sargent Report, after Sir John Sargent, who was its inspiration) published in 1944, that sustained thought had gone into how to provide India with a system of education approximating to those available in other countries.

> The Central Advisory Board of Education (CABE) have devoted their attention in recent years to surveying the main fields of educational activity with a view to ascertaining what would be the minimum provision required. Since their re-constitution in 1935, they have set up Committees to study and report upon the following among other subjects (i) Basic education (two reports) (ii) Adult education (iii) Special welfare of school children (iv) School buildings (v) Social service (vi) The recruitment, training and conditions of service of teachers in primary, middle and high schools. (vii) The recruitment of Education officers, (viii) Technical (including commercial and art) education. At their last two meetings they reviewed the recommendations of these committees with special reference to post-war needs and to the possibility of post-war developments, and they are satisfied that, subject to such modifications as will be indicated in this report, they provide the foundations upon which an efficient system of public instruction suited to the needs and circumstances of this country can effectively be erected . . .

The main conclusion of the Report's crucial first chapter was:

> A system of universal compulsory and free education for all boys and girls between the ages of six and fourteen should be introduced as speedily as possible, though in view of the practical difficulty of recruiting the requisite supply of trained teachers, it may not be possible to complete it in less than forty years.

Article 45 of the Constitution, referred to above, sought to reduce this period to a quarter of the time. Since 100 per cent enrolment in this age group has still not been achieved in 1974, the Sargent Plan has been demonstrated to be not unduly cautious.

IV TECHNOLOGY AND NATIONAL DEVELOPMENT

Capital, natural resources, foreign aid, international trade, government and social institutions play their respective roles in modernising a developing economy, but the most important of all factors in development is man. It is the urges and know-how of men that finally determine whether minerals and oil will stay underground or be converted into instruments of industry, whether roads remain tracks or become arteries of commerce, whether people remain hungry and naked or are fed and clothed. IN THE FINAL ANALYSIS ALL DEVELOPMENT STUDIES HANG ON THIS: THE EDUCATION, TRAINING AND ENGINEERING OF HUMAN RESOURCES.

Indian Industrial Commission 1916–18

Of the several Commissions and Committees convened before 1947 that advised the Government of India to train people on an adequate scale for modernisation, the most important was the Indian Industrial Commission of 1916–18. To the problem of industrial and technical education, the Commission devoted an entire chapter, analysing the role of education in the development of industrial societies in the West. Scientific research, it pointed out, had been encouraged and its practical application ran parallel with new industrial ventures by merchants and other entrepreneurs. There was no comparable activity in India and the Commission considered it essential that industrial and technical education should be provided to build up an industrial community capable of achieving industrial development for India.

Between 1847 and 1858 four engineering colleges had been established in India chiefly for the training of civil engineers for the Provincial and Central Public Works Departments. Other branches of engineering had also to be supported. The Commission said:

> . . . the higher branches of the engineering services in the country absorb but a very small proportion of the engineering students who pass through the colleges, and the rest enter the upper subordinate ranks or

find private employment of a not very remunerative character. The greater part of the work done in each college is the training of upper subordinates, lower subordinates, surveyors and draughtsmen. In the four principal colleges, increasing attention has in recent years been paid to the provision of instruction in mechanical and electrical engineering; but the measures adopted are inadequate and are conceived on altogether too narrow lines to meet the needs present and prospective of a rapidly expanding industrial system. In mechanical engineering which, outside the railway workshops, is mainly carried on by private enterprise, we find that in the absence of a proper system of training, they have seldom attained to positions of importance or responsibility. In practically all the engineering workshops which we have visited, we found the same state of affairs existing with regard to the superior staff as we had seen in the case of foremen. The former, whether assistants or managers, were men who had been trained as mechanical engineers in Great Britain.

The Commission proposed that higher technological education should be organised as follows:

It will be necessary in the immediate future for Government to consider the more general question of the part to be played by the existing engineering colleges and the Universities, in providing for the increasing need in India for scientific, technical and technological training. It is urgently necessary to prepare for a higher technical training, which will provide the means whereby the physical science students of the colleges affiliated to the Universities may learn to apply their knowledge to industrial uses. The simplest way of meeting this demand would be to expand the engineering colleges into technological institutes by the creation of new departments . . .

It will be necessary ultimately if not in the immediate future to provide India with educational institutions of a more advanced character, which no single Province could support or fill with students, yet which each Province will need to a greater or less extent. For some time to come the demand for this higher training can best be met by the provision of scholarships to enable students to proceed abroad, but as soon as our foregoing recommendations have had time to develop their full effect, it would be advisable to proceed further and establish an Imperial College of Technology of the very highest grade. Two at least will be needed, staffed with specialists of high reputation who must be provided with adequate equipment for both teaching and research work. One of these colleges should cover every branch of engineering, while the other should be devoted mainly to metallurgy and mineral technology, the developments of which are certain to be on a very extensive scale . . . If the ideal of a self-sufficing India is to be completely carried out, specialisation must be provided for, and this can only be achieved in colleges with a large number of advanced students.

The recommendations of the Commission stimulated industrial development and new enterprises started for iron and steel, textiles, chemicals and engineering goods manufacture. All these demanded more engineers and technicians. Provincial governments started new engineering colleges and polytechnics. Courses of study were diversified and more provision made to train mechanical and electrical engineers, metallurgists, mining engineers, industrial chemists and textile technologists.

War and postwar development

When the Second World War broke out India was in a position to support the war effort from within her own industrial infrastructure and her manpower resources. She became a major supplier of war materials. New industries were established and engineering colleges and polytechnics trained the necessary technical manpower. A War-time Technical Training Scheme was started to train craftsmen for the Defence Services.

The war ended sooner than expected and plans were formulated for postwar construction. Four decisions were made. *First*, the Government established in 1946 an All-India Council for Technical Education as a national organisation to coordinate development in technical education at all levels. The Council drew up comprehensive plans to improve existing institutions and to establish new ones. It formulated plans to reorganise courses to provide instructional facilities. It set up boards of studies and regional committees to watch continuously over the progress of technical education, to formulate developmental programmes and to establish liaison between industry and technical institutions.

Secondly, an expert Committee under the chairmanship of the late Nilratan Sircar was appointed in 1945 to formulate plans for the establishment of advanced technological institutes. Four higher technological institutes were proposed, one in each region of India, for advanced studies and research in engineering applied sciences. Each would have an enrolment of about 2000 students in first degree courses and about 1000 in postgraduate courses and research. Each would cover a wide range of important fields in engineering and technology and would provide for the effective interaction of science and engineering with fully-fledged departments of physics, chemistry, mathematics and the humanities and social sciences.

Thirdly, an Advisory Committee was appointed in 1944 to review the working of the War Technicians' Training Scheme and to recommend the lines along which it should be reorganised. The Committee recommended a comprehensive scheme to train young persons as craftsmen. A course of apprenticeship should follow a course of basic training at specially designed centres, and these should be organised and conducted on a national basis with provision for the award of National Certificates of Craftsmanship.

Finally, in 1947 a Scientific Manpower Committee was appointed to assess the requirements for various classes of scientific and technical personnel and to recommend measures to meet them. A plan was made to meet the requirements. The Committee established for the first time in India the concept and methodology of integrated manpower planning as an integral part of national development activities, with the capacity to foresee future requirements and meet them through organised effort.

By 1947 when India became independent an awareness of the importance of technical education already existed. A large amount of detailed planning for expansion and improvement of such education had already been done. The successive Five-Year Plans gave high priority to technical education and training and big financial provision was made for this. A phenomenal expansion of technical education took place in the course of the next fifteen years.

Measure of growth since independence

In 1947 there were 38 engineering colleges in India with an admission capacity of 2940 students each year for first degree courses. There were 53 polytechnics with an admission capacity for 3670 students a year for diploma courses. Today, there are 138 engineering colleges with an admission capacity of about 22,000 students a year for first degree courses. The number of polytechnics shot up to 238 and their admission capacity is 50,000 a year. The number of graduate engineers trained per year has risen from 1270 in 1947 to over 18,000 today. Similarly the number of diploma-technicians from polytechnics has risen from 1440 to over 25,000 for the same period.

A base of trained manpower for economic development has been correspondingly built up. There are 355 industrial training institutes with a total of 155,000 training places in 32 engineering and 22 non-engineering trades. Each institute turns out 50,000 trained craftsmen per year. Under the Apprentices Act of 1961 the further training of these craftsmen on the job is carried on. To ensure that the training is purposeful and oriented to continuing national needs the National Council for Training in Vocational Trades and the Central Apprenticeship Council were set up. These advise governments on training policies, standards of training, curricula for theoretical and practical instruction and the training of teachers. They award National Trade Certificates and National Apprenticeship Certificates.

Technological self-reliance implies that India must produce her own scientists and engineers for design, development, research, teaching and all other high-level scientific and technical activities. When the Second World War ended, a scheme of Overseas Scholarship was instituted under which brilliant young Indians were selected and sent to the United Kingdom, United States and other countries for advanced study and research. Under the scheme, over 1000 scientists and engineers were trained abroad and brought back to staff India's National Research Laboratories, her engineering institutions, industry and government organisations.

Moreover, the Five-Year Plans demanded a large number of high-grade engineers for design and developmental work in industry. A beginning was made to meet this need with the establishment of higher technological institutes planned by the Sircar Committee of 1945–6. The first was set up in 1951 at Kharagpur. This was followed by four more institutes within a period of ten years at Bombay, Madras, Kanpur and New Delhi.

The five IITs are apex institutions for the highest forms of engineering education and research. Incorporated as institutions of national importance, they conduct first degree courses in a wide range of engineering subject-fields, Masters' courses and research courses for doctoral degrees. The main emphasis is on postgraduate studies and research with an inter-disciplinary approach. First-rate departments of physics, chemistry, mathematics and social sciences interact with departments of engineering and technology. Student enrolment at each IIT is about 1500 at first degree level, and 800 at postgraduate and research level.

Foreign aid in technical education

India has received much valuable aid from foreign countries and international agencies in the establishment and development of her Institutes of Technology. The Bombay Institute was assisted by the USSR and UNESCO; the Madras Institute by the Federal Republic of Germany; the Kanpur Institute by the United States and the Delhi Institute by the United Kingdom. Each institute has assembled an excellent faculty of international expertise and has organised extensive facilities for advanced study and research. Each is developing peaks of excellence in selected areas. For instance, the Kanpur Institute is now a centre of excellence for systems engineering and computer science, materials technology, nuclear engineering and electronics; the Madras Institute emphasises production engineering, precision mechanics and heat power engineering. The Bombay Institute is an advanced centre for aeronautical engineering and is being developed as a centre of excellence for knowledge on aircraft propulsion technology, aircraft systems and aircraft production technology. At Kharagpur, the areas of excellence include metallurgy, structural engineering, electric power systems, naval architecture and ship building. The Delhi Institute concentrates on electric machine design, electronics, water power engineering and textile technology.

Another institute of national importance, with an accent on postgraduate studies in engineering, is the Indian Institute of Science at Bangalore that was established in 1911 through the foresight and generosity of Jamshedjee Tata. It has built up a high reputation in scientific research. In 1946 it was decided to develop it into an institute for advanced study and research in technology and to promote there the interaction of pure and applied sciences. Ten years from Independence the institute became a centre of advanced technology with emphasis on power engineering, aeronautical engineering, metallurgy, internal combustion engineering and electrical communication engineering. It now provides facilities for nearly a thousand postgraduate students and research scholars.

Technical institutions constantly exposed to the powerful influence of industrial development and scientific progress should have the capacity for growth to project themselves into the future and to anticipate changes, preparing their alumni to meet new challenges. A deliberate policy to develop as many engineering institutions as possible for postgraduate studies and research was formulated and implemented particularly during the third and fourth Plan periods. Today, a network of over fifty institutions in India exist that offer Masters' courses in a wide range of subject-fields with about 4000 places.

Need for managerial skills

For centuries an agricultural economy, India today has laid a strong industrial base for all rural development. She is setting up giant steel plants, machine building plants, oil refineries, petro-chemical units, fertiliser plants and a host of other manufacturing units. To support this base, she is expanding her infrastructure in terms of transport, communications and electric power. She is also reorganising her financial institutions. All this implies the development of modern technological know-how, sophisticated plant and engineering equipment, a big labour force including scientists, engineers and skilled workers trained with professional competence. We need the best managerial ability, foresight precision and cohesion exceeding anything we have yet known. Modern management implies special training. The modern manager must acquire the necessary skills to meet the challenges of a higher technological age.

Two fully-fledged Institutes of Management that conduct MBA courses and executive development programmes have been established at Ahmedabad and Calcutta. Two more are in the process of being established at Bangalore and Lucknow. Also, postgraduate departments of management studies have been set up at twenty-four university centres. An Administrative College, a National Institute of Industrial Engineering and other specialised centres of management studies have been established.

Expansion in higher science education

Alongside the development of technology since Independence, there has been a general expansion of general university education, particularly in the sciences. In 1947 India had only twenty universities with an enrolment of about 266,000 students. Today the number of universities has shot up to 101 and the enrolment to over 3·2 million. At Masters' level in science the number qualifying has risen from less than 800 in 1947 to over 15,000 today. The number of doctorates has increased from about 80 in 1947 to 1200 today. More important still, seventeen advanced centres of sciences have been developed at universities for the highest levels of scientific education and research. Each is equipped with the most modern and sophisticated laboratory facilities and staffed with outstanding scientists who can hold their own with their counterparts in the developed world. In the establishment and development of these centres of advanced studies Indian universities have received much valuable assistance from UNESCO and UNDP.

How valuable has foreign aid been?

As a developing country *par excellence* India has formulated and implemented four successive Five-Year Plans and is now poised for a fifth Plan. To support these Plans she has built up a vast infrastructure of human resources of which nothing comparable exists in other developing countries.

The questions that now suggest themselves are: how has foreign aid, whether from international agencies or on a bilateral basis from individual countries, helped in this development process? What considerations of policy have governed India in accepting and utilising foreign aid? Could we have pursued alternative strategies and achieved the same results without foreign aid?

Though India's economic development started after 1947, or more precisely after 1951, she had a well-structured public education system for well over a century before then. It was elitest, urban-based and restricted to a small section of the people. It had many of the defects typical of colonial countries. Nevertheless, an organised system of education and training did exist, which provided leadership in administration, industry, research and other important walks of national life. Engineering and technical education and training had made some advance, and India was becoming more self-reliant in technical and scientific manpower. Several industrial enterprises had been established that relied upon the raw material and manpower resources of the country. At Independence the base for industrial development and the necessary resources to train manpower existed. Upon these, India was able to build what was necessary for her Plans.

She recognised early that it is axiomatic in economic development that science and technology must play a vital role in increasing agricultural and industrial productivity. Also, that the mere availability of science and technology does not guarantee that economic development will automatically occur. If the productive processes are to be speeded up, men must be trained to apply science and technology on a broad front. This application in fact became a sheet-anchor of India's economic development Plans.

Scientific policy resolution

That manpower planning is an essential element of national development was recognised early and the need was seen to build up the skills, knowledge and competence required for economic progress and to provide industry with productive and socially useful employment. The articulation of this strategy as part of a national policy was extremely well expressed in the Scientific Policy Resolution passed by the Indian Parliament in 1958:

> 1. The key to national prosperity, apart from the spirit of the people, lies, in the modern age, in the effective combination of three factors, technology, raw materials and capital, in which the first is perhaps the most important, since the creation and adoption of new scientific techniques can in fact make up for a deficiency in national resources and reduce the demand on capital. But technology can only grow out of the study of science and its applications . . .
> 3. It is only through the scientific approach and method and the use of scientific knowledge that reasonable material and cultural amenities and services can be provided for every member of the community, and it is out of a recognition of this possibility that the idea of a welfare state has grown. It is characteristic of the present world that the progress towards the practical realisation of a welfare state differs widely from country to country in direct relation to the extent of industrialisation and the effort and resources applied in the pursuit of science . . .
> 4. The wealth and prosperity of a nation depend on the effective utilisation of its human and material resources through industrialisation. The use of human material for industrialisation demands its education in science and training in technical skills. Industry opens up possibilities of greater fulfilment for the individual. India's enormous resources of manpower can only become an asset in the modern world when trained and educated . . .
> 7. The Government of India have accordingly decided that the aims of their scientific policy will be:
>
> i. to foster, promote and sustain by all appropriate means, the cultivation of science and scientific research in all its aspects – pure, applied and educational;

ii. to ensure an adequate supply within the country of research scientists of the higher quality and to recognise their work as an important component of the strength of the nation;

iii. to encourage and initiate with all possible speed programmes for the training of scientific and technical personnel on a scale adequate to fulfil the country's needs in science and education, agriculture and industry and defence;

iv. to ensure that the creative talent of men and women is encouraged and finds full scope in scientific activity;

v. to encourage individual initiative for the acquisition and dissemination of knowledge and for the discovery of new knowledge, in an atmosphere of academic freedom;

vi. and in general to secure for the people of the country all benefits that can accrue from the acquisition and application of scientific knowledge.

It is in this situation that India has considered foreign aid as a means of harnessing modern science and technology from the developed world to her national economic development effort. However, she has also considered that to import modern technological know-how, along with sophisticated capital equipment and industrial plants, can at best be a short-term solution. The long-term strategy is to train her own scientists and technologists who can generate and help in applying scientific and technological knowledge to their country on a continuing basis. For this, too, foreign aid is regarded as useful to build up engineering and scientific institutions, but only to the extent to which indigenous resources fail to meet the needs of the institutions in full.

These are the considerations in policy that have informed India's acceptance of foreign aid in education and her utilisation of it in institution-building for science and technology. The years between Independence and today have proved her thinking and her decision to be wise.

V INDIAN INSTITUTES OF TECHNOLOGY

The first Indian Institute of Technology was started in 1951 at Kharagpur, West Bengal. Since at that time foreign aid had not entered into the Indian strategy of economic development, the Government of India decided to 'go it alone' in the establishment and development of the Institute. India provided all the resources needed, including foreign exchange for the import of specialised scientific and technical equipment for laboratories and workshops which were not manufactured within the country. India also recruited and appointed foreign specialists for senior faculty positions wherever adequately qualified Indians were not available. Fortunately, however, for most of the faculty positions at all levels competent Indians were available, particularly from universities and other well-established engineering institutions within the country. Further, a large number of Indian scholars who had been sent abroad by the Government of India soon after the war for advanced training under the Overseas Scholarships Scheme returned, and the Institute was also able to recruit them to its faculty. Thus, the Kharagpur Institute was an indigenous enterprise that did not use foreign aid. Within seven to eight years of its establishment, the Institute made a deep impression on high-level engineering education and research in India and became a model for four other institutes which were to follow.

The experience of the Kharagpur Institute was that to build a high-level engineering institution for advanced studies and research which has to be in step with world progress in science and technology much valuable equipment not manufactured in India would be required. India has an adequate number of young and competent scientists and engineers for middle and junior level faculty positions, but for senior faculty at the level of professors, who have to organise and direct postgraduate teaching and research, there would be difficulty in finding suitable persons in India. This difficulty would be felt particularly in new fields of engineering and technology which have not developed in India. Finally, young faculty members would need to be trained further to be entrusted with the responsibility of developing the institute.

It was precisely these constraints which were sought to be removed when the next four institutes were set up between 1958–62. The second and third Five-Year Plans demanded a larger number of engineers and technologists for national development and the establishment of more Institutes of Technology became imperative. Therefore, the strategy for these new institutes visualised foreign aid, particularly for equipment, experts and training facilities for the faculty. At that stage, foreign aid in various forms had also become a part of the overall national development planning processes.

There remained the question of from which countries, or from which multinational agencies aid should be sought for these institutes. It was evident that the aid must be from those countries which were scientifically and technologically more advanced than India, had institutions comparable in standard to the proposed Institutes of Technology, and which were sympathetic to the aims and objects of the institutes and willing to assist them. However, at no stage did India actively canvass for aid for the institutes from any particular country; it only explained its national development plans to all aid-giving countries, indicated its priorities and left it to the countries concerned to decide how they could help.

The first country to come forward was the USSR in 1957, but at that time India did not have any bilateral economic aid relationship with that country. The USSR, however, had placed at the disposal of UNESCO a large amount of roubles for the promotion of science and technology in the developing countries. UNESCO, which by then had accepted the broader objective of promoting science and technology for economic development, regarded India as the most appropriate country in which the Russian rouble fund could be applied. Accordingly UNESCO and the USSR proposed and India agreed that the Institute of Technology to be set up at Bombay (the next after the Kharagpur Institute) should be assisted in its establishment and development.

The *modus operandi* was that a UNESCO mission of experts came to India to discuss the plans for the Bombay Institute and the requirements of the Institute for equipment, experts and training facilities. The discussions with Indian experts led to a concrete plan of assistance to the Institute. The plan spelled out in detail the type and specifications of laboratory and workshop equipment to be supplied, the number of experts and their fields of specialisation and the number of Indian faculty to be trained abroad.

All these requirements of the Bombay Institute were met by the USSR through UNESCO. Almost all the equipment and experts came from the USSR and the training of the Indian faculty was also conducted in that country. In order, however, to give the project an international colour, UNESCO provided a small dollar grant for the services of experts from other countries.

The next institute to be established was at Madras in 1959 with the assistance of the Federal Republic of Germany which by then had made a remarkable economic recovery after the Second World War and evinced a keen interest in Indian economic development. An FRG mission came to India to discuss how West Germany could assist India in her efforts to promote the application of science and technology to economic development. The result was the decision of West Germany to assist in the establishment and development of an Institute of Technology at Madras.

The Kanpur and Delhi Institutes of Technology then followed in 1960 and 1962 respectively, with the assistance of the United States for the former and of Britain for the latter.

In all these cases the processes of formulation of the plan of assistance was the same. Teams of Indian experts and experts from the aid-giving countries discussed and settled the details in respect of equipment, faculty assistance and training of Indian staff for each institute. The processes also included identification of the specialities of each institute and determination of how advanced teaching and research in those specialities may be best developed.

From the beginning, it was visualised that the foreign experts for each institute would come strictly in an academic advisory capacity and that they would have no responsibilities for the administration and management of the institutes. Their main role was to assist and advise in organising teaching and research in their specialities and also to train the Indian staff ultimately to take over those responsibilities. The number of foreign experts for each institute was limited to those specialities in which senior Indian faculty was not readily available.

The period of foreign aid varied from institute to institute depending upon their progress, but all agreements provided initially for a five-year period which was considered the minimum for the development of an Institute of Technology. In practically all cases, however, this period was extended to eight to ten years when additional aid was given for the further development of the institutes, as new specialities were added and postgraduate teaching and research diversified.

The following table gives an analysis of the quantum of foreign aid for each Institute of Technology up to March 1972 *vis à vis* the expenditure incurred by the Government of India.

The proportion of foreign aid to the Indian Government's contribution for the institutes varies from 1 : 1·5 to 1 : 6 for capital expenditure which includes the cost of land, buildings, equipment and libraries. The highest proportion is by West Germany to the Madras IIT and the lowest by Britain to Delhi IIT. The Indian Government's contribution also includes annual recurring expenditure of about 64 million rupees for the maintenance of the institutes. In all cases, however, foreign aid for equipment with experts and fellowships constitutes a significant contribution to the establishment and development of the institutes because these accelerated the process.

Could India have managed without foreign aid for the Institutes of Technology? This is not an easy question, because it raises the general issue of whether less-developed countries can manage their economic development without foreign aid.

We believe that the less-developed countries can 'go it alone' in their development, but the process will take very much longer. More important, in order to accelerate the process, these countries may have to resort to drastic changes in their social, political and economic structure. The net zero aid level, if forced without ensuring self-sustaining economic growth, may accentuate the difference between the developed and developing world, which may express itself in international confrontation between them.

India established the first Institute of Technology at Kharagpur in 1951 all by itself. Almost eight years passed before the next institute started at Bombay in 1958 but the Madras, Kanpur and Delhi Institutes all came into being within about five years. It is therefore evident that the role of foreign aid was to accelerate the process. If India had to establish and

Government of India contribution (million rupees)		*Foreign aid*	
1. INDIAN INSTITUTE OF TECHNOLOGY, DELHI			
Land and buildings	57·16	Equipment	Rs. 13·24 million (rupee equivalent)
Equipment, library, furniture and fittings	18·56	Experts	number: 126 man-months: 1007
Total	75·72	Fellowships	number: 78
Recurring expenditure per year	13·28		man-months: 1490
2. INDIAN INSTITUTE OF TECHNOLOGY, BOMBAY			
Land and buildings	59·49	Equipment	Rs. 21·58 million (rupee equivalent)
Equipment, library, furniture and fittings	46·26	Experts	number: 132 man-months: 2169
Total	105·75	Fellowships	number: 63
Recurring expenditure per year	16·96		man-months: 1885
3. INDIAN INSTITUTE OF TECHNOLOGY, KANPUR			
Land and buildings	73·53	Equipment	\$7·42 million*
Equipment, library, furniture and fittings	34·64	Experts	number: 122 man-months; 2266
Total	108·17		£5·92 million*
Recurring expenditure per year	18·53	Fellowships	number: 47 man-months: 543 \$0·29 million*
4. INDIAN INSTITUTE OF TECHNOLOGY, MADRAS			
Land† and buildings	69·13	Equipment and library	DM 30·29 million
Equipment, library, furniture and fittings	18·83	Experts	man-years: 221
Total	87·96	Fellowships	man-years: 97
Recurring expenditure per year	15·23		

* Excludes rupee expenditure from US Trust Funds.
† Cost of land only approximate.

develop all these institutes all on its own, it would have involved a large outflow of foreign exchange for equipment and for the training of Indian faculty abroad. It would have taken India many long years to meet the foreign exchange needs of the institutes from its own resources.

The next important role of foreign aid is that it facilitated the induction of the latest technology from the developed world into the Indian system. The Institutes of Technology provide now the means of technological self-reliance for Indian industrial development. All five institutes together are training each year about 1500 graduate engineers and over 1000 engineers at the postgraduate and research level.

The foreign aid for the institutes is not uniformly considered as an unmixed blessing. Each institute has come to be identified in the general public image with the aid-giving country concerned. Thus, the Bombay Institute is regarded as a Russian institute, the Madras Institute as German, the Kanpur Institute as American and the Delhi Institute as British. This transferred identity implies that the institutes are the cultural colonies of these foreign countries.

The large foreign aid received has, it is alleged, made the Indian faculty incapable of developing their institutes further without more aid. And the faculty are afraid of losing their umbilical cord with the aid-giving countries lest their Institutes be equated with other Indian engineering institutions which are purely Indian enterprises. This is an echo of the general Indian belief that anything of foreign origin, including education, is better than Indian, which is also a hangover of British rule in India. There is some evidence that the faculty of the institutes are not intellectually completely independent of the countries from which they have received aid.

Lastly, it is also alleged that the Institutes of Technology are the training ground for Indian scientists and engineers who ultimately migrate to foreign countries in search of greener pastures and that they are therefore encouraging a 'brain drain'. True, a large number of Indian engineers trained at the institutes have migrated to other countries, but the problem of brain drain is not peculiar to the Institutes of Technology. Also, this problem needs to be examined from many other angles and in the larger context of the social and economic forces operating in India.

VI VOCATIONAL TRAINING FOR INDUSTRY

India, like other developing societies, is confronted with a twofold manpower problem: an abundance on the one hand of unskilled labour, with on the other shortages of skilled labour. Accordingly, manpower planning in India has two aims: first, to increase employment; secondly, to ensure that an adequate supply of skilled workers is available for industrial development.

Since 1950 the Government of India has made the industrial training of skilled workers an integral part of its developmental plans. The magnitude of the problem is well illustrated by the ILO in the following statement:

> Of the estimated 1961 population of 480 million, 17·7 per cent of the 158 million employed were working in manufacturing and mining. By 1976, when the employed population will have grown by 57 million, the largest increase of workers requiring some type of education and training will be in manufacturing and mining; this increase is expected to be 11·1 million to reach a total of 28·8 million. The factory labour force, around 3·5 million in 1961, will experience the greatest relative growth as the manufacturing industries increase their share of employed manpower from 11·2 per cent in 1961 to 13·4 per cent by 1976.

Background of industrial training

In the last twenty years India has created a nationwide network of facilities for industrial training, that consists of:

i. 357 Industrial Training Institutes (ITIs) with over 150,000 training places in 32 engineering and 22 non-engineering trades. Training varies from one to two years, depending on the trade.

ii. Apprenticeship or on-the-job training under the Apprenticeship Act of 1961 provides for about 60,000 apprenticeship places in over 5000 industrial establishments.

iii. Six Central Training Institutes (CTIs) at Kanpur, Calcutta, Madras, Hyderabad, Ludhiana and Bombay to train instructors for the Industrial Training Institutes. These have a capacity to train 2000 instructors a year.

iv. An Advanced Training Institute at Madras to upgrade the skills of craftsmen and technicians employed in industry in special areas such as tool design, tool and die making measurement techniques, heat treatment and welding.

v. A Foreman Training Institute at Bangalore.

vi. A Central Staff Training and Research Institute at Calcutta to train senior personnel of the government and industry who control and regulate training programmes and to conduct research in trade and training techniques, as also to prepare training aids and manuals.

The ITIs and apprenticeship are structurally related. The former provide basic training in trades under controlled conditions with related instruction in trade theory, mathematics and science. The graduates from ITI's may after this training be employed as semi-skilled workers or be apprenticed, and trained to be fully-fledged craftsmen.

The Central Apprenticeship Council determines the trades in which apprenticeships must be provided by an organisation, the number of apprentices to be trained and the training facilities to be provided. The Apprentice Act of 1961 made history in vocational training in India, representing the first organised effort at national level to harness the resources of industry towards training.

The success of the vast network of ITI's and apprenticeship facilities now depends on an adequate number of well-trained instructors being available on a continuing basis. They must be masters of their trades and must know how to impart their skills to young people scientifically and with some understanding of technological principles.

To meet this demand the Government of India set up six Central Training Institutes in or near industrialised areas to train craftsmen-instructors. The programmes of training were evolved to suit Indian conditions with instructors deputed by State Governments, private industry and other agencies in charge of vocational training and apprenticeships.

The ITIs had also to train craftsmen by simulating industrial situations. The CTIs did precisely this for their own instructor-training programmes, so that their instructors could create in the ITI's the atmosphere of a production organisation and the standards of national factories.

The heart of the problem

The production of first-rate instructors was and is in fact the heart of the problem of vocational training and the six CTIs had an urgent and vital national responsibility.

It was in this situation that the Government of India sought the assistance of UNDP and the ILO in 1959. Both organisations agreed to help the CTIs to develop the correct methodology to train instructors in training staff and in simulating industrial situations for training purposes. A Model Training Institute (MTI) was set up at each CTI to develop and test the new instructional methods and concepts of 'live' training environment.

Assistance from UNDP and the ILO covered the needs of five CTIs, at Calcutta, Kanpur, Madras, Hyderabad and Ludhiana. For the sixth CTI at Bombay, assistance was obtained from the US Agency for International Development (USAID). The main provisions of the Plan of Operations for the five institutes followed that of the Kanpur CTI:

i. The Institute is to offer theoretical and practical instruction in the instructor trainees trade and in the principles of teaching.

ii. Three types of courses will be given for two types of trainees: long-term courses for existing instructors in need of training; the same type of courses for candidates for instructor posts; and short-term refresher courses for working instructors; the Institute's capacity will be for 244 instructors.

iii. A Model Training Institute (MTI) will be set up with the CTI to serve for practical teaching purposes.

iv. Nine ILO experts will be assigned for a total of 184 man-months including Chief of Project for 14 months, an expert for teaching techniques for 20 months and seven trade experts for the same period.

v. Equipment tools and technical books required from abroad will be bought by the ILO to a value of $292,000.

vi. The Indian Government will pay the rupee equivalent of US $97,200 towards local operating costs. This amount represents 15 per cent of the total estimated cost to the special fund of foreign project personnel.

vii. The Government will provide the necessary technical counterpart personnel for the ILO experts as of the date they commence their duties. The (T) Principal will be the counterpart of the Chief of Project.

The terms of reference of the project personnel and the senior adviser who coordinated the work of the ILO teams at the CTIs implied two other objectives:

i. to train the national counterparts to serve as instructor trainees; and

ii. to develop the CTIs within the framework of the national vocational training schemes to serve as a source of instructors.

In consultation with UNDP and ILO, the Government of India accepted the principle of central coordination of the projects and a 'national component' was included in the Kanpur project, consisting of a senior ILO adviser based at the headquarters of the Ministry of Labour and Employment. His task would be to coordinate the work of all five projects at national level and to advise the Government on vocational training policies. A group of ILO apprenticeship advisers who would be assigned to work both at headquarters and in the states and who would help to implement the Apprenticeship Act were accepted. Another group of ILO experts would advise on aptitude testing, supervisory training and training special trades.

Relative foreign and home contributions

Total UNDP aid to the five CTIs and the contribution of the Government of India are as summarised below:

UNDP contribution	*(US $)**	*Government of India contribution*	*(rupees)*
1. Experts, 1286 man-months	1,824,204	1. Professional staff and non-professional staff	43,396,220
2. Equipment and supplies	1,659,673	2. Equipment and supplies	
3. Miscellaneous	70,762	3. Miscellaneous	
*Total gross project cost**	3,554,639	*Total contribution in kind*	43,396,220
		Total Government contribution $9,328,723	

* Excludes $334,400 of executing agency overhead costs or dollar equivalent of the contribution in rupees. Also includes Government's contribution towards local operating cost.

UNDP aid and the Government of India contribution (excluding land and buildings) were in the ratio of 1 : 2·6. UNDP inputs were chiefly in the form of services of experts and training equipment not manufactured in India

Evaluating foreign aid

Any evaluation of foreign aid to national projects such as the CTIs must be on a long-term basis, since the impact of the CTIs can be rationally assessed only on what the instructors trained under the project have in turn been able to contribute to the training of better craftsmen in their own ITIs and on how these craftsmen have been received by Indian industry. Clearly the CTIs were designed to have a multiplier effect, i.e. to train trainers and, through them, to improve the quality of vocational training in India. From this point of view, the CTIs have, during the period of UNDP assistance, trained about 9000 instructors. All six CTIs have a capacity today to train about 2000 instructors a year. The training programme seeks to upgrade the practical skill and technical competence of the trainees; to enrich their practical experience by involving them in real jobs and workshop situations; to provide the trainees with practical training and with teaching techniques; and to expose them to an environment in which they are required to organise trade instruction methodically.

These requirements are met today through a twelve-month instructor-training course of two six-month phases, the first to cover remedial work and skill development, the second to concentrate on teaching techniques.

Before the CTIs were established, India had very restricted facilities for training instructors. She could not have launched a programme for building up a network of ITIs without first training an adequate supply of instructors. Nor could the ITIs have developed and maintained standards of craftsmanship training without instructors of the right calibre. The CTIs are undoubtedly playing a vital role in the development of vocational training for industry in India.

In the initial stages, the ITIs depended on their own graduates to join the faculty as instructors. These graduates had had only an eighteen-month training course as contrasted with the three-year minimum of industrial experience given under the National Apprenticeship Scheme. The CTIs had the responsibility for training instructors in the shortest possible time and the effectiveness of the instructor-training programme was handicapped by the inadequacies of the professional background of the trainees. In time the CTIs will receive as trainees only those who have had the minimum of three years experience. In the interim period it remains their responsibility to upgrade and improve the ITI instructors through in-service courses.

The following UNDP summary of evaluation of its project of assistance to the CTIs is revealing:

1. Training national counterparts: the CTIs instructor-trainers

Within the five-year period during which the projects were implemented the profession of instructor-trainer was established in India. The number of CTI staff with the status of instructor-trainer rose from 40 to 300 highly-trained personnel with a knowledge of modern training methods and up-to-date industrial technology. This expansion was effected chiefly by recruiting CTI personnel from either the ranks of ITI instructors or from industry, and then upgrading them with in-service courses or on-the-job training while they actively participated in CTI development.

2. Training of ITI instructors

During the course of the projects 9000 instructors were trained at all six CTIs. The existing training capacity of the Institutes is about 2000 instructors a year. UNDP supplied assistance in the shape of modern machine tools and equipment. This was supplemented by equipment from the Government. USAID provided facilities for upgrading the skills of the trainees in subjects such as engineering drawing, craft, science and workshop mathematics. The Institutes have been equipped with modern apparatus to train in instructional techniques. They prepare instructors in techniques of visual education and workshop management that enable them to function more effectively in their ITI posts. They are equipped to meet new demands made on them in related instruction, apprenticeship training and language differences.

3. Establishing CTIs as functional units

Each CTI is now a modern training complex with well laid-out workshops and classrooms. Supporting facilities such as hostels for trainees and living quarters for staff have made each complex a self-contained community.

Workshop equipment is of the latest design and enables the layout to provide an environment for training in current teaching techniques.

Repair workshops and preventive maintenance systems have been introduced to guard against possible dislocation in training effectiveness. Workshop house-keeping, store keeping and safe working practices are stressed in the workshop organisation course.

Visual education is stressed in training. There are audio-visual projection rooms.

Draughting offices and craft science laboratories help to upgrade trainees' technical skills. Each CTI has a library.

4. Integration of MTIs in CTIs

A Model Training Institute has been established at each CTI and underscores the importance of instructor-training in a realistic training situation. Instructors are thus trained in the environment of actual problems. The MTIs 'live' training helps CTI staff to assess the value of their training methods in a truly 'model' trade-training programme.

India's own evaluation of the UNDP project with CTIs tallies with that made by UNDP. Today, the CTIs represent a well-developed system of instructor-training, that can be diversified and strengthened to meet the growing needs for industrial vocational training in India. In expertise, physical plant and lead time India has had the best inputs on lasting lines.

The CTIs may now diversify their activity by *inter alia* training supervisors in industry. According to present estimates, there are about 320,000 supervisors in Indian industry and they are increasing at the rate of about 7000 per year. Many of them have come up the hard way from the ranks of craftsman and after long years of experience. As vocational training expands, the excellence of workers will be determined not just by the quality of basic training at the ITIs but also by the standard of supervision that they receive in on-the-job training as apprentices. A well-trained supervisory force in industry is therefore vital to the success of the apprenticeship schemes. The CTIs must develop and implement a coordinated scheme for the technical upgrading and functional training of supervisors.

VII TRAINING POLYTECHNIC TEACHERS

At one end of the manpower spectrum are engineers, scientists and managers; at the other, skilled workers and operatives. In between, is a group of technical personnel that we refer to as 'middle level' manpower. They are technicians, supervisors, foremen, overseers, section officers, shifts-in-charge. They are responsible for a wide range of field operations such as testing and development, installing and running engineering plant, drafting and designing products, estimating cost and selling and advising. Often a technician acts as liaison between engineer and skilled craftsman. It is his job to interpret the engineer's plans and designs and to carry out a variety of jobs on his own initiative and under the general supervision of a professional engineer or scientists.

All developing countries need technicians badly. In the short run, shortages can be made good by importing foreign expertise or capital equipment. But we cannot make good a shortage of technicians in this way. We have to train and develop our own technicians. It is reckoned that four technicians are needed to every engineer.

Training a technician and developing his professional competence is not a course; it is a long process that takes place partly in a technical institute and partly in industry. In the institute the would-be technician must learn the basic principles of design, construction and production. He must be able to communicate his ideas to the expert and to the skilled worker below him. This education has to be cross-fertilised with practical experience in industry. He has to translate his engineering principles into processes. All developing countries have to evolve a system of technical education that can automatically accept from technical institutes the material produced there for apprenticeship in industry.

Polytechnics in India

India has established a network of polytechnics throughout the country. In 1947, there were only 53 polytechnics that conducted diploma courses. They admitted only 3670 students per year. Less than 1500 diploma holders were trained each year. Today, we have about 280 institutions capable of admitting 50,000 students a year which turn out 24,000 diploma holders a year. The total financial outlay on these institutions exceeds a billion rupees on buildings and equipment. Their annual budget for maintenance expenditures is over 100 million rupees. Over 250,000 diploma holders have graduated from these polytechnics. The present student enrolment is over 100,000; the faculty consists of over 10,000 teachers.

The diploma courses conducted by all polytechnics in India are uniformly of three years' duration after the matriculation or secondary school certificate, that is, the equivalent of the minimum required of ten years' school education. The curriculum and syllabus and all standards of instructional facilities have been laid down. These developments notwithstanding, there is some criticism of polytechnic education in India that tends to be made on the following lines: the polytechnic courses are essentially theoretical and their practical content is inadequate; the courses are a poor imitation of a university degree in engineering; no training is given in the many specialities of major engineering fields in which technicians are needed by industry.

In the final analysis, all improvement in polytechnic education depends upon the faculty. In 1955–60 when polytechnics were being set up in large numbers there was an acute shortage of teachers and 40 per cent of sanctioned faculty posts remained unfilled. Those teachers who were available were inexperienced and had little industrial experience. All faculty skills needed up-dating, their knowledge needing expanding and improvement in depth. This became a national problem.

In 1964 the Government of India formulated a plan for four regional Technical Teacher Training Institutes (TTTIs) to meet the needs of polytechnics for teacher-training facilities and the four Institutes were set up at Madras, Bhopal, Chandigarh and Calcutta. At first the Institutes offered two types of courses, one for teachers, who were graduates in engineering, another for those who held a polytechnic diploma. The former, which took eighteen months, included a twelve-month practical training. The diploma holders' course was extended over a two-and-half-year period and included the same periods in practical training in industry and in pedagogical methods as were required for graduates. For the remaining twelve months the candidates had an intensive training in basic sciences and technical content and skills in their speciality.

The TTTIs are still in process of development and adjustment to meet the changing needs of polytechnics. On the experience so far obtained, their teacher-training programmes have been improved. The vacant positions in polytechnic faculty have been filled. New and different courses are now conducted that include full-time integrated courses for eighteen-month periods for teachers with a diploma in engineering, and for twelve-month periods for graduate-teachers. Methodology and teaching skills are combined with in-depth training in selected engineering specialities. Then, there are short-term courses ranging from two to twelve weeks for groups of middle level and senior faculty, to upgrade and update their knowledge of polytechnic subject-fields and to equip them with new teaching skills. Finally, workshops and seminars to bring polytechnic faculty on to a common forum, and to discuss problems on content and method common to TTTIs, are continually held.

In addition, all four TTIs have undertaken a programme of curriculum development for polytechnics, the preparation of instructional materials and the development of new laboratory experience. They work in close collaboration with the Faculty of Polytechnics. The new curriculum and the new instructional materials are being introduced into all polytechnics in the country.

The case for foreign aid

The Government of India identified teacher training for technical and vocational education as an area of priority for foreign aid, because of the importance of technical manpower in economic development. India lacked the expertise to develop teacher training to meet the needs of a growing technical education system. Foreign aid was therefore resorted to.

The first choice for this was Britain, because there was a close similarity between the Indian and the British systems of technical education. Also, Britain had set up several technical teacher-training institutes that were regarded as a good model for India. Following the recommendations of the Commonwealth Education Conference, Britain agreed to assist developing countries within the Commonwealth in technician education and training.

British aid was obtained in 1966 for one of the four TTTIs. Substantial progress had by then been made by the Madras Institute, and this was earmarked for British aid. In 1967 the Netherlands showed some interest in technician education in India and offered to help another institute. This offer was accepted for the Chandigarh Institute.

Between 1966 and 1973 British assistance to the Madras Institute was provided and consisted of experts in technical teacher training who served for stated periods on the Faculty of the Institute. Their chief function was to help the development of the methodology of teacher training to suit Indian conditions and to train their Indian counterparts; to provide special teaching aids and instructional materials and demonstration equipment, including a closed-circuit educational television unit; to give fellowships for training selected members of Indian faculty in British technical teacher-training institutes.

Dutch aid to the Chandigarh Institute consisted of the same three elements as that from the United Kingdom.

The total foreign aid received by these two institutes is as tabulated below:

TECHNICAL TEACHERS' TRAINING INSTITUTE, MADRAS

Government of India's contribution		*British aid*	
Capital			
1. Land and buildings	Rs.3·68 million	Equipment and library	£33,427 (Rs.635,000)
2. Indigenous equipment and library	Rs.1·566 million	Experts	24 man-years (estimated cost: £53,204)
Total	Rs.5·246 million	Fellowships	62 man-months (estimated cost: £4,500)
Recurring	Rs.1·3 million per year		

TECHNICAL TEACHERS' TRAINING INSTITUTE, CHANDIGARH

Government of India's contribution		*Dutch aid*	
Capital			
1. Land and buildings	Rs.4·234 million	Equipment and library	600,000 guilders (Rs.1·2 million)
2. Indigeneous equipment and library	Rs.1·077 million	Experts	17 man-years
Total	Rs.5·311 million	Fellowships	90 man-months
Recurring	Rs.900,000 per year		

The precise amount spent by the Netherlands on the experts and fellowships for Chandigarh is not available. It is, however, clear that British and Dutch aid accounted for only a small proportion of the total expenditure on land, buildings and equipment of the Institutes. British aid to the Madras Institute was about 10 per cent of the total outlay. The main investment in both Institutes was made by the Government of India. In the present evaluation, it becomes relevant to measure the impact of the components supplied by foreign aid, namely the services of the British and Dutch experts and the training of the Indian faculty in both these countries.

Evaluation

The original purpose in setting up the TTTIs was to train a new cadre of teachers for polytechnics. In course of time, the scope of work of the TTTIs was extended to such matters as curriculum development, preparation of instructional materials, the in-service training of teachers and so on.

Altogether the Institutes have trained about 1030 teachers in their long-term courses and 2710 teachers in short-term in-service courses. The numbers are not impressive when compared with the present faculty strength of polytechnics, that is about 10,000. Nevertheless, it must be recognised that teacher training is a long and complicated process, that it takes time to break age-old habits and to change values. Educational innovation and practice are not achieved overnight. The Institutes have made a dent in technical education and may in time make a decisive change in polytechnic education.

Both the Madras and the Chandigarh Institutes confirm that the British and the Dutch experts have helped Indian faculty to understand the basic problems of technical teacher training, have structured long- with short-term courses, have developed appropriate methodologies and have set up laboratories and other necessary instructional facilities. The TTTIs consider that the foreign aid supplied has been vital to the development so far achieved.

All four Institutes have undertaken a comprehensive programme of curriculum reform in which large numbers of polytechnic teachers are participating. Chandigarh, for example, has developed totally new curricula, for the diploma courses in civil, mechanical and electrical engineering that have been adopted by polytechnics in four states. The curricula are accompanied by extensive instructional materials for teachers and textbooks for students. Inter-linking of theory with practice and the motivation of teachers are important aspects of these programmes.

Similarly, the Madras Institute has produced new curricula and instructional materials for engineering drawing, heat power engineering, production engineering, electrical engineering and engineering mathematics. It has also produced a new laboratory manual in industrial electronics. These materials are now being used extensively in polytechnics.

However, problems remain, for the teachers trained by the Institutes are confronted by resistance to change in their own polytechnics. While they value the importance of the work done by the two Institutes that have received foreign aid, they claim that they are finding it difficult to implement their own ideas in their polytechnics, because those in charge of administering the polytechnics are not willing to change. The polytechnics are affiliated to State Boards of Technical Education that prescribe the syllabus of the diploma courses and conduct the final examination. The rigidity of the system inhibits change in new directions and subordinates creativity in teachers to stability and uniformity. The TTTIs have still therefore a long way to go in breaking down impediments to progress. The strength to do this must now come from within themselves, for this foreign aid cannot help them to do.

VIII TEN YEARS OF EXPERIMENT IN SCHOOL SCIENCE EDUCATION IMPROVEMENT

> It is science alone that can solve the problem of hunger and poverty, of insanitation and illiteracy, of superstition and deadening custom and tradition, of vast resources running to waste, of a rich country inhabited by a starving people. Who indeed can afford to ignore science today? At every turn, we have to seek its aid. The future belongs to science and to those who make friends with science.[1]

The importance of science and technology to every nation of the world in the second half of the twentieth century does not have to be argued. With the explosion of scientific knowledge, it is possible to achieve a drastic improvement in a nation's economy, to bring to everyone more food and water, better clothing and housing, greater opportunities for education and a richer, safer and more rewarding life. But to do this, we need men and women capable of doing fundamental scientific research and of translating the knowledge so gained into the means of improving living conditions. For developing societies, this is true in a special way, for it is they who have today to move into the orbit of modernity that is a pre-condition of national survival.

Improvement in the standard of science and mathematics is a continuous process with three integrated steps:

i. developing a curriculum with concepts and understandings of subject-fields and an analytic study of fundamentals;

ii. preparing textbooks based on the new curriculum, teachers' guides and other instructional materials including experimental kits and apparatus;

iii. training teachers and equipping them to introduce the curriculum into the classroom.

A detailed survey of science education in Indian carried out by the National Council of Educational Research and Training (NCERT) revealed serious shortcomings: the curriculum did not include modern concepts on the understanding of science; the emphasis in mathematics was on developing skills, not on a disciplined understanding of basic principles; there was no organic relationship in the teaching of the biological and physical sciences and mathematics; textbooks were poor; teachers were not provided with manuals or instructional materials; laboratory apparatus was dated.

[1] Jawaharlal Nehru, Prime Minister of India.

Secondary school science teaching project (SSST)

The Government of India decided to launch a major programme to improve science teaching at all stages of school education and approached UNESCO for assistance. On the basis of recommendations made by a Planning Mission deputed by UNESCO to India in 1963–4, a UNESCO–UNDP project for the improvement of secondary-school science teaching was implemented. NCERT was nominated to implement the project and the Department of Science Education in NCERT became the venue for the project.

The long-term objective must be seen as part of a total effort to universalise science education and to improve educational standards. The means towards this objective were to make science and mathematics compulsory and to teach science in the form of separate disciplines from the middle school onwards. The project had the following components:

i. to develop model curricula syllabuses and textbooks for separate science subjects and mathematics for classes 6–11, that covered the middle and higher secondary stages of schooling;

ii. to design and produce simple sets of teaching equipment for demonstration to teachers and experiment by students;

iii. to develop teachers' guides and other instructional materials;

iv. to train NCERT counterpart personnel in the further development of such materials and on how to evaluate them;

v. to extend the new curricula and teaching materials progressively to all schools in the state after try-out in experimental schools.

UNESCO–UNDP inputs

Between 1963 and 1974 when the SSST project was implemented, UNESCO–UNDP provided the following assistance:

(a) Laboratory and workshop equipment	\$382·023 million
(b) Experts: 43 for 1087 man-months	\$2047·687 million
(c) Fellowships: 55 for 313 man-months	\$180·500 million
Total:	\$2610·310 million

Workshop equipment came from the rouble component and was mainly for the Central School Workshop of NCERT to produce science teaching kits and other teaching materials. The Government of India's contribution consisted of all other facilities for the project including counterpart personnel, local expenses on materials and supplies, publication of textual materials, production of laboratory equipment and kits.

Science curriculum developed

The SSST project was to be implemented in three phases, namely, preparation and tryout of experimental teaching materials, finalisation of these materials, dissemination of them to schools. Thirty schools in Delhi were selected and the experimental teaching materials were tried out in the middle classes, 6–8. A package programme consisting of syllabuses, textbooks, teacher guides, demonstration kits, pupil-experimental kits and so on were developed for physics, chemistry, biology and mathematics. The project team sought, in brief, to provide school children with a knowledge of the fundamentals of research in science and mathematics, i.e. the major discoveries, laws and theories in an easily intelligible form and so that they could be applied; to acquaint children with the major application of this knowledge to industry, agriculture, engineering, transport, health and the business of daily living; to provide students with progressive teaching materials to explain the development of scientific reasoning and its utilisation in living; to inculcate in students habits of observation, logical thought and the curiosity integral to scientific and mathematical knowledge; to correlate, where possible, knowledge so gained with schemes of vocational, physical and aesthetic education; and to contribute to an international outlook based on the universality of science.

The package programme was later adapted to classes 5, 6 and 7 so as to meet the needs of states in which these constituted the middle level of schooling.

Throughout, a major effort was made to develop prototypes of demonstration equipment and to secure their mass production in the Central Science Workshop of NCERT. The development of student kits was governed by the criteria that they should contain all necessary items in a prescribed course; that the equipment should be durable, cheap and produced out of local materials; and that it should be possible to produce kits locally with simple workshop facilities. The Central Science Workshop produced and supplied 7670 demonstration and pupils' experimental kits.

The third phase, dissemination of project materials, started in 1967 when 144 Central schools under the control of the Union Ministry of Education adopted the new curriculum for classes 6, 7 and 8. This was followed by 480 schools in Delhi.

UNICEF participation

In 1969, following agreement with the Government of India to assist with local funds to disseminate curriculum materials developed under the SSST project, UNICEF undertook the printing and distribution of all textual materials, the manufacture and supply of kits and the training of teachers. The textual materials were translated into various Indian regional languages and tried out in 700 selected schools in all the states of the

Union. UNICEF made available a package programme consisting of free textbooks, teachers' guides and kits. It also provided funds for training teachers.

The original proposal was that with $7 million earmarked by UNICEF, about 30,000 schools or about one-third of the middle schools of India would be covered by the package programme by the end of 1974. It would appear that the target has since been revised and only 10,000 schools for which the supply of kits has been arranged will be covered. UNICEF would also appear to be more interested in spreading science in primary schools, i.e. classes 1 to 4/5, in accordance with the curriculum and materials developed by NCERT separately. This being so, the Government of India and the State Governments have now to 'go it alone' in disseminating the SSST project materials in Indian middle schools.

Evaluation

Important as curriculum and instructional materials are, they constitute only a first step in science educational improvement. Teacher training and the introduction of the curriculum and materials into schools are also important. The first part of the SSST project has been completed, but the second part has not been implemented; the impact of curriculum and material has still to be felt.

The size and complexity of the problem make this a difficult undertaking. Nearly 100,000 middle schools with an enrolment of over 15 million students are involved. Education is a state subject and State Governments have to be persuaded to accept the project. Most middle schools are without qualified teachers; these have still to be trained and supplied. Existing teachers have to be refreshed on the basis of the new curriculum and modern teaching methods. Training facilities have to be created for these purposes. Printed materials have to be supplied and they cost a great deal. Unless the Central and State Governments in India are willing to bear this expenditure, to disseminate the new curriculum is not going to be practicable. Then, teachers' resistance to change requires to be overcome. Without the active participation of teachers, there is little that NCERT can do at ground level.

Begun with the aim of improving science education throughout the school stage, including classes 9–11, the SSST project after nearly ten years and an expenditure of 2·6 million dollars for UNESCO and UNDP, and at least a comparable expenditure by the Government of India, has produced new curriculum materials for the middle classes (6–8 or 5–8) only. Of the twelve textbooks planned for the higher secondary classes, only two have gone to press; the rest are still at various stages of planning. Teacher guides and other instructional materials have still to be developed. The feedback in experimental schools has still to be obtained before the materials are generally disseminated. If the time taken for middle school classes be a measure for the whole project, it will need at least as long to reach the original objectives of SSST. Can India afford to wait so long? Can UNESCO–UNDP provide another 2·6 million dollars' assistance?

All these considerations raise the basic question of whether or not India has evolved the correct strategy for school science improvement under the UNESCO–UNDP project. She has no dearth of top-flight scientists in her own universities and research institutes, though it is distressingly true that few have taken any real interest in school science and its need for improvement. School and university teachers appear not to meet at professional level and so the impact of the one on the other is not felt. Unless this gap is bridged and nationwide bridges are built between scientific research on the one hand, and school teaching and understanding on the other, schemes of school science improvement will be illusory. Take, for instance, the fine work done by the PSSC Physics Group, the SMSH Mathematics Group, the BSSC Biology Group and others of their kind in the United States in order to improve school science in American schools. The contribution of these groups to school science has attracted worldwide attention: they were serviced by university professors who recognised their responsibility to their country's schools and gave generously of their time with almost missionary zeal for several years, so that first-rate curriculum materials could be developed and disseminated in the American school system.

There is no reason at all why something comparable should not be done in India, on the basis of what has already been achieved elsewhere in the world. This, instead of a massive package programme funded by international agencies and on India's own initiative, is what requires to be done.

The recognition that this was the right strategy did, indeed, come in the course of the UNESCO–UNDP project though it came rather late in 1966 when NCERT convened a Conference of Science Educators in the shape of twenty-six university Professors of Science to formulate and implement a plan for school science improvement. The Conference decided to set up twenty-five curriculum development groups, five each in physics, chemistry, biology and mathematics at university centres. Each group would have a university professor as leader and forty-five university and school teachers as participants. The groups would be required to develop an integrated system of curriculum materials, try them out on an experimental basis in selected schools with the help of school teachers and, in the light of the feedback, would improve and finalise the materials for wider dissemination.

In the last four years, when the Curriculum Development Groups functioned, they produced a wide range of materials of great value, that were tested extensively in local schools. Unfortunately NCERT and the Government of India later considered that this programme duplicated the work done under the UNESCO–UNDP–SSST project and decided to withdraw their financial support from it. High prestige attached to the UNESCO–UNDP project possibly because of the international aid implied in it. Nevertheless, the entire question of the value of foreign aid in this project requires to be objectively evaluated. It is doubtful if such aid should be advocated when the work can be done satisfactorily within the country, using her own expertise and initiative and breaking new ground educationally by bringing the university to the school or taking the school to the university.

Now that the UNESCO–UNDP project has come to an end, and science teaching for the higher secondary classes has still to be dealt with comprehensively, it remains to be seen what strategy will be adopted by NCERT and the Government of India. Whether NCERT will complete the programme alone or will revise its own well-conceived Curriculum Development Groups at university centres to assist in its efforts, is also not clear at this stage. This case study would seem, however, to reflect the complications of having more than one agency involve itself in approximately the same project. Theoretically, there is a case for having several agencies engage in a proposition as vital and as 'sub-continental' as a school science programme for a country the size of India. From these, it may be argued, the best and most penetrating could be chosen with the assurance that it was likely to yield the most effective and enduring results. Yet it is an expensive way for a developing economy to meet an urgent need in national development. In terms of time-consumption and financial investment, we do not yet know whether school science in India has been fundamentally changed for the better. A ferment for change has certainly been created. The question is: how effective will this be, and has the investment in it been proportionate to the results achieved in the course of the last ten years?

IX BRAIN DRAIN

The term 'brain drain', used originally to describe the emigration of British scientists to the United States, came later to be applied to emigration of highly skilled or professional manpower from developing to developed countries. The twenty-second Consultative Committee of the Colombo Plan countries, at a meeting held in New Delhi in 1972, defined brain drain as a phenomenon which involves only the external migration of personnel at the skilled technician and professional levels for employment abroad under circumstances in which they could otherwise have been employed, at once or in the near future, productively at their proper, attained level of professional skill in their own countries, at work of national significance.

We need to examine the problem of brain drain from the standpoint of the group characteristics of those who emigrate, the impact of emigration on the economic and cultural development of the home country and the benefits to countries that receive such persons.

The important features of outward immigration would appear to be that there are numerous flows of professional personnel from developing to developed countries; that there are larger flows from a comparatively small number of countries like India to a smaller number of countries like the United States, United Kingdom and Canada; and that there are smaller flows from a larger number of developing countries at levels of development lower than India's. These flows have grown rapidly in recent years and they consist primarily of engineers, scientists and medical doctors. Among engineers and scientists, the largest component is of people who go to developed countries first as scholars and then stay there to take up employment. Medical doctors migrate mainly for employment as intern-residents in hospitals abroad.

The general conclusion for the person who emigrates is that of finding greener pastures away from home than he was able to find in India. Many seek a higher status by going to Europe or America. Colonialism has left a special cultural stamp on such countries as India and this is reflected in the ambition to 'go abroad'. The large number of foreign scholarships offered to India has reinforced the cultural influence inherited from years of foreign rule. Indian scholars still advertise such degrees as MA (Oxon), MA (Cantab), DPhil (Oxon), DSc (London), MS (Ohio), PhD (Wisconsin), MBA (Harvard) and so on, to emphasise their 'superior' qualifications. They rarely so much as mention the earlier degrees that they have secured at home.

From the standpoint of the receiving countries, brain drain clearly helps to make good the shortage of professional manpower that they may need for further development. Even more important is the fact that a substantial part of the expenditure on the education and training of potential brain drain has been incurred by the 'abandoned' developing country.

Certain studies indicate that foreign aid to developing countries for higher scientific, technological and medical education has encouraged a brain drain from those countries. Thus the donors would seem to take back with one hand what they have given with another.

For developing countries, and this is the most important consideration, brain drain implies the loss of educational costs incurred by them on persons who migrate and the loss of economic and social benefits from development, in the migration of professional manpower. The educational costs cannot be recovered. The economic and social benefits imply the depletion of human capital. This retards economic development in the developing country, as the emigration of exceptional persons deprives a developing country of those capable of providing new ideas and leadership.

As against this, it could possibly be argued that when such persons return to their own country after years abroad, they bring with them new ideas and varied professional experiences that do contribute effectively to developmental processes. They also enhance the prestige of their home country abroad and, when they remit part of their earnings, assist developing countries with much needed foreign exchange.

It may also be argued that several developing countries, such as India, have large surpluses of trained manpower that would be either unemployed or under-employed in the country, whereas they help to meet acute manpower shortages in the developed world. India, for example, has exported a large quantity of indentured labour to many British colonies in the past. These persons have found a new home, new opportunities for employment and have, in the course of time, projected Indian culture to those countries. India was not noticeably poorer for the loss of this labour. Indentured Indian labour for British colonies enabled India to send out her scientists and engineers to developed countries where they have had better opportunities and, incidentally, have helped to build cultural bridges between developed and developing countries.

All things considered, it is, however, possible to establish a connection between brain drain and foreign aid by developed to developing countries. The latter receive aid from many sources including the Communist countries such as the USSR, East Germany and Hungary, but there is no brain drain to Communist countries. It is restricted to some developed countries in the free world. Why? Is the pace and direction of the brain drain also influenced by the social, economic and political systems and their policy of aid-giving to such countries as India?

Among studies on the Indian brain drain, the most important are those conducted by the Institute of Applied Manpower Research (IAMR), New Delhi, and the Council of Scientific and Industrial Research (CSIR), New Delhi. The main findings of these investigations are summarised below:

IAMR study[2]

The purpose of this study was to determine the dimension of brain drain and to define its most important characteristics. IAMR analysed all passports issued between 1960 and 1967 to Indians with a degree or diploma in engineering and technology, a degree or diploma in medicine or nursing, a Master's degree in science, a Bachelor's degree in teaching, a PhD, and a degree in agriculture or veterinary Science. The analysis was restricted to passport holders who wished to go abroad for higher studies, training, employment or emigration.

[2] IAMR Report, no. 4, 1970.

The main findings were that:

(a) during 1960–7, 44,900 passports were issued for such categories. Though we do not know the number who went abroad, the number of passports issued represents the maximum out-flow for the period.
(b) Of the 44,900 passport holders, 44·24 per cent (19,863) were engineers, 23·63 per cent (10,608) medical doctors and 18·42 per cent (8271) Master's degree holders in science. The rest were teachers (9 per cent), nurses (2·10 per cent) veterinary scientists (1·22 per cent) and Doctorate degree holders (1·39 per cent) in the arts, humanities and commerce.
(c) Over 75 per cent of the engineers said that their main purpose in going abroad was study or training. Only about 16·2 per cent stated their purpose to be employment.
(d) Over 60 per cent of the medical doctors said that their chief reason for going abroad was higher study or training. Only 30 per cent gave employment as their purpose. This was equally true of postgraduate scientists.
(e) About 65 per cent of the teachers and a higher proportion of nurses stated that they were going abroad for employment.
(f) Assuming that all 44,900 passport holders went abroad between 1960 and 1967, the total position for these years is summarised in the table below:

Educational Category	*Number of persons given passports*	*Percentage of persons given passports to total stock*
Engineers (degree holders)	15,708	13·2
Engineers (diploma holders)	4,155	2·4
Medical doctors	10,608	10·8
Postgraduates in science	8,271	5·75
Teachers	4,045	0·4
Nurses	943	1·75
Doctorates in arts, humanities, commerce	622	Estimates of stock not available
Veterinary scientists	548	4·22

Clearly the largest depletion was in engineers and medical doctors, but this was only between 11 and 13 per cent. The assumption involved is that all passport holders went abroad and did not return to India. This is too large an assumption to be entirely acceptable, particularly when 75 per cent in these two categories went abroad for study or training. A small proportion may have obtained employment and settled abroad. The rest probably returned to India. The Indian brain drain could not therefore have retarded Indian economic development during this period in any significant way. There is no evidence in any report that a developmental project suffered for lack of adequate technical personnel.

This position is supported by another study conducted by IAMR entitled Migration of Indian Engineers, Scientists and Physicians to USA (Report No. 2/1968). The period analysed is 1954–66; the main findings of the study are that (a) the number of Indian engineers, scientists and doctors admitted to the United States as immigrants was 1958. About 68 per cent were engineers, 24 per cent scientists and 8 per cent doctors. (b) Most immigrant engineers, scientists and doctors were initially admitted to the United States on student visas.

If the United States is the most important recipient country of India's brain drain, the data would indicate that the outflow of Indian engineers to any one country during this period did not exceed one per cent of the total stock of such persons. The outflow of scientists and doctors is even less.

CSIR study[3]

CSIR collated its data from three different surveys: the Indians Abroad section of the National Register of Scientific and Technical Personnel, analysis of passports by IAMR, and UN Report on Brain Drain (1968). It made the following estimates.

i. The total number of Indian engineers, scientists and medical doctors abroad is about 30,000, consisting of 15,000 engineers, 6000 scientists and 9000 doctors.

ii. Of these 30,000 persons, 5000 had a Doctorate degree, 12,000 had postgraduate qualifications in their subject-field.

iii. Among the engineers, 3500 were mechanical engineers, the next largest group being electrical (2500), then civil (2000) and finally chemical (1500).

iv. Of the scientists, 2000 were chemists, 1100 physicists, 900 biochemists and 600 mathematicians and statisticians.

The study has its limitations. The estimates do not indicate how many in each group were merely pursuing higher studies or training abroad and how many actually settled down for purposes of employment. The latter is really the group that constitutes brain drain. From both studies, we know that a large proportion of these persons went abroad for study or training; that not all of them took up employment, and that many of them returned at different times to India. If we make allowances for all this, the brain drain could not have constituted more than 2 per cent of the total

[3] *Technical Manpower*, vol. XIII, no. 2, Feb. 1971.

stock of engineers, scientists, doctors and other categories of highly-qualified professional personnel in India.

Nevertheless, the public agitation in India on this score was not without value. The Government of India grew to be aware of the talented engineers and scientists who, having gone abroad for higher studies, research or training, then settled abroad for want of adequate employment opportunities at home. These professionals were willing to come home, if they could be assured of being absorbed within a reasonable time into suitable employment. The Government of India created a Scientists' Pool in 1959 so as to facilitate the return to India of Indian engineers and scientists from developed countries. Those who wished to come back to India were accepted in the Scientists' Pool, and given a salary depending on their qualifications and experience for periods up to three years. They were assigned to universities, research institutes, industry or other suitable organisations and given useful work. For that period they could compete for regular positions, and when they obtained suitable employment, be released from the Pool. In the event, the Pool not merely looked after returning scientists and engineers but also provided them with opportunities to involve themselves in research, teaching and other kinds of useful work while they waited for full-time employment.

So far, the Scientists' Pool has provided assistance for over 5000 engineers and scientists, all of whom are now employed in regular positions in the country.

Has foreign aid to the system of Indian higher education stimulated a brain drain? There is no evidence either way – yes or no. All that we do know is that a high proportion of the graduates of the Indian Institutes of Technology, which have received substantial foreign aid, are going abroad for higher studies or employment. Some figures from the Indian Institutes of Technology at Kanpur and Delhi respectively will give an indication of the situation.

For example, of the 2286* graduates leaving the Kanpur Institute during the period 1965–72, 1358 were known to have found employment in India and 236 were pursuing some form of higher studies in India – a total of 1594, or 70 per cent. The number of graduates pursuing further studies or actually in employment in foreign countries was 527, or 23 per cent. (The occupation of the remaining 165 graduates could not be ascertained.) The IIT at Kanpur receives assistance from the United States.

Figures from the Indian Institute of Technology in Delhi (which is assisted by the United Kingdom) for B Tech graduates leaving between

* Of this total 1324 had gained a B Tech degree, 587 an M Tech, 42 a PhD in engineering, 177 an MSc, and 156 a PhD in science.

1965 and 1970 present a similar pattern. Of the 983 graduates trained during this period, 563 were known to be employed in industry in India and 118 were pursuing higher studies there (a total of 69 per cent), but a further 209 graduates (21 per cent) were doing further studies abroad. Nothing was known of the status of the remaining 93 graduates.

On this analysis, between 21 and 23 per cent of the B Tech graduates of the IITs went abroad for higher studies or employment. This is certainly a high proportion but not all of them constitute a brain drain within our definition of this term. There is no record of how many came back, or how many settled abroad.

Why, however, do so many graduates from IITs go abroad? First, because the large number of scholarships and fellowships offered by various countries to Indian nationals are proving irresistible. Many of the scholarships are in fact offered through the Government of India which selects candidates in open competition, and on the basis of advertised conditions of eligibility. Secondly, the IITs attract the cream of Indian technical student-talent and offer education that compares with the best in the world. These graduates are therefore most competitive and most successful in scholar selections in technology. Thirdly, between 1960 and 1968 the IITs were still developing their postgraduate courses and resources and could not compete with the challenging opportunities for higher studies that were available in the developed world. Finally, for a developing economy and its students, there is always the glamour of going abroad to a developed society, and this is still very much in evidence with young Indian intellectuals, whether or not they have qualified at the IITs. For every foreign scholarship offered through the Government of India, there are at least twenty qualified applicants. Indeed, scholarship selection is a big undertaking in the Indian Education Ministry. India's missions abroad, particularly in such countries as the United States, the United Kingdom and the USSR, maintain large establishments headed by ministers (local rank) precisely to look after Indian scholars in these countries.

There is, it would appear, little real connection between the foreign aid given to the IITs and the existence of a brain drain. The most interesting feature of the present situation is embodied in the Report of the Reviewing Committee for the IIT, Kanpur, dated 8 March 1973:

> One gratifying feature of the situation is that of late the trend of the products of the Indian Institute of Technology, Kanpur, to go abroad, has been coming down. There is a positive improvement in the situation. But it does not mean that we can retain the cream of the products coming out from the Institute. The very best are still going

abroad. The only way to retain them in the country and make them available for various national projects is to offer better jobs and emoluments . . .

The reference to 'positive improvement' tends to give the impression that going abroad is still an Indian ailment, and that we have to locate the parasite and eliminate it. But such a conception is very much a matter of opinion. One section that is not likely to share this view are the graduates of the Institute.

X AID FOR AGRICULTURAL EDUCATION

Even today about 70 per cent of India's population depends on agriculture for a living but while the population has been growing at a rate of over 2·3 per cent a year, the increase in agricultural production required to provide foodgrains, edible oils and cotton (for clothing) did not exceed an average rate of about 4 per cent until the mid-sixties. In bad seasonal conditions, the fall in output could be very steep. Productivity per acre remained very low except in areas where chemical fertilisers came into use; in most parts of the country cultivation was practised on traditional lines and the results of whatever research was being undertaken in the institutes set up for the purpose were hardly carried to the farmer. Community development and extension services were first conceived in the early fifties and officially adopted towards the end of the decade under the second Five-Year Plan. Though a Grow More Food campaign was launched during the Second World War after the great Bengal famine of 1943, and food production was supposed to have been placed on a 'war-footing' whenever a crisis of shortage occurred, no real breakthrough was achieved until the beginning of the wheat revolution in 1967–8. However, the decade preceding this achievement was marked by sustained efforts to improve agricultural education and create links between the research worker, agricultural departments and farmers.

Five agricultural colleges had been set up even by 1907 to offer diploma courses and there were three veterinary colleges in the Presidency towns of Calcutta, Madras and Bombay. But subsequent progress was slow since enrolments were generally limited to the available government jobs. There were seventeen degree colleges and five postgraduate colleges in agriculture in 1947 and the annual enrolment was about 1500 students. In the field of research, there was greater concentration on industrial raw materials like cotton, sugar cane, jute and tobacco than on foodgrains. The University Education Commission (1948–9) examined this situation and felt that development of agricultural education on the pattern adopted in the United States after the Morrill Act, 1862 would be appropriate to

India. The Commission recommended the establishment of rural universities, each of which would include a ring of small, resident, undergraduate colleges with specialised facilities, but providing at the same time a common core of liberal education, with no field being excluded as being foreign to the rural university. No action was, however, taken on this recommendation during the next seven years. Meanwhile, a committee on higher rural education (set up by the Ministry of Education) recommended the setting up of rural institutes which could serve as training centres for development planning in rural areas, covering such subjects as rural hygiene, agriculture and rural engineering. The Government then proposed to set up ten such institutes in the second Plan (1956–1961) but later there were other developments which altered the course of events.

In 1954, the Government of India's Ministry of Food and Agriculture constituted an Indo-American joint team to inquire into the problem of strengthening agricultural education, after making a comparative study of the institutions in the United States and India. The team expanded the idea of a rural university recommended earlier by the University Education Commission in 1948–9 and suggested that agriculture, veterinary science, home science and arts and technology courses should be included along with agricultural research in the proposed rural university. At the same time, under an agreement between India and the US Technical Cooperation Mission in 1954, five American Land Grant Universities were drawn into the field (a) for providing 35 experts to assist Indian colleges of agriculture and veterinary science and the two research institutes, viz. the Indian Council of Agricultural Research and the Indian Veterinary Research Institute, (b) for training 35 Indian scholars in the United States, and (c) for supply of library, laboratory and field equipment. A second Indo-American joint team was set up in 1959 to examine the scope for further expansion of this collaboration. Taking note of the general demand in the states for the establishment of agricultural universities, but often without sufficient understanding of all the implications, the team recommended that assistance by the Centre should be made conditional on adherence to certain basic principles regarding status, integration of teaching and research, and location of all the faculties in the same campus.

By 1960, the number of agricultural colleges had increased to 51 and of veterinary colleges to 17, with a combined total enrolment of about 7500. One state alone, Uttar Pradesh, had more than a third of the colleges, of which several were private colleges which had mushroomed without adequate farm, laboratory and library facilites. The wastage rate was high, and as the graduates from these colleges were found unsuitable for most jobs many of them remained unemployed. The need for controlling this unregulated expansion had thus assumed great urgency.

Also by 1960, the Uttar Pradesh government had established the Agricultural University at Pantnagar after enacting special legislation. Later, the Punjab, Orissa and West Bengal also passed legislation for the purpose. At that stage, a committee headed by Dr Ralph W. Cummings, Field Director of the Rockefeller Foundation, was set up by the Government of India to examine the proposals made by the state governments for setting up agricultural universities and to scrutinise their draft bills. It was on the basis of the work of this committee and the Model Act drawn up by the ICAR that six universities were set up during the third Plan period (1961–6) at Ludhiana (Punjab), Udaipur (Rajasthan), Jabalpur (Madhya Pradesh), Hyderabad (Andhra Pradesh), Bangalore (Mysore) and Bhubaneswar (Orissa). The University of Kalyani (West Bengal) set up in 1960 under the West Bengal legislation was accepted as equivalent though it deviated from the recognised pattern in some respects. The main principles underlying the Model Act were later endorsed by the Education Commission (1966) which laid stress on single campus universities, creation of facilities for basic and applied research for postgraduate courses and separation of extension training from the purely supply functions of state agricultural departments. The Commission also supported the establishment of one university in each state.

Till now, nineteen agricultural universities have been set up, one in each of the major states, except Maharashtra which has the dubious distinction of having four of them. But only eight of these universities have had the benefit of foreign aid in the matter of supply of experts, books and equipment, and offer of facilities for participant training of their scholars. These are the seven universities set up by the end of the third Plan in Uttar Pradesh, Punjab, Rajasthan, Madhya Pradesh, Andhra Pradesh, Mysore and Orissa and the first university in Maharashtra which came into being in 1968. By 1969, USAID had provided about $10 million under its technical assistance programme, about two-thirds of which was expended on US experts sent to India and the balance for scholarships for Indian students and supply of equipment. In all, about 200 long-term specialists and over 100 short-term consultants were provided to eight Universities. Under the participant training scheme, 423 degree holders and 1300 non-degree personnel were given training until 1969.

In addition, the Ford Foundation and the Rockefeller Foundation supplemented the assistance in various ways; the Ford Foundation allocated in all about $20 million between 1956 and 1969, a major portion of which was given for the Intensive Agricultural Development programme to demonstrate how Indian farmers can combine their inputs to the best advantage ($12·6 million), to the IIT, Kharagpur to strengthen the PhD courses in agricultural engineering, for a water technology centre at IARI, New Delhi, for plant protection research at the University of Agricultural

Sciences at Bangalore and for a home science faculty at Baroda. The Rockefeller Foundation assisted the postgraduate school in IARI, Delhi in cereal improvement research, evolution of crop hybrids with high yield potential in maize, sorghum and millets, etc. and in providing supporting funds for travel grants and scholarships, all of which helped to demonstrate the value of linkages with leading institutions abroad.

Many useful lessons have been learnt from the drawbacks and shortcomings encountered in the implementation of the aided education programme. The integration of education with research, and of both with extension training, is still perhaps not all that it should be. Many universities have not yet developed to the point of playing a full role in research or in coordinating their work with the state agricultural departments' research activities, partly because of the latter's reluctance to part with or share their own responsibility. Multiple campuses have made the achievement of uniformity in standards of teaching and evaluation difficult. However, it is now accepted both by the donors and the Indian authorities that all the training facilities created within the country should be fully utilised before candidates are sent abroad for training and that these deputations should be limited to special fields where no facilities exist. It is also recognised that more incentives by way of pay or job opportunities should be given to attract students of higher calibre, especially from rural areas, to the agricultural universities. Similarly, home science courses in the agricultural universities should try to attract girls with a rural background who can provide supporting services in agricultural and rural development. Greater attention has to be paid to identifying local problems for research. On balance, the aid programme has provided an institutional basis for higher agricultural education, established useful links with work done abroad in relevant fields of education and research and taken the country far towards self-reliance in research and application of its results. The third Indo-American joint team clearly stated in 1967 that the eight universites established by then should aim at managing without any technical assistance from 1971.

An exception to this programme of self-reliance was considered necessary, and accordingly the Government of India applied to the United Nations Special Fund (later merged with the UNDP) for assistance in the development of the capabilities and resources of some selected centres of postgraduate agricultural training and research which had already acquired a reasonable status. These were expected to serve as Centres of Excellence, whose main object was to reduce the dependence on foreign training of staff for the Indian agricultural science institutions and to maintain collaboration with the research activities and contributions to knowledge of foreign institutions with outstanding accomplishments to their credit.

On the basis of the reports of three special missions sent by the UNESCO and FAO, the UNDP approved in June 1969 an exploratory project for two years, to lay the foundations for the creation of leading schools for postgraduate training and research in five fields (later raised to six) in an equal number of agricultural universities and research institutes. This involved a contribution of $539,436 by the UN Special Fund and an Indian counterpart contribution of Rs.2·3 million for allocations to the institutions concerned. The preliminary phase was completed in 1973 and the project is now in its second phase which will last until 1977.

The six fields of research and the respective institutes were:

1. Soil and water management at the Haryana Agricultural University at Hissar (in collaboration with the Central Soil Salinity Research Institute at Karnal).
2. Agricultural economics at the Indian Agricultural Research Institute, New Delhi.
3. Plant protection at the University of Agricultural Sciences, Bangalore.
4. Dairy sciences at the National Dairy Research Institute, Karnal.
5. Poultry breeding and production at the Indian Veterinary Research Institute, Izatnagar (Uttar Pradesh).
6. Agricultural engineering at the Punjab Agricultural University, Ludhiana.

Under this UNDP Scheme, the Agricultural University at Wageningen (Holland) has provided experts on soil and water management for the first project. The US Department of Agriculture has selected experts on plant protection. For poultry breeding and production, Japanese and American experts have been forthcoming. Other countries are also expected to send their experts during the second phase, thereby strengthening the international linkages in research and contributing to the improvement of higher education in agriculture, It would be premature to make at this stage any firm appraisal of the UNDP scheme. Since it is founded on the fruitful experience of past Indo-American collaboration, and there is no intention either on the part of the donors or recipients to increase the grants or the numbers of experts beyond certain limits, it may be assumed that this part of the aid will be given judiciously and made use of in appropriate ways.

The World Bank has also offered assistance during the fifth Plan (1974–9) to three of the newer agricultural universities in Bihar, Assam and Tamil Nadu. The amounts are substantial, $12 million for Bihar and Assam universities and much more for Tamil Nadu. The pattern of aid may be different from the Indo-American programme in the sense that greater importance will be attached to full use of training facilities and experts within the country. World Bank aid will be more a form of providing larger resources for balanced development of agricultural education than of foreign exchange for importing skills or equipment, or sending trainees abroad, on a large scale.

If an evaluation of the impact of foreign aid for agricultural education in the sixties is limited to the eight universities which were the direct recipients of such aid, the conclusion will be generally favourable, though four of them – the agricultural universities of Andhra Pradesh, Orissa, Rajasthan and Madhya Pradesh – have not fulfilled the expectations of the donors or the Indian authorities in respect of the quality of teaching or research. They have opened many postgraduate faculties without qualified teachers and their campuses are too far flung to enable coordinated direction. Appointments of vice-chancellors by state governments have not always been happy. On the other hand, the universities in Uttar Pradesh (Pantnagar) and Punjab (Ludhiana) have done well and that of Mysore (at Bangalore) seems to be catching up, judging by its choice as a Centre of Excellence under UNDP aid for plant protection research. The drawbacks of the former may have little to do with the forms of aid or the role of the collaborating US universities; for example, Illinois has been collaborating with both the successful Pantnagar University and the less successful Jabalpur (Madhya Pradesh) University, while Ohio State University has worked with both Punjab and Udaipur universities. Since state government's policies have been mainly responsible for bad appointments, location of too many campuses, and allocation of inadequate funds, it is clear that the Centre's efforts to evolve uniform principles through the Model Act have not succeeded. In Madhya Pradesh, for example, four campuses have Hindi as the medium of instruction while English remains the language in the other three, making confusion and deterioration in quality of research inevitable. The oldest of the unaided universities at Kalyani (West Bengal) is definitely in a shambles.

This raises the question as to how far foreign aid has contributed to institution-building as such, apart from the varying degrees of individual excellence of the Uttar Pradesh, Punjab, and Mysore universities. It is too early to judge the eleven new universities which came into being after 1968. The Haryana University at Hissar (1970) seems to be generally following the lines of the Punjab University, thus avoiding the pitfalls of the others. Maharashtra's decision to have four universities, on the ground of regional climatic variations, will probably result in spreading the available resources for education and research too thinly to enable purposeful research and may also dilute the quality of the graduates and reduce their job prospects.

The net contribution of foreign aid, however, is the increasing awareness at the policy-making levels of the conditions of success in higher agricultural education, the existence of the more successful institutions at Pantnagar and Ludhiana and availability of expert personnel from these institutions for manning other newer universities in their infancy or in

AID GIVEN FOR AGRICULTURAL UNIVERSITIES IN INDIA (1963–9)

Name of university, date of establishment, US university aiding it (1)	*US experts** *Long-term* (2)	*Short-term* (3)	*Nos. for participant training* *Degree* (4)	*Non-degree* (5)	*Total US aid ($000)* (6)	*Other aid by the Ford and Rockefeller Foundations and PL 480†* (7)
1. Orissa Agricultural University, 1962 (Missouri State University)	14	3	30	42	1235	
2. Mysore University for Agricultural Sciences, 1964 (Tennessee University)	13	8	35	29	1419	*Ford*, grant for plant protection department. *Rockefeller* travel grants. *Oxfam* grant for fertiliser supply for hybrid maize. *PL 480* grants for microbial and fungi studies.
3. Andhra Pradesh Agricultural University, 1964 (Kansas State University)	18	11	29	186	1646	*Rockefeller*, grant for equipment vehicles and seed for maize research station
4. Punjab Agricultural University, 1962 (Ohio State University)	15	10	31	102	1284	*Rockefeller*, grant for equipment. *PL 480* funds for research stations. *Ford*, for agricultural engineering college.
5. Udiapur Agricultural University, 1962 (Ohio State University)	12	3	33	136	1251	*Ford*, grant for extension wing of Rajasthan Agricultural University.
6. Jawaharlal Nehru Agricultural University, 1964 (Illinois University)	12	21	17	303	1344	*PL 480*, grant for research on maize-germ plasm.

7. Uttar Pradesh Agricultural University, Pantnagar, 1960 (Illinois University)	16	18	33	188	1820	*Rockefeller*, grant for experimental station. *Ford*, farm management IADP training. *PL 480*, grant for other research.
8. Maharashtra Agricultural University, Poona (Pennsylvania)	2	5	5	–	147	Nil

* Before 1963, 82 long-term specialists and 14 consultants were provided and 210 degree participants and 223 non-degree participants were trained on a regional basis.

† US Public Law 480, which allowed for the sale of grain to India, the rupees resulting from which were used in India for the financing of research.

difficulties. In the words of an Indian writer on the subject, the agricultural universities have had 'an impact in elevating the ceiling of comprehension, vision and determination in individuals'.[4] Mr O. P. Gautam, Deputy Director-General (Education) of the ICAR, expressed a similar appreciation.

> There is perceptible improvement in the quality of education. The reform in agricultural education introduced in agricultural universities besides improving quality has brought down to a large extent the wastage in higher education in agriculture. These institutions today are serving as fountainheads of new knowledge earned through a purposeful, problem-solving research and have become main centres of dissemination of useful knowledge to the farming community.[5]

Most of the weaknesses stem from political pressures in the states to start universities without sufficient resources or personnel; but these weaknesses are unrelated to the concept, quantum or basic strategy of the foreign aid provided during the sixties. Nor can it be said that aid should not have been sought for the universities which have failed to profit by it, since it was part of the national effort to create an active interest in agricultural education, set high standards and strive for uniformity in their application. Foreign aid came on the basis of a policy decision to adopt the land-grant college pattern as the most suitable for Indian conditions; USAID and the six American universities which have participated in this effort have done so after extensive consultations with the Government and periodical review of their methods of assistance. The annual conventions of the Association of Indian Agricultural Universities have provided opportunities for forceful and uninhibited criticism of the defects of agricultural education, like the two dozen notorious private colleges of Uttar Pradesh which are affiliated to the traditional universities, the serious under-utilisation of existing agricultural university facilities and of serious instances of under-staffing such as the lack of PhDs for heading the senior faculties in some institutions. The National Commission of Agriculture has offered some guide-lines for reform and the draft outline of the fifth Plan now under discussion has also underlined the need to rectify drawbacks like the regional imbalances in the intake of students, the high wastage and the unacceptable deviations from the prescribed pattern of integration of research, teaching and extension education.

XI THE INDIAN INSTITUTES OF MANAGEMENT

The case for expertise in management in a developing society such as India can be easily made out. After decades of stagnation in a predominantly

[4] K. C. Naik and A. Sankaran, *A History of Agricultural Universities in India*, Indian Council of Agricultural Research, New Delhi, 1961.

[5] *Indian Farming*, ICAR, Aug. 1972.

agricultural economy, India is laying the base for all-round industrial development. She is setting up giant industrial complexes; she is expanding infrastructure as well as reorganising financial institutions. All this depends on modern technological know-how, and a huge labour force. The process of this development demands not only capital and organisational ability; it also demands high managerial skill.

Problems of Indian management

The trade pattern of 'merchant adventurers' centuries ago brought in its wake British entrepreneurs who, with their capital and management, established business houses in order to exploit Indian natural resources, labour and growing markets. With British paramountcy in India, these enterprises grew with their own patterns of management. The later development of commerce and industry elaborated these patterns in response to local situations. The British tried to formalise the non-transferability of applied knowledge in terms of their own apprenticeship system. This influenced local entrepreneurs who took to the managing agency system and accepted its values.

Where communication is slow but daily decisions have to be made, those in authority often delegate their power to the 'man on the spot'. But for lack of communication, delegation, in the modern sense, cannot be controlled over short periods of time. Under the British, delegation of authority was high and the communication periods were long. People had, therefore, to be employed with a high measure of trust. In the personalised aspect of enterprise, this meant personal trust. There was, therefore, a tendency to employ relatives and people of one's own caste and nationality, and this continues to date in organisations of the same culture.

Several people in responsible managerial positions are in fact without formal training for their task. They have learnt their skill through experience. From some years of formal and informal apprenticeship, they have acquired personal qualities that appear to mark them down for leadership. They are promoted in the management hierarchy largely on the strength of their performance. They have learnt by trial and error and by emulating others by 'use and wont'. To them, new and improved methods of training that systematise and telescope experience, constitute a direct threat to their personal knowledge and authority. They continue to insist that tomorrow's managers shall come up through the school of experience.

Most Indian enterprises started as family or proprietary concerns in which the entire investment was made by the owners. As the firms expanded, partners were added from other members of the family, 'to take advantage of the loyalty and adhesion interest of the family group'. Soon the firms felt the need for trained employees with professional expertise in business affairs. They started recruiting persons from outside the family and caste groups. Organisations became more depersonalised and finally, many were converted into joint stock enterprises. Capital now came from outside the family group. A large number of partnership firms became managing agents to promote, finance and manage the affairs of other companies. The managing agency system did not make for better management since it perpetuated the proprietary character of the enterprises in other forms. Family members continued to participate; the head of the enterprise, also the head of the family, was cast in a highly paternalistic role *vis à vis* the employees, who came from outside the family. Responsibility for management rested with the owners of the enterprise. The managing agency system is being gradually replaced by boards of directors, but the fundamental management attitude towards enterprise has not undergone any radical change. Many aspects of this operation are, however, not appropriate because things have changed radically, and the system must progressively be eliminated through legal provisions.

A new element in India's management problem has been added by public sector enterprise. In the last fifteen years, public sector enterprises have emerged in a big way in manufacture, trade, commerce and distributive activities. These public sector enterprises have no tradition of management of any kind. Nor have they developed a style and philosophy of management that reflect the socio-economic goals of a socialistic state. Their management is dominated by the members of an aggressive civil service. The civil servant is without the necessary professional understanding of the complexities of modern industry, including its social and other implications, but he commands high prestige within the bureaucratic order and he develops a sort of magic quality or aura that stems from administrative experience. The need for India to professionalise her management of public sector enterprises is vital and urgent.

Management gap

What the country now needs is a new cadre of professional managers, equipped with the knowledge, competence and skills to manage modern enterprise. They require to have the right attitudes and the right values to respond effectively to the social, economic and political objectives of a developing country in India's stage of development.

Precise data are not available to quantify the management gap in India. According, however, to the 1961 census, about 56 per cent of managerial positions in private sector enterprise in urban areas were held by non-matriculates (less than 10–11 years of school education); 28 per cent by matriculates; 2 per cent by diploma-holders; and 14 per cent by graduates. In technical occupations, 38 per cent of the positions were held by non-matriculates; 36 per cent by matriculates; 6 per cent by diploma-holders; and 27 per cent by graduates. These figures indicate that nearly 40 per cent of managerial positions, technical and non-technical, were held by non-university persons. This was partly because managerial careers were not sufficiently attractive to young men and women of ability, and partly because such enterprises gave preference to practical experience among those who had come up the hard way. Caste and family loyalties also explain this position.

The aggregate ratio of managers to total workers is 1 : 100 in private as well as public sector enterprises. This indicates the heavy workload for each manager and the shortage of managerial power in the country. A large proportion of serving managers have not been educated or trained specifically for management. Since they have come up the hard way in the school of experience, they are constantly obsessed with the need to keep operations under them simple and unsophisticated.

The Economic and Research Foundation of the Federation of the Indian Chambers of Commerce and Industry has estimated that between 1969 and 1980, India will need about 34,000 new managers for the factory sector alone. If other sectors of the economy like banking and insurance, trade and commerce, construction, transport and communication are all taken into account, India's requirements will exceed 100,000 managers or about 10,000 managers a year.

Indian Institutes of Management

Against this background, the Government of India decided in 1961–2 to establish two fully-fledged Institutes of Management, one at Ahmedabad, the other at Calcutta, in close cooperation with private sector industry and commerce. The main objectives of the institutes were:

i. to provide educational facilities for training young men and women for management careers and for developing experienced administrators;
ii. to conduct research, to contribute to the growth of knowledge of management and administration and to provide consultancy services; and
iii. to provide for the development of teachers in management and administration.

During the 1950s, the Government assisted selected universities to set up departments of management studies to conduct postgraduate courses in business-industrial administration. Unfortunately, the university departments did not grow into vigorous centres of management education capable of meeting the country's growing requirements. Separate national institutions would have to be established outside the university system, that would have complete academic and administrative autonomy, and that could establish close links with industrial and commercial organisations.

The Ahmedabad and Calcutta institutes have sought to fulfil these objectives by conducting a two-year, full-time postgraduate course in management largely for fresh graduates, as well as by organising executive development programmes for junior, middle and top level managers. The programmes are supported by educational material developed by faculty members through research and consultancy services to industrial and commercial organisations. Each institute is designed to take in 100–120 candidates per year to the postgraduate course and a large number of participants for executive development programmes.

The two-year postgraduate course in management, the central activity, is designed to prepare students for management as a career. The course provides knowledge, develops skills and fosters attitudes for management expertise. The curriculum in the first year, which is common to all students, covers the basic functional areas of business. The basic disciplines of economics, behavioural sciences, accounting and mathematics are taught to the extent necessary.

Sandwiched between the first and second years of the course is practical training for about three months in an industrial or commercial house or a government department. In the course of this training, the student works on a specific project and submits a report on it. He gets the opportunity to understand management problems in actual situations. Employers are evincing some enthusiasm about summer training programmes and have been willing to pay reasonable stipends to students for their work during the practical period.

The second year of the course is devoted to specialisation. Here the student has the chance to explore in depth subjects covered in the first year. The areas include management economics; financial and management accounting; marketing management; organisational management; production management. The course is rounded off with a research project on which the student submits a thesis. The course is continually evaluated with a view to making it flexible, dynamic and imaginative in approach.

In addition, the institutes conduct each year several in-service executive development programmes for serving managers in management by objectives, materials management and financial management.

Ford Foundation assistance

The Ford Foundation has assisted the development of the Institutes of Management in a big way by arranging collaboration for the Ahmedabad Institute with the Graduate School of Business Administration, Harvard, and for the Calcutta Institute with the Sloan School of Management of the Massachusetts Institute of Technology. Both American institutes have deputed senior members of faculty to the Indian institutes for stated periods, to help to design and develop postgraduate programmes, to prepare instructional materials including case studies and training of Indian faculty. They have also provided extensive training facilities to the faculty of the Indian institutes in the United States. Ford Foundation assistance equipped the institutes' libraries; it also provided a computer to the

Ahmedabad Institute. The total assistance to the institutes of management is as follows:

Buildings	\$0·973 million
Library and equipment	\$1·617 million
Experts	\$1·66 million
Fellowships	\$0·87 million
Total:	\$5·12 million

The Government of India, the state governments of Gujarat and West Bengal and Indian industry and commerce have spent over Rs.30 million on setting up the institutes. The annual recurring expenditure of the institutes is about Rs.4 million. By comparison, the Ford Foundation inputs are in faculty support, faculty training and management literature.

Evaluation

Twelve years is a small period in the life of an institute, yet during this period the two Institutes of Management have made a big impact on management education in India. This is clear from the continually improving standards, the increasing number of applicants for admission, the enthusiastic response of industrial and commercial organisations to employing graduates in management positions and the growing volume of research activities and consultancy services. The institutes have established their own individuality and developed their stature and strength. Their success is due to several factors: (a) the institutes were set up as autonomous institutions and have been unfettered by traditional academic rigidities such as those which hamper universities; (b) the faculty is of excellent quality and is free to prescribe courses and determine content and standards as well as to modify courses in response to changing needs and to experiment with ideas; (c) each institute is administered by a high-powered board that includes representatives of industry and commerce, leaders from different departments of Indian national life and representatives of the academic community. The governing board has not merely conferred prestige on the institutes; it has also influenced the working of the organisations in many useful ways; (d) the institutes have been able to build up their faculty to the crucial size necessary for full-scale enterprise in teaching, research and consultancy.

Benefits have clearly accrued to the Indian institutes from their association with Harvard and MIT. In the last three years after the period of collaboration had ended, the Ahmedabad and Calcutta institutes developed on their own as viable national institutions.

Meanwhile they have not escaped criticism. The first is from our University Centres of Management Studies. These feel that there is no justification for setting up institutes outside the universities; that the latter are capable of meeting in full the demand for management education and research in India. Whereas, it is argued, the Central Government spends huge sums of money on the institutes, it is parsimonious towards the University Centres, and that the latter's performance could be as good as, if not better than, that of the institutes, if they received similar financial assistance. The Institutes of Managements' better resources have pushed the University Centres out of the forefront and are now claiming credit out of all proportion to their actual achievement. There is possibly an element of envy in this view.

The other criticism is general and relates to the failure of the institutes to serve the broader socialistic goals of Indian economic life instead of concentrating their resources on training managers for the larger and more powerful interests of the private sector. Most graduates of the institutes take up managerial positions in private enterprise partly because of the comparatively high salaries and 'perks' offered and partly because private sector enterprise is more alive to the need for professional management than is the public sector. Also, there is possibly a lack of national commitment on the part of the graduates to nationalised concerns.

The Institutes of Management are also criticised for their collaboration with Harvard and MIT which, so it is argued, have translated the management culture of the United States into India; it is claimed that this culture is one of a free capitalistic economy whereas India is wedded to the socialistic ideal. Conflict between private and public sectors is therefore inevitable.

In the last analysis, it is clear that the institutes have by their performance justified the investment made in them. Whether or not the University Centre would have done as well with the same investment is a moot point. There is also no evidence that the institutes are developing a predominantly private sector culture. In deciding to set them up outside the university system, the Government of India has legitimised their role, particularly in improving the level and quality of management practice in different sectors of the national economy.

XII INDIA AND THE COMMONWEALTH SCHOLARSHIP AND FELLOWSHIP PLAN

Among the recommendations of the First Commonwealth Education Conference held at Oxford in July 1959, was the proposal to institute a Commonwealth Scholarship and Fellowship Plan under which awards were to be offered by the several countries of the Commonwealth to citizens of other Commonwealth countries, both men and women 'who were of high intellectual promise and who might be expected to make a significant contribution to life in their own countries on their return from study overseas'. In addition, a limited number of Commonwealth visiting fellowships were to be made available to senior scholars of established reputation and achievement.

In subscribing to these recommendations the Government of the United Kingdom announced its intention of contributing 500 awards to the total of over 1000 awards which would be set up under the plan in its first few years. This study is an attempt to assess, to the extent possible, the value to India and Indian institutions of assistance received from the United Kingdom in the ten-year period between 1960 and 1970 from the Commonwealth Scholarship and Fellowship Plan administered by the Commonwealth Scholarship Commission, which came into being in 1959.

One of the largest single items in Britain's Education Aid Programme, expenditure on the CSFP has now grown to an annual figure of \$2·43 million (one million pounds). No separate figures are available for expenditure exclusively on India.

India an active participant throughout

India was represented at the first Commonwealth Conference, as she has been at the second, third and fourth Conferences held respectively in 1962, 1964 and 1968, and she has throughout been an active participant in the programme. Her share in it has, on her own initiative, grown with the years. As India's contribution to the Commonwealth Education Cooperation Scheme, the Government of India offers other Commonwealth countries 45 scholarships and five fellowships a year.

When the CSFP was first implemented, the chief considerations of the Commission in the United Kingdom in selecting candidates for awards were intellectual merit and a realistic and practical plan of study. Selections were, however, made in such a way as to ensure that various fields of study were included among the awards. In 1960 when the awards were made for the first time, the break-up for India's awardees was as follows: humanities 14; science 8; technology 12; medicine 3 – making a total of 37 awards.

From the inception of the scheme the Commonwealth scholarships to Britain have been the most prestigious available in India. Making allowances for the almost automatic popularity among Indian students of scholarships for study in developed societies, there would still be few external scholarship schemes among those administered by the Government of India, that could compete with the CSFP in the number of eligible applications received for it, the number of clear first-class academic records and the variety of fields and sub-fields in which applicants stake their claim for an award, or the chance to obtain one. The yearly applications from India have, on an average, been between 2500 and 3000 for a total of 80 nominations and 40 final awards. The number of applicants has continued to be very high over the ten-year period 1960–70, sometimes exceeding 3000; the quality of applicant has been consistently high. The business of preliminary screening, short-listing for interview and final interviewing for nomination to the Commission has challenged the patience and ingenuity of the administering authority in the Union Ministry of Education. The actual interviewing of potential nominees has frequently run into more than a week; and the organisation and maintenance of panels of experts in the varied subject-fields for which awards are available, has been refined to a speciality within the division administratively responsible for this item of work.

Special attraction of British awards

Part of the attraction of the United Kingdom, over the other developed countries in the Commonwealth who also offer scholarships in varied fields under the plan, is clearly the old colonial association with Britain, and the acquaintance with and confidence in the educational structure and prestige of her institutions at higher level. Both countries speak the same educational language. Because Britain is known in India, and because many employing authorities are conversant with British educational standards, even those would-be scholars who are not sponsored may consider a Commonwealth scholarship to Britain a sounder investment than one elsewhere. But perhaps the most resounding testimonial to the excellence of the British part of the scheme is that the scholars who went out in the initial years of its working, when it was largely experimental, were well selected, highly responsible, well placed and guided in the United Kingdom and almost invariably honoured their commitment under the plan to return to India when their awards expired. Many of them now occupy chairs and other focal positions in Indian universities and comparable institutions, and their influence through the multiplier has been educationally significant in their neighbourhood.

As the plan progressed, it was evident that the Commission was willing to learn quickly from experience of how to accommodate students from developing countries. In 1959 the leader of the Indian delegation to the Commonwealth Education Conference suggested that the British Council arrange, in addition to vacation courses of study and private hospitality, gatherings of Commonwealth scholars as a group to the principal university cities and towns of the United Kingdom, with a view to maintaining the corporate feeling fostered on their first arrival in London. This was promptly acted upon. *The Commonwealth Scholar*, a journal that appeared once a term, has continued to provide a forum for the views and impressions of individual scholars under the plan.

It was decided early to obtain reports, not merely from tutors and supervisors, but also from the scholars themselves. The scholars' reports threw much light on both general and particular problems and were a valuable guide. From the standpoint of the Indian agency, there have been few cases of discontent or maladjustment and many requests for extension.

Flexibility in the administration of the plan, and the regular assessment of the scholar on the basis of his report and his supervisor's report, confirmed that scholars in almost all cases made good progress academically and took full advantage of the opportunity to study in a fresh environment. The number of degrees and diplomas per year was large and impressive. The benefits that the scholars derived from their time in the United Kingdom were clearly not limited to the formal qualifications they obtained, but their examination results did provide some independent measurement of their performance and was the one to which, in most cases, the scholars themselves attached the prime importance. On their return to India, if they were not already employed, such qualifications which were plainly difficult to acquire would be the most promising factor in obtaining suitable employment.

In course of time the scholarships awarded to those who were likely to make 'a significant contribution to life in their own countries' were narrowed down to awards primarily for postgraduate study and research in any specific field in any of the universitics or comparable institutions of higher learning in Britain. Undergraduate study tended to be the exception; it was pursued at the Universities of Oxford and Cambridge, and more especially in such subject-fields as English, where the quality of a first-class Honours degree was, and is, uncontested. The qualifications actually obtained by Indian Commonwealth Scholars in 1962, only two years after the first awards had been made, are revealing both in regard to the scholars' academic excellence and to the varied subject-fields in which they had been trained: diploma in photogrammetry; MA English literature; diploma in bacteriology; Master's in metallurgy; diploma in electrical engineering; MSc in economics; FRCS (London); FRCS (Edin.); diploma in mineral exploration; BA English; Master in civil engineering; diploma in concrete structures and technology; diploma in advanced studies in science (physics); PhD history; diploma in tropical medicine and hygiene; postgraduate diploma in concrete technology; Bachelor of Law; diploma in public health engineering. Of the 39 awards made to India that year, 6 were for arts, 4 for social studies, 8 for pure sciences, 15 for technology and 6 for medicine.

Development considerations

As in all scholarship schemes, and particularly such schemes as the CSFP, in which the objective is to return to the home country scholars who will build up centres of higher education and so have a multiplier effect on those they teach or supervise, it was important for returning scholars to be suitably placed in employment. About this, the Commission could do little; it was essentially a matter for the nominating agency to weigh at the time of local interview and selection. Whether a scholar's field was, in developmental terms, valuable; whether sponsorship should be exacted in the interests of the economic and social development of the country – these questions have constantly exercised the Government of India. No scholar could, if not already employed, have been given a guarantee in the Indian situation that he would be employed when he returned to India. The difficulty that India felt in accommodating all returning scholars, was reflected in the preference that tended with the years to be given to sponsored applicants, so that the benefits of their training abroad could be quickly ploughed back into national development, and the scholar's own morale not be adversely affected by having to wait for suitable employment.

The decision of which predominant factor to nominate is not an easy one to make in purely educational terms, for outstanding intellectual ability is frequently demonstrated by young Indian men and women between the ages of 22 and 24 years (within the preferred age span) and before employment has claimed them. On the other hand, developing economies have of necessity to think in institutional, in preference to individual, terms and to reckon with the speed with which people can be absorbed into institutional positions. Leadership within an educational institution is a complex of many factors, of which outstanding intellectual ability is only one. The decision as to whom to nominate for a Commonwealth scholarship where first-class records abound and the sheer academic competition is so keen, has had increasingly to be made in conjunction with considerations that are external to the candidate's intrinsic merit: his subject-field; sponsorship by key institutions; level of professional experience already attained; and not least, the area of India from which he comes. A Commonwealth scholarship is a merit scholarship; it is not made on considerations of poverty as most national scholarships are. But some areas in India cry out for swift development more vociferously than others and, in the sub-continental, uneven Indian situation, the claims of even a locality cannot be entirely ignored. A developmental national situation in fact tends increasingly to take precedence over the individual's isolated calibre, or at least to weigh equally with it, but there has of course been no shortage of outstanding merit in most areas of India and in developmental fields.

Brain drain

From time to time in the operation of the plan, a fear has been expressed that it may exaggerate a brain drain to the developed world. In 1964 an analysis was made of the 370 scholars from all developing countries whose awards had been completed by 30 September that year. It was found that 281 (76 per cent) had returned to their own countries; 56 (15 per cent) had remained in Britain or gone to a third country, the period of deferment of return home approved by both home country and the Commission being still unexpired; while 18 (5 per cent) had made applications for deferment or payment of return fare which were still under consideration. The remaining 14 (4 per cent) for whom no deferment or payment of return fare had been approved, included 4 who had left for a third country, and only 10 who had remained in Britain. These figures showed that, with very few exceptions, Commonwealth scholars in the United Kingdom honoured their moral obligations to return home.

The second Commonwealth Conference held in New Delhi in 1962 and the third Conference in Ottawa in 1964 were both attended by Indian delegations, and on both occasions much time was spent critically surveying the plan. On both occasions India expressed her belief in the continuing value of the plan and endorsed the detailed proposals made for its improved operation. She also supported extensions that it would be desirable to introduce as resources allowed. At the third Conference, one of the two subjects chosen for public oration was 'The Commonwealth Scholarship and Fellowship Plan in relation to the needs of Developing Countries' and the guest speaker was the then Vice-Chancellor of the University of Kerala. The next few years, it was considered, should be a period of consolidation in the CSFP.

Seen in review, the attitude of the Government of India to the CSFP and other comparable schemes of external scholarships seems to have been responsive, rather than strictly selective or scientific. From the standpoint of national development and planning, policy ought early to have dictated a more precise line on offers of this kind. Areas of development might have been pinpointed and scholarships accepted in terms of what India most needed in the sixties, that she could use and apply most quickly to those projects and areas of her sub-continental expanse, that cried out for swift development. Instead, in the early sixties, India appeared to 'go along' with such schemes as CSFP (which were clearly aimed at identifying outstanding intellectual ability and grooming it for leadership) rather than take a positive stand in locating areas of development that demanded *a professional conscience*, even more than high intellectual ability. The two are not mutually exclusive and have been known in India to go together. Nevertheless, CSFP stressed as its objective the strengthening of universities and comparable organisations that would raise and maintain intellectual standards at a high level of excellence, and that might be presumed through the multiplier to make better students in crucial subject-fields. It did not, and could not, undertake to produce scholars with a strong social and professional conscience, who would be willing to plough back their expertise into backward areas of developing societies. This is clearly the responsibility of the nominating agency, that is also a planning authority. India needed, and still needs, the sort of professional leadership that is not merely intellectually outstanding but that will go where leadership is most needed in a developing society and will, for professional, if no longer for idealistic, reasons place social need above its own personal need.

By the end of 1964, it was possible to review the working of the plan. The educational scene in Britain had by now been enriched by the increased number of students of high calibre from overseas developing countries, which these scholarships had brought to its universities and colleges. Distinguished academic results testified to the high ability of many of those who had completed their courses. India's list of successful PhDs mounted in such fields as production engineering, textiles, electrical engineering, glass technology, metallurgy, organic chemistry, civil engineering, plant pathology and mathematics. A note of caution continued to be sounded: there was continued evidence that scholars were having difficulty in finding posts at home, in which they could return usefully the knowledge and training they had acquired in the United Kingdom. Countries overseas, including India, were urged to give closer attention to a resolution of this problem. More and more awards tended to be made in developmental fields – science, technology, medicine, agriculture, veterinary science. Below is a summary of awards to India made between 1964 and 1969 inclusive, which is self explanatory:

Year	*Number of awards*	*Arts*	*Social sciences*	*Pure science*	*Technology*	*Medicine*	*Veterinary science*	*Agriculture*
1964	45	9	3	10	17	5	1	Nil
1965	40	7	1	4	14	7	2	2
1966	38	6	2	10	10	9	1	Nil
1967	33	6	2	4	10	9	1	1
1968	33	2	2	9	9	10	Nil	1
1969	37	7	Nil	9	11	3	3	4

Medical awards

In 1966 new ground was broken by the institution of medical awards. The scheme had been the subject of public discussion on a Commonwealth-wide basis at the Commonwealth Medical Conference held in Edinburgh in October 1965. Its basic aim was to assist in the creation or expansion of facilities for medical education in the overseas Commonwealth. Four different kinds of award would be made: medical scholarships; medical fellowships; senior medical fellowships; and visiting professorships in medicine. Since senior fellowships and visiting professorships would necessarily be comparatively rare, the main emphasis was expected to be at the level of fellowships and scholarships.

Each year since the inception of the CSFP a number of Commonwealth scholarships, approximately fifty at any one time, had been held for training in medicine. It was out of these that Indian scholars had till 1966 won medical awards. These medical scholarships were now incorporated in the framework of the new scheme. Fellowships, however, formed a completely *new* element and would be more numerous henceforward than scholarships, eventually totalling ninety in any one year. Scholarships would be intended primarily for those preparing for a postgraduate qualification and would be primarily offered on similar terms to non-medical Commonwealth scholarships. Fellowships were basically for medical and dental *teachers* who had already obtained a postgraduate qualification, but who would benefit substantially from a specialised course of study or training, though research workers, teachers in basic medical science and medical administrators would also be eligible. The fellowships were normally tenable for twelve months, while scholarships would be held for longer periods, the average being eighteen months. The chief accent was on teaching at professional level. Through the multiplier, large numbers of medical students were expected to benefit from this scheme.

Of the nominations made for medical fellowships and senior medical fellowships received up to September 1966, a very high proportion, approximately 60 per cent, were on behalf of Indian candidates. In 1967, following an uneven response from developing countries to the Commission's request for medical nominations, the preponderance of fellowships and senior fellowships went to India. This is explained by the rapid development in the sixties of medical education in India. In 1968, it was recorded that the ordinary medical fellowships had proved particularly popular in India and nearly two-thirds of the awards that were offered in this category during the year came to Indian candidates. The need for training medical teachers from India was growing rapidly and would continue to do so as a result of the expansion of medical education in this country.

In 1969 over 50 per cent of the senior medical fellows and about 75 per cent of the medical fellows came from India, which had shown a keen interest in training its medical teachers and had been a major participant in the medical awards scheme from the outset.

In this year there was a total of fifty-two Indian medical fellows and thirteen senior medical fellows. The sub-fields are impressive in importance and range: haematology; genito-urinary surgery; gynaecological pathology and cytology; cardiology; neurosurgery; neonatal physiology; clinical immunology; nephrology; morbid anatomy; neuropathology; diagnostic radiology; photochemistry; endocrine surgery; orthopaedics, surgical anatomy; cancer research; cardiovascular surgery; bacterial and viral vaccines; plastic surgery; ophthalmology, etc. All medical fellows occupied important positions in medical education in India. The institutions to which the fellows belonged were in several widely-spaced parts of the country: Madras, Aligarh, Chandigarh, Trivandrum, New Delhi, Hyderabad, Agra, Bombay, Rohtak, Vellore, Miraj, Poona, Manipal, Ganjam, Mangalore, Indore, Nagpur. Among the fifty-two fellows were ten women.

The thirteen awards of senior medical fellowships were equally, if not more, impressive. These were Indians who held Chairs of Medicine or Surgery and their special fields included cardiac surgery, children's and neonatal medicine, coronary circulation and undergraduate and post-graduate teaching methods, neurosurgery, physiology, psychiatry, anaesthetics and gastroenterology.

It is still too early to assess the total impact that this has made on all-India medical education, but it would be difficult to escape the conclusion that its impact on the institutions to which the fellows and senior fellows returned must have been substantial. There was no evidence of brain drain. All the fellows and senior medical fellows were naturally sponsored people.

In medicine and surgery as in so many other vital aspects of national development, India is served primarily in her urban, not so well in her rural areas. Yet the sad truth is that the cities account for only 20 per cent of the country's population, whereas 80 per cent live in the large, sprawling and uncared-for rural areas. Medical fellows and senior fellows under the CSFP would normally belong to institutions of specialists which are located in urban areas, and in close association with hospitals that serve an urban public. Some part of this public is as poor as its rural counterpart and would need such expertise; but it is doubtful whether the expertise, even through a multiplier, can in the foreseeable future make a dent in India's total population of 550 million. It would be unrealistic to expect somewhat less than 200 awardees in specialised medical fields to make this dent, but here, as in the more general scholarships for arts, social studies, pure science and technology, it is important to stress that a developing society such as India must sooner than later make an impact on the entire rural community too, and these people would not normally come into contact with medical fellows and senior fellows. Perhaps the students of the CSFP awardees will channel the expertise to the rural areas, but such a hope would be reinforced if there were some indication that those who had benefited by the awards did something developmental in a rural health centre. This would, indeed, be a 'significant contribution' to the country, and not merely a contribution to individual expertise and prestige or to institutional status and efficiency.

Staff academic fellowships

After the fourth Commonwealth Education Conference held in Nigeria in 1968, a new scheme of fellowships was advertised with ten awards. These were to be available at post-doctoral level for periods of up to one year for training in a British university or comparable institution. They would be non-medical, in view of the large number of medical fellowships already offered, and would be intended for lecturers in universities in developing Commonwealth countries who, by this training, would be fitted for greater responsibilities.

It was clear that thinking within the CSFP was moving towards the need to groom middle-level personnel in universities and comparable organisations for top leadership. The Commonwealth Academic Staff Fellowships, as they came to be called, were designed directly to help to build the numbers and quality of locally-born staff in universities overseas. The scheme was started in 1969 and is still too young to be evaluated. However, the University Grants Commission of this country has cooperated in administering the awards for members of staff of Indian universities.

Evaluation

In the first decade of the CSFP, India utilised 376 scholarship awards. She had eight visiting professors; 144 medical fellows; 30 senior medical fellows. In 1970, a year beyond the decade, she had four academic staff fellows. Her returning scholars have brought home with them a first-hand knowledge and appreciation of the distinctive strengths of the university department where they have studied in the United Kingdom. Moreover, as stated earlier, many scholars of the early 1960s now occupy chairs and other positions of influence in their universities at home. There is in India a keener awareness of good opportunities spread through the British university system, and there is therefore less anxiety to cling to the old universities on the basis of their tradition and special character. India has been the developing society to take most advantage of the medical and senior medical fellowships; she has also been among the first to profit from the Staff Academic Awards scheme, making strong demands for the further training of her teachers of science and technology.

At the end of the ten-year period, the prestige of the plan was higher than ever before in India. This was partly due to the wisdom of an early decision to ensure the future success by safeguarding the high standards of the plan. If, for the sake of a quicker 'turn-round' of scholars, it had been decided to curtail the scholarships of those who were awarded them in the early years, and before they had reached their proper academic objective, the prestige of the scheme would have been damaged and there could have been a serious risk that the quality of education would fall. The interest of British universities would have diminished; the returning scholars would have been frustrated and of less value to India and themselves. The fact that quality was at no time sacrificed to a quick turnover in numbers, accounts substantially for the continuing prestige of the CSFP.

In accordance with a recommendation made by the third Commonwealth Education Conference, a survey of the results of the scheme was begun, circularising all former scholars with a questionnaire. Information was obtained on subsequent careers during the first few years of the scheme. Rather more than one-half of the number circulated replied. From the replies received, it is clear that the majority of scholars on returning home after completion of the tenure of their awards have taken up or resumed university teaching or research or government service.

Much of the success of the plan from India's standpoint has been due to the care with which, on the one hand, her own nominations have been made, and, on the other, to the constant responsiveness shown by the Commission in the United Kingdom to suggestions made by India and her scholars. The four Educational Conferences held in the course of the decade under report have paid dividends and their recommendations have been acted upon and have led to a substantial improvement in the initial scheme. The number of India's scholars and fellows, their universally acknowledged excellence and the fact that they have understood the full implications of their awards and honoured their pledges, have made the plan for us a substantial academic success. The awards have been made in fields in which national development, by and large, has been stimulated.

It would be a brave evaluator who could translate all this into measurable terms, for the awards have been designed to benefit teaching and research institutions, and not *directly* industry or agriculture or the health of a sub-continent. Also, it may fairly be argued that visiting professorships are largely prestige awards that honour individuals but do not necessarily contribute in any substantial way to national development. They are, indeed, too few to do so. Nevertheless, both in the cumulative impact that the scheme has made on our universities in science, technology and medicine in particular, and also in the arts and social studies, and in the growing self-confidence that academic success in open competition with candidates from developed societies must stimulate, we have undoubtedly gained. We have shown, too, an initiative and educational perception in going ahead of others to utilise medical awards and staff academic awards, that argues the determination to use all opportunities to provide this country with its own medical and administrative expertise. This in itself is an indication that CSFP has done something to meet India's needs for, if not, how could we explain the rush, *supported by all employing authorities in this country*, to take advantage of expanding opportunities under the plan?

As against this, since the CSFP has now entered its second decade and has already captured the imagination of the young Indian intellectual, there is clearly the need to stress that, in addition to benefiting the individual scholar or fellow or senior fellow, and the institution that he serves or will serve, CSFP, in conjunction with the Government of India, might aim at something larger as its contribution to a sub-continental society such as India. It would be impossible to say how many of the 500 or so awardees in various fields between 1960 and 1970 had so far brought back with them, in addition to their excellent qualifications, training and expertise, a professional conscience relevant to India's needs. For the first few years after their return to this country, they may be impressed by the need to give back some part of the invisible debt that a Commonwealth award to the United Kingdom represents. But what we need from such schemes cumulatively is the continuing assurance that an awardee brings back with him for good the professional and social conscience that implies some measure of willingness to sacrifice himself for the millions who so desperately require his expertise. This is more directly applicable to medicine and surgery than to pure science; more to technology than to the arts and social sciences. There is always a danger in sub-continental situations such as India's, in which people live in many centuries at one and the same time, that the rich urban areas will grow richer, and the neglected rural areas poorer through the expertise obtained abroad, which tends to localise itself in the cities and large towns of the country. This is no reflection on CSFP *per se*; it is a suggestion to Indian administrators and Indian educationists that they should articulate national needs in total national terms, so as to apply expertise acquired abroad where it is most required and so as to confirm on a long-term basis CSFP's initial far-reaching objectives.

XIII TEN YEARS OF STUDENT SERVICES IN INDIA

There has been a very considerable expansion of college and university education in India since 1947. There were then 18 universities with a student enrolment of 266,000. By 1968–9 the number of universities had risen to over 80 and it is now 101 with a student enrolment of 3·2 million. (It is expected to rise to 3·5 million by the end of the fourth Plan.) In arts, commerce and science courses, over 30 per cent of the colleges have an enrolment of over 1000 each. Both colleges and universities in many parts of the country suffer from over-crowding.

The bulk of the expansion has occurred at undergraduate level, implying that most students stop their education at this level. Many of the students at present up at college and university belong to sections of the population that have never before had the opportunity of higher education. They come of economically and socially backward families in urban and rural areas, and require help such as those who have taken higher education in their stride do not need.

Schemes of qualitative improvement have been made with the assistance of the Indian University Grants Commission. *Inter alia*, and in order to inculcate a feeling of belonging among students, campus amenities such as health services, recreational facilities, vocational and professional guidance centres have been provided. However, the large expansion of facilities for university education has, to a very large extent, neutralised the effect of various schemes of qualitative improvement. This is evidenced by the almost constant failure rate of about 50 per cent at the undergraduate level, the alarming proportion of third divisioners, particularly in arts and commerce courses, and the deterioration in the quality of the average university student as reported by the Education Commission.

The Student Services Programme started by the United States Educational Foundation in India in 1963 becomes relevant against this background. In the early years it involved organising seminars to interpret student services and their philosophy to college teachers and administrators. After holding introductory seminars in sixteen universities throughout India in the first three years, and conducting follow-up conferences, the programme moved into more specific training in such topics as orientation of new students, advising, counselling and hostel management. The Foundation has received invitations from institutions to evaluate their organisations for student services and to suggest new programmes or modifications of the present ones. In response to these invitations the Foundation has sent consultants to visit these institutions, observe the services in action and with the help of the staff in charge of various services, suggest changes or encourage the personnel in their specific roles. The project ended in 1973.

In sum, between 1963 and 1973 Indian educationists participated in 71 conferences held all over India with full or partial USEFI support, each conference averaging about 25 representatives of colleges and universities. In the summers from 1964 to 1968, 65 Indian teachers and administrators attended three-month seminars on student services in universities of the United States. Twenty-five American experts in student personnel work served as consultants in India over the ten-year period, four of them more than once. In addition, USEFI has published materials on student services: thirteen publications have been distributed to participants and administrators in Indian colleges and universities. In November 1966 the Foundation began the semi-annual publication of *Student Services Review* which is now published regularly and distributed to participants and other educationists involved in student services. A total of 2000 participants have been involved.

Student services are defined as 'all the organised services provided by colleges outside the curriculum, which assist in each student's overall development, physical, social and emotional, as well as intellectual. A comprehensive framework for student services includes selective admission; orientation of new students; an advising system throughout the year; foreign student assistance and advising; financial aids; remedial services to improve study habits and skills; counselling, both vocational and personal; student-centred activities and clubs – physical, cultural, social; hostel administration and advising; non-resident student centres or a general student centre with canteens; a health centre for students; a cooperative store; a student judiciary and grievance system; assistance for part-time employment and earn–learn programmes; placement services for jobs after graduation; alumni relations; provision for student participation and liaison with student government; cumulative records on students; and an office of Dean of Students to coordinate and develop all student services.

Under its programme of student services USEFI has emphasised orientation of new students, advising systems and administration and advising in hostels during the first phase of student services. Connected with even the early phase, there has also been administrative planning and some form of coordination. Therefore, experts have encouraged universities to establish student services or to appoint a Dean of Students.

Most universities and colleges in India already have hostels. The innovation emphasised by the USEFI programme is that hostels should not be viewed as mere places of residence. They should be considered educational units where students learn about how to live. A survey revealed that most hostel staff members see their responsibilities as being limited to upkeep.

The originator of the Student Services Project, the late Dr Olive Reddick, argued as follows:

> In what subject or area, which is under-developed in India, has there been substantial progress in the US? Student services for American under-graduates has been one of the areas that have received a great deal of attention in recent decades. Professional positions, research and development have grown from a belief that education is not confined to textbooks and classes, but that the student learns from the residence halls, the playing fields and all his associations. So the basic objective of education should include not only intellectual learning but student personal development in such areas as self-discipline, social responsibility, discernment in values – the cultivation of the physical, moral and social, as well as of the mind.

In short, the Student Services Programme should aim at providing the individual with opportunities for constructive personal growth and to be responsive to his search for support and improvement.

Interviewing of students, teachers and administrators of Delhi University revealed the following: a first priority would be to expand the library. A second, to provide as many day-centres as possible. Also to provide a health centre on the main campus. Of the 5000 subscribers to this centre at present, only 2000 are students; the rest are staff. There are 700 foreign students in the University but only one part-time person to talk to them. (They come, for the most part, from Thailand, Iran, Mauritius and Fiji.) Students are concerned about unemployment. 'I want a job', they say, 'not a degree'. There is a University Employment, Information and

Assistance Bureau that has registered 7000 people, but last year it was able to find full-time jobs for only 600. It helped about 700 to find part-time work. The Vice-Chancellor regarded 'over-population' as the University's main problem.

The total amount expended on the Student Services Project by the US Educational Foundation is approximately Rs.1,200,000. This includes expenditure on the seminars conducted in the United States. The Indian component, chiefly in the form of transporation for Indian participants from base to venue of seminars in India, would not exceed Rs.100,000 and would probably be substantially less. USEFI has now pulled out of the programme except for the journal *Student Services Review* that it continues to finance.

Reactions to USEFI student services project

Some people have criticised the student services project on the ground that the Americans are bringing something alien to Indian culture and that such services are not really needed. Others have argued that the programme of student services is uniquely Indian and harks back to the ancient Indian universities where there was a close relationship between 'guru' and 'shishya' – a total commitment, a mutual respect, a sharing and love for each other. Still others have argued that the Indian university today is really not Indian at all but a British import going back to the philosophy and operation of the University of London's external degree of 1857.

Reactions of participants and consultants are recorded below. After every formal workshop or conference, some form of evaluation was used – group discussion or written reactions. These were used informally in planning subsequent programmes and some formal tabulation was attempted. Some participants wrote most enthusiastically about the benefits of the seminars and conferences.

A USEFI survey[6] solicited comments and suggestions in open-ended questions. The investigators obtained about a one-third response from the 507 participants in three types of training courses: the three-month programme in American universities, the one-month summer course in India and the one- or two-week seminars in India. Three-fourths of the participants were in the short-training seminars and, in general, their response rate was lower and their reactions showed less involvement in student services. They reported changed attitudes about students towards more understanding, less authoritarianism and more recognition of the value of student services. Respondents expressed strong support for training of student service specialists, particularly of a practical nature. Nearly all the respondents indicated that their universities or colleges

[6] Howes and Parker, 1972.

needed more development of student services and recommended that USEFI continue to support training in this field. Some would have liked to see direct grants for student services. (Unfortunately this is not possible under the Fulbright programme which is primarily an exchange programme.) The publications produced were appreciated. The investigators formed the conclusions that 'training in student services seems to have borne fruit since the vast majority of responding participants were actively involved with student services at the time of the study and USA seminar participants appear to have done especially well'.

A survey conducted by Arnold and Pasricha in 1967 found that Indian institutions were beginning advisory services in a small but significant way. Among 70 respondents to a questionnaire, 40 had started the advising services within the last four years; only ten indicated their programmes were at least ten years old. Pasricha and George reported in 1971 on a small sample of 18 participants in an intensive course coming from 16 institutions. Although nearly all had orientation programmes, hostels and medical centre, the authors concluded that little was being done for students outside the classroom. Howes and Parker (the best survey) sent questionnaires to three samples of college and university totalling 272 and giving a 49 per cent response rate. The final report was based on 36 institutions from which representatives participated in the long course in the United States or India, 69 which had personnel in short seminars, and 28 which had no contact with USEFI projects. The study tested the proposition that greater contact with USEFI projects would be related to more use of student services. Intensive course institutions tended to provide more services being clearly superior to non-contact institutions in orientation programmes, use of student records, organised advisement programmes, counselling centres and vocational information and placement services. The inference drawn by the investigators was that 'in general institutions in which at least a few of the staff members had been exposed to USEFI student services seminars offered not only more student services but also better services than no-contact institutions did'.

The appointment of a Dean of Students was recommended by the Education Commission in 1966. Howes and Parker reported that the number of Deans of Students or equivalent in contact *versus* no-contact institutions in 1972 was about the same, i.e. half of the 133 institutions. Universities as compared with colleges were much more apt to have a Dean of Students and he was more likely to be full time. General agreement on responsibility, the highest frequency being general student welfare and coordination of services, was followed by individual advising, acting as advocate for students to policy-making bodies and initiating policies regarding non-class activities of students. Another survey sent to all 85 universities showed that of 57 correspondents, 13 had part-time and 23 full-time Deans of Students, a total of 58 per cent.

Consultants have reacted differently but always in some positive way to the USEFI student services project. Dr Thomas Schreck of the University of Indiana says:

> I feel very strongly that the Student Services Project has been very worthwhile. It has probably provided India with a leadership role in applying student services throughout Asia. I can think back to my experience in 1963–64 and contrast them to our summer workshop in 1969, and the progress and sophistication was obvious to any observer.

Professor Henry Weitz of the Department of Education, Duke University, Durham, North Carolina says:

> I am sorry to learn that the Fulbright programme in Student Services is being phased out although this does not surprise me. The structure of Indian higher education is after all hierarchic and authoritarian. This structure operates in such a way as to provide a means for the exercise of power, frequently political, by a relatively small number of educational officials. Please note that I do not say this is bad – or good either. I merely say that this appears to be the traditional Indian way of doing things and it has resulted in maintaining and enhancing Indian culture which is, after all, what an education system is all about.
>
> This system, however, leaves little room for the intervention of professional student services officers, for well-trained skilful professionals would divert and dilute some of the presently held power. Indians have not learned, nor have we in this country, that power shared is power enhanced.

Model for the future?

Can the USEFI project be said to have set up a model for the future in Indian colleges and universities? Will universities continue to support and develop student services in the coming years? Will a professional training programme be established? Will student services improve the performance of students both in college and later? These are some of the questions that must be asked, and answered to the extent possible, on a ten-year programme if we are to evaluate foreign aid in this activity.

In discussion with Dr Prem Pasricha, who has been chiefly associated with the project, it became clear that USEFI would have wished to continue the project if funds had been available, because it was still too early to be sure that student services had struck root in Indian university and college soil, and could move of its own momentum. The response, as might have been expected, has varied from institution to institution, having been particularly good at the SNDT Women's University, Sri Venkateswara, Calicut and Jaipur universities. Dr Pasricha considers that the most crucial point of the programme is the appointment of effective

Deans of Students. Once this has been done, one may be optimistic about achieving the objectives at which the project aimed.

It is hard to give a categorical answer to the evaluative questions that we have asked, for so much depends on the general economic health of the country and this lies outside educational administration or capacity. The University Grants Commission is clearly in favour of improved student services and no one fails to support the recommendations of the Education Commission Report on this subject. Nevertheless, as suggested earlier, we have to reckon with a rapidly increasing college student population that dilutes whatever progress has been made in many places. Educated unemployment is very great. Student violence is still prevalent. The polarisation of universities into political factions has done much to damage whatever consensus used to be present on the campus. Students, teachers and administrators have some difficulty finding common goals and working towards them. With this background, only a moderate expectation in regard to student services is realistic, but undoubtedly an awareness of what is necessary has been created and, if follow-up is lacking, it will not be because the philosophy propounded by Dr Olive Reddick is not accepted so much as that, with very limited funds and higher priorities in higher education, the funds earmarked specifically for this purpose are inadequate.

XIV THE CENTRAL INSTITUTE OF ENGLISH

The decision to set up the Central Institute of English at Hyderabad in 1958 was preceded by this announcement by the Government of India:

> Whereas, considering the falling standards of English in India, especially at the secondary school stage of education, it is deemed necessary to take steps to improve the teaching of English, both through organisation of research in the teaching of this subject and the training of teachers in the most suitable techniques, the Government of India hereby resolve to establish an English Language Teaching Institute of a sufficiently high standard. The Institute will function under the management of an autonomous body to be known as the Board of Governors, which will be registered under the Societies Registration Act of 1860.

The main functions of the CIE were summarised as follows:

> With a view to improving the standard of the teaching of English in India, to provide for the study of English Language and Literature, to organise research in the teaching of the subject, to train teachers, to undertake and facilitate advanced courses, conferences and seminars; to hold examinations and grant academic awards and distinctions or titles; to prepare suitable textbooks at various levels; to undertake and

provide for the publication of journals and periodicals in furtherance of its objectives; to establish, maintain and manage halls and hostels for the residence of students; to institute teaching, administrative, technical and ministerial posts and to make appointments thereto; to initiate and award fellowships and scholarships, prizes and medals; and to allocate grants to institutions with similar objectives.

Financing the Institute

The Ford Foundation during the first ten years of the Institute's existence met the expenses of the appointment of British and American specialists; provided specialised training abroad for some eight members of the Institute; gave substantial help in building up the library and radio studio, and assisted with short term rupee expenditure.

The British Council lent some of its best language teaching specialists. The late Mr J. G. Bruton, an Englishman, was the first Director of Studies. In later years British Council officers were available to the CIE under the Aid to Commonwealth English scheme. But as Dr Ramesh Mohan has written, 'the contribution from the Ford Foundation and the British Council can in no way be equated with the contributions of the Government of India'. This is highlighted by the fact that for the period 1960–9 the relative contributions of the Government of India and the Ford Foundation were as follows: grants from the Government of India, Rs.60·88 Lakhs; from the Ford Foundation Rs.33·55 Lakhs.

Academic courses

In the first four years of the CIE's existence, it ran two four-month courses a year for teachers of English from arts and science colleges, training colleges and schools, high and higher secondary schools, and for Inspectors of Education. Each course provided for 60 participants. Four months was found to be too short a period to equip teachers, other than those of exceptional ability, to work as efficient teacher-trainers or to organise language courses effectively in schools and colleges. The Government of India Review Committee in 1961 suggested a course of longer duration, not less than nine months. In 1962 a longer course was introduced, leading to a diploma in the teaching of English.

In 1966 the teaching programme of the CIE was reorganised and two self-contained courses were introduced:

i. a basic course leading to a certificate in the teaching of English, and

ii. an advanced course, leading to a diploma in the teaching of English.

The primary aim of the first was to improve professional competence, in particular of participants at school or college level. Admission to the advanced course depended on a satisfactory performance in the examination held at the end of the basic course. The advanced course was intended primarily to meet the needs of teacher-trainers. In 1967 the two courses were renamed respectively the certificate and the diploma course. In 1968, a diploma course in English studies was introduced to meet the needs of university and college teachers who had to teach both language and literature to BA and MA classes.

The CIE at present offers a postgraduate certificate in the teaching of English; a postgraduate diploma in the teaching of English; a postgraduate diploma in English studies and a postgraduate research diploma in the teaching of English. The certificate course is designed to improve professional competence of university and secondary teachers and teacher-trainers; the diploma course aims at producing specialists in teaching English as a second language at university and secondary levels. The diploma course in English studies has the same programme as the diploma in the teaching of English except that, instead of methods of teaching, practice teaching and a term paper, participants study the main trends in contemporary English literature (1920–60) and write a dissertation.

Short summer courses of two to six weeks in duration are organised in collaboration with the University Grants Commission for university and college teachers, and other special groups of teachers who are not able to attend regular courses. A one-year research diploma introduced in 1967 is for those who hold responsible positions at University Departments of English and English Language Teaching Institutes in various parts of India, of which there are now ten.

The Institute has now enlarged its activities to include foreign languages other than English, but this study will concern itself with English only for the period 1960–9.

Dimension of the problem

At various points between 1960 and 1969, authoritative comment has indicated that the standard of English at various levels of the educational process has declined steeply and that it is necessary in the national interest to do something effective to stem the decline. Thus Jawaharlal Nehru said:

> If we are going to keep up English, we must try to keep up certain standards in English. It is a fact, people tell me, that standards in English have gone down considerably in India. They are bound to go down as it ceases to be the medium of instruction. It is desirable to keep them up and the effort made here in this Institute [CIE] is a basic one and an important one and I hope it will succeed.

The Education Commission, appointed by the Government of India, reported in 1966:

> As English will for a long time to come continue to be needed as a 'library language' in the field of higher education, a strong foundation in the language will have to be laid at the school stage. We have

recommended that its teaching may begin in Class V but we realise that for many pupils, particularly in the rural areas, the study will not commence before Class VIII. The fact that English will be for the overwhelming majority of pupils only a second or a third language, makes it all the more necessary to ensure the adoption of effective modern methods of teaching the language by teachers who have been specially trained for the purpose. In this connection we would like to refer to a recent report (*The Study of English in India* by a Study Group appointed by the Ministry of Education). The group has supported the teaching of English on the basis of the structural approach which is now being used increasingly in different parts of India, and has suggested a detailed syllabus for the study of the language from Class V to Class XII both at the ordinary and at the advanced levels.

The Commission endorsed this recommendation.

The Commission was of the view that it was educationally unsound to begin the teaching of English in India at the level of Class 3. It said, 'The effective teaching of English in the lower primary classes where millions of pupils are enrolled required a very large number of trained teachers who are not available.' It was also of the view that to attempt to do this would be to incur a heavy drain on the funds allotted for education. 'In our opinion, this is a colossal task, the improper pursuit of which will lower rather than upgrade the standard of English at the school stage'.

The Commission further recommended:

i. Special units for teaching English that should be established in universities and colleges whose main objective would be to give a good working knowledge of English to new entrants by the adoption of modern teaching techniques and in as short a time as possible. A distinction has to be made between the teaching of English as a skill and the teaching of English literature. The teachers in this unit will therefore need special training on the lines of the pioneer work being done at the Central Institute of English at Hyderabad. Moreover, it has to be noted that the students who enter the universities will be at different levels of attainment in English. Some will have come from English-medium schools and will be well advanced. Others who come from urban schools with, comparatively speaking, good facilities for teaching English would be at an average level. But a large number who would have come from the rural areas or the weaker schools will be at a much lower level of attainment. No single course in English would meet the needs of all these students. It should therefore be a responsibility of the English units to adjust their teaching to the needs of the different kinds of students and to ensure that they are all given at least that essential command over the language which will enable them to use it efficiently as a library language.

ii. In Major universities it will be necessary as a rule to adopt English as the medium of education because their students and teachers will be drawn on an all-India basis. This is the only feasible approach if their all-India character is to be maintained.

The Commission was not averse to experiments in regional languages, but it made its position on the value of sound instruction in the English language clear beyond all ambiguity. This should have cured those who tend to be complacent about the level of English teaching in India.

By 1969 the Central Institute of English had trained a total of 1199 or approximately 1200 teachers. The map in the Appendix indicates the areas from which these teachers come, and the table supplies detailed information on the courses taken (pp. 285–7).

The CIE has given financial assistance to regional and state Institutes of English and to training colleges out of the funds placed at its disposal for this purpose. Several institutes and colleges have benefited through the creation of teaching posts in the Institution of English, through research projects aimed at raising the standard of English; through the preparation of teaching materials, audio-visual aids and through the library of books on the teaching of English.

Substantial work has also been done in the preparation of two series of textbooks for the learning/teaching of English at secondary level. The Institute works in close liaison with the National Council of Educational Research and Training, that publishes the materials which are now in use in all the Central schools of the country, and are being increasingly adopted and adapted by various state governments for schools under their jurisdiction. There are also the radio programmes developed by the CIE, which have been regularly broadcast for some years for schools in Andhra Pradesh, and are being extended to cover the whole of India. Special mention also deserves to be made of the research programmes undertaken at the Institute and its growing list of publications. As a measure of its rising status at higher level the CIE, which now has University status, is recognised as a research centre by more than twenty universities in India.

Evaluation

Some idea of the dimension of the problem that the CIE was called into being to solve, has already been provided in the statement of its objectives and the comment of the Education Commission. The Government of India has appointed review committees and two study groups, one in 1964 and the other in 1969 which have pronounced on the problems that confront the CIE. The comments of these committees and groups and the changes that have followed upon their analyses in the course of the ten years under review, indicate that this has been a period of constant adjustment to meet needs larger than the CIE appears to have been able, with its resources, to serve. If, for instance, the recommendations of the Education Commission were to be implemented, the CIE would have been responsible, directly or indirectly through its associate organisations for providing trained teachers for about ten million school children and for another two million or so at undergraduate level. In fact, as we have seen, only about 1200 teachers were actually trained by the Institute between 1958 and 1969. Even if we add to these others trained at the ten ELTI's in various parts of the country which received grants from the CIE, the number of trained teachers turned out would be only a small fraction of the number required to make the sub-continental impact on the teaching of English envisaged by the Commission.

The Gokak Committee reported in 1965 that the number of *additional* teachers required per year for the five years 1965–70 would be 16,000 at the middle school stage; 7000 at the higher school stage; 2800 at the higher secondary stage and 2300 at the undergraduate stage. This would make a total of about 28,000 additional trained teachers per year against the 1200 trained teachers produced in eleven years.

Dr Ramesh Mohan, the present Director of CIE, who has been in charge of the Institute since 1967 and whose forthright analysis of the problem is well worth our consideration, says:

> The entire strategy of planning and development of the Institute hitherto was based on the assumption that teachers from all over the country would come to Hyderabad for training and they in turn would train others. But although the Institute has so far [by 1972] trained about 1500 teachers in the various courses, the multiplier effect that was expected has not been achieved to any satisfactory extent. Because of the large distances in this vast country and regional variations, it has been difficult for the Institute to keep in close touch with institutions and to implement its programme of organised follow up work effectively from one centralised location. The Institute has therefore decided to set up a few regional centres.

(It has now been decided to set up a regional centre in Shillong in Assam. No ELTI's exist in this region at present. This regional centre will serve the needs of Assam, Maghalaya, Arunachal Pradesh and contiguous areas.)

Dr Ramesh Mohan continues:

> A careful review of the achievements and failings of the Institute during previous years has led to the conclusion that while the Institute's programme for work at the university level has been a move in the right direction, it needs to be intensified and properly planned to be more effective.
>
> To avoid the thin spreading of the Institute's assistance over a number of institutions and consequent wastage, it is proposed to begin with a concentration of assistance on some selected universities and extend it gradually to others. For this purpose, ten or fifteen major

universities may be chosen, preferably one from each state. These universities will have to commit themselves to a planned programme of work in joint consultation with the Institute. While the other universities or colleges may still be assisted through the Institute's participation in the University Grants Commission Summer Institutes, and the organisation of short courses and training of teachers, the Institute in collaboration with the UGC, should be able to provide full facilities and adequate financial support to these selected universities and autonomous colleges to strengthen their teaching and research components in the ELT fields.

The 1969 study group appointed by the Government of India, commenting on why important earlier recommendations had not been implemented, said:

> There is a grave shortage of trained and fully qualified teachers in English at almost all stages of the educational system.
>
> The State Education Departments have been slow in taking decisions, and even where decisions have been taken, enough resources are not available to carry them out. Often Departments have not been able to utilise fully the facilities available at various specialist centres and to organise their own courses for re-training or in-service training. In general, facilities available for reform and reorganisation have been inadequate. The result is that curricular changes have been very slow. In these circumstances even trained teachers have been unable to make any great contribution to the improvement of the teaching of the subject.
>
> The supervision of English teaching in schools has continued to be neglected with hardly any trained specialists engaged in this task.

From all this, it is clear that what was originally expected of the Central Institute of English has not been realised. Education is a state subject and if the state Departments of Education are not willing to treat the teaching of English as an area of educational priority and to depute their teachers of English regularly to the CIE for training, there is little that the Institute can do about it. The numbers involved even as teacher-trainers at school level are so large that no one institute with the resources that have been made available jointly by the Government of India and the Ford Foundation, would have been adequate to cope with them. If the multiplier effect is to be achieved at school level, the training colleges would require to be staffed by people with a clear command of the English language and modern methods of language teaching. Unfortunately, as Dr Ramesh Mohan observes,

> these establishments are not so staffed. Even if they were, their existing time-tables would not allow qualified teacher-trainers to do much good. Few of these establishments have exploited in substantial measure the

training facilities offered by the CIE. All too often there is only one lecturer concerned with training in English teaching and the training colleges do not find it possible to send him away for training of any really useful length.

When the Institute was set up, it was not of course envisaged that it would by itself be responsible for training or re-training all the primary, secondary and university teachers that India needs in the English language. There is a working arrangement by which the Regional Institutes of English at Bangalore and Chandigarh and the other ELTIs are responsible for training teachers in their own states, and the CIE helps to train only the key personnel that the regional institutes and the ELTIs need. Some of these organisations, notably the Regional Institute of English, Bangalore, the State Institutes of English, Maharashtra and the Regional Institute of English, Chandigarh, have done impressive work. Any evaluation of the CIE is bound to range further than its own immediate achievement, for the problem of maintaining and creating standards in English is sub-continental and takes in the work of the regional institutes and the ELTIs. It would be difficult and unfair to pinpoint responsibility for the inadequacy of what has been achieved as a totality in this field. The fact is, however, that the impact of foreign aid in this instance has been relatively small.

The conclusion is irresistible: the educational community in India – and this includes educational administrators in state governments as well as at universities – have not accorded to the teaching of English as a language the priority that Jawaharlal Nehru and the Union Ministry of Education hoped that they would give it. In consequence, and also because its resources have been small relative to the dimension of the problem it was required to tackle, the CIE's impact has been very small. Dr Ramesh Mohan's most recent proposal to concentrate the Institute's limited resources at ten or fifteen major universities may yield some fruit, but even so, there is unlikely to be a sub-continental change for the better in the teaching of English, and the sound recommendations of the Education Commission may well remain a dead letter.

The influence of the Central Institute of English has so far been seminal. It has played a not insignificant part in making universities and state governments aware of the need for ELT reform; syllabuses both at university and secondary levels have undergone much-needed changes as a result of the Institute's efforts. What has been achieved, has been achieved with the assistance of the Ford Foundation, and the contribution of the Government of India and the British Council has been substantial. Nevertheless, the high expectations with which the Central Institute of English was set up have not been realised and there is, therefore, reason to think through the problem afresh in order to see how aid can be more effectively applied in the seventies.

XV SUMMING UP

The historical introduction and background to economic planning that precede the selected case-studies on India make it clear that, from several points of view, India is in a special position. Her great age, with the continuity that is evident in her 3000 years of history, her sub-continental size, with all the variety and diversity that persist, and that are implied in her size and history, suggest that her educational problems are of a dimension and complexity rare in other parts of the modern world. The numbers involved at various stages of the educational process, the numbers which exist to be served through planning for national development set her apart, as does the fact that she is more developed than most developing societies, though less developed than the typical developed society. Her background of association with Britain and her determination since 1947 to make a democratic socialist society work, also distinguish her from societies that have either abandoned the democratic way of life or are still dominated by the ideal of free enterprise.

The reader may wonder what determined the choice of the case-studies. In part, this choice was dictated by the priorities that India has spelt out for herself in the process of national development. The logic of numbers dictates that in all planning the training of teacher-trainers is the most effective multiplier. Most of the case-studies exemplify this approach to educational planning and the application of foreign aid to the solution of educational problems. Thus, the development of the Indian Institutes of Technology, of teacher-training for polytechnics, of Technical Training Institutes, of science education improvement, of Agricultural Universities, of Institutes of Management are examples of aid accepted and applied to recognised areas of priority in a deliberate plan of national development.

There are, however, other recognised national priorities, notably universal, compulsory, free elementary education, in which foreign aid has never been given or taken. The omission of this item is explained by the fact that it was never considered for foreign aid, a gap that it is not easy to explain if the underlying principle governing the acceptance of foreign aid is to stress development in areas identified as being crucial to national development.

Some of the questions that the selected case-studies have posed are: was the need for foreign aid imperative at the time at which it was accepted and, if so, is it still necessary? If it was imperative, how thoughtfully and profitably has aid been applied to the solution of a national educational problem? If it was not imperative, why was it accepted and continued even when there was no evidence of significant gain? The purpose of the studies is to assess the success or failure or comparative success with which the decisions to accept and apply aid were accompanied and, since all developing societies have necessarily to be pragmatic, to learn from the experience of the sixties.

To ask whether or not India could have built up her Institutes of

Technology and other comparable educational organisations without foreign aid is to ask a not particularly useful question. If developing countries are willing indefinitely to prolong their period of development, it probably is possible to do without foreign aid altogether. Since, however, the time factor is of crucial importance to such societies, the acceptance of aid at a given point of time is often an indication that such assistance was considered necessary in order to accelerate a process of national growth and development. In deciding to accept a measure of foreign aid in some areas of priority, India was generally well advised. For instance, in accepting aid to train teachers of polytechnics, the Government of India applied aid to an area of priority in which she patently lacked expertise. Today, she would not require foreign aid in this area.

Science education improvement was also an area of priority, but aid here was accepted precipitately and without that careful preliminary examination of India's own resources that might well have met national needs more effectively. India had, and has, no dearth of top-flight scientists in her own universities and research institutes, though it is true that few had, or have, of their own volition, taken any real interest in school science and the need to improve it. Nevertheless, it was possible, as the National Council of Educational Research and Training demonstrated, to bridge the gap between scientific research at higher level, and science teaching in school. The recognition that this was the most sensible strategy in the Indian situation, came, while the UNESCO–UNDP project was already being implemented and the indigenous scheme, excellent as its results had been in the short period it worked, was then abandoned because it duplicated the work of the UNESCO–UNDP project. The moral would appear to be that where a developing society has the expertise to develop a scheme itself, it is unnecessary and even wasteful to go in for foreign aid. The experience of the science education improvement project at school level should provide a warning against the temptation to accept aid in similar circumstances in future.

Other case-studies have been included that are either only partially related to areas of national priority or deal with situations in which there has been little national investment, but in which a foreign country has had something to offer in experience and expertise; or in the development of a high-level institution that clearly has some educational importance, but less than recognised national areas such as science, technology, agriculture and medicine. India's participation in the Commonwealth Scholarship and Fellowship Plan is among these. Awards under the plan were made *inter alia* in areas such as the humanities and social studies that were not considered areas of priority for which foreign aid was necessary. The purpose of the plan was to strengthen universities and other comparable institutions at higher level and undoubtedly some solid gains were made in the ten years under review. In assessing such schemes today the difficulty arises of estimating their value in national or sub-continental impact. Individuals and institutions have both clearly gained from the plan, and educational leadership has been developed at higher level. It would, however, be difficult in the Indian situation to assess *national* gain. The awardees from such schemes tend to concentrate in urban areas and so to widen the gap that already exists between the relatively prosperous city and the backward countryside. In terms of national need, it seems advisable to introduce new conditions of eligibility into such schemes, that will ensure that those reaping the advantage of scholarships and fellowships under them are returned compulsorily to areas of India in which their services are most crucially needed.

Though the Education Commission stressed the importance of student services in the Indian university and college situation, and though the work done with the assistance of the US Educational Foundation in India over the ten years under review was substantial, this was not an area of priority in educational development. The project was too small to make a sub-continental impact, was sustained for too short a period to strike root in Indian university soil, and the danger that money will now not be available to continue it reduces its value as an important item for long-term educational investment.

Many of the projects selected raise the question of the comparative contribution made by the Government of India and the foreign country and/or agency in financing a developmental scheme in education. In general, the share of the Government of India has been substantially larger than that of the contributing foreign country or agency, and this is as it should be. There are notable exceptions such as the Commonwealth Scholarship and Fellowship Plan and the US student services project in which India has received more than she has given. Dr Ramesh Mohan, Director of the Central Institute of English and Foreign Languages, stresses that aid the Institute received, through the Ford Foundation and the British Council, can in no way be equated with the greater contributions of the Government of India.

A similar comment could be made on the other case studies that have been analysed, where the Indian component is very much larger than the foreign counterpart. The final evaluation is always of a collaborative venture in which the quantum of foreign aid must in each case be carefully noted. It is a matter of some satisfaction to India that she has generally borne the major burden of her own educational development.

The evaluations made in the case-studies selected exemplify changing attitudes on the part of educational planners as well as, possibly, of the Indian people. There is today a much stronger feeling *for* self-sufficiency and *against* the acceptance of foreign aid than there was in 1947, the year of Indian Independence. This is a change in the right direction, since it argues greater national self-confidence and a willingness to make sacrifices in order to evolve institutions that truly suit the character of the country. The acceptance of aid often implies the acceptance of a foreign social, economic, or industrial pattern. It is possibly wiser in the long run to make domestic mistakes and to learn from them, than to make the sort of expensive international mistake that appears to have been made in the evolution of a science education improvement programme. The sixties have been years of experiment in receiving and applying foreign aid; we should all be wiser for this experience in the seventies.

APPENDIX

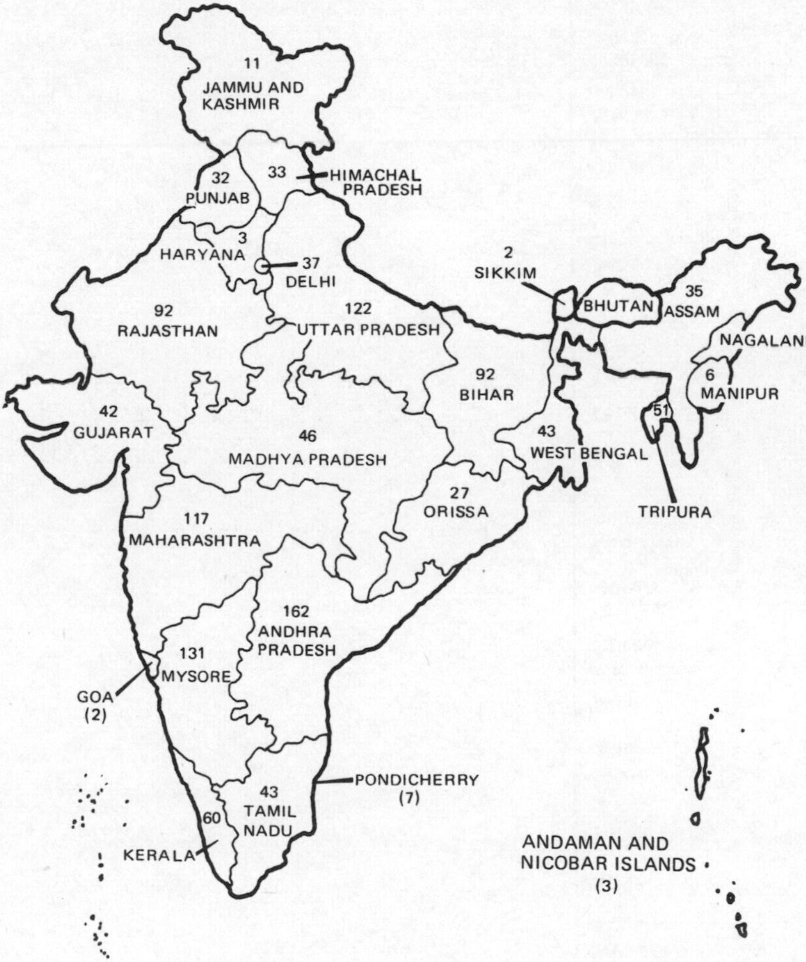
11
JAMMU AND
KASHMIR
32
PUNJAB
33
HIMACHAL
PRADESH
3
HARYANA
37
DELHI
92
RAJASTHAN
122
UTTAR PRADESH
2
SIKKIM
BHUTAN
35
ASSAM
NAGALAND
6
MANIPUR
51
TRIPURA
92
BIHAR
43
WEST BENGAL
42
GUJARAT
46
MADHYA PRADESH
27
ORISSA
117
MAHARASHTRA
162
ANDHRA
PRADESH
131
MYSORE
GOA
(2)
PONDICHERRY
(7)
43
TAMIL
NADU
60
KERALA
ANDAMAN AND
NICOBAR ISLANDS
(3)

Number of participants who attended CIE courses, 1958–69

States	*Diploma in the teaching of English*					*Diploma in English studies*		*Four-month courses*					*Certificate courses*					*Short summer courses*					*Total*
	Arts/science colleges	Training colleges	Secondary schools	Others	Total	Arts/science colleges	Total	Arts/science colleges	Training colleges	Secondary schools	Others	Total	Arts/science colleges	Training colleges	Secondary schools	Others	Total	Arts/science colleges	Training colleges	Secondary schools	Others	Total	
Andamans	–	–	–	–	–	–	–	–	–	–	–	–	–	–	3	–	3	–	–	–	–	–	3
Andhra Pradesh	28	4	13	7	52	1	1	32	7	14	4	57	1	–	2	1	4	21	9	7	11	48	162
Assam	7	2	6	–	15	–	–	3	1	7	–	11	2	–	–	–	2	4	–	2	1	7	35
Bihar	7	4	20	–	31	–	–	8	3	18	–	29	2	–	2	–	4	14	6	6	2	28	92
Chandigarh																							
Delhi	–	2	2	–	4	1	1	2	–	3	1	6	–	–	–	2	2	10	3	7	4	24	37
Goa	–	–	–	–	–	–	–	–	–	–	–	–	–	–	–	–	–	2	–	–	–	2	2
Gujarat	5	1	2	1	9	–	–	2	–	1	–	3	1	2	–	–	3	11	8	1	7	27	42
Haryana	–	–	–	–	–	–	–	1	–	–	–	1	1	–	–	–	1	–	–	1	–	1	3
Himachala Pradesh	1	–	5	–	6	–	–	3	1	13	2	19	2	1	2	–	5	1	1	1	–	3	33
Jammu and Kashmir	1	1	–	–	2	–	–	1	2	2	–	5	–	–	–	–	–	–	3	–	1	4	11
Kerala	1	3	9	7	20	–	–	7	5	8	–	20	2	–	1	–	3	2	10	3	2	17	60
Madhya Pradesh	2	2	8	1	13	–	–	1	3	2	1	7	–	–	–	1	1	10	5	2	8	25	46
Maharashtra	11	4	8	3	26	–	–	22	9	10	3	44	–	–	2	1	3	19	16	5	4	44	117
Manipur	1	–	1	–	2	–	–	1	–	2	–	3	–	–	–	–	–	–	1	–	–	1	6
Mysore	6	4	24	8	42	2	2	11	8	14	1	34	–	1	5	1	7	22	11	5	8	46	131
Nagaland																							
Orissa	2	–	4	–	6	–	–	1	–	10	–	11	3	–	–	–	3	3	1	2	1	7	27
Pondicherry	1	–	1	–	2	–	–	2	–	1	–	3	–	–	–	1	1	–	1	–	–	1	7

Punjab	2	1	4	2	9	–	–	2	–	–	–	2	–	–	–	–	–	12	3	6	–	21	32
Rajasthan	17	2	22	4	45	2	2	3	–	5	1	9	2	–	2	2	6	11	6	3	10	30	92
Sikkim	–	–	–	–	–	–	–	–	–	–	–	–	–	–	2	–	2	–	–	–	–	–	2
Tamil Nadu	3	2	–	–	5	–	–	1	–	–	1	2	1	–	–	1	2	17	10	2	5	34	43
Tripura	2	2	16	–	20	–	–	–	2	14	–	16	1	–	4	–	5	2	2	5	1	10	51
Uttar Pradesh	16	2	1	6	25	–	–	13	6	2	1	22	11	–	1	1	13	25	13	15	9	62	122
West Bengal	1	–	4	1	6	1	1	5	2	8	–	15	1	–	–	–	1	9	3	3	5	20	43
Total	116	34	150	40	340	7	7	121	49	134	15	319	30	4	26	11	71	195	112	76	79	462	1199

Note: On account of the division of certain states and the formation of new ones, the figures shown against all such states should be interpreted with caution. For instance, the figure 3 shown against Haryana gives only the number of people trained from that state *after* the formation of the state, the ones trained earlier from that part of the country having already been included under Punjab.

7 Turkey

Paul Stirling

I INTRODUCTION

Part at least of our problem ought to be hard and practical. How many skilled fitters, expert citrus growers, economic forecasters, textile chemists does Turkey need? How do, how should the donors contribute to their production? For all the experts and sophistication, even questions such as these are baffling; and often loaded.

But we are also involved in a massive, organised yet haphazard transfer of cultures, of ways of life, between nations. Science as a way of organising and thinking, moral and political values, legal codes, financial institutions, educational institutions, purposes and methods; in short, ways of perceiving, organising, understanding and constructing the world both physical and social, and ways of organising and controlling people and getting things done. Moreover, what is being transferred is itself changing, confused and teeming with contradictions and active conflicts.

Thousands of people are involved in hundreds of aid projects. Their perceptions of reality differ, often sharply. They do not present a consistent picture of what is happening, nor of what they and others are doing. In particular, official truth is never the whole truth. This record of and comment on a part of the technical assistance in Turkey up to 1972 plainly reflects these difficulties.

II TURKISH HISTORY

Modern Turkey inherits from the Ottoman Empire its geographical position as a bridge between Europe and Asia, between Christendom and Islam. The Ottoman Empire was the centre of a triumphant Islamic civilisation, conqueror of northern barbarians and infidels. Only with reluctance, in its declining years, did it borrow from the West. The Republic from 1923 set out consciously to join a triumphant Europe as a fully-fledged industrial national state.

The conscious import by the Ottomans of European knowledge and values is a vast theme.[1] Islam as a religious system embodies not only theology and morals, but specific legal, political, and social institutions. Education was entirely within the religious context. Western schools in Turkey by contrast meant secular schools, beginning with military sciences in the eighteenth century. The opposition to this cosmic innovation was fierce and the battle long. The control of education lay at the root of the attempted reforms of the nineteenth century, and the reformers were themselves products of the new educational institutions. Thus although many Ottoman reforms existed largely on paper, by the turn of the century the government had established a functioning Ministry of Education with a system of state primary, secondary and high schools and the University of Istanbul, besides the schools for military sciences, military medical services, and the Mulkiye for training civil servants. The European powers fell over themselves to offer advisers. The French were most successful, and the most famous school in Turkey is still the Galatasaray Lycée, which teaches mainly in French and is supported by the French government to this day. It is the Alma Mater of many influential Turkish Westernisers. Equally, America founded another renowned and influential institution, Robert College, in 1963 (p. 307).

The Ottoman Turks have never been ruled over by outsiders. But in the last years of the Ottoman Empire, they experienced a very large measure of internal interference from Europe. The famous Capitulations, introduced for certain foreigners by Suleyman the Lawgiver in the sixteenth century, gave foreigners extra territorial rights, especially economic ones. The Ottoman Debt Administration controlled directly some sources of government revenue. Foreign officers advised the armed forces and commanded the rural police; foreign capital owned a vast proportion of the factories, food-exporting industries, railways and mines. Finally in 1919, after the defeat of Turkey by the Allied Forces, came the plan to divide Anatolia between the victors, and the Greek invasion of the eastern seaboard. But in the same month, May 1919, Mustafa Kemal, later Ataturk, organised and lead opposition to the Allies and the Sultan. He succeeded in halting, and by 1922 in expelling the Greeks, and a year later through his lieutenant Inönü, in winning the diplomatic battle for absolute national independence within the present frontiers[2] with only a modest residue of Ottoman debt. The Republic of Turkey was established on 29 October 1923.

[1] H. A. R. Gibb and H. Bowen, *Islamic Society and the West*, 1957.
[2] The Hatay was acquired from the French authorities in Syria in 1939.

Ataturk had three objectives. First, to keep and defend national independence, and for this he needed an efficient army. Secondly, he needed to promote rapid economic growth, and thirdly, he set out to turn the new Republic into a European, liberal, rational, industrial democracy. The list of legislative and institutional reforms between 1923 and 1928 is as staggering as the military achievement which preceded it (see Appendix, Table 7.2).

Ataturk faced three dilemmas. Since the vast majority of Turks did not understand, let alone share, his aims, and many important and powerful men opposed him, Western-style liberal democratic institutions were for the time being out of the question. Secondly, to become an equal partner in Europe, Turkey needed knowledge, organisations, institutions, and capital and consumption goods from Europe. But after the experience of the Ottoman Empire and with the British and French empires still vigorous, and now holding mandated territories on Turkey's south-eastern frontiers, the new Republic was understandably nervous, not to say xenophobic. How could she imitate and get resources from the West without becoming dependent? Thirdly, two centuries of Western education had demonstrated that the Western educated always brought back, besides the much-needed technical knowledge, new and dangerous ideas with which to challenge the established order.

In spite of Ataturk's massive political, legal, educational, and cultural reforms, the Turkish economy grew, or so it is always said, only slowly.[3] By the early 1930s the government turned from hopes of private enterprise to a new economic policy of State intervention, Étatism or State Capitalism, and instituted in 1934 a five-year plan for the development of certain basic industries. The USSR and other countries helped the plan with what we would now call international aid. Nevertheless, the Second World War inhibited growth and from 1938 to 1950 the GNP per head hardly changed.

But since 1950, or thereabouts, the economy has been growing fairly fast, recently the GNP at 6–7 per cent per annum. Social changes, urbanisation, industrialism, new consumer habits, are now rapid. Popular demand for formal education is growing and the national shortages of many kinds of trained manpower are also growing. In spite of unemployment and rapid inflation, most Turks are materially much better off.

On the other hand, Turkey's development has been basically conservative. Ataturk's revolutionary movement was inspired by simple nationalism, and by the hopes of a prosperous future in the likeness of the European liberal democracies. Kemalism did not offer any kind of new

[3] It is likely that from the very low level in 1923, growth, if we could measure retrospectively the subsistence and local sectors, was rapid; but the effects were not conspicuous.

moral or political utopianism and was fiercely anti-Communist. No one suggested that Turkey should or could be an example to the world of social justice, or spiritual peace, or anything else. As it happens, the Western capitalist democracies are, or were then, pleased with their prosperity; and with their freedom, indeed many of us thought we were fighting for it against the totalitarian nationalism of Nazism and Fascism. Turkey has little ground for being pleased with prosperity, and no Turkish government has or could use freedom as a major political rallying cry. Even in the liberal period from 1963 to 1971, the freedom to foregather, to discuss, to publish, to teach and to conduct research was supported only by a dedicated minority among the educated; most of the nation was indifferent to, even suspicious of such liberty.

III TURKISH EDUCATION

The present main organisation of Turkish schools, colleges and universities is simple to outline. Children attend primary school for five years (aged 6–11), and middle school for three years, (11–14). After middle school a range of schools is available. The main academic stream leads through high schools, general and scientific, to university. A variety of more specialised schools, taking children from 11 to 18, are also available – secretarial, commercial, technical, religious. Middle school graduates may also go on to 'normal' schools for four years, in order to train as teachers. High school graduates may go to Institutes of Education to become school teachers for higher age groups.

The whole system is highly centralised, following the European model: France and Italy for example. The central government determines organisation, curricula, textbooks, timetables, appointments and budgets. Everything is in theory controlled by instructions and rules based on laws or ministerial regulations. Where these instructions and rules cannot be carried out for lack of skills and resources, or where they conflict with people's convenience, interests, or with obvious common-sense, they must often be evaded or thwarted. The result is a labyrinthine system, the complexity of which is seldom understood by observers or indeed by participants.

The system is authoritarian in two ways, both symbolised by the almost universal black tunics and white collars worn as uniform by school children all over Turkey. All procedures are in theory uniform; all decisions are referred to superiors, often overworked and necessarily unaware of specific local problems. Secondly, the children obey and conform. Learning is by rote, teachers are firmly in control and defined as always right; truth is whatever is taught. Arguing, questioning, thinking for oneself, are not encouraged; they are often perceived as dangerous.

The whole system rests on examinations. Every child must be deemed by his teachers to have reached the required standard each year, before promotion to the next grade; those who fail repeat the year. This rule applies up to and through university level, with two major effects. First, a resulting emphasis in training children for the achievement of easily testable performances strengthens authoritarian rote learning; secondly, children are very often older than they should be according to the norm and many, perhaps most, students lose a year or more on the way through. Late starters and late developers are not stigmatised. All educational statistics concerned with percentages of age cohorts (a cohort is all those born in one calendar year) are complicated by this body of students above the 'normal age'. The problem is further confounded especially for primary school statistics, because in villages a sizeable, unknown, and declining percentage of children are not registered at the moment of birth, but later, sometimes years later; or in a few cases, take over the registration of an older sibling who is already dead.

One major reservation must be made; such a simple stereotype is itself misleading, and just because it is so often said it may come to be believed without evidence. It does far too little justice to the warm devotion, originality and seriousness of thousands of teachers, educators and officials throughout Turkey. The causes are largely structural, and result from the vast and under-estimated problems of creating a modern system of education, based on alien models, more or less from scratch, in a nation where both material resources and mass comprehension were initially lacking.

Expenditure on education by the Government competes with massive other demands on government resources. Turkey has not devoted a strikingly large amount of the national income to education. It rose from about 1 per cent in 1938 to 2 per cent in 1952, and 3·8 per cent in 1962; in 1971 education accounted for nearly 6 per cent of government expenditure.

Within a limited educational budget, the alternative aims of educating an elite and of educating the masses are always in dispute. Around 1961, only some 3 per cent of those of high school age were in high schools and about the same number in universities. To these might be added a further 1½ per cent in higher teacher-training schools. At the same date, only 70 per cent of those of primary age were in school.

The 1960s were a period of very rapid expansion on all fronts. By 1972, primary education had achieved about 95 per cent coverage of all children; by 1971 middle schools of all types 35 per cent coverage, and high schools of all types 18 per cent.[4]

This very rapid growth inevitably imposed problems of maintaining quality and consistency. Primary and secondary education depends on the

[4] *Yeni Strateji ve Kalkınma Planı: Üçüncü Beş Yıl: 1973*, State Planning Organisation, Ankara.

quality of teacher education, which in turn depends on the staff of colleges and institutes for training teachers; and these in turn depend on the universities. It is virtually impossible to ensure competence in all sections of the system when demand outstrips the supply of qualified and competent people. Moreover, the legal formalism and centralisation make formal qualifications of paramount importance. Once qualified, a person is defined as competent, regardless of actual performance; some of necessity perform tasks for which they are not formally qualified. Rapid growth therefore tends to patchiness in quality under the formal umbrella of universal conformity.

IV AID TO TURKEY

After the Second World War, the emphasis in educational aid changed. The export of knowledge and resources was organised through international programmes and took on the moral overtones of an altruistic duty, something done in the best interests of the recipient rather than that of the donors. Turkey was in the centre of the new development, receiving postwar relief from 1946, and then Marshall Aid. Table 7.3 (p.329) shows the scale of the aid, in all over $7500 million from all sources for 1946–69; of this over $3000 million was US military aid. Even this vast sum is only a tiny proportion of Turkish government spending.

One consequnce, no doubt intentional (and to some extent a reaction to Russian pressure on Turkey in 1946), was the integration of Turkey into Europe and the Western camp. Turkey was a founder member of the Council of Europe (1949) and of the Organisation for European Economic Co-operation (1948), now OECD. American advisers, both military and civilian, have been in Ankara ever since, and Turkey's links, political, social, economic and personal, to Europe and the United States have grown steadily more binding and more complex.[5]

Around 1950 the Turkish government had not yet begun seriously to confront the problems of long-term centralised economic and social planning, nor indeed had any Western democracies. It is hardly surprising therefore if much aid in these early years was haphazard, mixed in its results, and badly planned.

Specific successes and failures apart, it is clear that these years provided at least one great, indeed incalculable asset – experience. Frequent changes in both American personnel and in Turkish politicians and administrators inhibited opportunities for learning by doing; but even so, ways of deciding how to spend resources relatively rationally were worked out and improved. The problems are illustrated by a USAID document which reports, incredibly, no available records on US mission activity in the educational field before 1959.

[5] Written before the rift between America and Turkey over Cyprus, in 1974–5.

It is difficult to quantify aid for education and technical assistance in money or any other terms because their defining boundaries are necessarily vague. Recent United Nations' reports on aid to Turkey for the years 1969–72 divide aid under two headings, pre-investment and technical assistance, and capital aid. Both include a subheading education, but almost all other pre-investment expenditure includes some element of training or educational activity. In 1971 on the other hand, capital aid includes US $13 million for education for building and equipment. Thus arriving at an accurate total for educational aid would involve complicated and arbitrary arithmetic. Approximately, in the year 1972, from a total of 195 projects, the number of different projects which appear to include some educational element was 92, and those which are clearly educational, 38.

The diversity of projects is vast and highly significant. The more technological, complex and developed the economy, the greater the range of specialisms needed. As development proceeds in Turkey, as elsewhere, new products, new techniques, new institutions are introduced and new weaknesses and shortages in productive skills, organisation and so on become apparent. Attempts to plug these holes, when home or official resources are already tightly stretched, lead people to turn to foreign donors. Thus successful development, far from diminishing the demand for educational and technical assistance, constantly increases its diversity and complexity, and even its total volume. As the growing economy becomes self-sufficient in one sector, so it finds itself short in new and more specialised sectors, and innovations constantly aggravate the problem.

It is difficult to see an end to this growth of demand. The donors may turn their attention to nations in greater need. But Turkey has close complex and growing links to the West, and technical assistance, rather than withering away, will be redefined as exchange between partners.

V CASE-STUDIES

1. The universities

Sizes and dates

Turkey now has nine fully-fledged universities. The numbers of pupils in 1971 and date of foundation are set out below. In addition to these, new faculties under the control of the established universities have been, or are being, established in three or four other towns, for example, a medical faculty under Ankara University at Diyarbakir, an agricultural faculty under Ankara University at Adana, a theological faculty under Ankara at Kayseri, and new medical faculties under Hacettepe at Kayseri and Adana. A new university at Bursa is also under construction.

Founded		*Men*	*Women*	*Total*
1840 or 1869	Istanbul University	29,156	8,000	37,156
1944	Istanbul Technical University	6,745	413	7,158
1946	Ankara University	12,202	3,898	16,100
1955	Aegean University	5,400	1,252	6,652*
1956	Middle East Technical University	5,564	1,936	7,500
1957	Ataturk University	2,255	225	2,480
1963	Karadeniz University	1,262	50	1,312
1967	Hacettepe University	1,911	1,113	3,024
1971	University of the Bosphorus† (formerly Robert College)	n.a.	n.a.	1,100

Source: Milli Egitim Istatistikleri Ogretim Yili, Basi, 1970–1, DIE.

* According to figures supplied by the University, the total for 1971–2 was 14,626 which included the new Faculty of Management, formerly the Izmir Academy, and eight other Institutes of Higher Education, some of them private, which were incorporated in the University.

† Interview with Professor Kuran, figures for 1972.

The older universities

Istanbul and Ankara Universities still dominate the university world, both in their share of total numbers – Istanbul has nearly one half, Ankara another fifth of all students – and in their control of university policies and resources. These universities, together with the Aegean, Black Sea and Ataturk Universities, are run on general lines laid down for Istanbul University when it was the only full university. German influence was strong when Istanbul University was reorganised in the early days of the Republic and was reinforced in the 1930s by the arrival of academic refugees from Hitler.

The rules are complicated, detailed, and allow little room for personal initiative. Everything is referred upwards. Reform or change from within is difficult; the high but at times flexible degree of formalism allows certain structural inefficiencies to persist, and makes for inconsistencies in academic competence.

Senior professors hold chairs, a personal position which is permanent and very powerful. Once appointed professor, a man can determine the policy, syllabus and promotions in his subject, and can enjoy if he wishes considerable services from his inferiors, especially the Assistants. As long as he avoids political provocation and any formal improprieties, he is fairly safe from criticism and attack; he is in a position to exclude anyone with views different from his own or anyone, it is often maliciously insinuated, more able than himself. First-class professors create first-class followings and first-class standards. But the system does not encourage first-class people.

Promotion is formal and rigid. The lowest grade of salaried staff are the Assistants, who, as one informant said, really do assist, rivalling each other to please their professor by every means at their disposal. They are formally forbidden to teach until they have their doctorate, which is supposed to take four years, and rests solely on a thesis. They may then teach, but only under 'direct supervision' of a professor, while they prepare a second thesis as a condition for promotion, after a further four years, to *Doçent.*

After another four years and yet another thesis, plus evidence of knowing two foreign languages, promotion to Professor is possible. The system can be breached in certain ways; for example it is possible to appoint someone who is not fully and formally qualified, as a '*chargé de cours*', or to appoint 'experts' for specific purposes; but these posts do not carry tenure. The system frustrates the able and ambitious, and suppresses or eliminates the unorthodox. It also fails in its main aim, to guarantee competence and propriety.

While chairs and department heads are permanent, Deanships of Faculties and Rectorships of Universities circulate among the senior professors. No one holds these powerful but often unpopular jobs long enough to formulate, promote, and carry through a long-term policy. More recent universities are either new versions of the older ones, with their own special laws and arrangements; or they are reformist universities. Hacettepe University is a personal and brilliant instance of one man's creativity. The Middle East Technical University is a multiple enterprise with wide international support. To these it is perhaps appropriate to add the new University of Boğaziçi, formed in 1971 by the purchase of Robert College by the Turkish Government, and still in a formative stage.

Aid to the older universities at present is limited to small and specific projects. Istanbul and Ankara are relatively self-confident and established universities who do not think of themselves as needing to reform or to innovate. The donors think of them as conservative, and uneven in quality. So neither side is likely to suggest any large schemes of aid.

The University of the Aegean, Izmir The main faculties of the University are now agriculture, medicine, and engineering. No law, humanities or social sciences were taught, but in 1971 the Izmir Academy, itself only founded in 1966, was added as the Faculty of Management. Most of the staff have studied overseas at some point in their career, and a few foreign teachers are scattered through the faculties. People commented that the main initiative, ideas, resources and plans were Turkish, and that they had received very little help. Projects which affect the University are specific, few and small-scale.

Nevertheless, the Rector is assisted by a Director of Foreign Relations, whose office provided a list of foreign assistance since 1960. The Agricultural Faculty alone listed 110 items, of which 62 were items of supply from CENTO costing from £30 to £2000, 41 came from Giessen University ranging from 330 DM to 18,000 DM, 5 were Fulbright teachers; and the French had provided a hydraulic laboratory costing 250,000 frs, discussed below. A similar list was supplied for the Science Faculty.

The Rector himself and several other professors praised the efficiency of the CENTO organisation for small-scale supplies. Requests through official channels for goods requiring import licences or custom duties might take months or years, but the CENTO organisation was able to circumvent red tape and supply urgent needs within weeks or even days.

French assistance to this University illustrates two extremes of aid projects. I was told in Ankara that a complete hydraulic laboratory had been donated by the French Government, to be installed with advice from the universities of Aix-en-Provence and Montpelier. After two years it was still in its packing cases. An informal French account of this project attributed the virtually total waste to a number of specific factors. The Turkish University had to find a share of the costs, which were not readily forthcoming; the relevant Dean changed, to one less favourable to the project; the Professor directly responsible was German-trained and unsympathetic to the French; the building allocated to house the laboratory was totally unsuitable; and in any case the laboratory had never been part of the University's planning.

By contrast a specific aid project in marine biology between Marseilles and the University, which was initiated by personal contact between French and Turkish professors, developed modestly, and in mutual understanding, and had proved highly successful.

By centralised rules, every Turkish student is expected to pass an examination in at least one foreign language. In this University the British Council provides some help for the teaching of English and likewise French and German native teachers provide instruction in their languages.

The syllabuses and timetables for all students are crowded and cover a range of subjects. Hence the University, dominated by its scientific staff, does not allow language teaching before 5.00 p.m. This rule, I was told, has a number of consequences.

First, the relative importance of foreign languages in the eyes of the senior professors is made plain to the students. Secondly, the students arrive tired. Thirdly, in order to fulfil their statutory time on university premises and nominally at work, the language staff are compelled to clock in at 1.30 p.m. and spend their afternoons in the department with virtually nothing to do.

The English students were taught by lecturers in large classes. Language laboratory facilities existed, but not on a large enough scale. Language teachers could not publicly announce their own failure to teach in these conditions and in any case students who had passed in serious scientific subjects could not be refused their formal qualifications because of inadequacy in a foreign language. So, in practice, in the end, virtually everyone passed, and the standard of the weakest tended to become the standard of the majority. Nevertheless changes were said to be in prospect.

The German Government supported from 1966 to 1974 a larger project in the Faculty of Management, costed in 1973 at just over 4 million DM. The project was to establish a training course for textile engineers, technicians and foremen, the first in Turkey, and also to establish a quality control unit, to supply relevant equipment, and to design a suitable building. The original plans from 1966 were for five years, but the project was extended to 1974, and negotiation for a further two years' extension was likely. The project had not gone smoothly. The buildings had not been built by 1972, the Germans had found recruiting suitable staff to send out difficult, the Turks had not succeeded in finding satisfactory counterparts. Some 30 German textile engineers had been involved altogether. The Germans had thought of withdrawing completely in the early days, but by 1971 both sides saw the project as likely more or less to achieve its objectives.

Ataturk University at Erzurum A university in eastern Turkey directly suited to regional needs and with the primary task of promoting development was conceived by Ataturk himself. Hence the University's name. It was founded in 1958 beginning with a Faculty of Agriculture, guided at first by the University of Ankara.

Under a major USAID project the University of Nebraska was contracted from 1955 to 1968 to give general advice and support in the founding of the new University. The total cost of the project is given in USAID documentation as $3,907,000.[6] The original project was comprehensive. A considerable number of American teachers mainly, but not exclusively, in agriculture came to Erzurum; Turkish university staff went to the United States for training; advice on administration and organisation was provided, with special emphasis on Nebraska University as an example of an American Land Grant College in a semi-arid environment. Equipment was provided for teaching and research; joint research was undertaken; and support was given to an extension services organisation for local agriculture to be based in the new university.

No detailed history and evaluation of the project seemed to be available. One official American comment calls it 'a frustrating project in many respects'. Turkish comment of an informal kind was equally mixed. The Americans were impatient, brusque and did not understand local problems, nor the local system. One Turkish informant remarked that at least Americans, admittedly for incomes princely by Turkish standards, were prepared to come and live in Erzurum for two to four years at a time,

[6] E. Frank Price, *A.I.D. Educational Assistance to Turkey 1957–70*, USAID, Ankara, July 1970.

which established Turkish university staff were not. He described them as friendly, and eager to get on with the job, to solve the problems by initiative, and to make themselves generally helpful. Their Turkish colleagues on the other hand were reserved, bound by official rules, and generally less willing to take risks and to put themselves out personally. At the beginning of the project there were many organisational failures, Turkish counterpart staff, and general supporting arrangements were not ready, buildings were not built on time, equipment ordered turned out to be unsuitable, or to lack essential parts; even in 1972 it was said that some equipment supplied during the project was still in its packing cases.

The decision to terminate the project and to sever relations between the two universities clearly implies a lack of success, since such a link once forged should surely have continued indefinitely. Nevertheless Ataturk University is established and running and undoubtedly owes a great deal to the American help, especially in the Faculty of Agriculture.

By 1972, the University had faculties of basic sciences,[7] agriculture, literature, management, medicine, sciences, dentistry and Islamic studies.

The Nebraska experience had not enhanced the image of foreign aid in the university, and no major projects were in operation in 1972. Most of the staff had been abroad at some point, many for their doctorates, or medical specialism. The Faculty of Medicine gave an impression of vigour and enthusiasm. It aimed to become the medical capital of eastern Turkey both for specialist needs and for training. It has close ties with Hacettepe University's campaign (see p. 304) for public health and preventive medicine as a major part of medical training. It is attempting to establish a chain of rural medical centres. Already all students have to spend a period during their training resident in a village and in a rural medical centre.

The Medical Faculty also has plans for a major innovation; namely to make intensive English obligatory in the first year of the course and then to use English as the medium for some teaching and reading throughout the medical training. The Faculty was also pleased to claim that it was training the nucleus of the new Medical Faculty to be established near Adana.

Erzurum has a long and bitter winter, and is a relatively small, isolated and conservative city. This relative discomfort and isolation makes the recruitment of staff and of students difficult. Both are controlled by the central government, and most of those who have the option of teaching or studying in Ankara, Istanbul or Izmir are likely to do so. Even the teaching of foreign languages received relatively poor foreign support.

The University of the Black Sea, Karadeniz University The reasons for the decision to found a university at Trabzon, and to make it a technical university in spite of the total absence of industry anywhere near

[7] This Faculty, found in several universities, is a service faculty teaching basic introductory science courses for the first year or two years before specialisation.

it, are complex. Though the decision was taken in 1955, the University was not set up till 1963. In 1972 it had four faculties, basic sciences, civil engineering and architecture, mechanical and electrical engineering, and forestry. A Faculty of Medicine was under construction, due to open in 1975. The total resident staff consisted of three full professors, one in civil and two in electrical engineering, and 12 *Doçents*, together with 17 temporary teachers, 7 Assistants with Doctorates and 90 without Doctorates who were not allowed to teach, and 21 specialists (p. 296). But the bulk of the teaching was done by 66 visiting professors and lecturers, almost all from Istanbul Technical University, who came by air once a week or once a fortnight to lecture.

Foreign aid played a very small part in the setting up of this University. Three foreign professors, two of them German, had helped to establish departments, including a German geologist from Giessen and a German mathematician. Most of the support and control had come directly from Istanbul Technical University, and the budget in 1972 was still directly controlled by the Ministry of Education; the University had therefore not achieved autonomy.

The Turkish Government had approached UNESCO for substantial aid to mount a project in mechanical, electrical and civil engineering; UNESCO responded in 1970 with a modest one-year project, later extended to 1972 and costing $292,000. Plans for a larger scale project were still under discussion in 1973.

The aims of the project were to advise on curricula, on the design of buildings for teaching, and the ordering and installation of laboratory equipment. The original team consisted of a Czechoslovak, a Scotsman, an Australian and a Norwegian, three of whom were civil engineers and one an electrical engineer. When the team arrived they found that as Karadeniz Technical University was under the control of Istanbul Technical University the syllabuses were fixed and could not be discussed. The Istanbul Technical University staff, who taught them exactly as they did in Istanbul, regarded them as perfectly satisfactory. The buildings had already been designed and the contracts signed, and hence any modification was legally impossible. The experts did order equipment for what they regarded as not entirely suitable buildings, and they did offer advice and help in some cases in installing it. They pointed out, however, that equipment dates very rapidly, and that delays in getting the equipment through customs and in getting the buildings ready for use had slowed matters down considerably. Moreover, the commuting teachers from Istanbul were mostly not accustomed to laboratory teaching, had no time in their brief visits for such activities and innovations, and had had no part in choosing the equipment. So it was doubtful what contribution the investment in laboratories was making or would ever make to the teaching of engineering.

The problems of the UNESCO team had been increased by their arrival in an interregnum between Rectors, which had virtually frozen all administrative action of any kind. A Rector was appointed, but then seconded to Ankara to play an important part in a commission on university reform.

The foreign experts were forbidden under Turkish law to teach, so that although they did not have a great deal to do they could not turn their hands to helping out in spite of the very serious shortage of local staff. They said they were able to make good relations in some cases with younger local teaching staff, and in particular to advise and inspire some of the army of assistants, who were sitting around trying to dream up and create research projects for their doctoral theses, or else simply waiting for their chance to go abroad.

This project illustrates a number of typical problems. The most serious one is the lack of coordination on the Turkish side between those planning and negotiating the aid, and those controlling the activities and environment in which the foreign experts were to work. Why spend international dollars in considerable quantities to get experts to carry out three tasks, two of which were legally impossible from the start? First, people in an organisation or ministry may genuinely not know what others are planning and negotiating. Secondly, they may know, but hope or believe that by the time the experts arrive the difficulties will have been solved. Thirdly, some officials may have a lot to gain by being seen to negotiate aid and very little to lose if the aid is not particularly successful. Although there had been, not surprisingly, some friction between the experts and the University, the effect of having the foreigners on the campus, talking to staff, making contact with students and assistants, and putting pressure on the authorities in various ways was generally agreed by all informants to have been highly beneficial. To evaluate the project in formal terms would be to miss these side effects. Do these unplanned pay-offs really justify hundreds of thousands of international dollars?

The innovating universities

Hacettepe Two universities which grew to maturity in the 1960s stand in sharp contrast to the three discussed so far, in that they were founded and developed as deliberate attempts at reform. Hacettepe is largely the result of the drive, ingenuity and vision of Dr Ihsan Doğramacı; the Middle East Technical University was planned as an international university with all teaching in the English language.

In an application dated 1951 for funds to establish a children's hospital in Ankara, Dr Doğramacı already foresaw, as the ultimate goal, a fully-fledged general medical training establishment with ancillary services including social work and other related activities. In the same document he also outlined a plan to establish a charitable endowment fund to support the venture, and to meet the running costs of the hospital partly by charging differential fees to those able to pay them. He also stressed in carefully diplomatic language the advantage of a private charitable initiative, especially if independent of the government and of the traditional medical schools of the existing universities.

By 1972, Hacettepe was a thriving university with a large teaching hospital, numerous faculties, over 3000 students and some 800 staff. Dr Doğramacı was President, and the central figure in a complex network of institutes, committees and foundations.

In an interview in 1972 Dr Doğramacı identified a number of shortcomings in the traditional system. All senior medical teachers depended for their main income on their fees from private practice, which were in turn related to their personal fame. No teachers in medical faculties and no doctors in hospital were full-time, and senior medical staff had no motive for attending to administration, organisation or reform. Yet these conservative professors of medicine had very great power. Although the system was enshrined in laws and regulations, Dr Doğramacı insisted that a great deal could in fact be done within the old framework. He had set up the Children's Hospital and an Institute of Child Health by 1958, and he gathered round him a group of doctors who undertook to do no private practice, but to work together and pool all fees. Thus his hospital and institute were manned by a devoted full-time staff. The loss of the opportunity to win a personal reputation in private practice was compensated by the reputation his enterprise soon acquired. By charging those who could pay for the services of the staff, he was able to set up a special fund for compensating the doctors for their loss of private fees. He expanded operations, and in 1963 he was able to separate his enterprise as a new Faculty of Medicine within Ankara University, and basic sciences, social studies, and foreign language teaching were added. He was thus able to present to the world what was in effect a university, and in 1967 a new and special law incorporated the whole complex as a new University in its own right. The University, in spite of special provisions, comes within the basic traditional legal structure of Turkish universities, but he claims that he is able to incorporate a number of new principles. In particular, junior staff members, the Assistants, are set specific tasks and goals, and are allowed, indeed encouraged, to teach; students are expected to read for themselves, and the University library had open shelves; curricula are free and flexible, and courses constantly incorporate new knowledge and the experience of the staff. A very high proportion, perhaps more than 90 per cent, of the teaching staff have studied abroad and many have close contacts with foreign universities. The University works on an American-type credit system, which contributes to the flexibility of curricula and of individual students' programmes.

In the course of the University's development, funds and foundations have been established with monies contributed voluntarily or by the fees of private patients, so that the whole complex enjoys greater financial flexibility than any other university. It rewards effort, excellence and loyalty, and escapes some of the formality of the old universities. But what are the criteria and who passes judgement?

The contribution that Hacettepe has made to medical care and to university education is without doubt enormous, though not surprisingly evaluations of the achievement vary sharply. Not everyone is equally willing to acknowledge the faults of the old system and applaud the claimed reforms of the new. The debt to foreign aid is vast. By his contacts with the private Foundations, Ford and Rockefeller in particular, and with USAID, Dr Doğramacı was able to win support from Turkish sources for his plans. Moreover, the sources of his ideas and standards were initially largely American, and in particular a grant in the early 1950s from the Rockefeller Foundation enabled him to send 25 carefully selected men to the United States for medical training. The effect of this was to reverse the brain drain; not only did all the 25 return to work with him but 50 other Turks who were in training or in medical employment in the United States also applied to join him.

Dr Doğramacı was eager to stress that though he had enjoyed a good deal of aid for a wide variety of purposes, the total proportion of his full budget that came from foreign aid was very small. As shown below the University budgets supplied by Dr Doğramacı are:

	1966	*1967*	*1968*	*1969*	*1970*
Total budget (US $000)	4,890	5,105	12,050	23,400	24,310
Current expenditure	2,350	2,890	4,650	10,300	13,260
Capital investment	2,540	2,215	7,400	13,100	11,050
Percentage from the Turkish State Treasury	95·4	93·6	85·7	90·9	88·0
Percentage from student fees, patient fees, publications, interest, etc.	3·0	3·0	3·1	2·0	2·0
Percentage from Hacettepe Foundations (Turkish) investments and finance	0·4	1·1	1·9	1·0	8·0
Percentage from foreign assistance	1·2	1·3	8·3	5·1	6·5

The medical faculty of Hacettepe University had been in the forefront of innovation in medical curricula. For example, in collaboration with the Government, Dr Doğramacı had played a major part in setting up the Etimesgut rural medicine experiment near Ankara. He had been able to use this to enforce a period of residence in the village for all students. He was thus able to give preventive and social medicine a much greater place in the syllabus than is normally the case, in a way most appropriate to a country with a gross imbalance of medical services between the large cities and the rural areas.

The effect of the success of this initative is that Dr Doğramacı and his senior staff claim to be leaders in international medical syllabus reform. He is playing a part in plans for a UN university, and has been brought in to discuss medical plans in other countries including those, he told me, of the University of Southampton. In no way does this indicate the end of technical assistance, but it does suggest the new stage in which countries participate as equals rather than as rich and poor, ignorant and well-informed. The emphasis on social medicine has produced two important institutes[8] within the University which, though distinct both legally and in their purposes, overlap in their Director and other personnel and work very closely together. These are first the Institute of Population Studies, and second the Institute of Community Medicine.

The Institute of Population Studies is extremely important in Turkey. It has initiated work aimed at improving and establishing basic demographic data, encouraged research on population control, and undertaken a major sample survey of the whole Turkish nation with questions on fertility and a whole range of other variables. The Institute of Community Medicine is involved in the organisation of the Etimesgut project, and in its use for teaching to medical students.

In both these institutes foreign help has been important; the Institute of Population Studies had been launched with a grant of $375,000 from the Ford Foundation in 1967, which was renewed for a period from 1973; this grant was used originally to import two foreign staff, to send ten students for doctorates, to organise seminars, to reprint publications, and for equipment; 40 per cent of the cost of the Institute was covered by Ford, 60 per cent by Turkish resources.

Aid to the other institute illustrates a contrasting case. The Institute for Community Medicine had received no more than a number of vehicles for the Etimesgut Rural Centre from UNICEF. Yet these were also vital to the working of the Centre. Due to complex legalistic rules, these could not be provided by any Turkish authority, yet the programme of integrating teaching and the community health service would have been impossible without them. Thus a small cost brought important benefits.

To sum up, the growth of the Children's Hospital established in 1957 into Hacettepe University owes a great deal not merely to foreign aid, but to the availability of aid from a variety of sources. While the vast bulk of the finance has come from Turkey, the role of foreign aid in breaking

[8] Written in 1973; events have altered the situation since then.

bottlenecks, providing examples and arguments, winning over private citizens and the government to finance support for the ventures has perhaps been indispensable.

If Hacettepe illustrates foreign aid at its most potent, it also illustrates two of its basic problems. The first is the unquestioned assumption that it is desirable to give virtually the whole staff foreign experience. The second is the increasing of national indebtedness to pay for universities, whose contribution to the increased wealth which provide the means of repayment is hard to measure, especially when it is heavily medical.

The Middle East Technical University The notion of an international technical university teaching in English, and aiming to serve the whole Middle Eastern region, goes back to the 1950s. METU was founded in 1956, with an architectural core, and the administrative and legal structure are completely separate from the older universities. Although at personal level cooperation has developed and senior members of the older universities are on the Board of Trustees, until 1972 service in METU was not recognised by any other university towards promotion and other rights. It is therefore difficult for teachers to move from METU into other Turkish universities.[9] A large site was made available outside Ankara for the campus. From small beginnings in temporary accommodation in the new parliament building, the University grew rapidly, student enrolment rising from 745 in 1960–1 to 6685 in 1970–1.

The University was both international and reforming. As such it received strong encouragement from the United Nations and other donors. It was modelled on American, and to a lesser extent on British, university ideas. For example, it provided libraries with readily available works, and expected students to read for themselves and to write; it stressed personal contact between staff and students, and, to make this possible, it set as its aim a ten to one student/staff ratio. Other aims were flexible and technically up-to-date syllabuses and a 'problem solving' approach to learning. There seems to be strong evidence to show that this educational approach had paid off, in that METU graduates were sought after by employers because of their greater articulateness and their ability to discuss and make decisions about problems and situations.

The University was divided in 1971 into four faculties: administrative sciences with 628 students, architecture with 605 students, arts and sciences with 1458 students, and engineering with 3646 students.

Most students take a whole year's preparatory course in English before beginning; the University, which had no less than 15,000 applicants in 1971, sets its own entrance examination independently of the other universities.

Foreign aid has come from a large number of agencies and sources, for a very wide range of projects. Most of them consist of grants covering a

[9] Current legislation may eventually change this situation.

specific academic subject or group of subjects, and include the cost of visting teachers, fellowships for Turks to study abroad, and books and equipment. The donors have divided up their responsibilities.

Thus USAID and CENTO have cooperated with the UNDP in the Engineering Faculty; the Ford Foundation supported the Faculty of Arts and Sciences, while OECD has supported the Departments of Economics and Statistics, Business Management and Public Administration in the Faculty of Administrative Science, as well as a course on regional planning in the Faculty of Architecture. The recurrent budget for 1967 showed nearly one-fifth of the costs coming from foreign sources; in 1970 and 1971 this proportion was around one quarter. The proportion of foreign staff has been high, and has declined only recently from 38 per cent in 1964 to 16 per cent in 1970.

Many of the foreign staff were American or British nationals, or were trained in the United States or the United Kingdom, because of the English language requirement. It has been said that about one quarter showed enthusiasm and friendliness, and inspired students and colleagues. About one half of them were competent teachers who contributed little except the technical task for which they were hired, and about one quarter were unsatisfactory.

The provision of equipment by donors was also uneven. Especially in the early days, the Turks accepted expert advice on their needs which was not always as expert as it might have been; or which was based on insufficient thought and local knowledge. But as the university grew, so did their own knowledge and experience and they were able to ask for and get more nearly that they wanted. The preparatory year of English study has presented many problems. USAID and to a lesser degree the British Council offered assistance. Teaching one student enough English in one year to understand lectures, to read, or write academically and to answer examinations is virtually impossible, let alone a thousand. Americans, British and Turkish ideas on methods did not coincide.

Foreign students are only 10 per cent of all students. The foreign staff is declining in numbers and likely to continue to do so. Thus the international hopes are likely slowly to wane, and in time the University may well switch to teaching in Turkish.

On a broad scale METU, for all the political difficulties of the period from 1967 on, has clearly been a great asset to Turkey. It has challenged the older universities and if not all new brooms sweep clean, at least some of the old sweepers looked at their old brooms to see how well they were sweeping. By 1970, the new University had produced 3000 graduates and 684 postgraduates, and by all accounts these had had no difficulty in finding employment. In spite of political upheavals, many administrative errors and some bad teaching, a complex, varied, and cooperative aid programme has made a major contribution to the University.

Boğaziçi University This University was created in 1971 by the purchase of Robert College from its American trustees. Robert College was founded in 1863 for boys of all creeds, languages and peoples, granting degrees under the laws of the State of New York, and the authority of the Ottoman, later the Turkish, Government. In the 1920s it set up a school to give boys a secondary pre-university education in English. A parallel girls college under the same Board of Governors was founded in 1971 and was combined with Robert College in 1958. In 1958 also, a preparatory year in English was established.

American funds have played the major part in founding and maintaining Robert College, and it has had great influence in Turkey through example and through its graduates. Since 1958, it has been receiving support through USAID and from the Ford Foundation. The final decision to transfer the whole campus and college as a going concern to the Turkish Government was in the end a way of keeping it viable financially. Clearly American government and foundation support will now decline very rapidly, but the close American ties, interest and influence will not disappear over night.

When I visited it in 1972, the University was only in its first year as a Turkish university. A large number of questions remained to be settled. I was told that on its beautiful but restricted site it could never expand above 3000 students, and that it planned to continue to teach in English, to retain its traditional outlook, and in particular innovative flexibility. One suggested aim was to maintain around one-third graduate student enrolment; such a plan would involve changing the traditional Turkish system of Assistants. This institution is a most striking and successful example of private and public foreign help, given in altruism, with long-term and immeasurable consequences for Turkey.

Aid to universities: some general comments

A century or more of innovation culminated in the final abolition, in the first years of the Republic, of all traditional Islamic Turkish higher education, and its replacement by a new system modelled on the West.

The Turks turned to Europe for models for higher technical and scientific education because they could not see how to adapt their own, nor how to devise new ones for themselves. In time, they also turned to the West for their models for humanities and social sciences. Once they had imported and naturalised a foreign system, they had within their own society no criteria for criticising and adapting it, for keeping it changing, evolving, improving. Those who were sent abroad to learn, in one university, one segment of a foreign system, brought that segment back to Turkey and made it their own. Their own security then lay in preserving it intact. Initially, which version of which Western tradition became established in which sector of the Turkish system was a matter of political or administrative accident. But once established, the sanctions supporting it against change were strong. When change did come, it came once more, directly or indirectly, from outside, not from within Turkey.

The motives of those who set out to import knowledge were originally purely instrumental. They wanted the knowledge for military, economic and welfare purposes. Later, they also wanted to create prestigious institutions comparable with those of Western nations. What the innovators wanted was technical capacity and its resulting power and prestige; what they got with it was a whole set of new ideas, the questioning of the unquestionable.

The designers of the new institutions faced two sets of problems. First, they sought to ensure the preservation of international academic standards in an imported institution. Secondly, they needed to prevent the new institution from fomenting radicalism. For both purposes, they fell back on making rules – complex detailed rules, with close central controls. Some Turkish professors still in 1972 defended the elaborate rules on the grounds of the continuing immaturity of the Turkish academy. But the multiplication of rules can never eliminate incompetence and self-interest. Almost everyone in the Turkish university system complained of the rules; though often the proposed cure for the abuse of rules is yet more rules.

Turkey now has had two generations of university teachers. But the input from the West remains high. There are five kinds. First, the training of students and staff in foreign universities. Secondly, the bringing of foreign staff to Turkey. Thirdly, the interest and concern for Turkey of foreign universities, and the provision of incidental expenses for maintaining contacts, including joint research projects. Fourthly, the provision of capital for buildings and equipment; and fifthly the provision of models of university life, academic values, assumptions, standards, organisation.

Research is a basic duty of university staff, and research programmes are central to any university. At present almost all able Turkish staff go abroad for their graduate research training. Roughly what happens is that the student abroad is set to work on a research project determined by the interests and resources of the university to which they have come. The more successful they are, the more likely is the university to encourage them to remain in close contact. Thus they return to Turkey with plans to carry out research in a specific topic arising out of the research of their foreign university. Either by capturing domestic or foreign aid resources in Turkey, or by managing to finance regular visits abroad, they launch on research related not to the activities of other Turks, nor to their Turkish university, nor to the needs of Turkey. Many of Turkey's best university brains are, in honorific ways, clients of foreign universities, contributing yet further to the colossal advantage which the rich nations already enjoy in knowledge and research; the academic analogue of the Turkish emigrant workers.

Foreign teachers supply three needs. They plug gaps where Turkey lacks trained people, in econometrics for example; they bring new knowledge, in computer science, or the medical application of nuclear physics; or they simply bring liveliness and stimulation for staff and students as with any academic exchange. By and large, all three objectives are achieved by some foreign staff some of the time. Renowned international scholars and scientists are unlikely to come for long enough to discover Turkey's peculiar difficulties; those prepared to stay for long periods are often the rather humdrum. Sometimes foreigners, who may have prestige simply as foreigners, are less expert than Turks who are available to do the job. But most foreign staff perform one great service: they establish at least some personal links of friendship and mutual concern.

One common way of recruiting foreign staff is the formal link between universities. These links are not by any means always successful. The only ones which appeared to be active after a period of time both involved the Agricultural Faculty at Eğe University. This had had a formal link for five years with Giessen in Germany, which it was renewing; and it was seeking an arrangement with Reading University in the United Kingdom. Several others, notably the general link between the University of Nebraska and Ataturk University and the link between Cornell University and the Middle East Technical University for Business Studies, had terminated in a lack of reciprocal enthusiasm.

A number of problems present themselves. First, the relative standing of the two universities. Turkish universities no longer, if they ever did, accept a relation of tutelage. The link must be between equal partners. Official British and German policy statements stress the same point. But the universities are not equal. Most universities in rich countries which are likely to enter into bilateral arrangements have more resources, more stable administrative and political systems, more research equiment, more autonomy and a higher level of consistency in staff ability. Turkish universities on the whole look for and welcome links, because they assume they will gain more than they give; reciprocally, individual universities in the richer countries are inclined to avoid links which are likely to bring in less than they cost. They often need inducement from their own governments. Secondly, formal links cover a vast range of possible arrangements, and it seems obvious and generally agreed that links between subjects or departments or research institutes for specific purposes are far more effective than wider programmes of collaboration. How these work depends both on the details of institutional and legal arrangements in different countries, on the personal compatibility of those concerned, and on the source and amount of resources available. Unless both sides benefit from and enjoy the relationship, it will not function.

One attractive and common suggestion is collaboration in research. The dangers and difficulties in practice are considerable. Much university research is in practice hierarchically organised. A man with a reputation and power initiates the project, obtains the funds, expects to give the orders and to take the credit. All academic Turks I spoke to complained of what is known as 'data mining'. Foreigners arrive, make a study with Turkish helpers, and publish it with their own name in large print. They build their own career, but Turkey gains little or nothing.

New knowledge and new ways of looking at the problems are at the very centre of development. On every front, technical and social, Turkey desperately needs more and better research. Yet research is difficult and expensive.

Joint research projects are often unsatisfactory simply because research is often unsatisfactory. But the hazards are increased by the need for autonomous organisations and autonomous scholars to agree on aims, hypotheses, methods and conclusions, and on the sharing of resources, results and applications, and in the end of the glory and the blame.

In spite of these formidable difficulties, indeed because of them, I would advocate directing a much larger share of expenditure on technical assistance into supporting joint research between Turkish nationals and foreign donors and institutions. The Turks would provide local knowledge and decide on local priorities; the foreigners would provide experience, knowledge and resources. Both sides would need to acknowledge and exploit the creativity and imagination wherever it came from. The high risk would be admitted from the beginning, but all projects would be designed to reward collaboration and to promote independent Turkish research capacity. Even relatively unsuccessful projects would at the very least arouse a wider international interest in Turkey's specific problems, and equip Turks with experience, even perhaps with knowledge. Instead of working on foreigners' problems in Princetown or Bonn or Paris, Turks would be working in Turkey on Turkey's own problems.

In less than half a century, Turkey has created a modern university system virtually from scratch, with nine universities; around six per cent of the young now reach university. At their best, they are as good as any in the world, although it is hardly surprising if the results of this half century of effort are uneven. But it is easy to forget just how much at ordinary day-to-day levels has been done and is being achieved by the efforts of thousands of teachers, administrators, librarians and students.

Since the Turkish universities are modelled on European, and not Islamic, traditions, the debt to foreign influence and resources is beyond calculation. The contacts remain close. Two universities teach in English. Ninety per cent of staff are said to have been abroad for training or experience. Hundreds of foreign teachers have worked in Turkish universities. Even schemes which appear to have failed may have contributed in unexpected and incalculable ways. On balance, small specific projects and close personal contacts work better than large and more impersonal ones. The larger the project, the greater the stake and at the same time the greater the problems of ensuring sensible and practical efficiency. We might perhaps suggest that the need for detailed foresight and meticulous planning increases with the square of the size of the project.

2. Turks abroad

The total number of Turks abroad for study or training at one time is difficult to find out accurately. It is probable that currently in the course of one year over seven thousand are involved all told, including short trips for specific purposes and those abroad for up to five years for higher education; the equivalent of a sizeable university. Education abroad for Turks may be well over a century old, but education abroad on this scale is new in this generation. If the following are added together: fellowships and bursaries offered by donors and by the Turkish government; fellowships and visits built into nearly every aid project; the Turkish government scholarships for study abroad; the university teachers on paid leave, and the professionals and managers who go abroad on their normal salaries or on special grants; and the unknown number who go abroad for private study at their own private expense, seven thousand in any one year seems a modest estimate.

Those who go abroad are roughly of two kinds. First, some go for study or research as university students, undergraduate and graduate, or as post-doctoral fellows, visiting scholars, or professionals, including medical specialists. Secondly, others go abroad for a specific course, often short, in a technique of immediate relevance; for example, to learn about newly installed equipment, or to observe methods or approaches, technical, administrative or social, directly concerned with their job.

The British, German, French, and Netherlands governments operate schemes for inviting Turks abroad. They all make their distinction between academic scholarships, and awards for technical assistance. The details of the donor's offers and arrangements go to the Turkish Foreign Office and thence to the State Planning Organisation. This organisation replies with detailed requests for training within the general offer. For Britain, technical training was formerly handled through technical training officers at the Embassy, but now the British Council deals with these as well with academic and cultural activities. Britain offers to Turkey about 100 opportunities in technical assistance, besides a few academic scholarships. France offers about 150 in all, some of them for more than one year, and Germany about 350. The Dutch invite Turks to compete annually with other nations for scholarships to Holland; officials of the donor countries in Ankara in each case claimed that the schemes run smoothly. They mentioned the difficulties of selection, especially the final selection; of ensuring that the visitors know the country's language sufficiently for their purpose; of ensuring they have an adequate background to benefit from the proposed visit; of getting precise and detailed information about their needs; and of making sure that the courses and arrangements provided in their countries are enjoyable, appropriate and efficient. The visitors must be made welcome and helped to sort out the many personal problems of life in a foreign environment. The donor officials agreed that follow up and evaluation is desirable, and some claimed that it happens.

The several hundred Turkish government scholarships offered through the Ministry of Education annually are not unduly generous, less than foreign-financed ones, and the decisions seem to be made in a fairly arbitrary way, often belated, and with insufficiently stringent tests of language. The studentships are for a maximum of five years: in theory, one for language learning, two for an MA and two for a PhD. The number abroad at any one moment must therefore be around 2000. The Ministry leaves students to make their own applications, gives them little help with finding a suitable course, and offers no orientation course.

Turkish university staff criticised the scheme on the grounds that the students chosen by the Ministry are seldom the most suitable or competent. It is precisely in this, the neglect of careful selection, orientation and detailed planning in this scheme which earns it a poor reputation.

A large number of those who go abroad do so as part of a definite project. Thus almost all UN projects provide 'man-months' of fellowships, which carry comfortable allowances and are much sought after. Each project makes its own arrangements to send people, and once again the administrative details of selection, orientation and reception in the host country and adequacy of the course to the purpose are crucial. Dr Fişek, who ran the Institute of Population Studies at Hacettepe University (p. 304), claimed that the undergraduate training at Hacettepe was good, and his own MA programme of a high standard. He therefore selected students who had done well already and sent them, by arrangement with the Ford Foundation, primarily to learn research techniques. For this purpose a brief visit was useless; they really needed about four years. His own high international reputation gave him contacts with centres of excellence and the guaranteed quality of his students ensured acceptance. Each case had precise and detailed plans worked out. Dr Doğramacı, on a rather larger scale, gave a similar account of the way he selected and planned the future staff of his Faculty and University (see p. 303). Those concerned with an entirely different project, the establishment of a research unit in the Ministry of Education, funded by USAID, had a similar method of selection and claimed to be sending exceptionally able students to the Michigan State University for doctoral work, to learn research techniques in educational planning.

The case for training overseas rests on two kinds of argument. First, in dozens of cases, specific knowledge and experience either does not exist in Turkey at all, or it exists in the wrong place or in totally insufficient quantity. Hence the solution is either to send people abroad to learn it, or to bring someone to Turkey to teach it. Secondly, much more controversial is the view put forward by Turks as well as by foreigners in Turkey that what is needed above all is a change in the style of thinking, in basic and unspoken assumptions. Knowledge should not be experienced as something precise and authoritative, which is simply increased by adding more of the same, but as something open, changing and developing to which the student must bring a critical, sceptical mind and a readiness to rethink what he already knows. The relevant attitudes and skills are to be learned only be working and studying among those who have them. Yet their growth in Turkey is a necessary condition for the development of an indigenous scientific and scholarly community. If we emphasise simply the acquisition of specific knowledge, the case for sending Turks abroad as against bringing foreigners to Turkey depends on the circumstances of each case. The second argument is not admitted at all by many of those involved on both sides, but if it is then it provides a strong case for sending at least some Turks abroad for a longish period.

Among the professional foreign aid administrators in Ankara, the Turks have a reputation of liking advice even less than most nations. Yet among the Turks themselves an overseas training seems to carry nothing but prestige, and often to bring promotion. Those who are jealous of their returning fellows are not against the principle; they simply wish to go themselves. Thus although Turks frequently claim that they can do things as well or better than foreigners, foreign training and foreign experience is highly valued, by those who want to go, by those who have been, and by those who distribute jobs and promotions.

This high valuation has several consequences. Everyone with a reasonably successful education wants to go abroad, and, for the successful, it is not at all difficult. I was told that some Turkish government studentships, as well as some fellowships offered by foreign governments, are not always taken up. Some ways of going abroad are preferable to others. Roughly, UN agency fellowships come first, other international fellowships next, donor government fellowships next, then fellowships of various Turkish agencies and finally the Turkish Ministry of Education studentships. From this point of view, the selection is not simply a matter of efficient choice for the efficient use of resources, but a micro-political competition for valuable privileges; a free trip abroad and a life time of higher earning. Those best at convincing the actual allocators of fellowship funds may well not be the most suitable or the most deserving candidates; and rules designed to prevent impropriety may sometimes impede efficiency. At the same time, those who succeed in winning opportunities for training of which they are incapable or which is inappropriate may be creating acute suffering for themselves. Many long-term foreign students experience periods of acute stress and misery.

A second more serious and more subtle result of the high volume of overseas training is paradoxically the devaluation of Turkish achievements. Many who have been abroad are scornful of Turkey's own institutions and achievements, yet they are automatically accorded a degree of extra prestige simply because they have been. Conversely, when a job is to be done, people often look first for a foreigner, or failing that a Turk with foreign experience. Able and competent Turks who have not been abroad may be passed over.

Thirdly, at any moment, a sizeable proportion of the educationally most successful young Turks are not working in Turkey on Turkish problems but learning to enjoy or adapt to life in a Western democracy with a much higher GNP; and others to learn dissatisfaction with, even despair of, the institutions, standards and customs of their own country. They may learn a more critical attitude to knowledge, and a more empirical approach to research. But they may also be deflected from any constructive interest in Turkey's own problems. Possibly Turkey's development would be helped rather than hindered if most of these well-qualified and able young people stayed at home.

Two even more serious consequences may follow. Fourthly, the close contact with European and American universities reinforces, even increases, the cultural separation of the elite from the masses of the Turkish people. Fifthly, how does a period abroad affect people psychologically? It can be argued that anyone who has studied abroad for any length of time has to face a dilemma. Either he has failed to fit in with the host country, and returns feeling that he has been a failure; or his time abroad has been highly successful, and then he returns to a country with which he finds it difficult ever again completely and unselfconsciously to identify. Sixthly, returning scholars may face practical problems. The Turkish government scholarships carry the obligation to serve the government for two years for every year abroad. Under another scheme, officials returning with doctorates in educational research had to enter the Turkish civil service at lowly grades, with a future of slow promotion under bureaucratic rules.

The final drawback to training students abroad is familiar, much discussed and virtually insoluble; some of them never return. Since highly trained manpower is expensive this desertion involves a double direct economic loss. Turkey has some severe rules, involving the provision of private guarantees before departure; these have some effect in some cases. All the same there are thousands of highly educated Turks living and working abroad. Dr Oguzkan[10] reported in a study he made of 150 Turks

[10] Oguzkan, 1971, p. 84.

with doctorates living abroad, that when they were asked to give three main reasons for their decision not to return, over half of the 450 'reasons' were classified by him as professional, and only 11 per cent as sociocultural and 10 per cent as economic.

One counter to permanent professional migration would be to organise strong professional communities in Turkey, able to provide good and stimulating working conditions with international standing. But the massive export of students is itself one factor which inhibits the growth of such national, professional, and scientific communities.

No total answer to this problem has yet been found; to apply sanctions which virtually deny the right of people to leave their country of birth is internationally unacceptable in terms of human rights, though a variety of penalties and inducements have been tried, and could be extended. But one unorthodox proposal has never been seriously canvassed. Since the importing of trained immigrants is an economic benefit to the importing country, any country importing a trained professional from a country with a lower GNP should compensate that country either in money, or in kind by sending a replacement at their own expense. But the simplest solution is to send fewer students abroad.

3. Schools, language and science teaching

The rapid expansion of the schools and of teacher training presents many problems which are not soluble by international aid. The main assistance at primary level has been to school feeding problems by the World Food Programme.

The growth of the 'normal schools' for training teachers has been supported by a UNICEF–UNESCO project, on which Guiton published a report in 1969 and 1972[11] making a number of administrative recommendations to avoid errors and waste, but reporting the combined operation as being a major success.

Such expansion required people capable of running and teaching in new or larger 'normal schools' and institutes of education, and a vast number of qualified students capable of becoming teachers. The original models for the '*lise*' level imported directly from Europe have been maintained in part by the continuing presence in Turkey of a number of foreign high schools, French, German, British, and especially American, and those of the Greek-speaking and Jewish minorities. Secondly, the American, British, French, and German governments have all helped the teaching of their own languages by various means; recently, both state and private Turkish schools have been established which teach science and mathematics in a foreign language, in most cases English, the most celebrated being Ankara Koleji, with pupils from eleven upwards. Most of these foreign teachers are

[11] UNESCO Report on Teacher Training in Turkey, Jan 1972.

paid by the Turkish school authorities and the foreign governments mainly help with recruiting.

The French are renowned for their enthusiasm in supporting French teaching; British and American support for English teaching has been substantial over a long period. So to a lesser extent has German support for German. But all the same, the recent expansion of *lycée* education has diluted resources at the very moment when the growing economic ties with Europe and the United States require sharp increases in the need for Turks to have technical competence in a European language.

International awareness and discussion of the problems led to the setting up of a project funded by the Council of Europe to improve English, French, and German language teaching in *lycée* schools in Turkey. The plan was to prepare special courses using modern methods, technical equipment and ideas, and to disseminate these courses and methods through a series of training seminars and special courses in different parts of the country. The British and German governments made experts available for the project, but France decided to rely on her four-man team of *Assistance Pedagogique* already working in Turkey. Problems arose because the Turkish authorities claimed that they could not legally second the Turkish members of the Commission, who must carry their new duties in addition to performing their normal stint of teaching, said to be eighteen hours per week. After argument, the British and German commissions accepted this decision; the French refused, but put a good deal of effort into organising seminars. They reported further difficulties in arranging these because the Turks declared that it was illegal for teachers to be absent from school in working hours even for training seminars or courses. These had therefore to be arranged in evenings or vacations.

In 1971, two rather different courses were devised by the British and German commissions, and the French had not begun. The project involved one international body, three national donors, and the Turks; the problems of financial and administrative coordination were considerable. Nevertheless, within limits, the project appeared successful. It seems probable that eventually much improved foreign language textbooks and courses for Turkish schools will result.

The Ford Foundation supported a very different project of aid for the *lycées* in a very different style. In the 1960s they established a special experimental science *lycée* in Ankara. With adequate resources and a clear intent, it was possible to muster a competent and interested staff for one school, and the project was a success. Around 1968, the science programmes used in this school were extended to fifty more schools, and in 1971 to a further 200.

The Foundation claimed this as an example of a success of their policy. They had selected an area neglected by others, won Turkish collaboration, put in the relatively modest sum of $2·3 million over some eight years, and achieved a major revolution in attitudes to the teaching of science in Turkish schools, likely to have considerable consequences. The new generation of young scientists, trained according to the new methods, will, it is hoped, approach science not as a set of truths to be learned by heart, but as a set of problems to be tackled and hypotheses to be questioned.

Set against the scale of expenditure on the Turkish school system, the amount of aid is minute. It is possible that it is crucial, more especially as it is concentrated at the elite levels, the most prestigious schools, the Institutes of Education, and is thus able to influence official policy and thinking about methods and organisation and standards of training. All national governments most closely concerned desired to switch from direct support in the form of teachers to support for teacher training. The costs to Turkey of paying foreign teachers above their own national scales and meeting their travelling expenses is a heavy burden; equally if the donor countries provide part or all of the cost, their capacity to give other forms of aid is diminished. Planting foreign teachers in schools where they are able to form close personal links with colleagues, pupils, parents and neighbours may have a host of unintended consequences, but these are bound to be highly variable according to personalities and circumstances.

Nevertheless, if aid is small, influence is not. The Turkish school system faces the dilemma that Turkey faces. Clearly, it is derived from European models. In policy terms, how far should Turkey use her present system to develop independently her own national contribution to her own, and perhaps, to world education? How far should she instead endeavour to keep close contact with developments in the industrialised countries? After all, primary schools are the only national institution to which all Turks must submit themselves for five years, and very formative years at that.

4. Education and industry

In absolute terms, and in terms of its share both of employed labour and of the national product, Turkish industry and commerce have been expanding very rapidly. Total employment outside agriculture rose from 2·7 million in 1962 to 4·6 million in 1972;[12] the third Five-Year Plan envisages further annual growth in industry of 11·3 per cent and in services of 7·9 per cent.[13]

This expansion creates a demand for managers and for technicians and skilled workers which the existing structures are not able to meet. A number of initiatives involving aid request and projects have recently been aimed to work towards eliminating these shortages. At the same time,

[12] UCUNCU BES YILC/PLAN. 1 (draft) Table 509, p. 723.
[13] Country and Inter-Country Programming, UNDP DD/GC/TUR/R. 1.

hopes have been expressed that Turks with experience of industrial Germany might contribute their experience and savings towards the development of Turkish industry, and some efforts have been made to encourage them to do so.

Turkey has for a long time possessed professional and technical schools from craft schools for boys and girls to teachers schools for primary teachers and for *imams*.

The technical schools clearly train very few of those working as craftsmen or skilled workers in industry; most of them learn by apprenticeship, which can be very informal, or simply by experience. On the other hand, what is formally taught is said often to have very little to do with practice. Even where boys and girls are taught specific practical crafts, there is still a gulf between what the teachers define as the proper way to do things and what people employed, or self-employed, outside school actually do. Moreover, much of what goes on is technically old-fashioned, and the technical schools do not on the whole adapt themselves to change. Although there is a fair amount of technical education, and some of it is excellent, it has little impact on industry.

In response to this situation the government set up a National Industry Training Scheme, with an elaborate plan for new institutions at different levels, and closer ties to industry. A project for assistance with this plan financed by ILO is to provide around half a million dollars over two years. The German aid at Izmir to textile teaching (p. 298) comes also under this heading, and much of the technical assistant bursaries offered by various governments are for specific purposes in specific industries.

The shortage of trained managers is also alleged to be a limiting factor on the growth of Turkish industry and similar enterprises. Nineteen university faculties and other institutions offer courses in business management, including the Middle East Technical University, Istanbul Technical University and Boğaziçi University. Of these one goes back to the nineteenth century; but all the rest have been established during the last fifteen years. The supply of trained managers is too small, the trainees receive far too little practical experience, and there is a marked tendency for the products of the schools to enter bureaucracies or to go back into teaching without gaining practical experience in managing.

In the late 1960s the Turkish Management Association, with help from the Ford Foundation, set up a Foundation for Management Education, the aim of which is to improve and expand management education, expecially by bringing together industrialists, practical managers and teachers of management. On the whole progress is slow. Private industry is not keen on paying for courses; academics are not keen on practical problems; and civil servants are not easily persuaded of the importance of business training. The Foundation is active and growing, and international support from USAID and other governments and agencies is forthcoming. The

Turkish Management Foundation had been running short courses in Istanbul and claims a high degree of success in alerting people to their problems. At a rather different level, but also with much success, the Management Faculty has been running three-month courses since 1954.

The United States seems the chief source of models and training in business studies, and appropriately support comes from the Ford Foundation and USAID.

Since 1963, Turkish workers have been going to work in Germany. The number of these rose to over 600,000 in 1972. From Turkey's point of view this exodus reduces unemployment, though by no means in a one for one ratio, and provides a large amount of foreign currency in the shape of remittances. Undoubtedly, one effect of the exodus is to deprive Turkey of trained manpower.

One obvious hope from migration is an increase in experience of industry and of an industrialised society. In one sense this may be true. It is possible to argue that people all over Turkey now have among their kin or neighbours someone who has been to work in Europe, usually in Germany. But in much more specific terms, the experience of working abroad is not an asset to Turkey. A study of returned migrants conducted by OECD reported on balance the reverse. Returning migrants often cannot find work which gives them the income or working conditions to which they have become accustomed. Some of them attempt to start small businesses, but these are often unimaginative, and frequently they simply lose their savings. Some of them invest in urban land, which is a virtually certain way of making money, thus accentuating one of the serious problems of steeply rising land prices.

Recently schemes have been set up between the German and Turkish governments to meet this situation. Selected Turks wishing to return permanently to Turkey are given a nine-month course at the German government's expense in running businesses, and then sent home to finish the course for three months in Turkey. They acquire rights to credit to add to their savings. The scheme covers small numbers and is hardly likely to have more than a marginal effect on the Turkish economy. But it does provide yet another source of training and sophistication, and possibly some of those so trained will help Turkey to acquire business skills.

5. Military aid

To discuss the range of educational aid and technical assistance in Turkey selectively is to leave one very large fact out of account. The total aid which has flowed into Turkey has included a very large amount of military aid (Table 7.3). The Americans, and to a much lesser extent, other NATO powers have trained Turkish troops to operate the equipment given. No doubt far more is spent on training regular officers than the ordinary soldiers, or the reserve officers. Nevertheless, Turkey's conscript army teaches thousands of men at all levels, from literacy, simple administration, driving lorries, radio operation and such for the conscripts, to advanced technology for army and air force officers. Without doubt Turkey's allies have made a very large contribution. Two questions about military aid can be asked, but not answered, here. How far have Turkey's defence strategy and military alliances diverted her own domestic resources and policies away from development? And – recalling the role of army officers in Turkey's liberal and nationalist revolution – how do foreign equipment, technology and training influence the ideas, beliefs and assumptions of the armed forces, and with what economic and political consequences?

VI THE POLITICS OF AID

As in any bureaucratic system so in Turkey, and in Turkish ministries and agencies, many procedures, assumptions and customs are shared. People are committed to their positions, policies, jobs and friends: their life-time careers are at stake. Long-term consistency of high-level policy within ministries is not easy to achieve because of rapid changes in national politics. Nor is consistency within political parties, since both the overall climate of opinion and the specific boss may change. The very success of rapid development is itself often a cause of this political instability.

All aid flowing into Turkey is channelled through the Foreign Ministry. The Finance Ministry is also closely involved, especially if the aid is sizeable and economically significant. So is the State Planning Office, established as part of the Prime Minister's Office in 1961; but it has no power to direct other ministries, to issue orders, or to execute policies. Nearly every project also concerns at least one of the more specific ministries, an arrangement which is often unsatisfactory for donors. At best it is cumbersome and slow, but it may also involve disagreements between Turkish officials and ministers. In Turkey's centralised system, detailed matters are normally referred to high levels for approval. Since many projects depend on precise timing for effectiveness, delays and uncertainties of this kind are expensive and frustrating.

It is not possible here to trace in any detail the relation between national political vicissitudes and aid. The setting up of the State Planning Organisation following the 1960 coup certainly seems to have impressed potential donors favourably. The formally liberal regime of Suleyman Demirel, Leader of the Justice Party from 1965 to 1971, with his majority based on an alliance of businessmen and peasants, must have influenced Turkish policies as to what kinds of aid were welcome.

From the late 1960s, and especially after the army called on Demirel to resign in 1971, the period was a troubled one. Economic problems and outbreaks of violence, especially in the universities, led to a widespread repression of people with left-wing opinions. The constitution was changed to increase government power, especially over the judiciary. A new University Law was before the Constitutional Court in 1972. This law makes universities less liberal; for example, giving government formal control of appointments of staff, and explicitly discouraging contacts between staff and students outside teaching hours. Such a law is contrary to the avowed purposes of many international aid projects, which seek to increase staff and student independence of thought and freedom to criticise, and informal stimulation and interaction.

No one seriously doubts that international politics are important in aid exchanges. Turkey has benefited greatly from her pivotal strategic position, which has brought her American military and civilian aid in large and continuing quantities. Her direct membership of European organisations, especially OECD, also gives her political advantages over many other poorer nations. International politics impinge on educational aid and technical assistance in three ways: the relation between Turkey and her donors, the implications of precariousness, and the multiplicity of donors.

In most cases, the donor, international agency or national government, has one set of ideas, and the Turks another. Issues are partly rational and administrative, partly political. The Turks want freedom of manoeuvre for rational reasons, but they also object not only to any explicit exposure of Turkish shortcomings but also to any implication that they cannot manage without international advisers or that they are under tutelage. Informally, donors comment that giving aid to Turkey calls for exceptional diplomatic skills. Formally they express the dilemma by asking how much pressure any donor is justified in putting on the Turks in order to ensure the efficient use in his own eyes of the resources he is supplying; waste is after all demoralising.

These questions can only be answered in specific contexts. The issues may range, for example, from techniques of language instruction or a guarantee of rapid passage of equipment through Turkish customs, to major questions of economic policy, political liberty, or population control. For example, the introduction of modern teaching techniques sounds uncontroversial, but new methods imply not only a 'problem-solving' approach to mathematics and science, but a questioning and argumentative approach to humanities and social studies. This in turn implies a less authoritarian role for teachers, and freedom for children to discuss traditional moral rules and national political issues. The Ministry of National Education, if they perceive these implications, may well find them unacceptable.

Aid may often serve purposes other than those officially envisaged. A donor may, by making resources available to one side in a dispute, alter the local balance of power in line with his own views. A small amount of resources at a crucial point may enable officials to evade a legal or political difficulty or break a deadlock in putting a particular plan into action.

The theoretically short-term commitment behind international agencies which rely on annual contributions from member governments for their incomes is a well-rehearsed problem. Many projects need support for many years if they are to be effective, but normally they are limited to two or three years, often with a late start, and usually with uncertainty about the future. Turkey has for political reasons perhaps fared relatively well in the continuity of aid in general; but specific projects suffer from the administrative complexities and mistimings implicit in this built-in precariousness. The problem of long-term finance is linked to that of monitoring and evaluating projects, a task which is far more difficult than is normally acknowledged.

Turkey receives aid from at least fourteen distinct United Nations agencies, the World Bank Group, OECD, EEC, the Council of Europe, NATO, CENTO, the Rockefeller and Ford Foundations, as well as from seventeen governments. Such a multiplicity of sources provides ample opportunities for overlaps, confusions, and falling between stools. Nations and agencies may be rivals in giving where conspicuous success seems likely, or anxious to pass responsibilities to others where a burden brings no prescribed reward. At the same time, an opportunity is provided for Turks with initiative to submit the same project to different sources; or rival Turkish agencies may submit similar projects, either to one source or to different sources.

Problems of this kind are discussed in the Jackson Report (1969–70) which led to the greatly increased responsibilities of UNDP as a coordinating channel for UN aid. The UNDP office in Turkey seems highly successful; not only does it publish an annual list of all aid and all projects except those of some socialist governments unwilling to disclose details, but it also appears to be succeeding to some extent in inducing both bilateral and international donors to coordinate their activities with each other and with Turkish agencies.

VII KNOWLEDGE AND CULTURE

Nations are notoriously and grossly unequal in material resources. The inequalities in knowledge and skill – including knowledge and skill in managing large-scale organisations – are no less gross, even though they are less conspicuous, harder to specify, and impossible to quantify. Any attempt, therefore, to reduce the inequality between nations must involve as well as the transfer of goods and capital, the transfer of knowledge and experience. Three questions can be distinguished, closely related and frequently confused. First, how much of Western culture, organisations, and institutions are a necessary condition for 'modernising' a nation technically, and managing a growing economy? Secondly, how much of Western culture is bound to be exported over and above this essential minimum? Thirdly, how far is it desirable that Western culture should be so exported because it is intrinsically 'good'?

Turkey has certainly gone far beyond the technical in her adoption of Western culture. Ataturk set out quite consciously to replace the Turkish script, clothes, customs, family morality, judicial, legal, political, military, and educational institutions by European ones. Now all Turkish men and all educated Turkish women wear European clothes; all children learn Latin letters; the government is a parliamentary democratic republic, and the economy planned capitalism. In short, at least in the cities and for the educated, Turkey is institutionally and culturally a European country.

However strong the argument for the material and economic necessity of aid, this wholesale export of Western culture has some questionable consequences, at least in the short and middle run.

I have argued that scientists and scholars who go abroad develop and maintain life-long attachments to centres of excellence abroad. They are virtually bound to remain marginal to these unless they migrate permanently; yet they are likely to be distracted from interests centred on Turkey on to problems of their international scientific or professional community. This situation may foster rivalry and secrecy among Turks, and impede the development of self-generating science and scholarship within Turkey.

How far does the fact that so much of Turkish life is directly linked to foreign enterprises, models, institutions and sources of finance prevent Turkey from developing an indigenous natural culture of its own? Except for those who migrate permanently many of her leading engineers, economists, writers, composers, and even industrialists, seek recognition in the international arena where all but a few of them, in the absence of a strong national culture in their own field, are bound to appear derivative and imitative. The Turkish intellectuals and professionals sit on the horns of a dilemma. They take their measures of excellence from the West, and they need to perceive themselves as at least equals of their international friends and colleagues. Yet for obvious structural reasons – finance, numbers and organisation – such equality is only possible for individuals with close personal ties to the West, and not for whole professional groups. They may tacitly admit by act or attitude an inferiority which in other contexts by act or word they explicitly deny. This very ambivalence is itself a break on their own autonomous development; and the constant flow of advice and assistance helps to perpetuate their problem.

A second consequence of the influence of Western society has been the increase in the gap between the majority of Turkish people and the Turkish educated elite (p. 314). The vast majority of the Turkish people are still villagers by birth and by social affiliation, even if not by residence. A further sizeable minority belong to the small towns, or to fairly traditional working-class sections of the larger towns and cities. Even those who know about German factories or German children's allowances do not normally share the pro-European views of the urban educated.

The gap between the villagers and recent urban immigrants on the one hand, and the Western-educated urban elite on the other seems, with rare exceptions, much greater than, say, the cultural gap in most industrialised countries between rulers and ruled within a single ethnic group. The differences in taste, in music and art, in leisure pursuits, political convictions and assumptions, in personal morality, in cosmology and religious belief are vast.

One serious consequence is the assumption by political leaders and administrators that they know what goes on, and do not need any empirical enquiries; and that in any case they know what is best for the village and the working class. People who challenge official facts are subversive, and paternalism without realism is anyway much simpler and more comfortable than finding out the facts.

People often say that aid is a temporary expedient aimed to render itself redundant. Yet measured in any economic terms, it is simple to show that unless growth rates for the rich drop to zero, and those of the poor remain high, the gap will persist indefinitely. Turkey is aiming to achieve by 1995 the level of economic production per capita which Italy enjoyed in 1972, in which same year she is to become a full member of the European Economic Community. Yet by then, even if Turkey keeps up the necessary growth rate of over six per cent per annum, parts of Europe, with the help of Turkish workers, may well have doubled their present standard of living.

The theory that aid is self-eliminating is implausible for another reason. At present rates of growth the Turkish economy should double in ten years or so. Such a rate of growth creates a constant series of bottlenecks. The more advanced the techniques, the more specific the technical skills needed. As import substitutions begin to cover basic requirements, so the need for more esoteric knowledge grows. Thus, far from withering away, the Turkish demands for educational aid and technical assistance are likely to grow and to become more specific, moving from general projects like that at Karadeniz (p. 300), to much more carefully defined and organised projects that aim to fill in specific missing links in technical chains.

I have argued that educational aid and technical assistance is not without very serious consequences for those receiving it. Yet aid is essential to the growth of Turkey, and it is likely to increase in quantity and change in character to more specific and technical goals. The present arrangements involve very considerable waste and inefficiency. More seriously, they seem to maintain the dependence of the Turkish elite on Western institutions, to emphasise through the constant export of students overseas the legitimation of foreign superiority, and to inhibit a sufficiently rapid growth of autonomous national centres of scientific, professional, business, and aesthetic creativity.

VIII CODA

One main impression of my study of aid to Turkey is of a series of cynical generalisations and critical anecdotes, interlaced with often plausible success stories from those directly responsible for running certain specific programmes or projects. Another is of the vast variety and complexity of what is going on. Any clear statement or analysis seems impossible. Some (e.g. UNESCO) have produced reports based on similar experiences consisting of recipes for organisational improvements, for avoiding troubles, errors and failures – but usually leaving it to the reader to decide whether the cap fits.

The practical implications of this tentative and brief analysis, which can only reflect a minute part of what is going on, are of three kinds. First, some pessimistic predictions that a certain level of waste and futility is inevitable. Secondly, recommendations to do things which everyone claims to have been trying to do for years. Thirdly, recommendations to change things which are an accepted part of the whole scene, and which a good many of those involved do not want changed. All three are likely to irritate those working at the coal face of development, the first two because they alter nothing and add little, the third because they threaten vested interests and challenge accepted dogmas. Nevertheless, I draw five specific conclusions.

1. Aid implies inequality. But sovereign nations are by definition equal. Hence the path of official aid is necessarily thorny. Moreover, all aid involves resources and advantages for someone, jobs, qualifications, trips abroad, markets, contracts, commission. Hence the negotiation of aid projects inevitably involves politics, the micro-politics of personal groups and institutions, as well as national and international politics. For example, Turkish politics, both national and academic, were major factors in preventing the UNESCO project in Karadeniz University from operating as planned. These factors seriously limit rationality and efficiency, and often put a premium on appearances, reports and politics rather than on real achievements, real consequences, and serious criticism.

2. The nuts and bolts of detailed planning and execution of projects gives vast room for improvement. In general small projects work better than large ones, and projects where the personnel on each side are retained for long periods and learn to work closely together do better than those with numerous changes of personnel. At the same time, long-term continuity and a built-in flexibility about the terminal date is likely to increase the ratio of benefit to cost. Pre-project planning requires the maximum degree of cynical, empirical checking. Plentiful anecdotal evidence suggests that in Turkey the existence of a complex set of administrative laws and rules and

the legalism of many officials who are more concerned to conform than to get things done provides more than ordinary bureaucratic obstacles to the planning and execution of projects.

3. Fellowships and studentships

a) Resources should be switched massively away from sending students abroad, and directed into training within Turkey. Fellowships and scholarships should be allocated only for highly specific objectives, and both candidates and foreign training establishments abroad should be carefully selected and checked. The present system of scholarships allocated by the Ministry of Education without detailed guidance and advice should be terminated. Students should be financed for undergraduate courses only where these are completely unavailable in Turkey.

b) No student should be sent on a course of study unless he or she is already highly proficient in the language in which the course is given. To follow lectures and discussions on intellectual problems demands an exceptional command of any language, let alone a foreign one.

c) Short and specific technical courses are excellent but only when directly relevant to the student's interests and occupation, and future.

d) Current rules limiting the time graduate students doing research in foreign universities can spend in Turkey on research should be abolished. Students should be actively encouraged to centre their research and training abroad on Turkish themes and problems in all disciplines.

4. It is often wiser to bring experts and teachers to Turkey. But experts and teachers should be trained in the problems of giving international instruction and advice, should learn at least some Turkish language and background, and should normally be prepared to stay at least two years. Contact and discussion between students and teachers should be encouraged, not discouraged. As far as possible, experts who come for short periods for highly specific purposes should either be experienced in aid-giving projects, or know something about Turkey, or both.

5. Two general objectives should underlie every project and programme. First, aid should move constantly towards a reciprocal exchange between equals. Secondly, every aid project should seek not simply to train one 'counterpart', but to build up in Turkey a body of self-replacing and self-improving experts in the particular field of knowledge concerned, and consciously to discourage individual and collective Turkish dependence on, and admiration for, foreign institutions. Priority should be given to the training of manpower planners, realising that this is a new and so far unsuccessful field of expertise in both developed and developing countries.

None of these recommendations resolve the basic dilemma. Turkey cannot maintain the pace of economic growth nor of cultural westernisation without the continuation of foreign education and technical assistance. Yet the existence of such a programme perpetuates the false belief that foreign is best and Turkish second best; it creams at any one time some 7000 able students and teachers, and brings them back, very often with attitudes, aspirations and doctrines which are in various ways contrary to Turkish interests, and which inhibit the growth of an indigenous, independent intelligentsia. But if the dilemma is clearly understood, seen and effectively faced, the results of this understanding can only serve to improve the programme of educational and technical aid.

APPENDIX

TABLE 7.1
Basic data 1973

Area	Total 780,976 sq. kms	
Population	37·2 million (mid-1972)	
Rate of growth	2·7 per cent per year	
Density	47 per sq. km of arable land	
Population characteristics (1967)		
Crude birth rate per 1000	39·6	
Crude death rate per 1000	14·6	
Infant mortality per 1000 live births	153·0	
Health (1967)		
Population per physician	2760	
Population per hospital bed	560	
Income distribution (1965–6, Istanbul)		
Percentage of national income, lowest quintile	7	
Percentage of national income, highest quintile	42	
Education (1970)		
Adult literacy rate	55%	
Primary school enrolment	90%	
Middle school enrolment	44%	
High-school level enrolment	13%	
Gross national product	*1967*	*1971**
GNP, total (million TL at 1968 market prices)	102,112·3 ($7,293·7)†	132,216·1 ($9,444·0)†
GNP, per capita (TL at 1968 market prices)	3,120 ($223)†	3,661 ($262)†

Source: United Nations Development Programme Report, June 1973.
* Provisional estimates
† $1 = TL 14,000 (as of March 1973)

TABLE 7.2
Important events

1919	Mustafa Kemal, later Ataturk, organises resistance to the Sultan and the Allies in Istanbul
1922	Final victory of Mustafa Kemal and capture of Izmir
1923	Independence negotiated and the Republic established
1924	Caliphate abolished. National secular educational system enacted. Remaining Islamic courts of law abolished
1925	Suppression of religious orders. The fez outlawed and the hat adopted as national head-dress
1926	Western legal codes

TABLE 7.2 (*Cont.*)

1928	The State declared secular. Latin script replaces the Arabic script
1934	First Five-Year Plan for industry. European-type surnames made compulsory
1935	'Etatism' becomes a principle of the constitution. Sunday becomes a legal day of rest
1938	Death of Ataturk. İnönü becomes President
1939–45	Second World War
1946	Democratic Party founded; opposition permitted in the Grand National Assembly
1948	Turkey becomes a foundation member of OEEC (later OECD). Beginning of US programme of aid
1949	Turkey joins Council of Europe
1950	First multi-party election. Opposition Democratic Party victorious
1960	Army seizes power
1962	New constitution and elections. İnönü heads coalitions
1965	Justice Party clear majority
1971	Army intervenes to restore order; non-party governments; martial law in cities and eleven provinces
1973	Martial law ended. Elections. Coalition government takes office

TABLE 7.3
Aid to Turkey
(million $)

1. US economic and military aid 1946–69				
	1946–8	1949–61	1962–9	Total 1946–69
(a) Economic aid (all US sources)				
Loans	44·5	418·9	907·2	1,370·6
Grants	—	914·0	270·0	1,184·0
Total of loans and grants	44·5	1,332·9	1,177·2	2,554·6
(b) Military aid	68·8	1,789·8	1,186·5	3,045·1
Total of economic and military aid	113·3	3,122·7	2,363·7	5,599·7
2. International agencies aid 1946–69				
		1968	1969	1946–69
		40·0	118·9	413·1
3. DAC countries aid 1960–8				
	1967	1968		1960–8
	71·1	77·0		460·2

4. UNDP reports for 1970, 1971 and 1972 do not give clear annual global totals, and include only non-military aid. But the 1972 report indicates approximate totals of capital aid in 1971 of 260 million dollars, and in 1972 of $470 million. This is in addition to a commitment for ongoing activities for Pre-investment and Technical Assistance of $165 million.

Source for 1, 2, and 3: USAID Programme, 1971.

8 Chile

Harold Blakemore*

I GENERAL INFORMATION

1. The influence of the past

The Latin American State of Chile, an independent Republic since 1818, has an area of some 740,000 square kilometres, and an estimated population (mid–1972) of more than nine million. Yet, in the country's evolution, size has been less important than shape. With its entire western boundary the Pacific shore-line, and its eastern frontier the mountain chain of the Andes, Chile extends more than 4200 kilometres in length but has an average width of only 200 kilometres, giving the country extraordinary variety of climatic conditions and great diversity of landscape. But, as a political and constitutional unit, Chile has had, for most of its independent history, centralised administration, with the government in Santiago holding the whole country in one single net of authority. The reasons for this paradox are many and involved: they lie, to a large extent, in the simple fact that for three hundred years as a colony of Spain, and for roughly half of its independent life, Chile consisted of a compact block of territory at the heart of the present Republic, some 1000 kilometres long and 200 kilometres wide, and its expansion north and south from this long-standing core in the last hundred years was simply the extension to much larger regions of well-established concepts of government and nationality.[1] And that central core remains, as it always

* The author is indebted for information, assistance and constructive criticism to a large number of informants in international and national organisations, but he would wish to acknowledge a particular debt of thanks to Martin Wilson in the United Kingdom, and to Oscar Aguero, Maria Angélica Junemann, Mario Leyton, Carol Pinto, Armando Uribe and Elizabeth Wicha in Chile. His opinions, of course, are his own.

[1] Harold Blakemore and Clifford T. Smith (eds), *Latin America: Geographical Perspectives*, London, 1971, pp. 475–6.

has been, the crucial part of the republic, containing today perhaps as much as seventy per cent of the national population.

The implications of centralised decision-making and of uniformity of administration for educational advance will become more apparent as this chapter proceeds. But there are other factors in the historical evolution of Chile, within its distinctive geographical framework, which remain significant in its future development, and which must be mentioned here, however briefly. Some of these factors are of general relevance to Latin America as a whole, and they derive from a colonial experience under Iberian powers which lasted some three hundred years. Other influences are more specifically Chilean, and they spring both from distinctive colonial features of this particular part of the Spanish empire in America and also from the highly individual development of Chile as a modern state. In general terms, Chile as a colonial appendage of Spain, like other parts of the Spanish empire, was subject over a long period of time to a system of government of which the characteristic features were absolute central authority, at least on paper, and bureaucratic control. In practice, as elsewhere, absolutism was tempered by circumstances, and the rigidity of regulations was often overcome by observing the forms but ignoring the intent. Nevertheless, Chilean colonial experience, like that of the rest of the Spanish American empire, left a legacy of bureaucratic formalism, dependence on instruction from above, and weakness of both individual initiative in government and of local autonomy.

As a colony, however, Chile evolved a racial and social structure which had much to do with its quite distinctive evolution after Independence. Unlike other Spanish American states with sizeable Indian populations (with the exception of Paraguay, which had a similar experience), Chile became independent as a bi-racial society. By 1800, pure-blooded Indians as a separate ethnic stock had almost completely disappeared from the central region, and the population was divided into a minority of whites, the dominant stock, and a majority of *mestizos*, the product of racial fusion which had proceeded for some three centuries. The Indians who were not absorbed lay far to the south, outside the real Chile, and they were not taken into the Republic until the last quarter of the nineteenth century. This largely two-tiered racial structure, compared with Andean America, Mexico and Central America, for example, made for a higher degree of homogeneity. The subsequent problems of these other states, and not least those of nation-building, the diffusion of skills for economic development, and the moral question of adapting education to different cultures derive, at least in part, from complicated racial structures in which Indian populations are sufficiently large to constitute a national issue.

Independence from Spain came to Chile, as it did to other parts of Spanish America, as the work of well-born leaders, conscious of an incipient sense of nationality which had been sharpened by resentment of colonial control. It was a political revolution, but not a social and economic one, and for the masses it made little difference. Here again, however, Chile was unique. Elsewhere in Spanish America, the abrupt removal of imperial power left a vacuum of authority which many sought to fill, and the post-Independence era of Spanish American history is largely a story of military control, dictatorship, and political instability. In Chile, events took a different course: after a decade or so of unstable administrations, the country settled down, under the combined aegis of Diego Portales (1793–1837) and the Constitution of 1833, a remarkable document which survived, though amended, to 1925. The genius of Portales, reflected in the Constitution, was simply to recognise Chile for what she was, a poor and backward country, ruled effectively by an oligarchy, which needed conditions of order without running the risk of tyranny. The answer was a system of government in which authority would be impersonal, administration honest, and the transfer of power from one president to the next a regular and peaceful process. It was an aristocratic system, but it was also a constitutional one, and while it sometimes, though rarely, broke down, the underlying continuities of a civilian tradition were fundamentally maintained. As Chile moved into the modern age, as its economic and social structure became more complex, so the framework of its institutional life had to be amended. The accommodation of new pressures was sometimes a painful process, notably in the 1930s when the Great Depression hit Chile harder than any other country in the world. Yet, the multi-party system which emerged in politics was a functioning one, and the extension of democratic rights proceeded slowly but surely. Chile retained in the twentieth century the reputation she had acquired in the nineteenth, that of an orderly republic which preferred the path of evolution to that of revolution.

Chile also possessed another particular advantage, compared with many of her Latin American neighbours, namely an educational tradition on which she could build as she entered the 'development decade'.

2. The educational heritage

High among the preoccupations of the first leaders of the Chilean Republic was the expansion of the country's educational provision. Not only were they conscious of Spanish neglect; even more they were concerned with the development of the infant Republic, and it is noteworthy that the Instituto Nacional, founded in 1813, even before Independence was secured, included, for the first time in Chile, natural science and economics in its offerings. Other institutions of learning were subsequently founded in the provinces, as well as in the capital, the National Library dating from 1818 and today one of the truly outstanding libraries of Latin America. At about the same time, technical assistance from abroad in the persons of distinguished foreign scholars, doctors, engineers and scientists, as well as teachers, began a tradition which continued. The Constitution of

1833 laid particular emphasis on the government's role in the development of education, and it was an expanding role throughout the nineteenth century. The University of Chile, the state university, was founded in 1842, its first Rector being the outstanding Venezuelan jurist and writer, Andrés Bello.

As government revenues increased with the development of the Chilean economy, so spending on education increased in proportion, and the range of provision expanded. To secondary and higher education was added technical education, beginning in the 1840s, again under the auspices of government, though also with private support. Chile, in fact, led the way in state education in Latin America, though this development was not an unmixed blessing: government control was a centralising force which imposed its own rigidities, and modern state education in Chile still suffers from this tradition. Yet, there was always diversity of structure and practice in Chilean education at all levels. This was largely because of the Roman Catholic Church, not constitutionally separated from the State until 1925. From the Catholic University of Santiago, founded in 1888, to the many parochial schools in Chile at lower levels, the Church remains highly significant in education, and is the principal factor in private education. Together with the foreign schools, British, German, French, and so on, which are permitted by government to function, the Church is responsible for the education of approximately one quarter of primary school children and about a third of secondary pupils.

Education in nineteenth-century Chile was still a minority privilege, but a major impetus to expansion and a frontal attack on illiteracy came with the Law of Compulsory Education in 1920, making primary education obligatory. A spate of reforms in the 1920s and 1930s laid the bases for the extension of education for those between the ages of seven and fifteen, and a significant development from the 1940s was the growth of rural education. Whereas approximately 50 per cent of the population was literate in 1920, over 86 per cent was claimed to be literate in 1970, putting Chile third, after Argentina and Uruguay, in this particular league-table in Latin America. Yet this achievement must be set in its proper perspective. The national literacy figure conceals vast discrepancies from province to province and between town and country. Logically enough, it is the rural provinces which have the highest percentage of illiterates, reflecting the demands of an agricultural economy on children of school age, and while more than 90 per cent of urban dwellers over the age of six are literate, less than 60 per cent of rural inhabitants are so blessed.

Despite such problems, which will recur in this discussion, the growth of educational provision from the birth of the Republic is a not undistinguished story.[2] Traditions of state concern and of private initiative

[2] See Amanda Labarca, *Historia de la Enseñanza en Chile*, Santiago, 1939, *passim*.

in this crucial field of activity were, at least, foundations to build on which many other developing countries lacked. But, quantitatively, as Chile entered the 1970s, there was still a good deal to be done, and even bigger questions surrounded the issue of quality of education, and its purpose at all levels. That the development of education depended on the development of the Chilean economy was a truism: how far the development of the Chilean economy depended on the nature, structure and objectives of the Chilean educational system was, perhaps, less obvious. But it was a question which needed an answer.

II CHILE IN THE 1960s

1. The Chilean economy

In the early 1960s, there was no better testimony to Chile's national preoccupation with economic and social problems than the writings of social scientists, national and foreign, both in the volume of their work and in the titles of their books. Even a random sample makes the point: *Chile, a Case of Frustrated Development*; *Chile, Disorganised Industrialization*; *Chile, a Difficult Economy*; and, a final example, *In Place of Misery*. They all expressed a basic frustration, that Chile was a developing, not a developed, country, and they pointed to the paradox that Chile was endowed with considerable natural and human resources, comprising abundant potential for economic growth, but lacking, apparently, suitable structures to promote it. Chile was, and is, rich in minerals: her copper deposits are the largest in the world, and she possesses iron ore and other industrial minerals in abundance. Her energy resources, notably hydroelectric power, are very large, and her agriculture, properly organised, should be capable of feeding twice the current national population. Communications are good, and Chile's industrial growth since the 1930s, notably since the Second World War, has been considerable. One of the major factors in the modern development of the Chilean economy on the basis of import-substitution has been the State Development Corporation (CORFO), founded in 1939 as an instrument of state planning and investment, and Chile also developed a large number of ancillary state corporations for the running of public utilities.

Since the Second World War, Chile's growth has lagged behind that of other Latin American states which had experienced similar economic changes, and it has been marked by wide fluctuations. Apparently endemic monetary instability was only checked by depressing economic activity to very low levels: when controls were removed, inflation soared again. One fundamental reason for this hard and persistent inflation was the slow growth of agriculture, as population increase outpaced it, and Chile was forced to import food to the tune of one-quarter of import costs. Agriculture's failure was, in part, a structural problem: the system of land tenure was one of high concentration of fertile land in large, unproductive estates, with most of the rural workers owning only small plots or no land at all. Low output from the land and the need to import food forced up prices, despite government attempts at control. Another acute problem stemmed from Chile's long-standing dependence on exports of her major primary commodity, copper. In the early 1960s, the government derived some 70 per cent of its foreign exchange, vital for essential imports, from copper, but it had no control over the world market which fluctuated widely, putting state revenues at risk. All these factors, together with an internal taxation system that was thoroughly inefficient, added up to budget deficits which were covered by well-established but dangerous measures, short-term borrowing, which increased the external debt, and increases in money supply, which fuelled the inflation. Nor was this all: inadequate investment had been made to provide productive employment for a growing urban population, fed, in part, by rural migrants, and, as a result, the service sector of the economy had increased at the expense of the industrial.

All in all, these economic circumstances, frustrating as they were in the light of Chile's potential, showed that the pursuit by government of both price stability and economic growth at one and the same time was simply not possible. A totally new approach to the problems of Chilean economic development was clearly needed, particularly since in education, health and housing the social consequences of economic failure were obvious.

2. Social and political pressures

Chile's economic problems in the 1960s were compounded, and, indeed, partly caused by the immense social pressures generated by two seemingly irresistible forces, population growth and rapid urbanisation. Between 1930 and 1960, the national population almost doubled to 7·4 million, but whereas the annual rate of growth had been 1·4 per cent in the early 1930s, by the 1960s it had reached 2·4 per cent. The universal phenomena of a declining death-rate, due largely to improved health measures, and a more or less stable birth-rate were the causes of this rapid increase. Moreover, the short time-span into which this change had been compressed imparted to the Chilean population an age-structure in which, by 1965, about 40 per cent of the population was younger than fifteen years old. The implications of this statistic both for education and employment are obvious.

Closely related to demographic growth itself was the Chilean expression of a common Latin American experience, urbanisation on an unprecedented scale. Natural increase in the cities and towns was paralleled by rural migration and, whereas in 1920 over 50 per cent of Chile's population was classified as rural, by 1960 it had fallen to 31 per cent. For the country as a whole, the proportion of the urban population increased from approximately half the population in 1930 to over two-thirds by 1960. The reasons for this are many, but a significant one in Chile was the failure of the agricultural sector to bring substantially more land into cultivation and thus retain more people in the countryside, and, at the same time a second 'push' factor lay in increased mechanisation on the land in the 1940s and 1950s. Very little attention had been given to positive measures to keep the rural population on the land by making life there more attractive, and it was clear that, if the rural migration was to be slowed down, the life of the agricultural labourer and the prospects for his children had to be improved.

Population growth and urbanisation on this scale created enormous pressures on housing, health facilities and education. In Santiago, whose population increased between 1930 and 1960 from 1 to 2½ million, from one-fourth of the national population to about one-third, the consequences were only too obvious in the large slum settlements called *callampas* (literally, mushrooms) which grew up in various parts of the city, and, indeed, no city in Chile lacked this scar.

Pressures on health facilities were no less acute. Qualitatively, the Chilean medical profession has always had standards as high as those obtaining anywhere else in the world, but it has always been under enormous strain. Access to facilities in 1960 varied greatly throughout the country. At that time, Chile had one hospital for every 30,000 inhabitants, but nearly half the country's hospitals were in its three richest provinces, and 60 per cent of all hospital doctors were working in the province of Santiago alone. Such disparity of resources naturally implied wide variations in effects: in 1960, while the infantile mortality rate in Santiago province was 121·8 – and this is very high compared with 'developed' countries – in Bío-Bío, a poor agricultural province, it reached the dreadful level of 234·9.[3]

Passing reference has already been made to educational disparities in Chile, which reflected the same lop-sided use of resources within a developing economy. While the measured national level of basic literacy was high, the six most urbanised provinces had literacy levels above the national average, the other eighteen provinces levels far below it. And, in the countryside itself, differences in schooling were no less wide: a sample survey of over 300 workers on 48 farms in two provinces in the Central Valley in 1965 showed that half the wage difference and productivity disparity between different groups of workers could be accounted for by schooling differences alone.[4]

[3] See R. Hoffman and F. Debuyst, *Chile, una industrialización desordenada*, Santiago, 1966, pp. 97–104.

[4] A. Valdés, 'Wages and Schooling of Agricultural Workers in Chile', *Economic Development and Cultural Change*, vol. 19, no. 2, Jan 1971, 313–29.

Such random indicators from related fields of social concern could be multiplied indefinitely for Chile in the 1960s, and by the 1960s the social tensions and economic pressures within Chile which the persistent stagnation of the economy had produced were also leading to a realignment of political forces which were to concentrate national attention on processes of change. By the presidential election of 1964, the country was faced with a choice between two types of reformist parties. On one side was the Marxist coalition of the Communist and Socialist parties with other like-minded groups in the Popular Action Front; on the other, the Christian Democratic Party. Both were committed to radical reform but by very different methods, and the campaign was fiercely fought.[5] In the event, Eduardo Frei Montalva, candidate of the Christian Democrats, won the Presidency by the biggest margin in modern Chilean history, and, in 1965, in Congressional elections, his party won a sweeping victory, gaining control of the Chamber of Deputies, and increasing its representation, but not winning a majority in the Senate. There were many reasons for these results, but of primary importance was the high degree of national consensus for a fundamental programme of change without the sacrifice, real or imagined, of the basic political freedoms which Chile enjoyed.

The programme of the Christian Democrats was a very ambitious one, and its details do not concern us. Suffice to say that among its main features were control of inflation, a sweeping agrarian reform, greater participation by Chile in its major resource, copper (then largely controlled by American interests) and a frontal attack on Chile's social problems. A primary concern of the Christian Democratic administration was education, to be dealt with in greater detail below, and regarded by the Christian Democrats as one of the keys to the wide range of problems with which the country was faced.

The advent to power of the Christian Democrats in Chile in 1964–5 was of fundamental significance in the country's own history and political evolution, but its impact was not confined to internal affairs. No assessment of the foreign aid programme to Chile in the 1960s, much less its relationship to education, can properly be made without reference to the international context in which it took place.

3. The international dimension

A few years before Frei's electoral victory in Chile, Fidel Castro had seized power in Cuba by a very different road, and launched the country on its revolutionary career, based on Marxist ideology, fervent anti-Americanism and tight internal political and social control. The threat of this example

[5] See E. Halperin, *Nationalism and Communism in Chile*, Cambridge, Mass., 1965, *passim.*

was certainly a major influence behind the Alliance for Progress, launched by President Kennedy of the United States in 1961. This was an idealistic programme of cooperative development which aimed to blunt the appeal of revolutionary doctrines in Latin America by a combination of internal reform there and large-scale foreign aid to promote it, and it was aimed particularly at the more democratic Latin American states whose governments showed a willingness to initiate and plan acceptable development programmes. As the most exemplary democracy in Latin America and as a country which had launched a ten-year plan of development in 1961, Chile was already well-qualified for such aid, but there can be no doubt that the triumph of the Christian Democrats in 1964–5 underlined its significance for all those who believed in the possibility of fundamental and necessary change within a framework of consent.

Other developed states were also interested, for a variety of reasons, in what had happend in Chile. Here, after all, the first Christian Democratic government to come to power in Latin America had an ambitious and exciting programme in a politically stable country, and its leaders had been profoundly influenced in their formation by Christian Democratic thinking in Europe. Western Europe could be expected to look favourably on Chile as a sound recipient of aid, and the challenge of development that Chile represented was to evoke a responsive chord from a variety of organisations, as well as from governments and multilateral agencies in the 'development decade'. In the mid-1960s Chile seemed to provide an excellent test-case for many of the assumptions on which outside aid for national development had been based, and a good deal of international hope had been placed on the new government. But, while Chile, no doubt, benefited greatly in the short run from this interest and assistance, it also had to carry the imponderable handicap of foreign, as well as national, aspirations. And that was something the Christian Demoratic government could well have done without.

III EDUCATIONAL REFORM

1. Before the reform

Chile has a long tradition of intellectual concern with the nature and purpose of education in general, and with the relationship between national education and the country's needs in particular. One of the classic early works on Chilean under-development, Francisco A. Encina's *Nuestra Inferioridad Econòmica*, first published in 1911, referred specifically to this issue, while Alejandro Venegas in *Sinceridad: Chile Intimo en 1910* made positive recommendations to the government of the day for reform of Chilean education at all levels. By and large, however, successive governments were either indifferent to such pleas, overwhelmed by other priorities such as the reduction of illiteracy, or simply unable to do much because of lack of resources. But by the 1960s there was general recognition of the absolute necessity for widespread reform, particularly in view of the accelerating economic and social pressures to which brief reference has been made.

In form, content and purpose, Chilean education was still partly imbued with the characteristics of a Hispanic tradition which survived, though in attenuated form, in much of Latin America: respect for well-established practices, dislike of innovation, suspicion of initiative, lack of coordination, and dependence on legally-constituted authority. Equally significantly, the educational system was geared to a social and economic structure in which hierarchy was rated more highly than equality of opportunity. Pyramidal in form, but rising from the broad base of compulsory primary education starting at the age of seven to a very narrow apex, the Chilean educational system was essentially geared for the production of a small elite which could afford to proceed, on a highly selective basis, from primary to university level.

The introduction of free, compulsory basic education in a six-year cycle from the age of seven in a society which was highly stratified economically and socially resulted in the primary stage, or, indeed, only part of it, being the sole educational experience of the vast majority of Chileans, who acquired a basic literacy but little else. The better-off minority proceeded to the secondary stage, and some of them to higher levels of education, but the primary level throughout was bedevilled by schizophrenic objectives: constituting a *total* education for the majority, and providing a *preparatory* education for the minority. Drop-out rates were very high at all stages, inevitable in a country with a highly-skewed pattern of income distribution where many children must become premature wage-earners if families are to survive. In effect, the primary level subordinated the aim of a good imaginative education for all as a preparation for life to the objective of selecting the minority for the secondary level, in other words, preparing an elite. The secondary level, in turn, was geared essentially to the production of candidates for the university and other institutions of higher learning, though its success in meeting even this objective was very partial.

The situation facing Chilean education in the early 1960s was not, then, simply a matter of devoting more resources to correcting deficiencies of both a quantitative and qualitative kind: it was no less a question of devising appropriate machinery for creating an educational system which, from top to bottom, would be more appropriate for a modern, developing democratic state, than the existing outdated, regressive and socially divisive structure which was increasingly unrelated to Chilean reality.

2. The philosophy of change

Like most great reforms, the Chilean educational reform of the 1960s had a long period of gestation behind it, and considerable investigation, deliberation and planning preceded the sweeping educational changes on which the Christian Democratic government of Eduardo Frei embarked. An important step had been taken in late 1962 when the government of President Jorge Alessandri set up the Commission for Overall Educational Planning (Comisión de Planeamiento de la Educación Chilena), a small committee consisting of representatives of relevant ministries, the legislature, the universities and the civil service, and assisted by groups of specialists drawn from different educational sectors and from the Latin American Division of the Education Department of UNESCO, headed at that time by a Chilean, Oscar Vera who, in fact, gave up that post to become co-ordinator of the Commission. Another key influence in the Commission's work was the then-President of the Council of Rectors of the Chilean Universities, and, later, Minister of Education under Frei, Juan Gómez Millas. The Commission was given an enormous brief, covering the whole field of education and more, as its terms of reference, which are worth quoting, indicate:

i. to undertake the study of those aspects of the demographic, social, economic and educational situation of the country which it is indispensable to understand for programming the overall planning of education;
ii. to study solutions to the administrative, pedagogical and economic problems posed by national education, its extension and improvement within an integrated plan;
iii. to propose the adoption and initiate the execution of specific measures which, within the context of the plan, may be applied immediately or gradually;
iv. to coordinate the international financial and technical assistance which the country receives in the field of education.

The Commission could not hope to complete so huge a task before the mandate of the Alessandri government expired in 1964, but, nothing daunted, it launched an impressive series of enquiries into existing provision, and made a number of positive recommendations on which the successor government was to build. No less important, it set out in a comprehensive document what it felt to be the primary aims and objectives of the Chilean educational system, a declaration of principles which, in effect, cut clean across many of the assumptions on which the existing system operated. The statement is far too long to quote in full, but its philosophy may be gathered from the following paragraph:

> The purpose of Chilean education, in its diverse forms and levels, is to facilitate the harmonious development of all aspects of the individual personality, in accordance with its capacities and interests, and to contribute in the acceleration of the cultural, social and economic development of the country. What this means is that the structure of

> the educational system and the content of teaching must be such as to strengthen national unity, emphasising integration and solidarity of different groups, and which, basing itself on the best traditions of our culture, will encourage values and stimulate activities which favour the development[6] of the man and citizen, make possible a higher level of individual well-being and of social and economic justice, and which will promote improvement in standards of living and increase production.

The Commission emphasised the necessity to strike a balance between individual needs and aspirations and the requirements of the State, stressing the broad human aims of education as well as its role in preparation for careers, and it argued for the importance of continuing general education at a late age, on the grounds that more lively, versatile and adaptable people would be produced, to develop their particular aptitudes and skills at a later stage.

The concrete recommendations of the Commission reflected these concepts. They included a major reform of the primary school and the first three years of secondary school by a new cycle of nine years of general education, compulsory for all children; and a flexible middle cycle of one, two or three years for those seeking technical or professional careers, and one of three years' pre-university education for academic training. Flexibility was emphasised throughout. The Commission also made many other specific recommendations, and Chile was ready in 1964 for the most exciting period of educational change in her modern history.

3. Implementing the reform

As we have seen, the Christian Democrat government of President Eduardo Frei came to power in 1964 on a very ambitious programme of reform which embraced almost every aspect of the national life – economic, social, administrative and legal. As events were to show, the programme was, in fact, *too* ambitious to carry out in its six-year term, and while there were many reasons for this, two deserve specific mention here. In the first place, there was the sheer weight of inherited structures and tradition, much more powerful in a country like Chile, where slow, evolutionary change was habitual, than in other states where political dislocation is the norm. Reforming regimes may make new laws, but they cannot easily change old habits, unless they are ready to use force. And force, in the Chilean tradition, was ruled out. Secondly, although the Christian Democrats secured control of the Chamber of Deputies in the congressional elections of 1965, the Senate remained in the hands of

[6] The Spanish word here is *formación*, for which there is no real equivalent in English. The notion behind the word is one of preparation and development of individual talent and personality.

opposition parties who could thus block or delay legislation. The sweeping electoral victories of Christian Democracy were not quite sweeping enough to give the government a completely fair wind for its programme.

Yet, there can be no doubt that a good deal was achieved, and not least in education, though, here again, education suffered from the overall inability to reach hoped-for objectives, and the necessity all governments face to adjust their priorities in the light of changing circumstances. But, at least, the basic infrastructure of educational change was well and truly laid, and the period 1964–70 saw the establishment of a large number of appropriate institutions and methods to improve Chilean education at all levels, in more strict accordance with the country's needs than ever before. Many of these had been adumbrated before 1964, but it was Frei's government which created them.

In fact, a number of quantitative objectives were surpassed. The reform had aimed, for example, to reach by 1971 a situation in which 95 per cent of children aged 7–14 would have entered a cycle of 8 years' basic education, and some 35 per cent of those between the ages of 15 and 18, a cycle of 4 years' of secondary education. By 1970, the first category stood already at 93 per cent, and the second at 54 per cent. In actual numbers, the total school and university student population in Chile rose between 1964 and 1970 from 1,808,663 to 2,759,080, a remarkable performance given the demographic pressure on education as well as the need to reduce the backlog of neglect. And, whereas in 1964, educational expenditure as a percentage of total national expenditure had stood at 14·6 per cent, by 1970 it had reached 21·4 per cent, having, in fact, attained 22·1 per cent in 1969. Great steps were taken towards 'democratisation' of education, by which Frei meant universal provision – education as a right – as far as possible. But the concept meant something more than merely the extension of scholastic opportunity: it also implied, at every rung on the ladder of education and advancement, the reduction of random advantages, wealth, family connection and even birth-place, and emphasis on individual talent as the basic criterion for upward mobility.

This implied not only restructuring the existing state system of education and also, incidentally, involving the private sector which depended, in part, on state funds, but also in establishing appropriate organisations with specific responsibilities for particular educational tasks. Prior to implementation of the many changes which were to take place, a good deal of investigation, discussion and report had occurred, some of it antedating Frei's accession to the presidency. Many of these reports resulted from co-partnership between the national government and international agencies, of which UNESCO was pre-eminent, being involved in aspects ranging from administrative reorganisation to technical training, for women as well as for men. Bilateral arrangements for the importation of expertise were made with a number of foreign governments, ranging from decentralisation of educational decision-making to teacher training, while foreign foundations and other private bodies were equally active, not least in the field of university education. These activities, or, at least, some of them, are considered in greater detail below. The point to be made here, however, is that the period was one of extraordinary ferment at all educational levels, as the 43 fundamental decrees on education promulgated between January 1965, and January 1970, testify.

Again, lack of space forbids a catalogue of actual achievements, let alone intentions, but certain examples may illustrate the wide-ranging scope of the reform in planning, administration and specialisation. The upper echelons of educational government were brought together under a national plan, and attempts were made to ensure coordination under the National Council for Education, to which new departments were added. For example, in 1967 a National Evaluation Service was created within the Ministry of Education, its functions being primarily to establish national standards at school level throughout the country and also to evaluate the effectiveness and relevance of educational programmes. The Ministry of Education itself was reorganised, and the functions of its different departments defined. Equally important, several specialised institutions were created, of which two of the most important were the Centro de Perfeccionamiento, Experimentación e Investigaciones Pedagógicas, the Centre for Educational Improvement, Experiment and Research, and the Instituto Nacional de Capacitación Profesional (INACAP), the National Institute for Technical Training.

The Centro, from its foundation in 1966, soon became a powerhouse of ideas and practice in teacher training, the application of modern teaching methods such as audio-visual techniques, and a focal point for discussion and publication in the pedagogical field, not only in Chile but in Latin America as a whole. Housed in new premises at Lo Barnechea, some miles from Santiago, the Centro stood, and still stands, as a highly creative force in education, a forum and a laboratory, to bring together teachers, administrators and specialists of many kinds for the fruitful exchange of ideas and experience. INACAP had a very different character, and it also had antecedents. But its progress was equally impressive. It was set up for vocational instruction, to help to remedy the situation whereby perhaps as much as 60 per cent of the Chilean labour force had less than six years of education, compared with about 2·1 per cent of the work-force in the United Kingdom. Established in 1966, not under the Ministry of Education, but under the State Development Corporation, the INACAP provides a wide variety of vocational training in its own centres, of which there are more than twenty throughout the country, on the premises of companies, at work-sites, and in other educational institutions, offering something like 150 different courses in such fields as mechanics, metallurgy, construction, manufacturing, agriculture and mining.

Under another educational innovation of the period, the setting-up of a national system of apprenticeship, INACAP became a partner with the Ministries of Education and Labour in catering for the vocational needs of young people between the ages of 14 and 16½. Given the two facts of a high drop-out rate and a shift-system in schools, many teenagers in Chile are working in industry while still completing their general education or soon after giving it up. This scheme was intended, to a large extent through day-release, to enable them to learn a trade while in this situation. So far as their elders are concerned, statistics indicate the success of INACAP. Between 1960 and 1964, some 19,000 workers in Chile received advanced training under arrangements which existed before INACAP was created: between 1965 and 1969, INACAP itself trained some 92,000.

This highly selective and brief survey of educational advance in Chile between 1964 and 1970 is intended merely to indicate the tremendous impetus given by government to education and training in these years. And in this process of challenge and change, foreign assistance was to play a part in the national task of educational renovation.

4. The role of foreign aid

External aid to Chile during the second half of the 'development decade' was a comparatively small proportion of total expenditure on national development purposes, as, indeed, it is with almost all developing countries. It amounted to some $25 million annually in the period 1965–70, approximately 0·4 per cent of Chile's GDP, and of the total expenditure of $150 million, some $70 million consisted of multilateral aid and $80 million of bilateral assistance. The Chilean contribution for the specific projects involved raised the total expenditure over the quinquennium to some $400 million. It is, of course, a truism that the significance of external contributions for development lies much less in the actual sums involved than in the nature of the projects financed and of their expected effects as multipliers, and in Chile's case particular human resources were much more significant than capital inflows. It was technical assistance in manpower and materials, experience and expertise which Chile lacked at her particular stage of development. Her educational needs were much less matters of tackling basic illiteracy than of slotting in resources at critical points to achieve maximum effect towards improving efficiency and raising economic potential.

By far the greater part of the multilateral aid was channelled through the UNDP, and largely through the Special Fund, with education as one of three priority categories – the others were energy and agriculture. Some of these multilateral projects are looked at in more detail below, but it is important to note here that the educational priority was also the major field for bilateral activities as well, not only by the donor countries considered specifically in this study but also by others, and by foundations and other voluntary organisations involved.

Another important prerequisite for effective technical cooperation was the establishment of appropriate machinery in Chile to plan and operate the new development resources coming in from outside. This problem of the capacity of developing countries to absorb foreign aid and technology with the minimum waste, distortion and muddle was, of course, the subject of the Jackson Report towards the end of the 1960s, by which time Chile had herself gone a long way towards providing national instruments for the same objective. And she had, again, a good deal to build on from past traditions – regular, functioning authority at the centre of affairs which was democratically responsive, an administrative structure which, while not entirely apolitical, was at least imbued with much of the civil service tradition, a considerable tradition of state intervention in the economy, and a proven capacity to respond to the challenge of change by creating new organisations to meet new needs, as when she set up the first state development corporation in Latin America at the end of the 1930s.

In 1967, the National Planning Office, ODEPLAN, linked directly to the presidency, was formally set up to create national economic aims and coordinate efforts at three levels – national, regional and sectoral. Under ODEPLAN, each region of Chile had its local office, ORPLAN, to put the national and sectoral plans into the regional context. It was within the new planning structure that organisations operated for the forecasting, administration and evaluation of foreign technical assistance. Most important of these was the Department of Technical Assistance, DATI, which, in fact, antedated ODEPLAN but was subsequently brought within it: this was the principal executive instrument for foreign aid, but it was also linked finally with the National Commission for Scientific and Technological Research, CONICYT, charged with global oversight of foreign technical assistance and with both long-term planning and evaluation. The specific relationships of these various bodies, both with one another, and with other relevant organisations, such as CORFO, the Ministry of Education and the universities, changed over time, but, throughout, DATI and CONICYT were the chief vehicles for the importation of foreign technical assistance and the export of Chilean trainees.

DATI itself became a highly expert organisation, drawing into its service well-trained Chilean administrators, many of whom had been educated, in part, abroad, and building up considerable expertise in aid administration. By 1970, it had a staff of some fifty people in its different divisions – programming, control and information, operations, awards, research and administration. CONICYT's involvement came primarily through its Division of International Affairs, DAI, which, in effect, acted as the supreme directorate for technical assistance within the national plan, while DATI was the executant.[7]

IV THE DONORS

1. Multilateral arrangements

So far as the UNDP was concerned, Chile ranked high as a recipient for projects in the Special Fund. Indeed, since the creation of the UNDP on 1 January 1966, Chile has been the fourth highest recipient of UNDP assistance, after India, the United Arab Republic and Pakistan.[8] At the beginning of 1971, Chile came eleventh in the world list of the Special Fund, in terms of expenditure, with 26 projects approved, of which 7 were essentially educational, though a number of others had obvious educational implications. The total cost of all Special Fund projects in Chile then was around $62 million, of which $36 million were counterpart contributions. Table 8.1 sets out data on the specific educational projects, some of which antedated the advent to power of the Christian Democratic administration in 1964.

Brief notes on each project will serve to show how they fitted into Chilean development planning in the second quinquennium of the development decade.

i. Faculty of Engineering, University of Concepción Concepción, with the nearby port of Talcahuano, is Chile's third largest city, the centre of the country's most important primary industrial zone.[9] It also contains Chile's third university, after the State and Catholic universities in Santiago, a university founded in 1919 on private local initiative, partly to counteract the magnetic force of the capital. By 1964 it had some 4000 students, and had already embarked upon a large-scale reorganisation, assisted by UNESCO, through the UN Expanded Programme of Technical Assistance.[10] The project with the Faculty of Engineering began at the end of 1961 and lasted until late 1968. It was intended to contribute in general to the economic development of the region, specifically to

[7] For a good description of the functions of DATI, see *La Asistencia Técnica Internacional. El Caso Chileno*, Santiago, Sociedad Chilena de Planificactión y Desarrollo-PLANDES, Boletín Informativo de PLANDES, no. 32, Mar–Apr, 1969, and especially pp. 79–96. For CONICYT, see its annual report of DAI activities for 1970, *Memoria 1970*, Santiago, CONICYT, DAI, 1970, esp. pp. 1–44.

[8] *Summary of Technical and Financial Assistance offered to Chile, 1970* 2 vols, mimeo, UNDP, Santiago, Dec 1970, ii, 1.

[9] See Blakemore and Smith (eds), *Latin America*, pp. 539–45, for a brief description.

[10] For details, see J. A. Lauwerys, *Chile, Reform of the University of Concepción, Mission Report*, EPTA/EDS/HE/CHILE 2, Paris, UNESCO, 1965, *passim.*

TABLE 8.1
Chilean Educational Aid Projects in the UNDP Special Fund Component, at 31 January 1971

Project	*Agency*	*Project costs ($m)* Total	UNDP	Government counterpart
1. Faculty of Engineering, University of Concepción	UNESCO	1,478,600	1,043,000	435,600
2. Instructor and Foreman Training Centre (CENFIS), Santiago	ILO	1,805,800	1,140,100	665,000
3. Institute for Training and Research on Agrarian Reform (ICIRA), Santiago	FAO	1,374,100	723,100	651,000
4. Telecommunications Training Centre, (CENET), Santiago	ITU	2,410,100	1,152,100	1,258,000
5. Training of Educational Administrators, Supervisors and Specialists, Santiago	UNESCO	2,674,600	1,294,600	1,380,000
6. ICIRA (Phase II)	FAO	2,653,000	982,000	1,671,000
7. Establishment of an Inplant Training Scheme	ILO	2,465,500	783,500	1,682,000

Source: Projects in the Special Fund Component, as of 31st January, 1971, DP/SF/reports, ser. B. no. 11, New York, UNDP, 1971, pp. 19–20.

strengthen the educational facilities for training qualified engineers by raising the level of instruction, increasing the number of students and broadening the range of courses, and, *inter alia*, offering specialised training to professional people in local industry. Modern equipment was an important part of the programme also, as was improving the facilities of both the Polytechnic School attached to the Faculty and of the Institute of Technological Research. Half-a-dozen foreign experts in engineering sciences worked at Concepción, the University being UNESCO's counterpart for the programme, devising, with their Chilean colleagues new curricula, organising the departments and installing the new equipment. In addition, thirteen Chileans received further training abroad as part of the scheme.

Clearly, this project fitted very well into Chile's particular needs in several ways. In the university context, it served both internal and extramural objectives in education and training; in the regional environment, it was linked specifically with the local economic structure, and nationally it made a contribution to providing highly-trained manpower in a crucial field at the particular stage of development which Chile had reached. It was also significant as a major project outside the capital city and the central valley, an exercise in decentralisation which Chile needed.

ii. Instructor and Foreman Training Centre (CENFIS), *Santiago* As with so many aid projects, CENFIS (Centro de Formación de Instructores y Supervisores) was but the final stage of a long gestation, though its origins do not concern us. But the thinking behind them does, for it was the same thinking which in Chile produced INACAP, the realisation that specific organisations for tailored training were necessary for middle and lower levels of industry, and that this training had to be closely geared both to shop-floor experience and to industrial needs. CENFIS was officially inaugurated late in 1963, but, in fact, it was with the formal establishment by the Chilean government of INACAP in 1966 that the project moved fully into gear. It aimed to produce instructors for INACAP courses, as well as some for more traditional schools at the middle level, and its targets at that time were 150 instructors and 120 supervisors each year, 100 highly-qualified workmen (foreman level) and about the same number of draughtsmen. Down to 1971, it had trained some 620 instructors for INACAP, 915 teachers for professional schools, 605 technical engineers for INACAP, 165 instructors for private enterprise, 320 supervisors, 2850 highly-skilled workers, 270 draughtsmen and 48 technicians, and finally, nearly 9000 workers to higher levels of competence. A wide variety of instruction was given – courses, both practical and theoretical, in industrial mechanics, automotive machines, welding, electricity, construction, industrial design, electronics, and so on, the classes being given in the workshops and classrooms of CENFIS. Instructors finishing training then went to INACAP's permanent training centres throughout the country, though, at the same time, CENFIS itself extended its operations to the provinces, providing experts, for example, at the San Fernando Agricultural Mechanics Centre.

Since INACAP was the counterpart for this programme and was itself, as we shall see, a major recipient of bilateral aid, middle-level training in Chile attained a good degree of integration, and with the ILO as the executive organisation, other benefits accrued. It is interesting to note, for example, that of the 42 countries participating in the ILO's programmes and seminars at its international training centre at Turin, Chile between 1965 and 1971 led the field with 176 participants, one of only four countries to send more than 100 students in this period. More importantly, instead of individual scholarships being given for Turin in diverse subjects, in recent years Chileans have gone as groups for specific courses: for one such course, for die-stampers in 1970, the expert from Turin visited Chile and selected candidates himself. And, finally, the CENFIS project was a major factor in up-grading the status of the middle-level, qualified technician by the establishment of a diploma moderated by the country's two leading higher educational institutions in the technical field with university status – the State Technical University in Santiago and the Federico Santa María University in Valparaiso.

iii. Institute for Training and Research in Agrarian Reform (ICIRA), *Santiago* Agrarian reform was a major plank of the Christian Democrat's programme, and by the time they gained power in 1964 it was widely recognised in Chile that problems of land tenure and agricultural production were among the crucial issues facing the country.[11] ICIRA was set up to carry out the planning and execution of a continuing programme of training and research in agrarian reform at all levels – short, practical courses for officials of the government's agrarian reform agencies, postgraduate courses for economists, agronomists and so on, and more general activities, including publicity and library services. Research and publication were also among its chief functions. Phase I of its operations was completed in June, 1968, and Phase II, funded largely by an Inter-American Development Bank (IADB) loan, was to expand its activities, not least on the training side, at both operational and policy-making levels, including group-instruction methods for farmers affected by reform. The executive organisation of the project for the UNDP was the FAO, which has its regional office for Latin America in Santiago: the Chilean counterparts were the Agrarian Reform Agency (CORA) and the Ministry of Agriculture.

Largely as a result of the establishment of ICIRA, Chile was a major beneficiary from the mid-1960s of FAO assistance. In Latin America, in the period 1961–70, Chile received more FAO scholarships than any other country except Peru, which received three more, and of the total of 106, 92 were awarded from 1965 onwards.[12] And in terms of foreign expert assistance, measured in expert-months, Chile came second only to Brazil.[13]

iv. Telecommunications Training Centre (CENET), *Santiago* Given the peculiar geographical configuration of Chile, it is hardly surprising that telephone, telegraph and telex links are of the highest importance. This project was designed to train the engineers, technicians and skilled operators needed to meet the demands of a large programme of expansion. It was estimated in 1968, when the project began, that some 1400 additional personnel would be required over the five-year period of the

[11] See Blakemore and Smith (eds), *Latin America*, pp. 501–4, for a general discussion.

[12] *La FAO en América Latina. Labor durante el decenio 1961–70 y actividades previstas para el futuro*, Santiago, FAO, 1971, p. 142, anexo III(a).

[13] Ibid., anexo II(a).

expansion programme. The executing agency in this case was the International Telecommunications Union (ITU), and the counterparts INACAP and the National Institute for Telecommunications (INTEC). The National Telecommunications Centre (CENET) housed the project, which organised a variety of courses at different levels.

v. Training of educational administrators, supervisors, specialists, Santiago This project, the most expensive educational scheme under UNDP in Chile, was closely related to the fundamental restructuring of education envisaged by the Frei government, as briefly described earlier in this chapter. The executing agency was, naturally, UNESCO which had been intimately involved in Chilean education in many ways for some years.[14] Indeed, in the development decade itself, UNESCO spent no less than $3 million in Chile both under the UNDP and on its own regular budget. UNESCO, moreover, had its regional centre for Latin America in Santiago. The Chilean counterpart for the project was the Ministry of Education, though the focus of its activities was to be the Centro de Perfeccionamiento.

The project was extremely broad in scope. It was concerned, in cooperation with the government, in organising the training of educational administrators, supervisors and specialists, the administrators for the headquarters and regional divisions of the Ministry of Education, as well as for the secondary, vocational, and other schools, and teachers' training colleges (*escuelas normales*); the supervisors at primary and secondary levels; and specialists in curriculum development, teaching techniques, audio-visual instruction, evaluation, academic and vocational guidance, school planning and educational research. With the assistance of a dozen foreign experts and half-a-dozen consultants, together with counterpart training on fellowships equal to a total of 138 man months, it was hoped by 1972 to be able to train about 900 people a year.

vi. Establishment of an in-plant training scheme In part, this project was a follow-up to the establishment of CENFIS (see (*ii*) above), though with quite distinctive objectives. That project provided appropriate training away from the bench: this scheme was intended to operate *within* the work environment. It was to emphasise the need for training directly with people on the job, to improve their skills and, indeed, status, at their actual work-place. Again, the executing agency was the ILO and the counterpart, INACAP, and the programme envisaged the utilisation of eight experts with consultants in particular fields, as well as thirteen counterpart fellowships for Chileans. Apart from assisting with the

[14] See, for example, *Chile, Educational Priority Projects for Development*, Paris, UNESCO, 1967; *Chile, Planning and Organization of Technical Education*, Paris, UNESCO, 1967; and, for UNESCO's activities in Latin America as a whole, *La acción de la UNESCO en los campos de la educaión, de la ciencia y la tecnología en América Latina y Región del Caribe, 1966–1971*, Paris, UNESCO, 1971.

planning of the training programme, the experts were also to help the particular enterprises involved in the establishment of a worker promotion system, to undertake both job analysis and job description. In addition, audio-visual methods, a mobile training unit and correspondence courses for industrial workers in isolated areas were envisaged. The project began at the end of 1969 and was intended to run until the end of 1974.

Chile, of course, was also a recipient of sizeable multilateral aid under other auspices, such as the provision of experts and the grant of fellowships by the International Atomic Energy Agency and the World Health Organisation. And it received a large number of foreign experts under the Technical Assistance Component of UNDP operations. No less significant were the World Bank and the Organisation of American States. It is worth noting that Chile, in fact, was the first country in the world to receive a development loan from the IBRD, in 1948, and in the twelve-year period to 1960 the Bank granted a total of over $250 million to Chile, as well as an International Development Assistance (IDA) credit of $19 million. Four million dollars of the total loans, made in two instalments in 1965 and 1970, were to CORFO for expanding the work of INACAP, which, by 1970, was providing 90 per cent of the country's vocational training. Indeed, the loan in 1965 helped INACAP to double its training capacity, and the second loan, of 1970, was intended to provide INACAP with 22 mobile units for agricultural training, and 7 mobile units and a boat for fishery training; to enable INACAP to construct 7 new buildings for various trades and equip them. This was an excellent example of channelling aid through the best agency, which was businesslike and realistic, and manned by enthusiasts. The World Bank then made a loan of $7 million to Chile in 1970 to support the government's ambitious programme of general educational reform. The borrower was the Ministry of Education, but the chief channel was the School Construction Company of Chile (SCEE) which planned to construct and equip one new primary teacher training college and extend ten others, and to build four new agricultural secondary schools and extend seven existing ones. The balance of the loan was to enable the Ministry of Education to provide overseas training for Chileans in the two fields of teacher training and agricultural education.[15]

No survey of multilateral aid for education in Chile, however brief, would be complete without reference to some of the regional projects based in the country and also coming under UNDP auspices. As we have noted, Santiago was the home of the regional offices of UNESCO and the FAO: no less significant for the UN family of organisations, the Economic

[15] For details of these World Bank loans for education in Chile, see IBRD (Washington), Press Releases no. 65/37 of 11 Aug, 1965, and no. 70/14 of 20 Mar, 1970.

Commission for Latin America (ECLA) had been based there since 1948. In 1962, the Special Fund established the Latin American Institute for Social and Economic Planning (ILPES) as an adjunct to ECLA, to provide training and advisory services within the geographical region of ECLA, and to conduct research, all with a view to raising the technical level of officials from member governments in planning and programming, and to assisting governments to establish and improve institutions and organisations needed for more efficient programming of policies of social and economic development in their own countries. Basic, intensive and special courses for Latin Americans have been provided ever since, and an enormous volume of research and publication has also resulted. In 1967, UNDP allocated over $4 million for the expansion of ILPES, member governments of ECLA pledged an additional $800,000 (of which Chile's share was $80,000) and the World Bank contribution on behalf of the government was $1,400,000. The total number of experts involved was 65.

A second example of this type of organisation is provided by the Latin American Demographic Centre (CELADE), set up in 1957 within the University of Chile by agreement between the Government and the United Nations. The agreement was renewed twice, but in 1966 UNDP took over the supporting role, and in 1968 made a contribution of $1,761,000 for the expansion of CELADE's operations, a further $361,000 coming from the thirteen supporting Latin American countries, including, of course, Chile.

This rather brief survey of multilateral aid in education in Chile during the development decade makes very clear the point that, whatever criticisms may be made on points of detail on the major projects, the philosophy and planning behind them were essentially correct. They were carefully-tailored projects with wide multiplier effects, operations of the 'plug-in' kind adapted to the needs of Chile at that particular time.

2. Bi-lateral relations

The United States

During the development decade, Chile was a favoured recipient of American aid in many forms, particularly after the launching of the Alliance for Progress. In fact, from 1961 to 1970, bilateral aid alone totalled some $720 million of which about $540 million took the form of AID development loans. From the point of view of this study, the most important component of AID funds were two sector loans made in 1967 and 1968, totalling $26·3 million for education, to accelerate, in effect, the Chilean Government's own reform efforts at the primary and secondary levels. Part of these loans was to cover purchases of educational materials, part to provide technical assistance and training in the United

States for Chilean educators, and, finally, the greater proportion was to generate Chilean currency to be used by the Ministry of Education in school construction, textbooks, libraries, teacher training courses, equipment and vocational guidance. In 1970, agreement was reached on a loan of $2·5 million to cover costs of research, study and specialised training of Chileans in the United States in fields considered essential to the overall economic and social development of Chile.

It was also under USAID auspices that particular Chileans received training in the United States or attended conferences, seminars and workshops. While the bilateral relationships between individual Chilean and United States institutions of higher education were more important here numerically (see below, pp. 357–8); in 1970, for example, over ninety Chileans benefited from short-term USAID assignments, while nearly twenty Chileans were on long-term graduate study in the United States, primarily in engineering, business administration, geology and economics. At the same time, Peace Corps operations in Chile were not insignificant. With an annual budget of $400,000, and between 100 and 150 volunteers in Chile, working in fields as diverse as forestry teaching and city planning, American aid at this highly personal level was particularly interesting in that it was concentrated on projects regarded as having a high priority by the Chilean government itself, and, in fact, the 'counterpart' agency for the American volunteer service in Chile was the National Planning Office.

France

French technical assistance to Chile was governed by a basic agreement made in 1962 and ratified by the Chilean Congress in May 1964, not long before President Frei assumed office. Between these two events came the visit of President de Gaulle to Latin America, including Chile, in 1963, a visit which, among other things, sought to emphasise France's continued interest in a continent with which she had had such close cultural ties in the past. The most visible expression of Franco-Chilean cultural relations had long been the colleges and schools of the Alliance Française in Chile, and the sizeable role played by French educators in Chilean universities and similar institutions. Indeed, it is interesting to note that the French *lycée* in Concepción is called the Lycée Charles de Gaulle, founded in 1944, and that the amount of space devoted to Chile in the Annual Reports of the Ministry of Foreign Affairs in France increased markedly after the French President's visit there.

In Chile, French aid was essentially technical, taking the form of French experts in a variety of fields and receiving Chileans for training in France. For example, in 1970, forty-four French teachers were working in Alliance Française institutions in Chile, together with sixteen French volunteers, while well over one hundred Chileans received fellowships for study in France. Technical cooperation costs to France falling under the

Ministry of Economy and Finance rose from 320,000 frs in 1961 to 1,578,000 frs.

While it can, of course, be argued that French assistance in education in Chile of the kind described above was essentially to promote the French presence in accordance with well-known and long-standing emphases on French culture and civilisation, a glance at some of the specific projects operating in Chile with French assistance in more direct developmental tasks presents a different picture. Thus, experts were assigned for industrial planning to the CORFO, in administrative organisation to the Chilean Central Office of Organisation and Method, in agricultural training and management to the four principal national agencies concerned with the countryside, in electricity with the State Electricity Organisation (ENDESA), in electronics to CENET, and so on.

Experts were also attached to the INACAP, to assist in training in electricity and electronics at its regional centres in Santiago, Valparaiso, Concepción and Arica, but a more interesting experiment with INACAP was the training school in applied sciences operated jointly with West German assistance, but under a Chilean director, from 1969. This tripartite organisation, CENFA (Centro Franco-Alemán) is unique in Chile, with France in charge of certain operations – electricity and electronics – and Germany in charge of others. In 1970, there were seven long-term and two short-term experts from France at CENFA.

French and Chilean university contacts are an important expression of aid cooperation, and in 1970 no fewer than forty-eight French missions were operating in Chilean universities.

Federal Republic of Germany

West German aid to Chile in the 'development decade' was substantial, amounting to more than DM. 350,000,000, a large proportion of which was on earthquake relief and infrastructural projects. In technical assistance for education, experts were assigned from the mid-1960s to a number of institutions, with the emphasis on forestry, industrial training and irrigation. Thus, the Chilean–German Industrial High School at Nuñoa received not only its equipment from Germany, but also a sizeable number of German experts – seven in 1970 – and two fellowships for counterpart training; the Apprentices School at Frutillar had two experts in residence in 1970, while seven experts were teaching in forestry at the Austral University, Valdivia, and at the Forestry School near Concepción.

As almost all donor countries, Germany had specific links with the INACAP, through the joint French project, CENFA, with responsibility for mechanics: in 1970, three German experts were teaching there, eight fellowships had been granted to Chileans, and seven more made available. By that time also, CENFA was capable of training 120 Chilean students a year. In addition, forty-five German volunteers were working in Chile under the bilateral programme, in a variety of schools, universities and other institutions. On the scholarships side, fifty-six Chileans were studying in Germany in 1970 on direct government grants, administered through the DATI.

As with the United States, German bilateral assistance to Chile on a government-to-government basis was strongly complemented by a large number of German educational institutions, including universities, some of whose schemes are specifically mentioned below.

The Netherlands

Chile is not one of the countries singled out by the Netherlands government in accordance with its policy of concentrating its aid effort – remarkable for a country of its size – on specific countries in the Third World. Apart from bilateral financial assistance for projects under the CORFO, its main thrust has been in technical assistance, sending Dutch experts to Chile, and awarding scholarships to Chileans for study in Holland.

The number of experts sent to Chile on bilateral schemes has been small – one in 1967 in sociology, who remained in 1968, eight in 1969, and six in 1970. These, however, were complemented by experts seconded to multilateral programmes, ranging from nine to twelve, and by associates, about the same number. Many Chileans, however, have benefited from Dutch scholarships during these years, fifteen Chileans going to Holland in 1970 for training in fields ranging from housing, engineering and aerial photography to industrial management and statistics. Two Chileans also received Dutch scholarships to attend courses in other Latin American states. In fact, between 1961 and 1970, inclusive, 72 Chileans received Dutch grants for study in Holland, 15 in economics, 13 in social sciences, 11 in agriculture, as the major fields.

The United Kingdom

British preoccupations with the liquidation of empire in Asia and Africa in the post-war period, not the least of which was concerned with aiding the newly-independent countries, had, as one corollary, the comparative neglect of Latin America as a recipient of British aid, and, in fact, it was the last area of the developing world to contract agreements with Britain for technical assistance, starting in 1961. A formal bilateral agreement between Chile and the United Kingdom was signed in 1966, the latest testimony at that date of the strong historical ties of friendship between the two countries.

So far as the British bilateral aid programme in Latin America is concerned, gross disbursements to Chile between 1967 and 1970 on the technical assistance side were second only to those allocated to Brazil and approximately one-seventh of the total assigned to the whole of Latin

America. This fact indicates the significance attached by British policy-makers to Chile in the Latin American continent. And, of the total of £232,000 set aside for Chile, no less than £188,000 was spent on personnel – income Chilean students and trainees and so on, and outgoing British experts. In other words, the emphasis in the British technical assistance programme in Chile was on education in one form or another. Nor is this surprising: the flurry of educational reforms in Chile under the Christian Democratic adminstration came precisely at the time when a similar process in the United Kingdom, though earlier, was the subject of much discussion and dispute. British experience dovetailed with Chilean aspiration in particular fields, and it was widely sought in others which were highly relevant to Chile's needs at that particular time.

There were three fields in particular in general education on which a good deal of British technical assistance was expended, in line with Chilean requests – primary education, and particularly teaching methods and teacher training; secondary education, including the comprehensive school; and the decentralisation of Chilean educational administration. In the late 1960s, individual exchanges of personnel were systematised: five British teacher–demonstrators were sent to Chile to work in primary schools for two years, and two specialists in teacher training were sent to work in *escuelas normales* (teacher training colleges). At the same time, a group of Chileans were sent to England for concentrated study of primary method and organisation, one of four such groups from Chile to study different aspects of British education ranging from school architecture to comprehensive schools.

The third major emphasis was placed on the attempt to create in Chile a much more decentralised system of control in education, a formidable task in view of the inherited tradition of bureaucratic formalism and centralised administration, whereby even a request for short-term leave by a teacher in the far north of Chile had to be approved at the top in Santiago. After a first stage of considerable discussion, the Chilean government approved, under British advice, a pilot-project based on the Bío-Bío zone, with a regional office at Concepción: this led to legislation for national decentralisation through the establishment of ten zones throughout Chile with a regional coordinator for each. Again, British experts served in Chile on this plan: the national adviser, a man of great experience in British education who had previously worked in Chile for UNESCO, spent two-and-a-half years in Chile, while a Chilean team of educationalists, including the regional coordinator for the Bío-Bío zone came to the United Kingdom to study the organisation of local education. At the same time, another British adviser on the project for primary education was working in the zone itself on a long-term mission, and his contributions there re-inforced the decentralisation project. The two-way flow was crucial: in the words of the senior British adviser: 'it was a specially valuable feature of the group-visits to England that they took place at about the same time, and that these Chilean primary teachers, secondary teachers and administrators were in contact together ... so that all became aware of the common philosophy underlying British practices and of the interconnection between the areas in which each specialised: *the dynamic of professional responsibility in the teaching sphere could be seen to be related to that of local initiative in the administrative sphere*'.[16]

Under bilateral auspices, British experts also worked in Chile in activities as diverse as slaughterhouse management, forestry, egg and poultry marketing, ports management, employment placement, agricultural mechanisation, mining, nuclear energy and technological research. Relations with the INACAP were close: apart from gifts of equipment for its management training courses, experts in specialised subjects, such as foundry operations, worked in Chile, and programmes of training for Chileans in Britain for INACAP personnel were provided.

By 1970, the British Council was offering fifty awards for Chileans for study in the United Kingdom in a wide range of subjects, and thirteen British volunteers were working in Chile. University and other links are dealt with separately below (pp. 358–9).

3. Private aid and regional possibilities

The emphasis in previous pages has been placed on government-to-government aid in education: here, it will be placed on assistance to Chile provided by individual organisations, such as universities, private foundations, and so on. While, however, in some cases the distinction is unequivocal, in others it is not. For example, with American aid, the sizeable operations of the Ford Foundation in Chile, and the multifarious links between Chilean and American universities can properly be regarded as separate and distinct from American *official* aid; with British universities the matter is not so clear cut, since most of them operating these links did so with assistance from the Overseas Development Administration (ODA).

Not all the organisations operating from the donor countries in Chile can be mentioned here in view of their large number and diverse operations: only those most significant in education are specifically mentioned, however briefly.

In terms of finance and range of operations, the Ford Foundation has been the most significant individual, extra-governmental agency operating in Chile for many years, and its activities have been with universities, inter-American institutions and ministries, as well as administering and funding its own projects. A few examples will suffice to indicate the range of its programme and the financial commitment in Chile. Between 1960

[16] Personal communication.

and 1971, the Foundation supported eight projects at the Catholic University of Chile in Santiago, primarily to develop or strengthen existing faculties – physics and maths, sociology, economics, education, planning studies, and so on. Over $3,000,000 was earmarked for this programme. At the University of Chile, the State University, the Foundation backed twelve major projects, committing some $10,500,000 to such schemes as the development of regional university colleges, graduate programmes in economics, research projects in education, graduate training in business and public administration, and, far and away the most costly single item, a programme run jointly with the University of California for the comprehensive strengthening of the University of Chile. Assistance of a similar kind was offered to other universities. In addition, the Foundation actively supported projects at the Ministry of Education, the Ministry of Agriculture, in collaboration with the University of Minnesota, on the development of agricultural extension schemes and rural education.

A similar report could be provided on the activities of the Rockefeller Foundation, which was very active in Chile in the 1960s, particularly in population studies at the University of Chile. The Foundation had over twenty projects with Chilean universities running in the middle years of the decade, and its disbursements amounted to an annual figure of $500,000. Other American foundations and agencies operated in Chile throughout the period, but lack of space forbids a catalogue.[17] As for university links, these were extremely diverse and numerous. About twenty American universities had institutional links with Chilean universities, while the amount of sponsored research on Chile in American universities increased enormously in the 1960s.[18] Over 600 Chilean students and trainees were working in American universities in the academic year 1966–7, a figure which rose to over 700 the following year. By 1970, in fact, some 42 per cent of all Chileans studying abroad were in the United States.

Similarly with the other donor countries considered here – university links between Chile on the one hand, and France, the Netherlands, West Germany and the United Kingdom on the other grew significantly in the 1960s. Selective examples must suffice to illustrate their range and nature. Thus the Technical University of Berlin had a partnership with the Federico Santa María Technical University of Valparaiso, while five other German universities had cooperative agreements with the University of Chile, chiefly in medicine, agrarian studies and technology. Among the many links involving British universities was one for training Chilean

[17] For details, see the annual publication *United States Non-Profit Organizations in Technical Assistance Abroad*, Washington.

[18] See, for example, *Survey of U.S.–Chilean Educational Relations at the University Level* mimeo, Education and World Affairs and Council on Educational Co-operation with Latin America, New York, Sep 1967.

political scientists to doctoral level between the Catholic University's Institute of Political Science and the University of Essex, and an interchange scheme between the Departments of Chemistry of the Universities of Chile in Santiago and Exeter. Like the political science scheme, this was a genuine interchange and partnership arrangement, British chemists working in Santiago and Chilean staff working in Exeter.

In addition, of course, a number of foreign institutions were active in educational aid programmes in Chile. One of the more interesting was the programme of the Konrad Adenauer Foundation in West Germany, a private foundation concerned with technical assistance in the general field of social action. Here, the emphasis was on the choice of individual potential leaders, Chileans who were offered scholarships to German universities for three years' study. Courses were also organised in Chile by the Foundation, especially in sociology and youth education, with the assistance of German experts serving for two to three years. There were also sponsored programmes of joint research with Chilean institutions.

Another important German institution in Chile was set up by the Friedrich-Ebert-Stiftung: this was the Instituto Latinoamericano de Investigaciones Sociales (ILDIS), a teaching and research organisation, which in recent years has produced an impressive flood of publications on Latin American, and Chilean, problems, partly the outcome of joint seminars organised in Santiago.

Reference has already been made to Chile's important role as a base for many inter-American and international organisations which had their regional offices for Latin America there. And Chile herself was a recipient of significant amounts of aid from other, similar institutions for educational purposes. A few deserve mention. Financially, the most important has been the Inter-American Development Bank (IDB), which made its first loan to Chile in 1961 and which by the end of the 1960s had loaned Chile almost $300,000,000, of which over $18,000,000 was for educational projects. These are set out in Table 8.2 below. The Inter-American Institute of Agricultural Sciences, a specialised organisation of the OAS has also been very active in Chile, in programmes of both higher education and agricultural research. Apart from organising courses in Chile itself, and inviting foreign experts to the country, the Institute has also fostered third-country training for Chileans in other Latin American states, where, of course, the problems are analogous to those of Chile and there is no language problem.

Twenty-eight Chileans studied abroad on IDB scholarships in 1970, most of them in engineering and drawn largely from the State Technical University.

The OAS has also been important in this respect, and not least for scholarships to Chileans to study in other Latin American countries.

TABLE 8.2
IDB Loans to Chile for Educational Projects, at 30 September 1970

Borrower	*Date*	*Purpose*	*Amount ($000)*
University of Chile	1962	Technical instruction	2300
University of Chile	1964	Sanitary instruction	1214
Catholic University	1964	Physical sciences, maths	1050
University of Concepción	1965	Social sciences, education	1200
Technical University Federico Santa Maria, Valparaiso	1966	Technical instruction	2500
University of Chile	1966	Agricultural instruction	5000
State Technical University	1967	Technical instruction	1000
State Technical University	1967	Technical instruction	4000

Source: UNDP, *Summary of Technical and Financial Assistance*, i, 100.

Fifty-four scholarships were awarded in 1970 in the fields of education and science, of which thirty-nine fell into this category, the average study-time spent abroad being a little under ten months.

The regional possibilities for effective use of funds in educational aid for a country like Chile which shares a common language with almost all the Latin American states, and has analogous problems to most of them, has become increasingly important for international and inter-American organisations. Unfortunately, it has hardly yet impinged on the thinking of bilateral donors, though there are a few exceptions.[19]

V SOME PROBLEMS OF THE RECIPIENT

1. The weight of tradition

The electoral victories of the Christian Democrats in 1964–5 testified to the wide consensus for fundamental change in Chile, and the government had a programme to satisfy it. Unfortunately, it was seriously hampered by its failure to secure control of the Senate, where the opposition parties could, and did, obstruct and delay its legislation, and not always for valid reasons. The consequences of this situation were a growing sense of frustration among its younger and more radical members, and ministerial distraction from the continuous task of running their departments. As one

[19] In the sixty-one pages of the CONYCIT *Memoria* for 1970, listing all bilaterally awarded scholarships to Chileans for that year, there is only *one* case of a grant from a foreign country on its official aid programme for a Chilean to study in another Latin American, Spanish-speaking state.

foreign expert, responsible for a major project in education, discovered, marked fluctuations in the order of priorities for the bureaucracy resulted.

A contributory factor here was another strong Chilean tradition, particularly in education, that of centralisation of decision-making. The Government had embarked upon a major educational reform but everything had to wait on the green light from above, and it might only flash sporadically, or, no better, flicker constantly in all directions. And, of course, while the higher officials, many of whom were acquainted with the latest developments in educational thought and practice, were anxious to move with the times, their colleagues in the schools and *escuelas normales* needed tremendous inspiration to go along with them. Many, if not most schools worked on a shift system, and few teachers, especially at the secondary level, though less so at primary level, were completely full time. The school as a community and the teacher's involvement in it naturally suffered. Moreover, materials were short, and the natural practice of English teachers, for example, of using their ingenuity with simple materials to make instruction more exciting – a process of discovery – was very rare.

Another important factor bound up with these traditions was the common attitude to the foreign 'expert'. Given a pedagogical tradition in which hierarchy and learning by rote were the norm, Chilean teachers and students often expected to be taught by the 'expert' in much the same way as they taught their own pupils: they did not see him necessarily as a partner in a joint enterprise, as he should have been. And, for his part, the 'expert' might well have been inadequately briefed about Chile, not given a sufficient command of Spanish to establish quickly and easily that necessary first rapport. It was a frequent comment of many Chilean educationalists that these two prerequisites for foreign advisers were the most crucial, and that foreign 'experts' in education were often imported simply because they were foreign, even when nationals were quite capable of doing the job. Whether, in fact, they could have done it better alone rather than in partnership with foreigners is another point.

This natural attitude was encountered much less in technical education, where the material of assistance is more concrete, and the language of transfer from developed to developing is much more a common one than that of educational philosophy in general and educational methodology in particular. Moreover, for a country at Chile's considerable level of development, the transfer of technology through foreign educational assistance was perhaps more obviously necessary – at least, to many Chileans – than the more controversial and sweeping reforms of the basic educational structure on which the government had embarked.

So far as those reforms are concerned, however, and whatever detailed criticisms may be made of Chile's experience in the 'development decade' – and there are many – considerable progress was made, not only in quantitative but also in qualitative terms. For example, the British-supported scheme for decentralisation of education – a project which ran counter to the strongest Chilean traditions – did get off the ground, and certainly the expansion of technical training, not least through INACAP, was one of the major achievements of Eduardo Frei's government.

2. The brain drain

Many Latin American countries – and Chile is no exception – suffer from the migration of professional people abroad. In Chile, two factors have been significant – a persistently high rate of inflation and political change. The former, of course, erodes the standard of living, and affects the attitude of the well-trained whose expectations are disappointed: in Chile, the latter has been much more significant. Chile's highly-politicised system – at least, until the military intervention of September 1973 – means that the spoils system operated quite widely. While much of the administrative structure remained intact through changes of government, personnel moved or were moved for political reasons, or themselves took the initiative to leave the country. This migration, though not massive, showed a tendency to increase in the later 1960s, and, on the election of a Marxist government in 1970, accelerated rapidly. Although, as for many other Latin Americans, the United States was the preferred objective of a majority of Chilean professionals leaving the country, many went to other Latin American states which were both Spanish-speaking and, like Chile herself, suffering a dearth of needed intellectual capital.[20] The loss to Chile was more in quality than in numbers but, given the major factors behind the migration, it could not easily be stopped.

3. The balance sheet

The evaluation of aid is a notoriously difficult exercise, since the criteria for measuring its effectiveness are necessarily, in part, subjective. Moreover, educational aid is by its very nature a type of long-term investment, the return on which cannot be measured in the short run. It is not difficult, in the Chilean case, to provide detailed statistics which would provide some measure of success – amounts expended, experts received, scholarships awarded for study abroad, and so on. But getting behind the figures is a different matter. Such conclusions as can be drawn from the experience of the 1960s are, therefore, necessarily tentative, but they may have some value, though the present situation in Chile is somewhat clouded by the events of 1973 and their aftermath which are summarily discussed below.

[20] An excellent study of the Chilean 'brain-drain', though giving statistics only down to 1967, is a study produced under the direction of Inés Reca, *Algunos aspectos teóricos y empíricos del exodo de profesionales chilenos*, mimeo, FLACSO/ODEPLAN/UNESCO, Santiago, 1970.

The first point – in part a reiteration – is that Chile is the most distinctively 'westernised' of all the receiving countries in this study. Turkey may have had a longer independent history, but Turkey is Islamic, and there is a deeper cultural divide between civil servants in Ankara and villagers in Anatolia than there is between bureaucrats in Santiago and peasants in Bío-Bío. In economic terms, Chile is far and away the most urbanised and the most industrialised of the countries surveyed here, as a comparison of both agriculture and industry as a percentage of GDP would show.[21] And the percentage of her population in the primary sector is markedly less than that of any other of these countries, the percentage in the service sector significantly higher.

Given then the very different nature of Chile's development needs and, as the survey of educational aid in Chile makes clear (see above, *passim*), critical appraisals of her experience are less concerned with major issues of policy than with modest suggestions for improvement. For example, the now common assumption that developing countries should devote a greater proportion of their educational investment, including aid, to middle-level training rather than to producing highly-qualified research staff with PhDs, was precisely the thinking behind the establishment of INACAP. It must, however, be stressed that, at Chile's stage of development, a balance between the two types of trainee had to be struck, if advanced technology produced outside the country were to be imported into Chile; the country's capacity to absorb it was no less important than the training of middle-level operatives to work the establishments and industries using more advanced techniques. Hence, the rationale behind the Ford Foundation's massive programme of support to Chilean universities was largely correct, and the amount of foreign aid – such as, for example, the projects in the Special Fund of the UNDP, or the bilateral efforts of France, West Germany and the United Kingdom in technical education – was fully justified. Similarly, the two-way flow of personnel, incoming experts and outgoing Chileans, was a proper policy to pursue, though certain criticisms can be made of its operation.

In the first place, not enough use is made of third-country training in Spanish America, both to reduce the size of the language problem for Chileans, and also to reduce the costs of studying abroad. No doubt there is an important psychological factor here for Chileans wishing to have further training abroad, in that the long-standing *cachet* of a higher degree from Chicago, the Sorbonne or the London School of Economics is difficult to replace with the attractions of Bogotá, Lima or Mexico City, despite the excellence, and relevance, of a number of institutions there. This may increasingly be resolved by the development of the Andean

[21] See, for example, *Partners in Development. Report of the Commission on International Development* (the Pearson Report), London, 1969, p. 362, Table 3.

Group – Chile, Bolivia, Ecuador, Colombia, Peru and Venezuela – a sub-regional attempt at economic integration which offers enormous scope for the expansion of third-country training, highly geared to development needs.[22]

Language considerations for Chilean scholarship-holders (*becarios*) are another area for improvement. The practice of donor countries on language competence varies widely, and the British system of testing in Chile came in for a good deal of criticism particularly, as a somewhat arbitrary selection process in the absence of standardisation of testing English-competence throughout the world. No doubt the British Council, the mediating body for *becarios*, is under pressure from receiving institutions in the United Kingdom on this issue, but here a leaf might be taken from the book of the Konrad-Adenauer Foundation: all *becarios* must undertake three months' language instruction at the Goethe Institut or at *colegios alemanes* in Chile, but if they fail the language test, they are not, as they are with English, immediately rejected but are sent on other courses.

But language is a much more crucial issue for outgoing personnel from developed countries, and most informants were agreed that their own states were deficient in this respect. In the Chilean case, there is no doubt that this is a very important factor in the effectiveness of the expert, particularly in the field of education. Communication is crucial if new ideas and techniques are to be appreciated, and much damage has been done to the image of aid by comparative failure to appreciate this point. And, paradoxically perhaps, this is particularly true of the long-term expert with inadequate language preparation, since he tends, much more than the short-term visitor, to become radicated in the expatriate community.

Equally important for the incoming expert is a prior understanding of the country, and, while no amount of orientation courses are a proper substitute for living experience, far more could be done here to prepare people for what is in store for them. Latin American habits of bureaucratic behaviour, deference to authority, adherence to traditional practices and, most frustrating of all to those whose acceptance of a foreign assignment is its own proof of their eagerness to impart, an indifference to time – all these factors can be highly frustrating and productive of much misunderstanding. What first strikes the European visitor to Latin America is the absence of public clocks, but the difference from his own country in this fact covers a totally different historical experience. If he is aware of this, and of the reasons for it, he will not ascribe the failure of *rapport* to the stupidity or backwardness of his counterpart or audience, but will come to

[22] For interesting material on this, see *Rol de Chile en el Pacto Andino y en la Integratión Latinoamericana,* Boletín Informativo, número unico, Santiago, PLANDES, 1971.

understand that technical assistance is also an extension of humanity and also, perhaps, a lesson in humility.

This discussion leads on, naturally, to the question of appropriate goals for donors in the case of a country like Chile. The growing assumption that there should now be for developing countries generally a greater concentration on teacher trainers, rather than teachers themselves, may be questioned in Chile's situation. While it is certainly the view of UNESCO, whose experience in this field is formidable, there is an alternative argument with regard to developing countries whose educational growth is less a question of absolute input to correct fundamental deficiencies, e.g. large-scale illiteracy, than adapting the educational system to national needs. So far as Chile is concerned, it seems, in fact, to be more efficacious to train in *subjects* than to train in *training techniques*, on a kind of Lancasterian monitor system. There may be exceptions, of course, in particular instances, such as the Chile–UNESCO project for educational administrators. But third-hand instruction introduces distortion: there can be no doubt that the British-supported scheme for decentralisation of education in Chile was effective because the expert in the Bío-Bío pilot project, who, incidentally spoke good Spanish, was a long-term influence on a wide range of educational and administrative personnel in the region, and the expert adviser had been in Chile before, and had contacts at all levels in the educational hierarchy. The permanence, in comparative terms, of these contacts could not have been replaced by short-term training of Chileans to do the job, given the political volatility of administrative appointments, the fundamental re-thinking required for the particular project, and the need for semi-permanent personal stimulus and encouragement. In other words, national counterparts may not always be appropriate in themselves alone, and they must, like foreign advisers, be very carefully selected.

Whatever protestations may be made to the contrary, aid is a highly political subject, both on the part of the recipient and of the donor. This is no less true of multilateral than of bilateral arrangements, and it is no disparagement of the selfless dedication of many international public servants to say that the *raison d'être* of their employing institutions may be partly to perpetuate their existence. And a good deal depends, of course, on those who take the decisions: it seems highly unlikely that they will not have a political philosophy of their own. Spokesmen of receiving countries such as Chile frequently aver that they prefer multilateral to bilateral aid: in practice, they like both, to maximise their value to all. And, of course, they wish to receive bilateral aid from as many donors as possible, to give them the maximum freedom of manoeuvre. There is nothing intrinsically wrong about this, any more than there is anything immoral in donor countries expecting some return in the tangible form of ultimate capital projects or investment opportunities, or merely in the natural desire to be liked. The worst of both worlds is exemplified in the British Labour government's decision in 1974 peremptorily to cut off aid to Chile for purely emotional reasons which had nothing to do with the needs of the Chilean people. British aid in Chile had a high reputation as 'aid for aid's sake', which was largely, but not entirely, true, though it could properly be regarded as having minimal political implications: its abrupt severance seriously harmed that reputation and not only in Chile.

Politics apart, the balance-sheet on educational aid to Chile in the 1960s is a favourable one, certainly in comparison with many other countries in the Third World. Waste and frustration there certainly was, which comparatively minor adjustments might have done much to correct. But the priorities were basically correct, and the programming, in a fallible world, fundamentally sound. There is, however, one final point on coordination which needs to be made in the case of Chile in particular and of Latin America in general. The Jackson Report has been widely acclaimed as making recommendations to improve the coordination of aid efforts in developing countries, and its proposals might well be valid for many recipient countries. But it was based heavily upon the experience of Asia and Africa, and, in the investigations of the capacity committee, Latin America was comparatively neglected, despite the extraordinary experience, extending over twenty years, of the ECLA on *Latin American* development problems. As this *country* study of Chile in the development decade has emphasised, the problems of technical aid revolve around many issues, but perhaps the crucial one is the *distinctive* nature of the recipient. While lack of space precludes a detailed discussion, there is something paradoxical in the recommendation of *global* remedies to improve coordination, based on the experience of only part of the developing world. Attention to regional and national susceptibilities is, after all, the first prerequisite for effective aid cooperation.

VI POSTSCRIPT: CHILE 1970–1974

The advent to power in Chile in 1970 of a democratically-elected Marxist government and its three-year tenure of office had immediate implications for Chilean education and for foreign aid to Chile. In its pursuit of what it called 'the Chilean road to socialism', the government of Popular Unity (UP), a heterogeneous coalition of left-wing parties, included in its sweeping programme plans to accelerate changes in the existing educational structure, reflecting the simultaneous changes in the economy brought about by the rapid extension of state control, and with added emphasis on social change. Its priorities included greater attention to the pre-school child, under six years of age, heavy emphasis on middle-level education and not least technical training, and an expansion and reorientation of university education to put more stress on technology and science. In two years, if official figures are to be accepted, the numerical results were certainly impressive, with pre-school provision (i.e. nursery-type facilities) raised by over 65 per cent intake, primary education by 13 per cent, middle-level education in the humanities by 33 per cent and in technical/professional schools by over 50 per cent and in higher education overall by some 83 per cent. Social supporting measures, such as free milk to minors, school allowances and so on, were also implemented. Some months after its take-over of power, the Government also announced plans for a total restructuring of education through the National Unified School Plan (Escuela Nacional Unificada), designed to eliminate completely the separate streams in Chilean education and create a unified through-system. There was also a good deal of talk about the new socialist man to be developed for the new society, and much energy and more time was spent in political and ideological meetings by the teaching profession.

So far as the UNDP was concerned, the new Government in its programme for the period 1972–6 proposed to carry forward as ongoing projects inherited schemes accounting for 40 per cent of its own programme, and it hoped to continue to receive bilateral aid on no less a scale than in the past. The political difficulties into which the Government ran, and concomitant economic problems, do not concern us: suffice to say that the velocity of economic change brought about by government extension of control over the private sector could not be matched by the educational output in terms of highly-qualified managers, engineers and technicians – an important contributory factor to the sharp decline in the economy from late 1971. In addition, the administration became top-heavy and highly unprofessional, the consequence of attempting to keep all parties in the Government happy by allocating jobs to their representatives. In education, for example, new men were appointed to top posts, many of them for political rather than for professional reasons, and in most organisations a good deal of time was spent in political meetings rather than getting on with the job. The Government's plans for education ran into very stiff resistance from the opposition parties and the Church, and majority public opinion, strongly opposed to the Government on other grounds as well, resisted attempts to inculcate Marxist doctrines in many spheres of activity. The country, in effect, became polarised as Chile had never been before, and bitterness took the place of accommodation in politics and society. As the country slid towards anarchy, in September 1973, the armed forces and the police seized power in a bloody coup, much criticised at the time and since but, in all probability, the only real alternative to civil war.

Not surprisingly against this background, many of the educational projects surveyed above ran into heavy weather. In the Government's first two-and-a-half years, for example, five Ministers of Education held office, three of them in the space of ten months, and the increased politicisation at all levels led to a sizeable increase in the brain drain, as well as making cohesive development almost impossible. Thus, for example, on the UNESCO-supported project for the training of educational administrators, policy vacillations on the type of administrator to be produced and what functions he should perform – ideas far from clear even when the project was approved by UNDP in 1968 – totally circumscribed the project's effectiveness.

The future of Chile at the time of writing is far from clear, and much of what has been written above may be totally irrelevant to it, both in terms of development aid and education. But one lesson of the last few years is abundantly clear: revolutions cannot be made in a day, except at a terrible cost. And the results are unpredictable. Chile's development has been set back years, if not, indeed, decades, by men in too much of a hurry.

Part IV

9 General Conclusions and Recommendations

The purpose of this chapter is to draw together the main threads of the 'country' surveys, and to present conclusions. To try and cover such a width of work and research by different people in one chapter is like assuming that because you have had conversations in your own country about the problems of another land, your conclusions are as soundly based as those which are made after visits to countries, and discussions with people in them; this is as true for developed as developing countries.

THE DONORS

The donors include most of the major countries of the Western World and in addition the majority of the United Nations' Agencies and the Ford and Rockefeller Foundations.

BACKGROUND AND POLICIES OF THE FIVE COUNTRIES INVOLVED

FRANCE and the UNITED KINGDOM share a common factor which affects their pattern of aid, namely their past roles as centres of empires. French aid is accepted as a normal part of French governmental activities, particularly in relation to Francophone Africa south of the Sahara, where French influence in aid is overwhelming, and by no means unwelcome in the countries concerned.

In the United Kingdom aid is a subject more debated in Parliament and more apt to have fluctuations in the finance available. Although it is true that a high proportion of aid goes to the countries which previously had colonial status, these states also receive a great deal of aid from other developed countries.

THE FEDERAL REPUBLIC OF GERMANY began aid on a major scale in 1961, and was able to draw intelligent conclusions from the mistakes of others. Similarly THE NETHERLANDS expanded its aid programme considerably in the early 1960s, and now does a remarkable amount for a small country. Policy is based on the United Nations Declaration of Human Rights and lays particular stress on the idea of partnership in aid programmes between developing countries and the Netherlands. Aid is deliberately concentrated on certain countries and areas. In general their aid is welcomed, humane, and well administered and has always been subject to forward planning for sensible periods of time.

The development of aid from the UNITED STATES OF AMERICA has of course been formidable in proportions and a tremendous force in the world. This comment is brief as, at the time of writing, US official aid does not seem to have found its true rationale, or total self-confidence in the task it carries out in the development field. The Ford and Rockefeller Foundations, particularly the former, are repeatedly mentioned favourably in the chapters on the developing countries, and are quite clearly doing outstanding work in educational aid.

THE ADMINISTRATION OF AID

In most countries the administration of aid is subject to 'convulsive' and constant changes which frequently serve to confuse all concerned. It must be remembered that there are two sides, the policy makers and the operators, both of equal importance in making aid successful. FRANCE has perhaps suffered more than most in changes in administration and a certain lack of internal cooperation and coordination.

The organisation of aid in the FEDERAL REPUBLIC OF GERMANY is as complicated as in some other countries. The Federal Ministry for Economic Cooperation (BMZ), being the source of so much finance for numerous organisations in the aid field, leads to some simplification and coordination. Vigorous steps are taken to explain the administration, notably through the German Foundation for Developing Countries, in such publications as 'The Organisation of Development Aid'. A complicating factor is the existence of the eleven *Länder*, who also have a role in aid administration and spend quite considerable funds on development aid. Here again the BMZ takes steps to coordinate this aid with the Federal and voluntary aid programmes.

The NETHERLANDS' administration is simpler than that of other donor countries, although the Dutch would find this hard to believe. This is not so much because the country is smaller, although this may be a contributory factor, but mainly because there is a high degree of coordination both between ministries and between voluntary bodies themselves and the ministries.

THE UNITED KINGDOM's administration has also had its share of convulsive change, but chiefly in the area of administration, relating to its colonial past. The Department of Technical Cooperation after a series of administrative reorganisations became the Overseas Development Administration (ODA) of the Foreign and Commonwealth Relations Office. In 1974 it again secured an independent Minister of Overseas Development.

A unique aspect of the administration of educational aid is the existence of the British Council, a purely British conception of an independent body with a Royal Charter, handling millions of tax-payers' money coming both from the Foreign and Commonwealth Office and the ODA. The Council has gradually taken over most of the administration of educational aid in developing countries, and in the United Kingdom; the ODA remains in collaboration with the main policy makers.

In the UNITED STATES the main organisation of aid administration, USAID is in a state of uncertainty because there have been three government inquiries into aid, none of which has been totally accepted, and all of which affect USAID; consequently the organisation must have been in a state of suspended animation over too many years. Many government agencies, some financed by USAID, take part in the aid programme, together with a large number of voluntary organisations. The Ford and Rockefeller Foundations, included in the survey, are the most notable voluntary charitable organisations in the field of educational aid.

THE IMAGE OF AID

The *image* of aid is an increasingly important factor which affects the policy making of governments both on administrative and international levels.

In FRANCE, aid, particularly to Francophone Africa, is accepted without much question, though probably if there were a tendency for aid to be increased, there would be more resistance.

A good job of informing the public is done by the FEDERAL REPUBLIC OF GERMANY on the problems of development aid: there is a ramifying set of organisations taking part in this work, well supported by the mass media, television, radio and newspapers. It is felt that the interest is not so vigorous, however, except amongst the young (Chapter 2, p. 59).

THE NETHERLANDS are successful in having the backing and interest of the public partly because of the way in which they base their development aid programme on the United Nations Declaration of Human Rights. A survey in April 1973 showed that 91 per cent of the public could be said to be in favour of development cooperation (Chapter 2, p. 60).

There is perhaps a more casual attitude in the UNITED KINGDOM because they are not particularly good at saying what they are doing in any field; they are not so coordinated as the Netherlands, or the Federal Republic, nor is aid so accepted by the public as it is in France. Recently the position has improved with the setting up of the Voluntary Committee on Overseas Aid by the main fund-raising organisations; this committee receives a grant from ODA. A study by the Office of Population Censuses and Surveys in 1969 on the public attitude, and opinions and knowledge about aid, showed that a knowledge of the true nature of aid was rudimentary up to 1971, and that the public tended to confuse aid with famine, droughts or other natural catastrophes (Chapter 2, pp. 61–3).

The difficulty of ascertaining a national view on any subject in such a vast country as the UNITED STATES OF AMERICA is obvious. There is one advantage, however, namely the foreign origin of many Americans, including, of course, the negroes. This inclines Americans, on the whole, to be sympathetic to the problems of developing countries, and to the provision of aid. A recent survey showed that one-third of the American public was basically sympathetic, and a quarter unsympathetic.

Methodology of donors' aid

Training

Training is one of the major forms of educational aid, as will be seen from (Chapter 2, pp. 23 ff).

In FRANCE training is considered of paramount importance: stress is placed on *sur place* training, and awards are not given in subjects available in the country of origin. Industrial training, certainly in the early 1970s, had been well organised.

The NETHERLANDS receives about a thousand fellows a year; until now they have mostly been placed on the courses organised by the Netherlands Universities Foundation for International Cooperation (NUFFIC), although this position is likely to change in the near future (Chapter 2, p. 38).

The FEDERAL REPUBLIC OF GERMANY granted 21,517 awards for study in the Federal Republic in 1971; this is the highest figure for any donor country. Much is done in the field of industrial and middle-level training by the Carl Duisberg Gesellschaft (CDG). Another unique institution is the German Academic Exchange Service (DAAD) which works globally, financed by both the Foreign Ministry and the BMZ, and deals with the placement of Germans overseas at the postgraduate level, and the sending abroad of university staff as experts, and senior lecturers (Chapter 2, pp. 30–7).

In BRITAIN the great majority of awards tenable in the United Kingdom are handled by the British Council, be they financed by the ODA, UN, UN specialised agencies, the British Council, or through Commonwealth Education, and by a wide range of smaller awarding schemes, and some awards by developing countries. It is probable that Britain has given more attention to the welfare of overseas people, be they young students coming to study, or researchers at the postgraduate level, senior visitors of the standing of the rector of a university, and Ministers of Education (Chapter 2, pp. 45–6).

The numbers in the UNITED STATES OF AMERICA are large: 17,639 students and trainees received awards in 1971. Quite a number are placed in third countries for training, and a smaller number are trained *sur place* in their own countries. Many official and voluntary organisations have training schools.

Nothing that has been said should be taken as meaning that study abroad is not of value in itself. The old conception of the wandering scholar is still true, and in a world in which every country is dependent upon others, the necessity of knowing how things are done in other lands, and why, is more essential than it ever was; to know and understand does not necessarily mean automatic copying.

Experts, teachers and advisers

The provision of experts, advisers and teachers is another obvious educational activity. FRANCE provides such aid on a massive scale, probably greater than any other donor; concentration is chiefly on North Africa, and on Francophone Africa south of the Sahara. Endeavours are made not to send experts or advisers when indigenous people are available (Chapter 2, pp. 25–8).

In THE FEDERAL REPUBLIC OF GERMANY also this activity is carried out at a high numerical level, by a variety of official and voluntary bodies including both the Catholic and Protestant churches (Chapter 2, pp. 33–4).

In 1972 half of the 1415 experts from THE NETHERLANDS were concerned with some form of agriculture. The Young Associates Experts Scheme is a Netherlands innovation, now much used by the United Nations (Chapter 2, pp. 38–40).

BRITAIN is second to France in the numbers of people sent overseas. In 1972 the main responsibility was transferred to the Crown Agents for Overseas Governments Administration from the ODA. Other recruiting bodies are TETOC, IUC and the British Council, the latter concentrating to a great extent on the teaching of English as a foreign language (Chapter 2, pp. 47–9).

More money is spent on this activity than on any other by the UNITED STATES, where considerable numbers are recruited from universities and a maze of official and unofficial agencies. Numerically fewer experts go from the United States than from France, or Britain (Chapter 2, pp. 54–5).

Volunteers

FRANCE is not yet as active in the volunteer field as the other major donors; the main effort is the Volontaires de Service National Actif, when aid service at a French Embassy in a developing country can be undertaken instead of military service. A voluntary scheme, Volontaires du Progrès, operates only in Africa south of the Sahara.

The GERMAN Volunteer Organisation is an efficient body financed entirely by the BMZ, but is also an independent company. The age of the volunteers ranges from twenty-one to thirty-five, the great mass being in the middle twenties, having had two years training after leaving school. Practically none are academics, the majority are technicans or junior professional people (Chapter 2, pp. 33–4).

THE NETHERLANDS Volunteer Organisation is a part of the Ministry of Foreign Affairs. The age range is similar to that of the Federal Republic of Germany, as are the professions of volunteers and recruitment and briefing processes. The Dutch expect no contribution from the developing country, paying one hundred per cent of the costs and small salaries to the volunteers (Chapter 2, pp. 39–40).

In BRITAIN the Volunteer Programme is more voluntary in the normal usage of that term than is the case of The Netherlands, or the Federal Republic of Germany. Seventy-five per cent of the costs are borne by government sources, the other twenty-five per cent coming from industry and charitable foundations. Originally the great majority were school leavers, but now they are graduate volunteers; the position may well change to a type of volunteer rather nearer that of Germany and the Netherlands (Chapter 2, pp. 47–8).

From 1961 to 1971 the Peace Corps handled UNITED STATES' volunteers; but for reasons outside their own control the Peace Corps, as such, became in 1971 the International Division of the Domestic Programme of Volunteers 'Action' Federal Agency. Even so in 1972 there were 8500 volunteers serving in 56 countries in a very wide spectrum of trades and professions (Chapter 2, p. 55).

The teaching of languages

For many years the teaching and spreading of the French language has been a major concern of French policy, both for reasons of *civilisation* and of aid and trade. The same can be said of Britain and the United States, who often collaborate together.

The teaching of German is a considerable activity of the Federal Republic of Germany, the main instrument being the Goethe Institute.

University links and research into development aid

FRANCE is not very active in the field of university links; development research on the other hand is prominent. The Office de la Recherche Scientifique et Technique d'Outre-Mer (ORSTOM) is exceptional although so far not many people from developing countries are involved in joint research projects (Chapter 2, pp. 28–9).

University and other links have been a well-developed feature of the GERMAN FEDERAL REPUBLIC's aid, and are frequently mentioned in the chapters on developing countries. They are also a part of aid which is subject to considerable evaluation. Research is well developed. Much of it is financed by the BMZ, including research projects into the value of university links; many individual research institutes at German universities are concerned with development aid (Chapter 2, pp. 34–5).

In the early 1970s money was made available by the NETHERLANDS' Ministry of Foreign Affairs to the Netherlands Universities Foundation for International Cooperation for an extension of links and research between institutions of higher education in the Netherlands and developing countries (Chapter 2, p. 40).

Until recently active partnership links between British universities and those in developing countries have not been a very important part of educational aid backed by official funds; recently however more official money is being made available, notably through the Inter-University Council. Development research is a fairly vigorous part of Britain's development operations both through university finance, through ODA, research councils, by voluntary bodies such as the Overseas Development Institute, and by major foundations like the Nuffield and Leverhulme Trust Funds (Chapter 2, p. 49).

Undoubtedly more is done by the UNITED STATES both in the spheres of university links and development research than elsewhere. Much money and manpower is available through official, university, and private sources.

Evaluation

A good deal of lip service is paid to the importance of evaluation, but so far of the five developed countries concerned only the FEDERAL REPUBLIC OF GERMANY, THE UNITED STATES and THE NETHERLANDS seem to devote money, thought and research into evaluating the effectiveness of projects. OECD in 1972 published a booklet on evaluating development assistance, and the list of evaluated research projects done by the United States is formidable (Chapter 2, p. 56).

Professional migration

FRANCE and THE NETHERLANDS do not appear to be worried about the migration of professional people from developing countries. Two countries which do show concern are the FEDERAL REPUBLIC OF GERMANY and BRITAIN. In the former case the nationalities chiefly concerned are from Iran, Turkey and Greece, and in the latter from India, Bangladesh, Pakistan, Sri Lanka and a growing number from the Middle East. Both countries share a common feature in their shortage of medically trained people and migrant medicals are therefore welcomed, often to replace German or British staff who have 'migrated' in their turn, usually to North America.

THE UNITED NATIONS AND UNITED NATIONS AGENCIES

As the survey has proceeded, more particularly the case-studies of the developing countries, several points have emerged that are general, but which affect the United Nations in particular. In the first place, governments of developing countries normally say that they would like more assistance through multilateral channels, although they do not mean necessarily that they want less aid through the bilateral ones. In practice, the slowness of multilateral agencies in the actual implementation of agreed projects sometimes causes a bilateral scheme to be chosen instead, because it can be done more speedily. An example of multilateral slowness is the time-lag caused by recruitment and clearance procedures under the United Nations Volunteer Scheme, which causes a high withdrawal rate of candidates; this is commented upon in the report of the Administrator of UNDP for 1973, published in 1974. Cumbersome machinery and slowness cannot be avoided entirely when governing bodies may represent as many as 138 states; there is also the fact that the agreement of a project, and recruitment if that is involved, normally depends upon the cooperation of a developing country, the UNDP, the executing United Nations agency, and one or more governments of developed countries. UNDP is taking steps to speed 'project approval and delivery' and to improve communications between UNDP in the field, at headquarters and with the agencies.

The Jackson Report recommended an increased coordinating and financial role for UNDP, and in the writer's view this is already having an effect, but as has been said in an earlier section on the United Nations (Chapter 2, p. 65) the final success will depend on enough staff of the right calibre in the right places.

Another factor which is impressive is the very wide variety of projects which come under one or other wing of the 'UN family'. Many are of much imagination, which is some cases have not met with the success the original innovation deserved.

Some of the comments which now follow are based on the UNDP's Administrator's Report, 1973, this being the most up-to-date overall picture of UN activities in the aid field.

The Administrator refers to the uneasiness amongst both developing and developed countries on the future of aid assistance: some developed countries are showing signs of 'donor fatigue', coupled with 'donor alarm', caused by rising prices, especially for petroleum. These deep worries have however had a positive 'back lash' in spotlighting concern for development issues and stressing the interdependence of the nations of the world upon each other, be they developed or developing. This has led many to realise that the classic signs of underdevelopment – inadequate educational facilities, unemployment and low productivity and population growth – are not in any way helped by curtailment of external aid, either multi- or bilateral. Rather surprisingly in view of world comment there was an overall increase in bilateral aid in 1973, but an even larger growth of UNDP resources, this being due to some extent to the Jackson Report, and also to UNDP's fairly general political acceptability, its size and global experience.

It is acknowledged, and this is a point that this survey has shown, that despite all the aid to development in the past, the population of many countries in absolute terms is worse off now than it was ten years ago; this has focused attention on projects aimed at the immediate improvement of the lot of people in these countries, and more particularly in the twenty-five countries now termed 'the least-developed countries'.

Since 1967 UNDP has been concerned with, and to some extent has carried out, evaluations; in 1973 a system was started whereby all large-scale UNDP-assisted projects are reviewed once a year, jointly by the government authorities concerned, representatives of UNDP and the relevant executing agency; the results seem to be that a proper appreciation of the effectiveness of a project, and its application in practice, are both fundamental to the success of UNDP assistance, or any other assistance for that matter, and both depend on evaluation in depth. Stress has also been laid by UNDP on the development of inter-regional projects – for example, a study on the feasibility of the trans-Saharan road, a project which could be technically possible, a programme of joint studies on Latin America's economic integration, and on an East African civil flying school.

The fact that contributions to aid development by voluntary sources rose to one billion dollars in 1973 caused UNDP to have a survey made by selected representatives in collaboration with non-governmental organisations (n.g.o.s) engaged in technical assistance. This survey showed that UNDP had not been aware of the extent and professional competence of the voluntary effort. As a result UNDP field staff, UN agencies and major n.g.o.s are jointly making suggestions which will lead to better collaboration between UNDP and competent n.g.o.s (Chapter 2, pp. 11–13).

OTHER INTERNATIONAL AND REGIONAL ORGANISATIONS

Only Commonwealth organisations are commented upon in this section, as the Sixth Commonwealth Education Conference held in Jamaica in 1974 concentrated upon the problems facing educational development.

The Commonwealth Secretariat is to examine the possible establishment of a Commonwealth Programme on a regional basis by subsidising existing institutions to help train planners and administrators, and personnel in other fields, according to the needs of individual countries.

The Secretariat is also to consider appointing resident regional representatives. Greater flexibility under the Commonwealth Scholarship and Fellowship Plan's operations is envisaged, to enable developing countries to participate more fully in the plan as awarding countries, possibly with assistance from the Commonwealth Fund for Technical Cooperation (CFTC), and also to see if through the CFTC more aid can be provided to developing countries of the Commonwealth on a multilateral basis.

THE DEVELOPING COUNTRIES

Comments on the methodology of aid

Training

Training is a prominent feature in educational aid. In KENYA lack of coordination means that training abroad is not always undertaken with Kenya's needs in view; large numbers go to Britain and the United States on scholarships provided by those countries. There are, too, numerous Kenyan government awards and United Nations fellowships. Considerable numbers go, particularly to Britain, at their own expense; so far a fair percentage of the estimated manpower has been met through such training (Chapter 3, p. 93).

SENEGAL receives grants for study mainly in France for subjects that cannot be studied locally, or regionally, though it is very rare for a Senegalese to study in the West African region (Chapter 4, pp. 146–8). Again in TUNISIA, as in other spheres, France is by far the largest provider of fellowships and courses. There has been concentration chiefly on vocational and managerial training. The same is true for the Federal Republic of Germany. The ILO has coordinated the training of hotel and tourism staff, hoping to establish an institute for this training in Tunis (Chapter 5, p. 183).

Inevitably a country as vast as INDIA receives an overwhelming number of offers of fellowships and scholarships, all coordinated by the Union Indian Ministry of Education. This form of aid is well detailed and discussed in the chapter on India (Chapter 6, pp. 195 ff.). One point however is fundamental: there are no lack of applications of merit for the wide range of scholarships, on average there are twenty well-qualified candidates for each award, rising to 2500–3000 for 80 nominations for the 40 awards offered to India by the United Kingdom, under the Commonwealth Scholarship and Fellowship Plan (Chapter 6, pp. 256 ff.).

Another important point is that the Indian Government exercises close control of currency for those students going abroad to study at their own expense, priority being given to certain subjccts; a steadily lessening number of undergraduates now receive foreign currency for study abroad.

It is probable that in any one year over 7000 TURKS go abroad for either long periods of study, or for short visits for specialist purposes. An overseas training is often sought for reasons of prestige, frequently leading to better career prospects in Turkey; this latter point may lead to an unsatisfactory denigration of Turkish institutions and achievements. Training abroad can thus increase the gap between the elitism of the more highly-educated portion of the population and the less-educated sectors (Chapter 7, p. 327).

CHILE has had considerable aid in the field of training, both from multilateral and bilateral sources. The United Nations projects are coordinated by UNDP and a Chilean government department provides the counterpart funds. The UNITED STATES award many fellowships, particularly to educators, engineers, geologists and business advisers, whilst FRANCE, BRITAIN and THE FEDERAL REPUBLIC OF GERMANY give more modest assistance in the training field (Chapter 8, pp. 352 ff.).

Experts, teachers and advisers

Nearly all the case-studies stress the inadequacy of selection of experts and teachers, and point out that expatriates fill positions which could often be perfectly well filled by indigenous people. Expatriates of one sort or another are found as individuals, or as members of projects, throughout all aspects of educational aid.

The main exporter of personnel to KENYA is Britain, for in the mid-sixties Kenyans felt it would be disastrous to reduce the number of expatriates in the educational system. Experts, however, are not always able to judge what changes are needed, are influenced by their own home experience, and do not normally stay long enough to implement the relevant innovations. They are often expected to accomplish much in too little time, and frequently have inadequate training themselves and little insight into Kenya's needs.

The difficulty of finding the right counterparts is stressed and many lack flexibility because of attitudes due to 'foreign training' (Chapter 3, p. 110).

In the case of both SENEGAL and TUNISIA, the overwhelming majority of expatriates at most levels are French. Experts and advisers abound from many sources in INDIA, as can be seen from the various sections of the Indian chapter. Expatriate teachers are not used except to a very minor extent at the school level, but experts and advisers figure prominently in many bilateral and multilateral projects.

TURKEY too has a large number of experts and the chapter stressed that too often they are employed because they are foreign, so leading to devaluation of Turkish achievements (Chapter 7, pp. 311–15).

In CHILE many experts are imported because they are foreign, even though there are completely competent Chileans to do the job. It is stressed several times in the Chilean chapter that too many experts, while expert enough in their subject, lack either good orientation or have inadequate knowledge of Spanish.

Languages

The knowledge of foreign languages is a constant thread through all the case histories, be it lack of knowledge of the language of a developing country on the part of experts, or inadequate acquaintance with the relevant language for study abroad on the part of award holders. The teaching of foreign languages throughout an educational system is a subject of political importance. The KENYA chapter stresses that the teaching of English at the school level already brings in its train an alien culture and medium, and begins the process of the educated sections of the population becoming isolated from their human environment (Chapter 3, pp. 101–6).

The French language, as elsewhere in Francophone Africa, is a binding force in SENEGAL. President Senghor has, however, on several occasions said that he attached importance to the teaching of English, and that Senegal should be bilingual. Apart from the English teaching provided by the United Kingdom, the Canadians, being bilingual in French and English, provide various forms of educational aid, including the teaching of English (Chapter 4, pp. 151–2).

In TUNISIA the language problem seen in the light of the country's cultural experience and social development is as acute as in India, although obviously the scale is vastly different. French is, of course, pre-eminent, but there is an increasing demand for English, and there is significant cooperation between the Ford Foundation and the British Council (Chapter 5, pp. 180–1).

In INDIA the problem of the English language is obviously frequently a highly political and sensitive subject. The importance of maintaining adequate language competence to match such projects as the major scientific developments is important, and has not always been achieved. The section on the Central Institute of English demonstrates well the fact that the Indian financial contribution far outweighs that of any external aid (Chapter 6, pp. 273–80).

In TURKEY the United States, the British, the French and West German governments all have considerable schemes of long standing for teaching their languages. French, German and United States high schools are still active. The Turkish authorities pay the teachers, while the sending countries do the recruiting. All are aware that at this time when economic ties are strengthening with the West, an even greater need exists for the learning of European languages. For this reason the Council of Europe initiated a project involving the British, Federal Republic of Germany and Turkish authorities to improve the teaching of English and German in the *lisa* schools (Chapter 7, pp. 315–17).

SOME GENERAL CONCLUSIONS

In Chapter 1 five major issues affecting development aid are mentioned. These are:

1. Educational expansion.
2. Problems of newly independent states post the Second World War
3. Lack of coordination and cooperation
4. Increase in population and pollution
5. The widening gap

There now follow some of the principal problems which seem to have emerged under these five headings during our surveys, and which are discussed in Chapters 2–8; a section on agriculture and rural training has been added.

1. Educational expansion

Educational expansion has to be seen against the background of development problems as a whole and obviously the large increase in populations has been fundamental to these; this factor along with the urge of people themselves, both children and parents, to gain education as a key to lives less submerged in poverty, hunger and many other miseries, exerted overwhelming pressures. Governments of developing countries, too, believed that it was education which would produce more civil servants and other professionally trained people, and be the way for nations to achieve true independence, particularly in the economic field.

Unfortunately the 'key' was frequently conceived in terms of Western forms of education, so donors implanted their educational systems, often already out-moded in their own countries, on developing countries. The latter wanted Western forms of education, believing that these had led the developed nations to economic success and a much higher standard of living, and also because 'the elitists' of the developing countries had themselves obtained education in the West, or through Western methods. It was reasoned by them, and those less fortunate, that they had obtained positions of power through this type of education.

The disastrous consequences of superimposing an alien system of education on a country with totally different methods and standards of life were not always foreseen by the developed countries who were concerned with educational aid. This was particularly so in the case of those countries to which educational development came at a relatively late stage. Inevitably an educational system brings with it many other influences, linguistic, cultural, and modes of living which were too often assumed to be better than those of the developing country, which often came to be denigrated, quite wrongly, by the people for whom historically they had formed the background of life for centuries.

Now the cry on all sides is for educational systems of developing countries to be attuned to their current needs within their own heritages and indigenous skills. In Chapters 3–8 these facts are discussed and some of the major points now follow.

The KENYAN chapter goes in the greatest depth into the effect of the transference of a Western educational system, notably in this case from the United Kingdom, on to a developing country. It stresses that the Kenyans assumed a direct relationship between education and economic growth, and, therefore, great emphasis was laid on expanding the high levels of the educational system to produce more trained people, including civil servants. The conviction also existed that the monopoly of high positions held by Europeans and Asians was the result of the Western-type education they had received. Inevitably therefore this formal education was proliferated, particularly at the higher levels which were to a great extent manned by expatriates. This state of affairs continued after Independence, but coupled with the long-term need for greater Africanisation of many of the professions.

The time has now been reached when Kenyans have to decide which elements of Western education and culture they will accept, and which African standards they will retain and strengthen. A related problem is manpower needs, the calculation of them and the action to meet them; but the dangers of a rudimentary manpower planning organisation are pinpointed, for clearly the results of miscalculation of manpower needs are greater and more pervading in less-developed countries. The expansion of education depended not only on expatriate staff but on the training abroad of Kenyan students. Even with so vast an expansion the great majority of the young did not go beyond the primary level, and there were many 'drop-outs'; huge numbers of young people were therefore unemployable, and the concentration on the provision of education in the urban areas led to the deepening of the urban/rural divide (Chapter 3, pp. 98–101).

In SENEGAL France plays by far the major role in education, and as in other spheres this is accepted by the Senegalese. The education system was created by the French and is French, but this fact must be seen against the beliefs of President Senghor in his form of African socialism, believing that Africans should play a leading role in the shaping of tomorrow's civilisation and with a firm belief in the importance of African culture as shown by his establishment (with Césaire of Martinique) of the Négritude Movement. The influence of the *marabouts* has also to be remembered, and their fear of the *animation movement*. Like Kenya there are ever-growing numbers of unemployable youth starting at the primary school level. It was hoped that by 1973 50 per cent of children would get some form of schooling. The University of Dakar is totally modelled on a French university, and even though Senegal took over full responsibility for the University in 1971 80 per cent of the teaching staff were still French in 1972–3 (Chapter 4, p. 146).

TUNISIA's educational development has been affected, as has all development aid to Tunisia, by the political conditions in the country. If correct political decisions and identification of national priorities are made, there will be a very positive effect on all aid programmes, including education. There has been a huge 'linear' expansion since 1957, probably too ambitious and usually at the expense of quality. Here again the problems burgeon at the lower educational levels, not so much because they have been neglected but because it was necessary to achieve so much, and the failures have been correspondingly greater. Clear-minded and coordinated donors could have brought some useful pressure to improve this situation (Chapter 5, pp. 186–7).

The INDIAN chapter perhaps gives the broadest and best documented picture of educational development; what stands out very clearly is the enormous financial contributions that India herself has made to educational development. Although the external assistance may look puny in comparison, if well directed it can be essential and of value far beyond the money involved.

There has been great concentration of development aid to India in the 1960s in the general field of education: namely science, technology, industry and management training and agriculture. The section headings of Chapter 6 on the contents page, particularly Sections 4–15, will make this clear. Some of the qualified success stories have been the teacher training programmes in the polytechnics and the Institute of Technology and Institutes of Management. Here positive results have been realised; progress has been slow, but it has been made.

The great majority of the development aid for education was concentrated on the higher level, and it is admitted that elementary education has not really been considered as a candidate for development aid. This is an example of incorrect recognition of national priorities on the part of both India and the potential donors, and something which must contribute to the 'widening gap' between the urban and rural populations. This is a dislocation in the concentration of efforts on different levels of education. The fact that many of the most pressing problems remain in the lower levels has parallels in other of the case-studies, for example Chile, Tunisia and Turkey, although the lower levels have not necessarily been neglected to quite the same extent as in India. In many ways this uneven concentration has lessened the potential achievement of the great 'scientific leap forward' which was planned. On the whole attempts to improve science teaching in secondary schools seem to have been a failure so far. There seems to have been little or no cooperation and communication between the UNESCO–UNDP projects and the indigenous potential in this particular instance; surely intelligent, informed, and altruistic outside experts could and should perform more capably (Chapter 6, pp. 230–5).

In TURKEY originally educational expansion was entirely within the religious context; the first Western secular establishments began with military sciences in the eighteenth century. In recent years the highly centralised structure of Turkish administration and the huge linear expansion since 1957, based on European models such as France, have been too ambitious, particularly at primary and secondary levels, so that the need for qualified teachers far outstripped the possibilities at the high level to produce an adequate supply of qualified and competent people. Of the nine universities only the University of Istanbul was created in the nineteenth century, and this had much German help and influence when it was reorganised in the early days of the Republic. The other universities were established between 1944 and 1974, and all had considerable external aid: the University of the Aegean from Germany, CENTO, France and the United States; Ataturk University had major USAID through the University of Nebraska; Karadeniz had no external aid until UNESCO was asked by the Turkish Government to assist with a faculty of mechanical, electrical and civil engineering. Hacettepe's finance came mostly from private foundations, in particular the Ford, Rockefeller and Turkish Foundations, and also from UNDP, CENTO and OECD; the University was modelled mainly on American lines, but to some extent on United Kingdom ones. Boğaziçi, previously Robert College, financed by USAID, was purchased by the Turkish Government to become a university in 1971.

Like other parts of the Turkish educational system the universities are bedevilled by central control, rules and regulations. The section of the Turkish chapter relating to universities shows both the benefits and restrictions of so much external aid (Chapter 7, pp. 294–311).

When CHILE became an independent Republic high priority was given to education. The history of educational reform in the 1960s in Chile seems, as in other countries, to have been too ambitious, but because of the long-standing educational development it was built on a far firmer base, and impressive quantitative results have been obtained.

The section of the Chilean chapter 'The International Dimension' (p. 337) provides one of the clearest examples of the political aspects of aid-giving and receiving, and is particularly apt because of the unique Chilean experience in Latin America. In the mid 1960s serious attempts were made to coordinate activities within education itself – Chile in fact anticipated much of the Jackson Report on her own accord. In great contrast to many countries, Chile in the last few years has taken vigorous steps to decentralise the control and administration of education. This has been done in cooperation with the United Kingdom over a period of years. Chilean educational administrators at all levels have gone to the United Kingdom for discussions and training, and United Kingdom experts on the subject have spent long periods in Chile. As in all other fields Chile devoted large sums of money to this project which by the early 1970s was being successfully operated by trained Chileans with no external aid (Chapter 8, pp. 338–44).

2. Problems of independent states post the Second World War

These are the historical and political problems which are constantly mentioned in the preceding chapters. The relevance for this book is that these problems indicate both that they are global but also that the uniqueness of each country's experience must not be overlooked, even though there may exist more common factors between countries such as Tunisia, Kenya and Senegal. Yet it would be misguided to consider these as any more than superficial resemblances in the historical experience. There are few if any common factors between Turkey, India and Chile. The uniqueness of each historical experience means that the aid must be individually tailored to individual problems. There must be avoidance of all models or patterns or transposable solutions to theoretical problems. This has implications for the following points which are relevant:

i. The numerous complaints about the quality of the 'experts' involved in the aid-giving process probably arise because of the great individual variety of each and every country. There are probably not enough truly regional experts in a very local sense who are also free enough from internal political pressures or sympathies to take the right decisions.

ii. Every consultant mentions the past and immediate present political situations which affect aid projects both inside the recipient country and outside in the interests of the donors. These pressures may have either a positive *or* a negative effect on the efficiency of the aid programmes.

iii. All this probably underlines the urgency of the Jackson Report's recommendations for the regional organisation of aid programmes with a considerably greater degree of local responsibility than has been the case in the past, and a significantly enlarged coordinating and financial role for UNDP. There are signs that this is beginning to have an effect.

3. Coordination and cooperation

The obvious problems of the lack of coordination and cooperation between the less-developed countries and those which provide aid are too well known to need reiteration here. There is not only the gap between countries, but within countries, be they developed or developing. In the case of developed countries it is indeed rare to find one where there is coordination and cooperation between official sources themselves, between voluntary agencies, who frequently work in a vacuum, frightened of anyone poaching on their preserves, and far too often no knowledge in official spheres of the role voluntary organisations can and could play. Developed countries should be able to solve this, and also see that all their relevant official and unofficial agencies for aid know what is being done by multilateral and regional organisations. Developing countries should see that their various ministries are aware of what is done by each other, and in an ideal world the developing country should coordinate all the activities of donors, be they official bilateral, multilateral, regional, or voluntary organisations. In the interval, before a developing country has adequate trained manpower for such tasks UNDP should be recognised as the most informed and neutral source of such coordination, and bilateral agencies should take greater steps to see that they are aware of what other donors are doing before a project is started. They have much to learn from each other, and could often jointly tell a developing country why a certain type of project or methodology of aid has failed, or could be improved.

4. Population increase and pollution

The question of pollution is not of immediate relevance because most developing countries cannot yet see this as a problem which requires their urgent attention. Responsibility for this must rest squarely on the donors, as only they have experience of it as a problem and therefore the capacity to advise against its worst pitfalls. Yet it remains a responsibility which must not be shirked wherever it seems important.

Every case-study at some stage discusses the population increases which have occurred during the United Nations' first 'development decade'. These are an inevitable result of health programmes and lower mortality rates. Obviously the population factor will militate against national development in a 'scarce resources' situation, whether aided or unaided. Until people actually enjoy a higher standard of material well-being and can be persuaded of the economic benefits to them personally (and not to national statistics) of having fewer children, they will go on having children. If one exists at subsistence level, or just above it, children will keep on appearing. This is only part of the whole problem of development, including education. The population increases are important from the point of view of this survey for two reasons:

i. They make agricultural progress a crucial necessity. If the mortality rate drops, then the agriculture which is the basis of even a subsistence economy cannot afford to remain stagnant. Otherwise more food has to be imported and this causes either inflation or a total lack of financial viability, or relying totally on food aid which is a highly uncertain and short-term non-solution.

ii. The population increases have placed crippling statistical demands on the educational systems of developing nations, all of which led to the dramatic 'linear expansions' of the 1960s taking place, usually at the expense of quality.

The dangers are recognised by developing and developed countries and United Nations agencies alike, but solutions are hard to come by. The lower mortality has meant a vast increase in the number of school-aged children. In Tunisia from 1930 to 1960 the population almost doubled, and 40 per cent were under 15 years old. The population explosion intensifies the urban/rural gap, which is discussed below. In the course of the preceeding chapters the population problem is mentioned frequently, but there is not much reference to action in individual countries. One of the most imaginative schemes is perhaps in Turkey, where the Institute of Population Studies at the University of Hacettepe was launched with a grant from the Ford Foundation, which met 40 per cent of the cost, the other 60 per cent being met by the Turkish authorities.

5. The widening gap

This problem can be understood in two ways: it often refers to the discrepancy in wealth and living standards between developed and developing countries, or could refer to the privileged and under-priviledged sections of the populations of the developing countries, which are in receipt of aid in various forms. If we take the first sense of the 'widening gap', it is probably true that the rich countries do get richer and the poor poorer *in relation to each other*. This is doubtless the cause of life in an inflationary world, and certain types of aid programme probably contribute to this trend.

As far as the second sense of the widening gap is concerned, it occurs because of corruption, poor administration, bureaucratic chaos, and incorrect identification of national priorities. All these things are referred to implicitly or otherwise in most of the case-studies. Corruption and bad internal administration are lergely the responsibility of the recipients, but woeful lack of enough trained manpower is not always their fault. Such features can also be perpetuated by irresponsible aid giving, often undertaken for the wrong reasons. The guilt and responsibility for incorrect identification of priorities must be shared between both sides. In all these matters, the quality and local knowledge of the 'experts' are of paramount importance.

But the major cause of this widening gap within countries is the overwhelming amount of aid, and educational aid not least, which has been devoted to the urban sector, as against the far larger and poverty stricken rural areas. Within a few kilometres of the sophisticated cities – Nairobi, Dakar, Tunis, the major cities of India, Ankara and Santiago – there exist different worlds, with different values and very much lower standards of living, many people indeed living in conditions similar to those of long ago. As is said in the Senegalese chapter, the salaried classes are based on Dakar, the rest of the population living mainly on the produce of their fields – an uncertain livelihood, subject to the calamities of nature (Chapter 4, pp. 139–41).

These discrepancies between the urban and rural standards and opportunities have led to the enormous drift from the land to the towns, causing all the obvious problems of shanty towns and thousands of untrained and unemployable boys and girls, men and women. The particular 'widening gap' as interpreted as the main concern of this book has been deepened by the increase in populations, particularly of school age, and this with the inevitable drift to the towns has caused much mention of rural education and agricultural problems in the preceding chapters and is briefly discussed in the following section. From time immemorial the majority of people, particularly rural dwellers, have been deeply under-privileged, but there can surely be some improvement made, and faster than in the past.

6. Agricultural and rural education

There are now numerous and mostly profitable projects and research programmes on the betterment of agricultural production, which would of course be of benefit to the whole country, but would have the side effect of creating more and better employment on the land, and might therefore contribute towards stopping the drift to towns. That this will not always be the case has already been proved by some vastly improved production schemes under the Green Revolution, where farmers with very small holdings and tenant farmers and labourers have become unemployed. In Chapters 2–8 reference is made to many schemes of research by the FAO under bilateral schemes, and by foundations, in particular the Ford Foundation.

A project of note is a UNDP one in Senegal, jointly organised by the Senegalese Ministry of Technical and Vocational Training, the FAO and ILO. The project has three aspects, the training of agricultural teachers, handicrafts, and the education of women in rural areas (Chapter 4, pp. 152–3).

This leads to comments on the problem of rural education, really our main concern in that far too little has been done to keep people on the land. This can only happen if they see that for themselves and their children life in rural areas will be pleasanter and more profitable than shanty-town dwellings and unemployment. There seems little evidence at present of vigorous action; in the educational field there has clearly to be a great deal more thought given and action taken on the increase of school education in rural areas, and what form it should take. It must be profitable for teachers to teach in rural areas, and further, to be specially trained for such a profession.

The educational adminstrator in a city must often find it hard to imagine what sort of amenities teachers, parents and pupils need in rural areas, which he has possibly never visited. There may perhaps be a clue in the 'out of school training' adapted to the rural environment which was foreseen in Senegal's third Four-Year Plan of 1969–73, but whether it happened and what success is foreseen is at present unknown (Chapter 4, p. 143).

In India, at the tertiary level much has been done with the creation of new agricultural universities, while USAID with the cooperation of six American universities has participated with the Indian Government in the establishment of land grant colleges. There is however little said in the chapter of any notable achievements in rural schools, primary or secondary (Chapter 6, pp. 242–50).

RECOMMENDATIONS

At the outset of this chapter it was said that it was not intended to repeat the reasoning and conclusions of the preceding chapters; this is also true of recommendations, although some are mentioned in all the preceding chapters, and it is these with which this section is mainly concerned; others however are particular to one country or region and not applicable elsewhere.

1. Training

In a previous section in this chapter (p. 374) reference is made to the vast sums that have been spent, mostly on training, in developed countries. It is a truism to say that with the creation of any new programme of official bilateral, multilateral or regional aid, or of a new voluntary organisation, the first activity is nearly always the offer of scholarships or fellowships; mainly because a quicker return can be seen for this type of activity to justify expenditure of funds. For too long developed countries and UN agencies have offered the same type of awards which have been accepted unquestioningly. Now both the donors and the developing countries accept inevitable changes, and that the wholesale provision of scholarships without careful manpower considerations is wasteful and dangerous; far more thought now is being given to training '*sur place*', although both in the case of the Federal Republic of Germany and in the Turkish chapter such training is shown to be complicated by language difficulties. Third-country training and regional training have obvious difficulties, but the time has now come where the advantages tip the balance more in their favour. It is generally accepted that study abroad should be at the postgraduate level, and only at the undergraduate level when there is no relevant course in the developing country. One point which does however need further examination is that where there is a course available but perhaps with ten places for one hundred equally well-qualified candidates, some students then have to go abroad at the undergraduate level. Would it be more desirable in the long term for the donors to help expand the faculty concerned in the developing country? The level of study is inevitably linked with manpower problems; this means, or should mean, that sometimes awards both for study abroad or in institutions provided in developing countries should be aimed at the training of far more technicians and fewer PhDs. Lack of good well-paid and respected technicians often means that the knowledge of those who have achieved the level of PhD is wasted, as they have no trained staff to back them up. But the stress for the technical level must be on a well-paid and well-respected profession. Another trend which must be strengthened is the training of teacher trainers of all levels and professions, so that more and more of the actual teachers and trainers are indigenous. Coupled with this is the need for pride to be taken in the facilities and resulting qualifications available within the developing countries themselves. This point is stressed in both the Turkish and Indian chapters.

Not enough attention is given in developed countries to their guests, be they senior academics, other professional people, or the great mass of 'foreign students'. A fellowship, scholarship, or a short visit by a more senior person involves a lot of money, all of which can be wasted if the individual is not treated as an individual, receiving a friendly welcome at air or seaport, and being assured of suitable living accommodation and of opportunities in his free time to meet his opposite numbers, to visit and explore his country of temporary residence. In the case of the more short-term senior visitor a well-coordinated programme is essential, along with guides and interpreters who can foresee the visitor's needs, and who are capable of vanishing quietly from the scene when not needed at an interview. These points all sound most obvious, but certainly at the student level enough of the right things are not done at the right time, nor is it always appreciated that professionals are needed to do such things – and above all they must be those who like people, from wherever they may come.

Amongst more specific points from Chapters 2–8 which seem to have a general application, a massive switch of resources is recommended, from awards of scholarships and fellowships abroad, for tenure in developed countries, to *sur place* training, 'third-country' or regional training. In Kenya's case the switch should be to training for lower and higher technical levels; in the former case only simple workshops and trainees with elementary education would be needed (Chapter 3, pp. 123–5). The value of the training of teachers as a 'multiplier' example is stressed in the Indian chapter, as is the development of the training of supervisors for 'on the job training' of workers; all such training comes within a deliberate plan of Indian National Development, and the Indians' financial contribution to them is substantial (Chapter 6, pp. 281–2).

The Commonwealth Scholarship and Fellowship Plan is recognised as a prestigious one, and brings undoubted gain to Indian awardees and to institutions in India, but it is more difficult to assess the national gain. As returned fellows and scholars are apt to concentrate in urban areas, and this increases the gap with the rural areas, it is recommended that returned fellows and scholars should be sent compulsorily for given periods to areas of India where their services are most needed. This touches upon the problem of personal advancement as against national need (Chapter 6, pp. 259–60).

In most chapters it is strongly recommended that study abroad should only be for highly specific objectives. The selection of candidates needs in many cases to be done with greater care, and probably when feasible by a joint committee of the sending country and the host country. The latter should exercise similar care in ascertaining that the fellow or scholar is placed in the institution best fitted to equip him to fulfil the object of his award.

Chile cites both third-country and regional training in Spanish-speaking countries of Latin America as a matter which could be more vigorously pursued. The point is also made that in any form of training it is training in a specific subject, rather than in training techniques, that really matters (Chapter 8, pp. 343–65).

2. Experts, advisers, teaches and counterparts

There is overwhelming evidence that the need for a far better selection of experts, advisers and teachers is paramount. Selectors should always bear in mind the essential qualities that all forms of expatriate personnel should have, such as acquaintance with the realities of the country to which they will go, knowledge of its language and social context, and obviously the necessary professional skills and human qualities which will enable them genuinely to aid the people whom they will be serving; they should also have the capacity to act as both counsellors and students. Far more should be done to prepare selected candidates for their job before they leave for their posts, and when in the developing country they should have advice available to them, both from experts of the country concerned and their own nationals.

It is generally felt that the well-placed expert, adviser or teacher should serve for at least two years in a country, and preferably longer.

Another general point of universal concern is that the training of teacher trainers, and of other professions, should replace the massive supply of individual teachers; this is undeniably the right policy, but the timing of such a change needs to be most carefully planned with developing countries, so that no sudden gap is left in the educational infrastructure, where indigenous teachers are not in adequate supply to replace the expatriates. On the other hand consideration should be given, particularly at the lower levels of further education or operational skills, to well-equipped experts being attached to training institutions in developing countries, in place of large numbers of students at low levels going for overseas training; examples are secretarial skills, junior ranks of hotel and catering trades, and of industry. At the start such a scheme may be more expensive than sending people abroad, but long-term it should be cheaper, and more indigenous people would be employed.

Counterpart students are an important element, but developing countries need to see that they have people of the necessary calibre, and the right numbers at the right places. Too often the expert or adviser finds that there are no counterparts. It is for the developing country to decide for which projects they need experts, advisers and teachers; the donors must decide if they can produce candidates, and 'job description' should whenever possible be undertaken jointly by the developed country and the potential host to avoid the difficulties which arise when the expert finds himself in a post for which he is not suited.

The Netherlands scheme for junior associate experts is an admirable one, and a method of ensuring that a pool will exist of people with a knowledge of the language and needs of particular areas, or countries.

3. Volunteers

It is clear that developing countries now need volunteers who are trained in an occupation, and can undertake work at the lower and middle technical levels, or are graduates who can assist as junior teachers, particularly perhaps in language teaching. Developed countries must realise that developing countries DO develop, and a post which might be satisfactorily filled by a volunteer could in time be better filled by a junior associate expert.

Selection and preparation are as important for the volunteer as for an expert. Immense care in this field is taken particularly by the Federal Republic of Germany and the Netherlands Volunteer Schemes. It is essential, too, that the young volunteer can feel that constant advice is available to him, both as regards the job he is doing and his own welfare. The willingness of young people to serve in developing countries is unbounded but much care must be taken to see that both the sending and receiving countries appreciate the spirit of the volunteer, the former seeing to it that he is properly selected and briefed, and the latter that he is well received and not treated as cheap trained labour.

4. Languages

The need for experts to know the language of the country they are to serve in, and for the student going abroad to know the language of his host country, is a constant and recurrent theme in previous chapters. In the long run it might be better in some cases to reduce the number of awards made and increase the facilities for the teaching of the relevant language, and thus avoid some total failures and much human misery, when a scholar or fellow has inadequate knowledge of the language of his host country. The knowledge of language is clearly the key to other countries 'civilisation', and also to trading relationships. Hence the teaching of some languages such as French and English is widespread. German is taught well, but on a smaller scale, through the Goethe Institutes.

Mention is made in the Indian chapter of the relatively small amount of foreign aid in the field of teaching English, neither has the Indian educational community given as much attention to this problem as it should (Chapter 6, pp. 277–80).

5. University links and research

University links between developing and developed countries should increase, provided it is realised that they are costly and that official funds must be available, although the academic content should be left to the partner institutes concerned. It is also essential that there is some form of 'mixed commission' to oversee a link, so that difficulties can be avoided because of too much dependence on the enthusiasm of one individual, who for one reason or another may disappear from the scene. Other essentials for university links are that the object of the link should be clear, and that a time limit is set for its achievement. The need for more people of developing countries trained to do research is obvious, and one reason why joint research projects are valuable is that more junior levels of the team from the developing country learn research methods as they work on the project; but care must be taken to see that research will be of value to the researchers' own country, and that he will go back there.

6. Evaluation

A great deal of lip service is paid to the importance of evaluation, but in many cases not a great deal is done; the fact that evaluation of much educational aid is inevitably long-term makes for greater difficulties. 'Follow-up' means remaining in contact with the results of projects, or individual fellows, and is part of evaluation. It is a truism to say that the bond between fellows who have studied overseas is not necessarily the bond of studying in a particular country, but that they have studied the same subject in the same country, and this should be born in mind when follow-up schemes are under consideration. A major element should be to assist the returned fellow or scholar to keep abreast of developments in his profession.

UNDP and some UN agencies now have some fairly thorough evaluation schemes, as have some donor countries, but frequently in the latter case too little money is available for evaluation, and consideration should be given to ways in which more money could be 'switched' for these purposes. It is assumed that most evaluation will be a partnership process between the developing country and the donors, and for this purpose to be successful more training of evaluators for developing countries might well be considered; the use of 'outside' experts for evaluation as well as officials is of paramount importance.

7. Professional migration

This does not seem to be such a subject of concern as it was some five years ago, when it often became a subject of political difficulty. It is still in some instances a worrying matter. Setting on one side those who migrate for political reasons, the only eventual cure is for the facilities and financial rewards in their own countries to be adequate enough for these reasons not to exert the 'magnetic pull' to developed countries, in particular the United States, United Kingdom and the Federal Republic of Germany. In the case of all these countries, however, shortage of medically trained people means that there is recruitment by them of doctors from developing countries, which does not help the latter countries already poorly staffed in the medical field. In the case, however, of India, there is no evidence that professional migration has to any significant extent retarded economic development. It is calculated that not more than two per cent of the total stock of engineers, scientists and doctors migrate, and many do so only temporarily. The danger, as is stated in the Indian chapter, is that too often it is the 'cream' of the graduates who go abroad, and the only way to retain their services in India is for better jobs and emoluments to be available in their own country (Chapter 6, pp. 240–2).

8. Coordination and cooperation

The need for coordination and cooperation betwen developing countries and developed ones is now recognised as basic to the success of aid programmes. The need for similar action within developing and developed countries, between developed countries themselves, or on a regional basis, is obvious. There has been an almost purposeful lack of coordination in some developing countries in the past, so that the input of aid can be maintained; on the other hand donors have been indiscriminate in their offers of aid and have been too often unwilling to say no. Coordination and cooperation would improve both these failings.

The most significant step towards better international coordination lies in the increased responsibilities in the field of UNDP, arising from the Jackson Report. In one or two countries the UNDP's role of coordination has covered not only the United Nations multilateral agencies, but bilateral schemes as well. Clearly this should be extended in full cooperation with the developing countries, who should play an even greater part as they achieve more trained manpower for such work.

9. Multilateral and bilateral aid

The wish of developing countries for more multilateral aid, (though not necessarily less bilateral aid) is constant, and normally coupled with the difficulties envisaged in more multilateral aid being achieved. It has however increased, and the 'UN family' is trying to put its administrative machine into better order; if educational aid is given on a more selective basis, with carefully chosen priorities, more will be achieved. The difficulties are enormous – slowness of decision making, the complication of an international civil service, and of international teams on field projects are obvious, but should not be beyond solution. Bilateral official schemes do not have the same difficulties, but rightly or wrongly their operations are often regarded as mainly political. It must however be said that the multilateral or regional operations have the same national ministries involved as in the bilateral operations, and the money all comes from the same sources – the national treasuries of the developed countries.

The obvious recommendation is for the greatest possible coordination and cooperation between multilateral and bilateral operations at all stages, for an increased coordinating role for UNDP in partnership with the developing countries, the developed ones, as well as the 'UN family' and regional organisations.

10. The voluntary or private sector

The recent UNDP survey of voluntary organisations (n.g.o.s) discovered that apart from one billion dollars being provided for aid from voluntary sources, much of the work was very competently done. Governments do, in some cases, provide money for such organisations, and this should be increased, but not to a point where a government contributes the major part of the funds, and the voluntary body becomes an agent of government.

Both bilaterally and multilaterally the process of 'farming out' projects to universities, or other institutions, including industry, should be increased rather than decreased, with the necessary safeguards on quality of staff to undertake the project and a target date for completion.

11. The switching of funds

Reference has already been made in several of these recommendations to the 'switching' of funds under various methods of educational aid. It would seem that both the developed and the developing countries should give serious thought to switching funds in relation to capital expenditure, from such prestigious projects as airports, universities and other institutions, when buildings have often been very expensive and unnecessarily luxurious. In the case of institutions at the tertiary level the students may spend three to four years under living conditions quite different to those from which they have come, and to which they will return, particularly if they work in the rural areas. The funds released might be devoted to projects concerned with evaluation, coordination, university links and joint research.

It is not recommended that there should be any reduction in funds available for the construction of roads and other means of transport, particularly those that will improve amenities in rural areas – indeed such projects could well merit more funds. The reader is referred to the Kenya study for some other detailed switching of funds (Chapter 3, pp. 122–5).

12. Administration

Some improvement in the administration of developed bilateral and multilateral organisations including voluntary ones, also within developing countries, have been mentioned in the preceding sections of this chapter. There are some common factors needed, such as a truly massive attempt at better cooperation and coordination amongst all elements in the aid picture. At the official level there is too much jealousy between government departments, and this is not confined to developing countries, but affects developed ones, and also parts of the United Nations family. Voluntary organisations, too, jealously preserve their own 'pads', often really terrified that another organisation will take over a part of their work, and receive funds from official sources. UN agencies have in the past 'ventriloquised' requests from developing countries, to keep their positions strong and well financed; this should be less of a problem if UNDP play their coordinating role properly. Many of the evils which beset the administrations in developing countries are caused by lack of adequate manpower, and in this instance part of the training should be overseas, preferably in more than one country, including developing ones with fairly advanced administrations. This overseas training is recommended so that the potential administrators in developing countries can have a comparative basis on which to formulate their own administrations. Another facet of administration which needs to be vastly improved is the almost total centralisation of administration on capital cities. The dangers of this are detailed in the chapters on developing countries and notably Tunisia and Turkey (Chapters 5 and 7). An example of the practice of decentralisation is the Chilean educational system as described in Chapter 8 (pp. 338–44).

Consideration should be given to the consortium method, a free association of developing countries, and multilateral, bilateral, and voluntary organisations. The nature and purpose of such a consortium is clearly spelt out in the final recommendation of the Kenya study (Chapter 3, p. 126). The suggestion is made here that a consortium, though complicated to get off the ground, would lead to intensive coordination and cooperation between many facets of official and unofficial bodies concerned with aid.

Some developed countries might well consider adopting the British method of having a body like the British Council, almost totally financed from government sources, the authority for its work vested in a governing body composed of men and women of distinction, representing not only education but all the major professions and arts, industry and the trade unions. The fact that the British Council has a degree of independence from Government; that the staff are not civil servants, and overseas many are indigenous; that staff are interchangeable between offices overseas and those in Britain, which ensures that staff at home have first-hand knowledge of developing countries – all this means that the educational work the Council undertakes (and this now represents the bulk of Britain's efforts in this field) can be done in more complete partnership with developing countries from the grass roots upwards, a task not so feasible for officials of British embassies, however dedicated they may be. It also automatically means that the Council is a considerable coordinating force, certainly in the field of fellowships and scholarships tenable in the United Kingdom.

Donors of all types should in each country have agreed forms of as simple descriptions as possible, as to whom does what in their particular country, including voluntary organisations, and UN agencies coordinated by UNDP. The documentation should be as free from aid jargon as possible, and readily available and clear to all concerned with the administration of aid in all countries and multilateral agencies.

Regional organisations such as the Commonwealth Education Scheme, OAS, etc. have not been included in this section, the basis of their existence being peculiar to the region or countries concerned, and their activities in the aid field being fairly well known.

There is in most of the chapters on developing countries an overall strong recommendation for much more self-reliant initiative and planning to come from developing countries themselves. Included in such initiatives must be sober appraisals of all projects, and as is said in the chapter on India, an awareness must be exercised of the extensive damage which can be caused by the unthinking acceptance of the wrong sort of foreign aid in the field of education. Within the local initiative should come schemes by which there will be an improvement in the social and cultural context of life, particularly in poverty-stricken rural and urban shanty areas, but yet which are based on the historic customs and cultures of each individual country.

Throughout Chapters 2–8 we have treated many diverse aspects of educational aid. In this our final chapter we refer to some of the more prominent mistakes of the past (for example, the wholesale implantation on a developing country of an outmoded system of education from a developed country, or the consortium method) and inevitably the recommendations at the end of each case-study in Chapters 3–8 have their basis in educational problems of one sort or another, seen against the general development scene. Many of these recommendations are referred to again here, with page references, but are not repeated in full.

The conclusions and recommendations in this chapter are made from the same roots of educational development in the past and the hopes and beliefs for the future.

This final paragraph is the end of a long road of explanation with many people in many countries, and with a wide variety of organisations giving the author and consultants stepping-stones across many rivers and valleys. At the end of Chapter 1 we said that we hoped that our labours might help the people of developing countries. At the end of the road I would like to quote Harold Blakemore, the author of the chapter on Chile, who hopes when writing about the expert that 'he will not ascribe the failure of *rapport* to the stupidity or backwardness of his counterpart or audience, but will come to understand that technical assistance is also an extension of humanity and, perhaps, a lesson in humility.' The practice of humanity and humility would well be the basis for a motto for all those working in the donor field; I leave it to someone with a greater capacity and elegance of writing to devise such a motto.

Glossary

CHILE

CELADE	Latin American Demographic Centre
CENET	Telecommunications Training Centre
CENFA	Centro Franco-Alemán
CENFIS	Instructor and Foreman Training Centre
CONICYT	National Commission of Scientific and Technological Research
CORA	Agrarian Reform Agency
DATI	Department of Technical Assistance
ECLA	Economic Commission for Latin America
ENDESA	State Electricity Organisation
IADB	Inter-American Development Bank
ICIRA	Institute for Training and Research on Agrarian Reform
ILDIS	Instituto Latinoamericano de Investigaciones Sociales
INACAP	National Institute for Technical Training
INTEL	National Telecommunications Centre
ILPES	Latin American Institute for Social and Economic Planning
OAS	Organisation of American States
ODEPLAN	National Planning Office
SCEE	School Construction Company of Chile

COMMONWEALTH

ACU	Association of Commonwealth Universities
CELC	Commonwealth Education Liaison Committee
CFTC	Commonwealth Fund for Technical Cooperation
CSFP	Commonwealth Scholarship and Fellowship Plan

FRANCE

ACTIE	Agence pour la Coopération Technique Industrielle et Economique

ASMIC	Association pour l'Organisation des Missions de Coopération Technique
BELC	Bureau pour l'Enseignement de la Langue et de la Civilisation
CCCE	Caisse Centrale de Coopération Economique Central Fund for Economic Cooperation
CIES	Centre International pour les Etudiants et Stages
CIS	Centre International des Stages
CNOA	Centre National des Oeuvres Acceuil
CREDIF	Centre de Recherche et d'Etude pour la Diffusion Française
CST	Culturelles, Scientifiques et Techniques (Relations) (Département de Ministère des Affaires Etrangères)
OCAU	Office de Coopération et d'Accueil Universitaire
ORSTOM	Office de la Recherche Scientifique et Technique d'Outre-Mer
S.d'E	Secrétariat d'Etat

FEDERAL REPUBLIC OF GERMANY

BFE	Bundesstelle für Entwicklungshilfe Federal Agency for Technical Assistance
BMZ	Bundesministerium für Wirtschaftliche Zusammenarbeit Federal Ministry for Economic Cooperation
CDG	Carl-Duisberg Gesellschaft Carl Duisberg Society
DAAD	Deutscher Akademischer Austauschdienst German Academic Exchange Service
DED	Deutscher Entwicklungsdienst German Volunteer Service
DSE	Deutsche Stiftung fur Entwicklungsländer German Foundation for Developing Countries
GAWI	Deutsche Forderungsgesellschaft für Entwicklungsländer German Company for the Furtherance of Developing Countries
GTZ	Gesellschaft für Technische Zusammenarbeit The Society for Technical Cooperation

INDIA

CABE	The Central Advisory Board of Education
CIE	Central Institute of English
CSIR	Council of Scientific and Industrial Research
CTI	Central Training Institute
IAMR	Institute of Applied Manpower Research
ICAR	Indian Council of Agricultural Research
IIT	Indian Institute of Technology

ITI	Industrial Training Institute
MBA	Management Business Administration
MTI	Model Training Institute
NCERT	National Council of Educational Research and Training
SSST	Secondary School Science Teaching Project
TTTI	Technical Teacher Training Institute
USEFI	United States Educational Foundation in India

KENYA

CPE	Certificate of Primary Education
KANU	Kenya African National Union
NPA	New Primary Approach

NETHERLANDS

CESO	Centre for Education in Changing Societies
NUFFIC	Netherlands Universities Foundation for International Cooperation
NVO	Netherlands Volunteer Organisation

SENEGAL

CEG	Collèges d'Enseignement Général
CES	Collèges d'Enseignement Secondaire
FAC	French Aid
FED	European Development Fund
NB	National Budget
OCAM	Common African and Malagasy Organisation

TUNISIA

CERES	Centre for Economic and Social Research
CPI	Centre for the Promotion of Investments
ISGE	Business School
OFPE	L'Office de la Formation Professionnelle et de l'Emploi

TURKEY

METU	Middle East Technical University

UNITED KINGDOM

ACE	Aid for Commonwealth English
CEDO	Centre for Educational Development Overseas (now part of the British Council)
CIIR	Catholic Institute for International Relations
IUC	Inter-University Council
ODI	Overseas Development Institute
ODM	Ministry of Overseas Development

OSFAS	Overseas Students Fee Awards Scheme
TETOC	Council for Technical Education and Training for Overseas Countries
VCOAD	Voluntary Committee on Overseas Aid
VSO	Voluntary Service Overseas

UNITED NATIONS AND UNITED NATIONS AGENCIES

FAO	Food and Agricultural Organisation
IAEA	International Atomic Energy Agency
IDA	International Development Association
ILO	International Labour Office
ITU	International Telecommunications Organisations' Union

Jackson Report – 'A Study of the Capacity of the United Nations Development System', by Sir Robert Jackson, 1969

Pearson Report – 'Partners in Development': Report of Commission on International Development, by Lester B. Pearson (published by Pall Mall Paperbacks, 1969)

UNAIS	United Nations Association for International Service
UNCTAD	United Nations Committee on Trade and Development
UNDP	United Nations Development Programme
UNESCO	United Nations Educational, Scientific and Cultural Organisation
UNICEF	United Nations International Children's Emergency Fund
UNIDO	United Nations Industrial Development Organisation
UNITAR	United Nations Institute for Training and Research
UNV	United Nations Volunteers
WHO	World Health Organisation
WMO	World Meteorological Office

UNITED STATES OF AMERICA

AID	Agency for International Development
NPA	National Planning Association

OTHERS

CENTO	Central Treaty Organisation
DAC	Development Assistance Committee of OECD
EDF	European Development Fund
EEC	European Economic Community
GNP	Gross National Product
n.g.o.s	non-governmental organisations
ICVA	International Council of Voluntary Agencies
IVS	International Voluntary Service
NATO	North Atlantic Treaty Organisation
OECD	Organisation for Economic Cooperation and Development

Index